Maureen Junker-Kenny
Self, Christ and God in Schleiermacher's Dogmatics

Theologische Bibliothek Töpelmann

—

Edited by
Bruce McCormack, Friederike Nüssel
and Christoph Schwöbel

Volume 192

Maureen Junker-Kenny

Self, Christ and God in Schleiermacher's Dogmatics

A Theology Reconceived for Modernity

DE GRUYTER

ISBN 978-3-11-111089-9
e-ISBN (PDF) 978-3-11-071598-9
e-ISBN (EPUB) 978-3-11-071606-1
ISSN 0563-4288

Library of Congress Control Number: 2020942951

Bibliographic information published by the Deutsche Nationalbibliothek
The Deutsche Nationalbibliothek lists this publication in the Deutsche Nationalbibliografie;
Detailed bibliographic data are available in the Internet at http://dnb.dnb.de.

© 2022 Walter de Gruyter GmbH, Berlin/Boston
This volume is text- and page-identical with the hardback published in 2020.
Druck und Bindung: CPI books GmbH, Leck
www.degruyter.com

To Peter
In gratitude
for being such a rock

Contents

Preface —— XV

Abbreviations —— XVII

Introduction —— 1

I The Conception of an "Introduction" as Part of an Account of Christian Doctrine after the Anthropological Turn

Introduction —— 7

1	The Tasks and the Layout of the "Introduction" in the First and the Second Editions of *The Christian Faith* —— 9
1.1	"Philosophical theology" as a framework for dogmatics in the *Brief Outline* (1811) —— 10
1.1.1	The enquiries constituting "philosophical theology" —— 11
1.1.2	Dogmatics as part of "historical theology" —— 11
1.1.3	Issues requiring clarification —— 14
1.2	The Introductions of 1811 and 1821/22: Continuities and differences —— 15
1.2.1	Continuities between the Lecture course and the first edition of the *Glaubenslehre* —— 17
1.2.2	Differences —— 18
1.2.3	The systematic reason for beginning the *Glaubenslehre* with a definition of dogmatics —— 19
1.3	The final ordering in 1830/31 —— 20
1.3.1	The new sequence of the propositions —— 20
1.3.2	The effect of the reorganisation —— 23
1.4	The final shape of the architecture of the *Glaubenslehre* in current debate —— 25
1.4.1	Schleiermacher's discussion of his planned revisions in the 1829 Letters to Lücke —— 25
1.4.2	Counterarguments to reversing the sequence of Parts One and Two —— 27

2	**Determining the Essence of Piety by Two Distinct Methods in the First and the Second Editions —— 29**
2.1	The original version: A phenomenological approach —— 29
2.1.1	Feeling as the location of piety (^{1}§ 8) —— 30
2.1.2	The feeling of absolute dependence as a consciousness of God (^{1}§ 9) —— 32
2.1.3	The need to keep "partial" and "absolute" dependence distinct in the interpretation of both editions —— 34
2.2	The transcendental turn in defining the essence of piety in ^{2}§§ 3 and 4 —— 36
2.2.1	The first step: The analysis of actual self-consciousness in its dual constitution —— 37
2.2.1.1	The deepened account of ^{2}§ 3 for the place of "feeling" in relation to thinking and acting —— 38
2.2.1.2	Actual self-consciousness as marked by the distinction between "positing" and "posited" —— 40
2.2.1.3	The essential structure of the subject as the functional unity of activity and receptivity —— 41
2.2.2	The second step: The impossibility of founding the structure of finite freedom either on itself or on the world —— 42
2.2.2.1	Comparing the key terms of the second edition with their English translations —— 42
2.2.2.2	Enquiring into the origin of the subject's structure —— 45
2.2.3	The third step: The immediate self-consciousness of utter dependence as an innate relation to God —— 46
2.2.3.1	The lack of foundation in the finite as the basis for claiming a "Whence" —— 47
2.2.3.2	Immediate and inaccessible as an object? —— 48
2.2.3.3	The feeling of absolute dependence as the hermeneutical basis of the concept of God —— 49
2.2.3.4	Self-authenticating claim or a careful identification of the anthropological foundation for the question of God? —— 51
2.3	Disputes about the interpretation of the analysis and of its results —— 52
2.3.1	Questions to a transcendental reconstruction —— 53
2.3.1.1	Different understandings of "transcendental" —— 54
2.3.1.2	Objections to reconstructing Schleiermacher's argument as an analysis of facticity —— 57

2.3.2	The immediate self-consciousness as pre-reflective, and its divergent interpretations as monist or as egological —— 61
2.3.2.1	Comparing Schleiermacher and Dieter Henrich on an immediate or "pre-reflective" consciousness —— 63
2.3.2.2	The "pre-reflective familiarity of the Ego with itself" as the first principle of a theory of subjectivity —— 64
2.3.3	Questions to the result of the analysis of ²§ 4 —— 65
2.3.3.1	Distinguishing between the key findings and the choices made in their interpretation: facticity as "absolute dependence" from God —— 65
2.3.3.2	Questions to the "immediacy" of the self-consciousness as a God-consciousness —— 67
2.3.3.3	The issue of what is being claimed: the possibility or the actuality of a God-consciousness in all humans? —— 69
3	**The Definition of the Essence of Christianity —— 71**
3.1	The functions of the essence definition of Christianity —— 71
3.1.1	Establishing the theological principle of the dogmatics —— 71
3.1.2	Replacing the method of proofs from the Bible —— 73
3.1.3	Striving for a consensus in the face of inevitable disagreements —— 76
3.2	Methodological reflections and key terms for defining the essence of Christianity in the Lectures of 1811 —— 78
3.3	Steps, explication and implications of the definition of the essence of Christianity in the first edition —— 81
3.3.1	The general and the individualising principles for capturing historical religions —— 81
3.3.2	The relation between a constructive and a comparative, historical-critical approach in the first edition —— 84
3.3.3	The explication of the concept of redemption —— 85
3.3.4	Implications of the essence formula for drawing limits —— 88
3.3.4.1	Deriving "natural heresies" from the concept of redemption —— 88
3.3.4.2	The "natural" and the "supernatural" regarding revelation —— 90
3.3.4.3	"Inner experience" as supra-rational, its secondary dogmatic conceptualisation as "rational" —— 92
3.4	The corrections and the new emphases of the second edition —— 93
3.4.1	Clarifications of the hermeneutical procedure —— 93
3.4.2	The relation between the sensible and the higher self-consciousness —— 96

3.4.3	Redemption – historical event or construction of reason? —— 97
3.4.3.1	The limits of construction by a philosophy of religion —— 97
3.4.3.2	Changes regarding the relationship of reason to revelation —— 99
4	**Critiques of the First Edition and Evaluation of the Changes to the Introduction as a Framework for the Dogmatics —— 102**
4.1	The reception of the first edition among rationalists and supernaturalists —— 103
4.1.1	Rationalist objections —— 104
4.1.2	A supernaturalist critique —— 107
4.2	F. C. Baur's interpretation of the *Glaubenslehre* as an "ideal rationalism" —— 109
4.2.1	F. C. Baur's early critique —— 110
4.2.2	The final shape of the critique since Baur's turn to Hegel —— 117
4.2.2.1	The method of inferring backwards from the effect to the cause —— 118
4.2.2.2	The intertwining of the archetypal and the historical —— 119
4.2.2.3	The determination of the content of redemption —— 121
4.2.3	The renewal of Baur's critique by Alister McGrath —— 125
4.2.3.1	On the road to Feuerbach? —— 125
4.2.3.2	Lacking a historical foundation? The method of inference in the dogmatics —— 128
4.3	Evaluation: The Introduction as a framework for the dogmatics. Directions of the revision, ongoing debates, and questions to Part Two —— 131
4.3.1	Key orientations in the revision of the first Introduction —— 131
4.3.2	The enduring bond of redemption to the person of Jesus Christ —— 134
4.3.3	Questions for the dogmatics —— 136

II Schleiermacher's Reworking of Christian Doctrine in his Material Dogmatics

Introduction —— 141

5	**The Theological Anthropology of the *Glaubenslehre*: Original Perfection, Sinfulness and Receptivity for Redemption —— 143**
5.1	Theological anthropology in its role of mediating in two directions: to the doctrine of God and to soteriology —— 143

5.2	The basic conception of a humanity receptive for redemption —— 145	
5.2.1	Original perfection as the world's openness to enquiry —— 145	
5.2.2	A model for combining natural determination with receptive and self-active individuality: Leibniz's theory of monads —— 148	
5.2.3	The interpretation of human sinfulness —— 154	
5.3	The revised argumentation of the second edition —— 156	
5.3.1	The relationship of human sensibility to the God-consciousness —— 157	
5.3.2	The content and the standing of human freedom —— 160	
5.3.3	Objections to a naturalising concept of sin —— 162	
5.4	Consequences of the revised subject theoretical foundations for the approach to Christology —— 166	
5.4.1	Can a sinless existence be constructed a priori? —— 166	
5.4.2	The completion of the creation of human nature and Jesus as "Second Adam" —— 169	
5.5	Taking stock of the doctrines of human perfection and sinfulness —— 170	
6	**A Christology from Two Perspectives: the Consciousness of Redemption, and the Single Divine Decree —— 172**	
6.1	The basic outline of Christology —— 173	
6.1.1	The inconsistencies of the two-natures terminology in Christology —— 173	
6.1.2	The arguments for the unity of the archetypal and the historical in the person of Jesus —— 177	
6.2	The final outline of Christology —— 180	
6.2.1	The historical nature of the archetypal Jesus —— 180	
6.2.2	Christ as the completion of creation —— 184	
6.2.3	Evaluations of the turn to a Second-Adam Christology in the history of reception of the second edition —— 188	
6.2.4	The mediation of redemption —— 190	
6.3	The liberation of human God-consciousness by a sinless redeemer: Enough to secure the ongoing significance of Jesus Christ? —— 193	
6.3.1	Jesus' distinction: the unique strength of his God-consciousness —— 193	
6.3.2	The under-determination of Jesus' concrete relationship to God —— 197	
6.3.3	Continuity of natural forces versus contingency of history —— 201	
6.3.4	The balance between Christology and ecclesiology —— 203	
6.4	Summary and guiding questions to the doctrine of God —— 206	

7	**A Doctrine of God Developed from the Feeling of Absolute Dependence —— 208**
7.1	Foundational points from the first edition onwards: God as absolute causality —— 209
7.1.1	God and the "interconnected process of nature" (*Naturzusammenhang*) —— 209
7.1.2	The priority of preservation over creation —— 212
7.1.3	The view of personalistic concepts as limiting for God —— 214
7.2	Clarifications in the final elaboration of the doctrine of God —— 217
7.2.1	The status of Part One: not a natural theology —— 218
7.2.2	The role of the *Dialectic* —— 220
7.3	Ongoing disputes in the reception history —— 222
7.3.1	The general and the specifically Christian attributes of God —— 222
7.3.1.1	The canons of divine unity, simplicity and infinity, and the identity of essence and attributes —— 222
7.3.1.2	Love as a complete definition of God's essence, or as a modification of divine causality? —— 224
7.3.2	The God-world framework: metaphysics of monism or of individuality, Spinoza or Leibniz? —— 225
7.3.2.1	Arguments for a Spinozist reading —— 226
7.3.2.1.1	Subordinating creation to preservation —— 226
7.3.2.1.2	Tying God to the world —— 227
7.3.2.1.3	Declaring 'will' and 'can' as identical in God —— 228
7.3.2.2	Points incompatible with Spinozism —— 228
7.3.2.2.1	The definition of piety itself reached in an analysis of subjectivity —— 229
7.3.2.2.2	*Creatio ex nihilo* as indicator of the difference between God and world —— 229
7.3.2.2.3	The explication of the attributes of omniscience and of eternity —— 230
7.3.2.2.4	Individuality not as transition point, but as constituted in itself —— 230
7.3.3	Consequences for the concept of human freedom in relation to the world and towards God —— 231
7.3.3.1	Freedom as the backstop against a reduction to materialism —— 232
7.3.3.2	Not recognised: the unconditionality of human freedom —— 232
7.3.3.3	A test case: The reasons for endorsing an *apokatastasis panton* —— 235

8	**Conclusion: Creation and Redemption in Categories of Freedom —— 237**
8.1	Key theory decisions and achievements of Schleiermacher's *Glaubenslehre* —— 237
8.1.1	The choice of thought form: human freedom —— 238
8.1.2	Renewing Christology —— 238
8.1.3	Recasting theology as a project of elaborating the core truth of Christianity in critical interaction with modernity —— 240
8.2	Problems with specific argumentations and solutions —— 241
8.2.1	Overdrawing the result of the analysis of self-consciousness —— 241
8.2.2	Underdetermining the content of Christology —— 242
8.2.3	Making the case for a changeless God —— 243
8.2.4	Underrating the critical contribution of theological perspectives to the dialogue of the humanities with the natural sciences —— 245
8.3	Opening up a new era: Duns Scotus's conception of a God who creates free counterparts and risks an open history —— 247
8.3.1	The distinction between *potentia Dei absoluta* and *potentia Dei ordinata* —— 248
8.3.2	The addressees of God's love: Human beings in their freedom —— 249
8.3.3	The *haecceitas* of Jesus —— 250
8.3.4	The outcome of history as an open theological question —— 252

Bibliography —— 255
1. Sources —— 255
2. Secondary literature —— 256

Person Index —— 270

Subject Index —— 273

Preface

Thanks are due to the persons and institutions who have enabled me to return to the pioneering work of Friedrich Schleiermacher for theology in modernity: Trinity College Dublin for a sabbatical in 2014; Professor Wilhelm Gräb and Professor Christian Albrecht for kindly acting as hosts and conversation partners at the Humboldt University of Berlin and the Ludwig Maximilians University of Munich as well as the German Academic Exchange Service (DAAD) for awarding a Senior Research Fellowship in 2014. The Colloquia of the *Internationale Schleiermacher Gesellschaft* at the Leucorea in Wittenberg have offered insightful and motivating encounters. Dr. Katharina Hell is to be thanked for helping to commence the final phase of the project by providing a calm retreat in June 2019. I am grateful to Dr. Albrecht Döhnert and to the co-editors of Theologische Bibliothek Töpelmann, Professors Bruce McCormack, Friederike Nüssel and Christoph Schwöbel, for including the book into the series, and to colleagues at De Gruyter for their collaborative spirit and attention to detail. My family has made the completion of the book possible in manifold ways from everyday tasks to highly specific competences. Fiona Kenny has again provided her proofreading and copy-editing skills, managing tight deadlines with professionalism and patience. Kilian Kenny enabled the turn to online teaching due to the Covid-19 crisis which has accompanied the ultimate phase of completion. Dr. Peter Kenny is to be thanked for his immense support and humour over the past three decades of my exploration of Schleiermacher's work: from his desktop publishing of the manuscript of my PhD thesis on Schleiermacher, to many philosophical and theological discussions, stores of bibliographic materials, and for sourcing new publications. This book is dedicated to him.

Dublin, June 2020

Abbreviations

KGA	Kritische Gesamtausgabe
BO	*Brief Outline of Theology as a Field of Study* [1811 and 1830], trans. with an introduction by Terrence N. Tice (Lewiston, N.Y.: The Edwin Mellen Press, 1988).
¹§	*Der christliche Glaube* 1821/22, 2 vols, ed. by Horst Peiter (Berlin/New York: De Gruyter, 1984) (= KGA I/7.1 and I/7.2).
²§	Der *christliche Glaube,* 2. Auflage 1830/31, ed. by Rolf Schäfer (Berlin/New York: De Gruyter, Studienausgabe 2008).
ET 1928	*The Christian Faith,* English Translation of the Second German Edition, ed. by H.R. Mackintosh and J.S. Stewart (Edinburgh: T. & T. Clark, 1928; 1986).
ET 2016	*Christian Faith. A New Translation and Critical Edition*, 2 vols, trans. by Terrence N. Tice, Catherine L. Kelsey and Edwina Lawler; ed. by Catherine L. Kelsey and Terrence N. Tice (Louisville, KY: Westminster John Knox Press, 2016).
Letters	*On* the *Glaubenslehre. Two Letters to Dr. Lücke*, trans. James O. Duke and Francis Fiorenza (Ann Arbor: Scholars Press, 1981).
LS	*Leitsatz* (Lead Sentence / Proposition).
Marg.	*Der christliche Glaube, 1. Auflage (1821/22), Marginalien und Anhang. Unter Verwendung vorbereitender Arbeiten von Hayo Gerdes und Horst Peiter* ed. by Ulrich Barth *(Berlin/New* York: De Gruyter, 1984) (= KGA I/7.3).

Introduction

The publication of Schleiermacher's *The Christian Faith* two hundred years ago has inaugurated a new era for theology.¹ With the appearance in 1821/22 of this first account of Christian doctrine that responds to the new epistemological conditions of the "Copernican Turn" effected by Immanuel Kant's critiques of reason, decisive departures are implemented. Whether they are to be judged as breakthroughs, or as delivering Christian dogmatics over to a modern framework that will end up in the critique of religion and secularisation, is an ongoing debate. Exchanges continue on the legitimacy of the anthropological turn and on the place a justifiable account of the Christian faith is to give to insights from the historical and natural sciences. Two English-speaking readers of Schleiermacher illustrate the range of theological views with their opposite conclusions. Roger Haight expresses what he appreciates as follows:

> Schleiermacher broke the hold of the mythological views of redemption in which something was accomplished between God and God, or Jesus and God, and then extrinsically received by human beings. By contrast, Christian salvation begins historically in each person who absorbs Jesus' message and person in such a way that this consciousness becomes internalized.²

Alister McGrath considers the *Glaubenslehre* "unquestionably one of the most significant works of systematic theology ever written"; yet, he traces a direct line from its "theological programme" based on "introspection" to Feuerbach's unveiling of religion as projection:
"Feuerbach's critique of religion called into question the propriety of inferring the existence or nature of 'God' from religious feeling, in that this feeling

---

1 Friedrich Daniel Ernst Schleiermacher, *Der christliche Glaube* 1821/22, 2 vols, ed. by Horst Peiter (Berlin/New York: De Gruyter, 1984) (= KGA I/7.1 and 2) [marked hereafter ¹§]. *Der christliche Glaube, 1. Auflage (1821/22), Marginalien und Anhang*. Unter Verwendung vorbereitender Arbeiten von Hayo Gerdes und Horst Peiter ed. by Ulrich Barth (Berlin/New York: De Gruyter, 1984) (= KGA I/7.3). *Der christliche Glaube*, 2. Auflage 1830/31, ed. by Rolf Schäfer (Berlin/New York: De Gruyter, 2008) [marked hereafter ²§]. *The Christian Faith*, English Translation of the Second German Edition, ed. by H.R. Mackintosh and J.S. Stewart (Edinburgh: T. & T. Clark, 1928; 1986) [hereafter ET 1928]. *Christian Faith. A New Translation and Critical Edition*, 2 vols, trans. by Terrence N. Tice, Catherine L. Kelsey and Edwina Lawler; ed. by Catherine L. Kelsey and Terrence N. Tice (Louisville, KY: Westminster John Knox Press, 2016) [hereafter ET 2016].
2 Roger Haight, "Take and Read: The Christian Faith", in *National Catholic Reporter*, May 23, 2016, accessed March 1, 2020. https://www.ncronline.org/blogs/ncr-today/take-and-read-christian-faith.

could only be interpreted anthropologically, and not theologically."[3] Since then, the *Glaubenslehre's* "unsatisfactory foundation" has been "exposed, its inadequacy" has become "obvious to all."[4]

In view of the discrepancy between these two programmatic assessments, one rejecting an extrinsic account of salvation, the other the starting point in human subjectivity or "feeling", the aims of this study are three: One, to reconstruct Schleiermacher's argumentation, including the revisions carried out in the second edition of 1830/31. Two, to follow up key questions in the nuanced investigations of the history of reception and critique which cannot simply be divided up into responses from liberal and from dialectical theologians. Three, to identify alternative directions on issues that will remain unresolved due to their foundational character. These include the consciousness of freedom and individuality, the contingency of existence, the human capability of being addressed by God, the role of historical consciousness, and the conception of a Christology in response to these terms in their relevance for practical self-understandings in the late modern age. In pursuing these three aims, I will relate German- and English-speaking sources and scholarship to each other. The questions, positions and exchanges that developed in the last thirty years are followed up, building on my comparison of the first and the second editions' theory of religion and Christology published in 1990.[5]

The title has been chosen to reflect the order of enquiry. It was Schleiermacher's acute realisation that theology had to be reconceived if it wanted to avail of the insights of the philosophical turn to the human subject and to justify its faith stance publicly within a diverse contemporary culture. This meant that theological truth claims could no longer be based on arguments derived from theoretical reason for faith in God as creator. Yet the dismantling of proofs for God's existence by Kant in keeping with the critical insight into the limits of reason did not spell the end of a meaningful, justifiable faith orientation. A different avenue could be taken, human self-reflection, beginning with a philosophical analysis of self-consciousness. The themes of theology could only be reached from the starting point of the self. Speaking of Jesus Christ and God without examining the anthropological presuppositions of such insights lacked the condi-

---

[3] Alister McGrath, *The Making of Modern German Christology. From the Enlightenment to Pannenberg* (Oxford: OUP, 1986), 19.
[4] McGrath, *The Making of Modern German Christology*, 47.
[5] Maureen Junker, *Das Urbild des Gottesbewußtseins. Zur Entwicklung der Religionstheorie und Christologie Schleiermachers von der ersten zur zweiten Auflage der Glaubenslehre*. Schleiermacher-Archiv 8. (Berlin/New York: de Gruyter, 1990, reprinted 2013). Translations from sources in English, unless otherwise indicated, are my own.

tion for defending the truth of such claims, a reflection on their epistemological possibility. Correspondingly, the only avenue open to understand the significance of Jesus Christ was to explain his relevance, based on the human need for redemption, and his identity through his relationship to God as well as to humanity. This approach avoids what Haight describes as an "extrinsicist" account in which divine relevation is taken in instruction-theoretical terms as an unveiling of contents cognitively unavailable to the human creature. Instead, Schleiermacher's doctrine of faith (as the literal translation of *Glaubenslehre*) invokes the "total impression" of Jesus as the origin of faith in him. Finally, in view of the limits of human knowing, any reference to God must be aware of the inadequacy of concepts taken from the finite human sphere. At the same time, the author of *The Christian Faith* was confident that an analysis of "immediate self-consciousness" would be able to identify the elementary experience in which the dogmatic statements on God are ultimately anchored. The motivation was to explicate to an age that was reaping the insights of in-depth enquiries and brimming with intellectual alternatives that "redemption", a term many would have preferred to declare "traditional" or bygone, was still a live possibility. "Satisfying our longing for redemption" was exactly not something to which the human person should "renounce as being too elevated to be reached" (^{1}§ 121,1. II, 67).

Part One deals with the "Introduction" and with the changes it underwent in the second edition. Chapter One discusses the tasks assigned to this account of the structured procedure chosen for the dogmatics and its clarification of key concepts; the different layouts of the model devised already in 1811 for a lecture course at the newly founded university in Berlin, in the first and in the second edition are compared. Following the treatment of the definitions of religion and of Christianity in Chapters Two and Three, the early reception of the work is analysed in Chapter Four and linked to questions that have continued to be raised.

Part Two examines self (Chapter Five), Christ (Chapter Six) and God (Chapter Seven) in the material dogmatics. It is a sign of the exact methodological consciousness at work that Schleiermacher divides the treatises on theological anthropology and God into a first treatment abstracted from its Christian specificity and a second part where they are studied as determined by the Christian consciousness of sin and grace. Christology appears under "grace" in the second section of this Second Part. The doctrine of God is treated in three distinct locations of which I will discuss the first two, before the final part on the Trinitarian constitution of God: in the abstracted First Part, and in the second, specifically Christian part on the divine qualities as they appear from the consciousness both of sin and grace.

The two parts of the material dogmatics have provoked questions in particular about the God-world relationship: whether the connection devised between God and the nexus of nature is envisaged in a monistic way; how it influences the distinction between anthropology and Christology; what the relationship between creation and redemption in the one divine decree implies for the freedom of God and the underlying concept of history. Chapter Eight provides a summary of achievements and problems and concludes with an alternative outline in which these questions are taken up from the same starting point as Schleiermacher's: intending to reconceive Christian dogmatics through the categories attained by the turn to the subject and from the perspective of human freedom.

I The Conception of an "Introduction" as Part of an Account of Christian Doctrine after the Anthropological Turn

Introduction

The new departure which Schleiermacher's *Glaubenslehre* constitutes for dogmatic theology as a discipline becomes clear from its "Introduction". What contemporaries would have expected was, depending on the author's allegiance to supernaturalist or rationalist foundations, either a defence of the authority of Scripture, or a clarification of the Bible's relationship to reason.[6] What the Introduction to the two volumes offers instead is an unprecedented mapping of the place of *religion* as one of only three key human pursuits, and that of *Christianity* among the other historical religions. The new access chosen by Schleiermacher is a response to the new intellectual requirements of his age: to legitimate faith in God as an anthropological possibility in its own right, as neither irrational nor reducible to other human functions such as moral agency or theoretical reason. This first enquiry into the essence of religion – or, as it is termed, "piety", capturing the personal commitment of the believer – is followed by locating Christianity in a framework that classifies its type and then determines its self-understanding through its historical origin and its key content: redemption by Jesus Christ. The implications of these two essence definitions as well as the architecture resulting from the second are spelt out in the remaining propositions, ¹§§ 23–35 and ²§§ 12–31. Through them, the newly created entry point of an "Introduction" elucidates and clarifies the ensuing terms and tasks, steps and methods that select and organise the distribution of the material dogmatic content.

The originality of this starting point with its intention of providing "the specification of the place of Christianity" (*Ortsbestimmung*)[7] in an anthropological and a historical framework has given rise to debates that have continued since its publication. As Chapter 4 will show, some of the earliest critiques are still unresolved and key issues remain contested. Chapters 2 and 3 will deal with the definition of religion as an irreducible element of human life, and with the determination of Christianity through the Christian consciousness of redemption by

---

[6] In *Friedrich Daniel Ernst Schleiermacher* (München: Beck, 2001), 101, Hermann Fischer explains the difference of the new unified dogmatic principle which Schleiermacher put forward with the Christian determination of the pious self-consciousness to the previous starting point, Scripture, and, since the Enlightenment, both Scripture and reason. "Holy Scripture and tradition are presupposed, yet no longer serve as immediate points of reference but only in the medium of the Christian pious self-consciousness … It is the task of dogmatics to transpose (*überführen*) Christian experience – under the premises of Holy Scripture and tradition – into a conceptual-reflective shape."
[7] Schleiermacher, *On the Glaubenslehre. Two Letters to Dr. Lücke*, trans. James O. Duke and Francis Fiorenza (Ann Arbor: Scholars Press, 1981) [hereafter: "Letters"], II, 76.

Jesus of Nazareth. Chapter 1 will examine the differences between the first and the second editions regarding the order of the propositions and the reasons given for its revision, as well as their effects as far as they become visible at this stage.

1 The Tasks and the Layout of the "Introduction" in the First and the Second Editions of *The Christian Faith*

The second edition of *The Christian Faith* (1830/31) represents the most thought-through elaboration of Schleiermacher's mature theology. It owes its final shape to the critical reception that the original version (1821/22) had encountered. The clarifications and corrections of his philosophical and theological argumentations mainly concern the internal ordering of the Introduction, the theory of subjectivity in which it anchors the concept of religion, and the Christological section in the second main part of the material dogmatics. While the modifications carried out in his theological anthropology, Christology and doctrine of God will be analysed in the second part of this study, it will become clear in the first part that his reconstruction of Christian doctrine reflects the theory decisions made in the Introduction. Its task is to develop a systematic outline for the contents of the Christian faith that respects the insights of the self-critique of reason.

Since also the first edition, beginning with its first proposition, refers to the *Brief Outline*, the conception of theology that was developed in this formal encyclopaedia will be explained first.[6] In order to understand the function of dogmatics and the definition of its content given in § 1, it is important to keep in mind the underlying designation of theology as a "positive science" and the threefold structure it was given in the earlier book dedicated to theology as an academic subject. First published in 1811, it allocated both exegesis and dogmatics to "historical theology" which already at that time was preceded by "philosophical theology" (1.1). Secondly, the original order and function of the Introduction as it takes shape in the lecture course of 1811 in the newly opened university of Berlin is compared to the first edition of 1821/22 (1.2). The substantially revised ordering in the final version of 1830/31 is explained and assessed in its effects in the third subsection (1.3). Among the points of contemporary debate that are treated in conclusion are Schleiermacher's deliberations on whether to change the complete layout of the

---

[6] *Brief Outline of Theology as a Field of Study* [1811 and 1830], trans. with an introduction by Terrence N. Tice (Lewiston, N.Y.: The Edwin Mellen Press, 1988), with the second edition as the main text and the first supplied as notes. Tice's instructive comments help clarify their contents and their relations within Schleiermacher's work. References to the respective edition's paragraph and page number will be included in the text.

Glaubenslehre and reconstruct the architecture that had led to such misunderstandings and principled objections (1.4).

1.1 "Philosophical theology" as a framework for dogmatics in the *Brief Outline* (1811)

By aligning theology with other "positive sciences" like law and medicine, Schleiermacher's conception locates the unity of this subject in its practical purpose: to equip its students who will be future church professionals with the knowledge and judgement necessary for serving in leadership roles. This functional determination of the academic character of theology implies that the types of enquiry it needs to conduct belong to different domains with their own distinctive purposes and methods[7] – for example, history, philology, comparative cultural studies, and "technical", application-oriented disciplines like hermeneutics and pedagogy. It is only in the second edition of the *Glaubenslehre* that the statements belonging to such fields of enquiry are explicitly classified as "borrowed propositions" (*Lehnsätze*) from their home subjects: a structural theory of human subjectivity and culture entitled "ethics", a comparative framework for the historical religions called "philosophy of religion", and a conceptual-historical enquiry named "apologetics". Their different origins and status are presupposed but not spelt out in 1821/22. Of the three strands into which the *Brief Outline* divides theology, the first two are relevant for the *Glaubenslehre:* "philosophical", and "historical" theology, to be complemented by a third, namely "practical theology". How the new discipline, "philosophical theology", is devised as a sequence of distinct enquiries is treated in the first section (1.1.1), followed by an analysis of the allocation of both exegesis and dogmatics to "historical theology" (1.1.2). Judging from the reception of the *Glaubenslehre*, the third section will identify the issues that called for clarification due to the decidedly new lines being drawn which cut across the structuring of the subject that its practitioners were accustomed to (1.1.3).

---

[7] The first, fifth and sixth propositions of the 1811 publication on pp. 1, 3 and 4 make it clear that the principle which holds the disciplines of theology together is not an internal one, but a practical task: "¹§ 1. Theology is a positive science, the various parts of which join into a cohesive whole only through their common relation to a particular religion, Christian theology, accordingly to Christianity... ¹§ 5. Christian theology is the assemblage of scientific knowledge and practical instruction without the employment of which a Christian government of the Church is not possible. ¹§ 6. Without this relation this same knowledge ceases to be theological and each aspect of it devolves to some other science."

1.1.1 The enquiries constituting "philosophical theology"

A specification that sums up the status of the new discipline is the indication of its starting point: it is located "above" Christianity (^{1}§ 4. 20), a term that is clarified in the second edition of the *Brief Outline* as being meant "in the logical sense" (^{2}§ 33. 19). To be able to define the "distinctive nature" requires "comparing what is historically given in Christianity with whatever regularity (*Gesetzen*) is lodged in the idea of religion and of the church as changing entities" (^{1}§ 2. 19). The disciplines required are first, "ethics" as "the science of the principles of history" (^{1}§ 6. 21) for a general concept of religion and religious community (or "church" in a comprehensive, not specifically Christian sense); second, "apologetics" to investigate the "essence of Christianity" (^{1}§ 2. 27 of Apologetics) both from a comparative perspective with other religions (that will later be called "philosophy of religion") and from its "inner consistency" (^{1}§ 3. 30 of Apologetics); finally, "polemics", which is to safeguard this core from misinterpretations, heresy and schism (^{1}§§ 1–11. 32–37). Thus, being able to take one's standpoint above one's own religion does not imply that one cannot at the same time judge the internal coherence – which an observer from the outside could not accomplish. But it entails the assumption of a constitutive ability to be, so to speak, bilingual or no less competent in the philosophical reflection of the element shared in all religions. The philosophical, comparative and critical internal enquiries inaugurated here point forward to the elliptical structure established in *The Christian Faith*, with its two focal points: a philosophical principle consisting in the concept of religion that is reached from an analysis of human subjectivity, and the theological or dogmatic principle, consisting in the essence of Christianity.

1.1.2 Dogmatics as part of "historical theology"

Beyond its functional definition of theology, however, the *Brief Outline* also puts forward a substantial definition of the content of dogmatics, as Hermann Fischer points out. It is the "systematic presentation of doctrinal concepts that now have currency in the Church *(mit der zusammenhängenden Darstellung des in der Kirche jetzt grade geltenden Lehrbegriffs)*" (^{1}§ 3. 97). The subject area is a critical elaboration of currently accepted, or valid doctrine.[8] Two aspects need to be highlight-

---

8 In his comment on the term "*geltend*" in both editions of the *Brief Outline* and of the *Glaubenslehre*, Tice points to the range of meaning from "enjoying a degree of acceptance" to "properly understood, justified and formulated". BO, ET, Ed. note, 97.

ed: First, it anchors the systematic reflection on the content of the Christian faith in history, obliging it as an ongoing development of doctrine to maintain the connection to earlier elaborations. What "historical" indicates in this context is a need to attend to the dimension of continuity for acquiring "knowledge of the present condition of Christianity", as the heading to Part III, "Dogmatic Theology and Church Statistics" (97) specifies. There are divergent views on how binding the tie between inherited and "currently accepted" doctrine was meant to be for Schleiermacher. On the one hand, its link to the "visible church" allows the rejection of the label of "subjectivism".[9] Hans-Joachim Birkner points out the degree to which it kept the historical doctrines as the key reference point and corpus of dogmatics.[10] It makes the dogmatics a place for critically scrutinising, but not for abolishing existing doctrines, for example on eschatology, and seeks a different location, namely the sermons, for a more outspoken critique and replacement. On the other hand, the renewal of doctrine through the interplay of history and the present era in the equal tasks of heterodox and orthodox elements, can result, as Hermann Fischer points out, in a most radical critique, such as no longer including the resurrection into the doctrine of Christ.[11] Thus, [1]§ 3 of the third part of the *Brief Outline* of 1811 (and [2]§ 195 of 1830) with

---

9 Regarding the critique of "subjectivism" by Karl Barth and Felix Flückiger, John Thiel comments that they "promulgate the erroneous view that the subjective orientation of Schleiermacher's theology overlooks, ... even denigrates, the importance of tradition for theological reflection. In Schleiermacher's view, the theoretical and practical dimensions of the theological task derive their unity from a 'certain mode of faith', from a particular confessional commitment." John Thiel, *Imagination and Authority: Theological Authorship in the Modern Tradition* (Minneapolis: Fortress Press, 1991), 40.
10 In *Schleiermachers Theorie der Frömmigkeit. Ihr wissenschaftlicher Ort und ihr systematischer Gehalt in den Reden, in der Glaubenslehre und in der Dialektik* (Berlin/New York: de Gruyter, 1994), 198 n. 6, with reference to Hans-Joachim Birkner, Christian Albrecht points out that the "allocation of dogmatics to historical theology is by no means a devaluation but exactly its opposite; the intention is to upgrade dogmatics by relating it to the present." Hans-Joachim. Birkner, "Beobachtungen zu Schleiermachers Programm der Dogmatik" in *Neue Zeitschrift für Systematische Theologie und Religionsphilosophie* 5 (1963) 119–131, 124–126.
11 While Hermann Fischer notes the departures both from biblical sources and from the dogmatic tradition in some of Schleiermacher's key decisions that represent a "considerable radicalisation of the critique" (*F. D. E. Schleiermacher*, 114–115), Martin Weeber underscores the continuity: Martin Weeber, "Schleiermachers doppelte Eschatologie", in *Schleiermacher und Kierkegaard. Subjektivität und Wahrheit*, ed. by Niels Jørgen Cappelørn et al. (Berlin/New York: de Gruyter, 2006), 577–598. Claus-Dieter Osthövener also underlines how much Schleiermacher kept to ecclesial limitations at the expense of innovation, in Osthövener, "Dogmatik II: Materiale Entfaltung der 'Glaubenslehre'", in *Schleiermacher Handbuch*, ed. Martin Ohst (Tübingen: Mohr Siebeck, 2017), 362. 383.

which the first edition of *The Christian Faith* begins as ¹§ 1 of the Introduction can be assessed differently in the scope it allows for innovation. The emphasis on the role of theological authorship that John Thiel points out constitutes a new starting point for developing

> a tradition's self-understanding, coherence, and integrity. This conception of theological authorship stands in sharp contrast to the classical paradigm's suspicion of all nonsupernatural authority and sanctions an understanding of theological responsibility that the classical paradigm would have judged ecclesially anomic. ... It was Schleiermacher's theory that introduced the conception of theological authorship to the Christian tradition. ... It is in Schleiermacher's *Brief Outline* ... that one discovers the first consideration of doctrinal development as a methodological principle of Christian theology.[12]

What the *Brief Outline* accomplished in the period from 1811 to 1821, and the *Glaubenslehre* took over subsequently, was the replacement of the previous systematic justification of the authority of Scripture by two tasks: it was to work out the definitions of two "unknowns", namely of the essence of religion, and of that of Christianity. They take two perspectives, the first "above", the second both above and within Christianity. Regarding the status of philosophical theology and its relation to historical theology, Eilert Herms clarifies the distinction between the two enquiries. The specification of ¹§ 3 of the first and ²§ 33 of the second edition of the *Brief Outline*, to take its starting point "above" Christianity, does not relate to "the concept of the essence of Christianity, which is fundamental for theology as such, but rather the concept of religion taken universally as a constant trait of human existence, a concept belonging in the context of philosophical ethics (and arguably psychology)".[13]

The contested term, "above", was dropped in the Introduction of the second edition of the *Glaubenslehre*. This was possible because the starting point for the conception of dogmatics was now a definition of the Christian church, instead of

---

12 Thiel, *Imagination and Authority*, 23 – 24. 35. A distinct question to the historical character of the doctrinal system, to be followed up at a principled level, is what relation does the Christian message itself have to history? This angle arose from the reception of the first edition of the *Glaubenslehre*. Beyond the changing forms of Christian self-consciousness which are expressed in the doctrinal system, the key point Schleiermacher emphasised was that it had been determined historically by the founding figure, the person of Jesus.
13 Eilert Herms, "Schleiermacher's Encyclopedia, Philosophical Ethics, Anthropology, and Dogmatics in German Protestant Theology", in *Schleiermacher, the Study of Religion, and the Future of Theology. A Transatlantic Dialogue*, ed. by Brent W. Sockness and Wilhelm Gräb (Berlin/New York: De Gruyter, 2010), 361– 374, 366.

Christian pious stirrings that were under dispute and needed to be identified also by enquiries located "above" the concrete historical tradition of Christianity.[14]

1.1.3 Issues requiring clarification

With the new division of disciplines and tasks within "philosophical theology" as proposed by the *Brief Outline*, a new direction beyond rationalism and supernaturalism had been indicated. Both the rationalist subordination of Christian specificity to an uncritical regard for reason as sufficient in itself, and an extrinsicist concept of revelation – as promoted, for example, by a Biblicist approach – had been challenged and superseded by a new integrative vision. Yet the status of the connection between the Christian faith, as specified in apologetics and polemics, and philosophy as the general consciousness of truth, diversified into reflective-analytic and comparative aspects, remained unclear. Those readers of *The Christian Faith* who criticised that Christianity had been turned into a philosophy evidently assumed a difference in principle, diagnosing a problematic subordination of faith to its counterpart, human reason. Other scholars have doubted in recent comments whether there can be a "pure" philosophy and whether a properly cultural-historical view does not reveal the time-bound exercise of reason as the dependent part, having originated on Christian ground:

> But does this mean philosophical reflection takes place on neutral ground, and as such, is indifferent to Christianity? Or does it tacitly imply that philosophy can only be done at all on the basis of certain historical conditions (which, for Schleiermacher, are the conditions of Christianity)? ... does this then mean that philosophy in general is *not* a performance of 'pure' reason, but of historically conditioned reason? And what does it mean for theology that one of its essential disciplines is a philosophical one? Does it mean that insofar theology moves on foreign ground?[15]

Thus, the profile of the different dialogue partners needed a sharper focus. Misunderstandings were also facilitated, as Schleiermacher later saw, by the unclarified genre of the Introduction itself. Reasons for mistaking it as the beginning of the systematic treatment of Christian doctrines lay not only in its lack of struc-

---

14 Martin Rössler, *Schleiermachers Programm der Philosophischen Theologie* (Berlin/New York: De Gruyter, 1994), 157. He investigates the different understanding of "philosophical theology" in the first edition of the *Brief Outline* (106–113), the distinction between philosophical and historical theology (135–140) and the "fragmentary unfolding" of the former in an abbreviated form in the *Glaubenslehre* (150–202).
15 Herms, "Schleiermacher's Encyclopedia", 66.

ture, but crucially in starting off with a definition of dogmatics. Being aware of these pitfalls in advance, the organisational layout and sequence of the first two outlines, the Lectures of 1811 and the book of 1821/22, can be appreciated with greater clarity for the fundamental decisions and specific turns they take.

1.2 The Introductions of 1811 and 1821/22: Continuities and differences

The first realisation of the organisation of Schleiermacher's dogmatics into an Introduction and two material parts predates the 1821/22 edition of *The Christian Faith*. The architecture of the future *Glaubenslehre* becomes visible already in the title of the first lecture course on dogmatic theology that Schleiermacher gave in the summer term of 1811 at the university in Berlin which had only been opened in the previous winter term. Announced in the University Calendar as "Dogmatic theology, besides (*nebst*) prior philosophical investigations on Christian religion", it already contains the division between the material parts of Christian doctrine and an introductory part.[16]

In the development of Schleiermacher's reconstruction of core Christian doctrines, the 1811 teaching course stands in the middle of a timeline between the "Speeches" and his full outline of the contents of the Christian religion in the different genre of an academic course book on dogmatic theology in 1821/22. The *Brief Outline*, published at the beginning of 1811, had offered the first occasion to put his conception of the unity of theology in the diversity of its disciplines into circulation. It is instructive to note regarding dogmatics the continuities and the modifications which Schleiermacher considered necessary after ten years of teaching in both the Theology and the Philosophy Departments of the new university.

The Introduction of the first edition of the *Glaubenslehre* shows no subdivision in its 35 propositions, organised in paragraphs headed by a summarising thesis or

---

[16] Matthias Wolfes, "'Ein Gegensatz zwischen Vernunft und Offenbarung findet nicht statt'. Friedrich Schleiermachers Vorlesung über Dogmatische Theologie aus dem Sommersemester 1811", in Ulrich Barth and Claus-Dieter Osthövener (eds), *200 Jahre "Reden über die Religion"*, 629–667, 630. Cf. also Wolfes's introductory remarks to his edition of the transcript of these Lectures by Schleiermacher's student and later successor to his Chair in Berlin, August Twesten, "Friedrich Schleiermacher: Einleitung zur Vorlesung über Dogmatische Theologie (SS 1811). Nachschrift A. D. C. Twesten", in *Zeitschrift für Kirchengeschichte* 109 (1998) 80–99, 82. Quotes from the 1811 Introduction will state the number of the proposition, followed by a page number referring to this text.

Leitsatz; yet in effect it proceeds in four steps.¹⁷ It begins with a definition of dogmatics (¹§ 1), relating its contents back to the pious Christian feelings (¹§§ 2–4). It then explains the concept of piety (¹§§ 8 and 9), and moves on through a typology of religious communities and their specifying factors, to offer, thirdly, a definition of the essence of Christianity (¹§ 18) which will function as a critical standard for the treatment of the dogmatic material. The final section then outlines its implications for the specific content and shape of Christian dogmatics (¹§§ 23–35). As the Christian religion is characterised by faith in Jesus Christ as the Redeemer, which presupposes a prior state of sin, this core conviction needs to be spelt out in two parts, one treating the consciousness of sin, the other that of grace as made available by the Redeemer. Yet since this specifically Christian understanding of God's activity implies a prior, general conception of God as the cause of creation and preservation of the world, the subdivided Second Part is preceded by a treatment of the doctrine of God as it is implied by and contained in the Christian faith in redemption. Thus, the First Part of the dogmatics proper is dedicated to an abstracted, yet valid exposition of the Christian God's activity and attributes.

What is remarkable about this approach is the stringency with which it develops a coherent, critical and comprehensive understanding of Christian dogmatics from its definition of the essence of Christianity. How the key terms – such as feeling, consciousness of God, redemption, sin, grace – are interpreted, will be a matter for discussion both in the current and in the second part of this study. The decision, however, not to begin an exposition of the content of a historical religion with the ordered series of dogmatic treatises themselves but to lead into the history of Christian doctrine with steps of clarifying and justifying the premises contained in the key categories, testifies to a marked methodological awareness and circumspection. Before analysing in Chapter 2 the argumentation of the first edition regarding the

---

17 The marginal notes in a copy of the first edition used by Schleiermacher for lectures in subsequent years and a student transcript give clues to his reasoning. Marg. 9 of the printed version explains: "Introduction presentation of its schematism 1.) In the explanation § 1–4 the doctrine as expression and word is related back to an internal moment, namely the pious inner constitution (*Gemüthsverfassung*) of the Christian. This is why 2.) this has to be characterised § 5–18. Yet since the Christian one is only type (*Art*) or modification, one has to go back to the general. § 5–11 and then to the principles through which it becomes pluralised (*vermannigfaltigt*) § 12–17 3.) After the explanation in § 18 additions follow in § 18 19–22 which define the relationship of Christianity in its content to other manners of faith (*Glaubensweisen*). [About] some significant concepts. 4.) After these from 18 and 1 in § 23 ensues the explanation of dogmatic perfection in individual detail; likewise in § 24 its ecclesial nature. The first formally, the latter materially § 25 Heretics § 26 Protestant : Catholic – § 28, § 29 Plurality in the Protestant. § 30 Documents of proof § 31 Other element the perfection of the academic (*wissenschaftlichen*)." *Marginalien und Anhang* KGA I/7.3, 4–5.

concept of religion, I will compare the continuities (1.2.1) and the differences (1.2.2) between the Lectures and the book and conclude with an assessment of the reason for the decision in 1811 and 1821/22, reversed in 1830/31 due to the misunderstandings this placing gave rise to, for putting the definition of dogmatics in front (1.2.3).

1.2.1 Continuities between the Lecture course and the first edition of the *Glaubenslehre*

The key continuity between the Lecture course of 1811 and the first edition is its innovation of accounting in philosophical terms for the concepts and methods to be used.[18] In the Lectures, the Introduction opens with a definition of the purpose of dogmatic theology which is followed by propositions 2–10 grouped under the title, "Indication (*Aufweisung*) of what is characteristic in Christianity". They contain a reflection on religion in general as being located in "feeling" (proposition 2. 86) and as consisting of "the consciousness of the relationship of the human person to God" (proposition 3. 86). All humans are assumed to be religious.[19] In the Christian religion, the element that "modifies all other feelings" is here named as "the idea of reconciliation" (proposition 9. 87). Crucial distinctions that will continue to structure the work and the elucidation of key terms set forth in the Introduction are already present in the text of 1811.[20] The distinction between the doctrine of sin and the doctrine of grace already constitutes the "formal principle of construction of the total extent (*Gesamtumfang*) of Christian dogmatics". Further continuities are evident in the fact, though not in the specifics, of the distinction between religion and theology; already stated are the understanding, set down in the *Brief Outline*, of dogmatics as belonging to the given continuous reflection that historical theology is to investigate, and the double task of theology to impart a biblically and historically informed scientific or academic certainty (*wissenschaftliche Sicherheit*) as well as an "intuition" (*Anschauung*) of the whole in its necessary connection (*Zusammenhang*) (proposition 1. 85–86). What has

---

18 Wolfes, "Einleitung 1811", 82. In "Gegensatz", 640, Wolfes sees " indications … that precisely the lecture course of 1811 marks an important turning point within the development of Schleiermacher's theological conception. It seems that for the first time, he has decided to preface the exposition (*Entfaltung*) of the dogmatic material with an integrated discussion (*Erörterung*) of central problems in the theories of religion and theology." He judges that "Twesten's text offers a singular insight into the oldest currently accessible stage of Schleiermacher's reflections on the theory of dogma and on doctrine" ("Gegensatz", 632).
19 Wolfes, "Gegensatz", 642.
20 Cf. Wolfes, "Gegensatz", 649–651.

been consistent since the *Speeches* is Schleiermacher's rejection of "natural religion" which is now, however, further explained in his concept of revelation. All religions are "positive", that is, historically individualised. Schleiermacher insists that it is necessary to show that the original revelation from which they begin is not at odds with reason. Thus, it is crucial to conceive of divine revelation in a way that does not treat it as an "external" (proposition 23. 91) or "foreign authority"[21] imposing itself on human consciousness. Both the task of defining a concept of religion and his explanation of the specific difference of Christianity try to steer clear of a stark opposition between the supernatural and the rational. They are marked by the aim to avoid a contradiction between reason and revelation, knowledge and faith.

1.2.2 Differences

Decisive differences, however, in how this shared programme is to be achieved can be seen in specific points of its realisation: in the description of the interface between doctrinal and philosophical statements, and in the actual transition between the Introduction and the first part of the material treatment of doctrine.

Firstly, in 1811, the relationship between dogmatics and philosophy is conceived as one of validation, indeed, of complete transferability to the perspective of the other discipline. Yet after ten years of co-existence with an understanding of philosophy in the neighbouring Faculty that absorbed religion as a stage to be superseded into reason, the aim from 1821 onwards is to keep both separate.[22] This intention is reinforced by modifications in the second edition of the *Glaubenslehre* relating to the difference between the original Christian pious feelings and their reflected dogmatic form, and will be returned to below.

Secondly, a principal change which affects the architecture envisioned from the beginning is owed to a clearer realisation of the demarcation between the

---

[21] Wolfes, "Einleitung 1811", 91. Wolfes, "Gegensatz", 644 and 644, n. 37, with reference to proposition 23 and to a note in A. Twesten's diary.
[22] In 1811, the aim is to "dissolve" (*aufzulösen*) religious feeling into "the reflexive form of scientific intuition" (*wissenschaftliche Anschauung*) (proposition 43. 95), based on the concern that keeping the two apart would mean to split the integrity of the human person. Wolfes points out that "ten years later under the impression of the confrontation with Hegel" ("Gegensatz", 645) "precisely the harmonistic relation through which Schleiermacher coordinates the immediately given religious consciousness and the critical effort of reflection of scientific intuition in 1811 cedes to an analysis in the theory of science that focuses mainly on highlighting the differences instead of indicating commonalities" (666).

"Introduction" and the first main part of the dogmatics. Even if the First Part explicates the concept of God as it is "presupposed" by the opposition between sin and grace in the Christian faith, thus abstracting from this concrete determination, it has to be distinguished from the general concept of religion that was put forward in the Introduction.[23] The reason why it was possible to confuse the two distinct locations and levels will be examined in Chapter 2 which treats the determination of religion as an inherent "consciousness of God". Before this can be done, the argumentations behind the sequence of the Introduction and its subsequent reordering and attribution to distinct disciplines in 1830/31 need to be assessed.

1.2.3 The systematic reason for beginning the *Glaubenslehre* with a definition of dogmatics

By starting with a definition of dogmatic theology that relates it "to the doctrine that is valid at a specific time in a Christian church community" (^{1}§ 1. I, 9), Schleiermacher wanted to avoid a problematic solution of the systematic problem posed for any such treatment, of having to begin with as yet undefined terms. Being aware of what an Introduction can and cannot deliver, he begins with defining dogmatics by its subject, as the church doctrine of a certain time, rather than as a discipline. This would have required giving a complete overview of the disciplines that make up theology. Yet the proper place for such decision-making on the ordering of the different theological sciences is not the Introduction to a dogmatics. Thus, even the opening explanation of dogmatics is geared towards the specific remit of an Introduction. The fact that an analysis of the scientific unity of theology in the plurality of its enquiries would have been out of place at this point is also the reason why he does not take the concept of religion as his starting point. Both in the marginal notes and in a lecture transcript, alternative avenues that could have been chosen are compared. One possibility would have been to begin with the concept of religion and to move towards the concept of dogmatics via the intermediate notion of theology as the "scientific concept" of religion. However, the comprehensive ex-

---

[23] Wolfes sums up the initial failure to show "enough consequence in distinguishing between reflections on the feeling of dependence and the internal connection of dogmatic-theological matters". These reflections, "according to their theoretical status are supposed to precede the material dogmatics, since they present the feeling of dependence as the defining characteristic of the religious consciousness in general; in effect, they are linked to explanations of the doctrines of creation and preservation in a way that has not been clarified sufficiently in its method" ("Gegensatz", 654).

position required for this makes theology unsuitable as either an intermediate or as a starting concept. The procedure chosen instead is to use as his point of departure a content-related definition of dogmatics. Schleiermacher characterises this entry point, defining doctrine as expressing the faith statements of the Christian pious consciousness, as reaching religion "from below".[24] By tying doctrine closely to its basis in the consciousness of the believers, he makes the latter the elementary fact of the entire doctrinal enterprise. While it led to the misunderstanding that with it, the dogmatics itself was being unfolded, making this statement in ^{1}§ 1 is meant to show that what is fundamental are positive, historical, concrete verbalisations of Christian piety. The general concept of religion that is implied in these expressions is to be reached in the subsequent analyses of ^{1}§§ 8 and 9. Reverting to philosophy for this task ensures that the doctrines of a faith community are not merely taken as a matter of social or cultural fact requiring only a description and an elucidation of their internal connections. Instead, this step provides a justification of their truth claim by reflecting on the relationship of the expressions of faith with their roots in history to the human subject as a bearer of reason. The methodological awareness with which the treatment of the tradition of Christian thinking is allocated to "historical theology", and the clarification of the basic categories operative in the entire project given to philosophy or "ethics" as a prior task, already governs the outline of the Lectures and of the first edition. However, only the second edition points out expressly the distinctions between the types of enquiry: access to a general concept of religion is through an analysis of human consciousness; a description of the specific shape it takes among Christian believers requires historical and hermeneutical tools.

1.3 The final ordering in 1830/31

After elucidating the new sequence in which the propositions of the Introduction are ordered (1.3.1), it will be possible to sum up at least the external impression conveyed by the reorganisation (1.3.2).

1.3.1 The new sequence of the propositions

In response to the critical reception of the first edition, Schleiermacher devises a new ordering that ends a sequence which had been operative from 1811 onwards.

---

[24] Cf. Marg. 11, in KGA I/7.3, 5, Script (*Nachschrift*) Heegewald, 2–3.

Since he found ¹§ 1 to have been misunderstood as the opening of the dogmatics proper, in the second version he places the previously first paragraphs (¹§§ 1–4) after the definition of the essence of Christianity (²§ 11) as ²§§ 15–19. At the same time, he also provides "headings for the smaller sections to indicate where the propositions that precede the constitution of the concept of dogmatics properly belong".[25] Thus, the first chapter (²§§ 1–19) containing the "Definition of Dogmatics" *[Zur Erklärung der Dogmatik]* is now explicitly divided into "*Lehnsätze*", topic sentences "borrowed" from the sciences of ethics, philosophy of religion, and apologetics. With the definition of dogmatics moved from its former opening position as proposition 1 to a place after the definition of Christianity, that is, proposition ²§19, the danger that the Introduction would be confused with the material dogmatics has been eliminated. The second chapter (²§§ 20–31) treating the "Method of Dogmatics", that is, the selection of its material and its division, retains the old sequence already followed by the final part of the Introduction of the first edition.

Regarding the view of the role of philosophy, a reversal had already taken place between the 1811 Lectures and the original edition of 1821/22. Philosophy or "intuition" first appeared as the target language for translating the content of religious feeling, while ten years later, they were destined to keep their independence. Yet in the reviews of the first edition, Schleiermacher still found himself in need of responding to the perception that it had turned Christianity into a philosophy.[26] Thus, the sections dealing with the scientific shape and dialectical language of dogmatics (²§§ 15–19. ²§ 28) are the result of further changes that minimise the influence of the systematising conceptual treatment by the philosophical means used in their exposition. The task to reformulate his statements also gives him the opportunity to elaborate on the theme of religious language formation.[27] According to the first edition, the presentation of Christian doctrine in the *Glaubenslehre* was marked by two purposes, the first "ecclesial", "to represent the stirrings of the Christian pious mind-state (*Gemüthes*) in doctrine", the second "scientific", "to bring what is expressed as doctrine into a precise connection (*Zusammenhang*) (¹§ 3 LS. I, 16). In ²§ 18, however, the "interconnecting (*Zusammenstellung*) of dogmatic propositions done for the purpose of conjoining them and relating them to each other" is derived from "the very same need that leads to the forming of such propositions themselves" and depicted as "a natural outcome" of the former (²§ 18 LS. ET 2016, 128). The second edition thus clearly portrays the forging of the connection

---

25 Schleiermacher, "Letters", 80. German original: *Sendschreiben*, KGA I/10, 378–382.
26 This was the main impression Karl Gottlieb Bretschneider took from the *Glaubenslehre*. "Ueber das Princip der christlichen Glaubenslehre des Herrn Prof. Dr. Schleiermacher", in *Journal für Prediger* 66 (1825) 1–28, reprinted in *Marginalien und Anhang*, KGA I/7.3, 369–383, 369.
27 These reflections are already expressed in "Letters", 81–83.

between the doctrines as a dogmatic, not a philosophical activity. What distinguishes the dogmatic *doctrines* now from the original Christian pious stirrings (*Gemüthserregungen*), is not their "connection" or their "scientific presentation", but the "defined" or "determined" nature (*Bestimmtheit*) of their "presentational-didactic character" (²§ 16. ET 2016, 119).[28] "Christ's self-proclamation (*Selbstverkündigung*)" is clearly distinguished as the "only *one* source from which all Christian doctrine is derived (*abgeleitet*)" from the "one way (*eine(n) Art*) in which Christian doctrine is pursued,... based on (*entsteht*) religious (*frommen*) consciousness itself and on the immediate expression of it" (²§ 19. ET 2016, 138). By contrast, the first edition had put the doctrines of the dogmatics and Christ's own teaching on the same level: "In the area of Christianity there cannot be two but only one way in which doctrine originates as the expression of piety and of faith: and the ecclesial doctrines are completely similar (*ganz gleichartig*) to the doctrines of Christ and the Apostles also in their origin (*Entstehung*), only different through their scientific presentation" (¹§ 1,4. I, 12).[29]

The first lead proposition in the new "first chapter" offering an "explanation" (*Erklärung*, ET 2016, 3, definition) of dogmatics over 19 paragraphs directs the reader towards the need to establish a concept of the Christian church. This task requires the establishment of a general concept of church or of religious community. The reason for entrusting the enquiry into human piety as their foundation to "ethics" is also given in ²§ 2: a church is "a community (*Gemeinschaft*) that arises (*entsteht*) only through free human actions and that can continue only by means of such actions" (²§ 2,1. ET 2016, 5). Having added to the characterisation of "piety" in ¹§ 8 LS that it "constitutes the basis of all ecclesial communities" (²§ 3 LS), not only the first and second but also the last proposition of the "definition"

---

28 Theodore Vial uses "descriptively didactic" for "*darstellend-belehrend*" in Vial, *Schleiermacher. A Guide for the Perplexed* (London/New York: Bloomsbury T. & T. Clark, 2013), 84, Matthias Gockel, "representative-didactic" in *Barth and Schleiermacher on the Doctrine of Election. A Systematic-Theological Comparison* (Oxford: OUP, 2006), 38, n. 2.
29 Despite his overall assessment of Schleiermacher's argumentation as "naturalistic", Georg Wehrung, a Schleiermacher scholar in the first decades of the last century, makes an insightful observation in *Die Dialektik Schleiermachers* (Tübingen: J.C.B. Mohr, 1920), 239–240: in order to counteract the criticism that "he had handed over his *Glaubenslehre* completely to worldly wisdom (*Weltweisheit*)", that is, to philosophy, Schleiermacher in the second edition now "strives to limit the remarks about the extent of dialectical thinking in the constructive order (*Aufbau*) of dogmatics which seemed to have been too frank (*offenherzig*): the most dangerous places are either transformed or weakened (cf. ²§ 28 and ¹§ 31); only a logical-formal and architectural collaboration of the pure striving for knowledge to the work of theology is admitted in an exterior way (cf. ²§ 16 Postscript, ²§ 19 Postscript); even the coining of dogmatic sentences is rendered as far as possible ... as a completion of religious language formation (²§ 16.3)".

or "explanation" of dogmatics (²§§ 2–19) frame the task of constructing a coherent system of doctrines as an activity in and for the church.

1.3.2 The effect of the reorganisation

Having noted the individual changes, a preliminary answer can be given regarding the combined effect of the corrections to the order of the Introduction, compared with the intentions for reworking it. The differences affect the architecture of the work mainly in making the distinction between the prolegomena and the treatment of the doctrinal substance more visible. A more substantive judgement – especially in view of the relative weight of the key propositions – on whether the result of shifting blocks of paragraphs to different locations fulfils or counteracts the intention, can only be made in Chapter 4.

The advantage of the new organisation, besides highlighting its status as an Introduction, is that the connection to the general sciences is made more evident. The allocation of the steps of enquiry to their home disciplines makes the subjects and methods of the Introduction more transparent and more controllable. The sequence of speculative, critical and hermeneutical reflection that will be further elucidated when treating the steps towards identifying the essence of Christianity is conducted in an explicit consideration of the limits of each discipline and of the need to change to the subsequent method.

In both editions, the methodical sequence of steps towards identifying the element that gives internal coherence to Christianity begins with determining the concept that functions as a framework to all the historical realisations. Already in 1811, Schleiermacher located "the religious" as an irreducible function among the fundamental pursuits of human conscious life. Proposition 2 stated: "The religious element (*Das Religiöse*) has its seat in feeling; the outward appearance (*Hervortreten*) in intuition through the medium of reflection is secondary."[30] The "proof" for giving feeling the same foundational rank as speculative thinking and agency was its equally originating capacity: "Speculating also about the object of religion and acting from this insight is only called religious when it is not merely accompanied by feeling but is at the same time seen as having originated from it." He then drew an analogy between the lived and the reflective levels of being religious, good and patriotic, which do not require people to have "philosophy", a "moral system" or "a

---

30 Wolfes, "Einleitung 1811", 86.

developed idea of the state". He concluded: "Religion thus does not lie in the field of knowing (*Erkenntnis*) but of feeling".[31]

The first edition goes beyond this brief external comparison by offering an "analysis of the souls in which we find the pious stirrings". They are the "only given elements" (^{1}§ 7,4. I, 25) in an investigation into two essences which are each "unknown" (^{1}§ 7,1. I, 23). As the locus of the pious stirrings, the "souls" are to be considered both "on their own" and "in community", and in two respects: first, regarding the way in which "pious states of mind (*Gemüthszustände*) in several such individuals who do not belong to the same ecclesial community and therefore appear as dissimilar in this respect, are different from other states of mind in relation to which those individuals belong not to different but to the same community". This investigation will lead to the essence of piety. The focus of the second enquiry is on "what unites those belonging to the same ecclesial community of the Christians amongst themselves, and by which they are separated from others who belong to other ecclesial communities", thus leading to what is "peculiar" (*eigenthümlich*) for the Christian mode of faith (*Glaubensweise*)" (^{1}§ 7,1. I, 25).

From the essence of Christianity – redemption from sin by Jesus of Nazareth – the principle of construction for the dogmatics is concluded: the analysis of "sin" and of the "grace" of redemption that structure the concretely Christian consciousness in the Second Part, and the conceptions of God, humans and the world presupposed in the First Part. Besides the statements that directly reflect the Christian self-consciousness, the anthropological ones, two other types are concluded: those on God, and on the world. The steps are the same in both editions: concept of piety, specification of Christianity, organisation of the material system of doctrine drawn from the factors determining the Christian pious stirrings.

At the same time, the question remains whether the new structuring of the Introduction into two chapters achieves its purpose: to establish the "definition" (*Erklärung*) of dogmatics in the first chapter and the principle of its construction – in two main parts and by three types of statements – in the second. Is this formal division not overshadowed by the weight of the two central definitions, of the essence of piety, in ^{2}§§ 3 and 4, and of Christianity, in ^{2}§ 11? The impression, at least externally, is that the focus has moved to the first third of the Introduction. When the first edition set out from the definition of dogmatics in ^{1}§ 1 to find the essence of Christian piety in ^{1}§ 18 and to develop the schematism for the material part in ^{1}§§ 33–35, the key organising paragraphs were placed at the beginning, in the middle and at the end of the Introduction. While the essence definitions also in the second edition are meant to have only a subsidiary function as steps towards

---

[31] Wolfes, "Einleitung 1811", 86.

the definition of dogmatics in ²§ 19, the question will have to be examined whether their argumentative weight does not give them an independent status. On the one hand, the Introduction can no longer be confused with the dogmatics; yet, *as* an Introduction it may have acquired a function that is more than preparatory. Through its position near the start, the claim to having shown the existence of a consciousness of God in ²§§ 3 and 4 acquires a significance which, despite Schleiermacher's express intentions, can easily be mistaken as a speculative foundation of dogmatics in the Introduction.

1.4 The final shape of the architecture of the *Glaubenslehre* in current debate

While the opposing judgements on Schleiermacher's project and its achievement can only be understood when the contested conceptions will have been analysed, one proposal can be dealt with already: the question, considered by Schleiermacher himself, of reversing the order of his reconceptualisation of dogmatics. This matter has been raised again recently in a significant place: the new English translation and critical edition of the second edition. From their first encounter with the text, students of the *Glaubenslehre* are thus reminded of the ambiguities that its structure has encountered since its first reception. It is not only the order of the Introduction, but of the entire work that is under debate. Yet the Introduction is affected in a major way, and the thorough and serious reflection for choosing this sequence in the first place and then for also maintaining it in the final version must be recalled. By highlighting the choices that were open to Schleiermacher in his already substantial revisions of the first version, the editors lay open the seminal decisions that went into the structure of this work (1.4.1). The critical response by the philosopher Peter Hodgson to their suggestion to "read what he gave us, section by section, backward!" will be presented and supported with further reasons (1.4.2).

1.4.1 Schleiermacher's discussion of his planned revisions in the 1829 Letters to Lücke

In their editorial comments, Terrence Tice and Catherine Kelsey refer to Schleiermacher's two open letters sent to his friend Lücke when they summarise the problem he was faced with and its possible resolutions as follows:

"One large quandary that he found no clear resolution for … was whether he should try largely to reverse the order of the book itself. This would chiefly require that he start with Scripture and the core doctrines regarding Christ and the church, then move to using the Part 1 propositions, and somewhere work in the introductory matter. Adopting this arrangement, however, would lead to confusions of its own making and would not obviate difficulties inherent in the matter to be considered. So, he gave up the whole idea (OG 55–60). That leaves us to make only one recommendation to readers, one definitely not for beginners, however. Be sure to identify where the core of doctrine lies (not a set of detailed bits and pieces), then perhaps you really would like to try to read what he gave us, section by section, backward!"[32]

Which alternatives would Schleiermacher have had, and what made him stay with the solution he devised before? One is depicted by the editors of the new English translation: return to the accustomed starting point with the Bible, which presumably would have been taken as the foundation for "the core doctrines regarding Christ and the church". But this way out would have given up on the whole enterprise of offering a justification of the truth claim of Christianity and its Scripture that was adequate to the contemporary level of the critical exchanges of his age. This era no longer accepted mere authority assurances regarding the Bible nor attempts to prove the existence of God from the outside world. If the revision not only reversed the order of Parts One and Two of the material dogmatic but also gave up on the Introduction as such, attaching some propositions – maybe those on the natural heresies derived as the key contradictions from the essence of Christianity – elsewhere, it might indeed have led to quite another level of misinterpretation. In view of the "scrupulous, at times almost mathematical style",[33] pointed out by the 2016 editors, such a random and patchwork procedure would have been out of character for Schleiermacher. Doing away with the Introduction is not something he considered; the only remedy against the misinterpretations of its function was, as we have seen, to order it differently and structure it more clearly. Yet these clarifying and correcting measures would still have allowed the sequence of Parts One and Two to be reversed. Treating the Christian self-consciousness under the "contrast" (*Gegensatz*) of sin and grace as the first part of the system of doctrine would have made it abundantly clear that this was not a philosophical but a Christian treatment of God, Jesus Christ and humanity, and the more general points could have been left to the new second part. Richard R. Niebuhr's judgement is similar to Tice's and Kelsey's: "As we know, Schleiermacher's compromise is to keep the conventional

---

[32] Tice and Kelsey, "Concerning this translation", xxi, with reference to "On the Glaubenslehre" [= OG], "Letters", 55–60.
[33] Tice and Kelsey, "Concerning this translation", xxii.

order, but he does his best to mitigate the consequences... had he yielded to his inclination to reverse the order of doctrine, the structure of his theological thinking, as distinguished from the order of his exposition, would be much clearer to the reader."[34] What spoke against this straightforward solution?

1.4.2 Counterarguments to reversing the sequence of Parts One and Two

In his greatly welcoming review of the seminal work of the new translation, Peter Hodgson comments: "Fortunately Schleiermacher decided not to make this change which would have caused even more confusion about his underlying theological agenda. But Kelsey and Tice seem to suggest that readers might try to identify the core of doctrine and then read the work backward. From my point of view, this would be a mistake."[35]

What rationale – apart from the "whim" (*Grille*) Schleiermacher refers to self-deprecatingly of wishing to avoid an "anti-climax" in the structure of the work[36] – supplies the backbone that could not be turned on its head without consequences for its stature and balance? Since the completion of this epoch-making edifice, theologians of different approaches have copied the basic order it pioneered, as Thomas Pröpper observes: for example, Gerhard Ebeling, Eberhard Jüngel as well as Karl Rahner, Hans Urs von Balthasar, and Walter Kasper.[37] He explains the alternative starting points with their respective gains and losses that have to be weighed up. If one followed the *ordo cognoscendi*,[38] the second main part would have to come first: the consciousness of redemption by Jesus Christ could be covered in its range and depth, providing the recognisably Christian doctrines as the epistemological entry point and moving from there to a further part dedicated to explaining, justifying and connecting the key concepts. The gain of going *medias in res* of the doctrines closest to Christian experience by starting with the history of redemption would be offset, however, by the disadvantage that the overarching statements on God, the human person and the world would have to be brought in at a second stage although they had already been presupposed in the explanation of the salvific significance of Jesus. The other possibility is to

---

34 Richard R. Niebuhr, *Schleiermacher on Christ and Religion* (New York: Ch. Scribner's Sons, 1964), 28. 33.
35 Peter Hodgson, Review of *Christian Faith: A New Translation and Critical Edition*, in *Modern Theology* 33 (2017) 692–697, 692.
36 Schleiermacher, "Letters", 4–11.
37 Thomas Pröpper, *Theologische Anthropologie* (Freiburg: Herder, 2011), 2 vols, vol. 1, 84.
38 Pröpper, *Theologische Anthropologie*, vol. 1, 82.

begin with the "abstract", but nonetheless accurate concepts that capture the human person in her ability to be addressed by God, the concept of God as creator, and a general understanding of "world" under these premises. They are further determined by the Christian understanding of salvation but can be justified as not irrational with philosophical reasons. Thus the "Original Perfection of the World" and of "Humanity" (^{2}§§ 57–61) are treated prior to the factual sin that can only be accessed from the Christian consciousness as it is defined by this contrast. Without this distinction between the two parts, the only content theologians could treat would be new interpretations of biblical terms and their use in the different eras of the tradition. But there would be no location for examining the conceptions as such, although their premises would make themselves felt in the interpretations they offer. Looking back on the sequence of paradigm changes in the Christian tradition, it should be clear that "sin", "grace", "freedom", "evil", "salvation", or "church" have been subject to diverse readings that require conceptual analysis. Pröpper's conclusion with Schleiermacher is to provide the reflection and precise definition of these conceptions first. This means speaking of the "human destination for community with God"[39] in theological anthropology and in the doctrine of God before the decidedly Christian qualifications are examined. Opting for the "logical" order[40] comes at the price of arguing at a remove from the concrete, historical level of Christian experience; but it also provides a level of general understanding that enables exchanges across faith communities, cultures and diverse self-conceptions.[41] From these considerations, the proposal to undo Schleiermacher's well-thought-out sequence by reading the two parts backwards and cancelling his major structural innovation appears counterproductive. Could it not also count as a sign of confidence in the capability of the readers with their Christian-determined pious self-consciousness that he expected them to hold out on the supposedly arid long route through Part One to reach the familiar pastures of Part Two?

---

39 Pröpper, *Theologische Anthropologie*, vol. 1, 79–104.
40 Pröpper, *Theologische Anthropologie*, vol. 1, 83.
41 For the cross-cultural potential of theology as "*scientia*", as distinct from the other three modes (theology as commentary on a sacred text, as wisdom, and as praxis), cf. Robert Schreiter, *Constructing Local Theologies* (Maryknoll: Orbis, 1985), 75–94.

2 Determining the Essence of Piety by Two Distinct Methods in the First and the Second Editions

Schleiermacher's argumentation for determining the essence of religion constitutes the anthropological turn in Christian theology. It is not surprising that his steps of enquiry in the first and the second editions have been subject to the greatest attention and dispute among scholars. In contrast to the *Speeches* which defended "religion" against its cultured despisers, he now uses the term "piety" which emphasises the subjective dimension. Together with the order of the Introduction and the Second Part's Christology, it is the analysis of self-consciousness and the argumentation for the God-consciousness implied in it that have undergone the most fundamental corrections. The first section will present the original argumentation (2.1), the second the rigorous revision for the new edition that amounts to a complete change of method: from a phenomenological description to a transcendental enquiry (2.2). By interpreting the changes as a breakthrough to a transcendental level of analysis, I am following one line of interpretation that has been challenged and needs to be explained in view of other reconstructions. The third section will compare this interpretation to other readings put forward in the ongoing debate by theologians and philosophers, including the alternative between a monist and an egological understanding that marks part of the German-speaking discussion (2.3).

2.1 The original version: A phenomenological approach

In order to assess the first edition's development of a theory of subjectivity which culminates in a consciousness of God, it will be necessary to examine the steps of his analysis in detail: the location of piety in "feeling" (2.1.1), and the identification of the "feeling of absolute dependence" as a God-consciousness (2.1.2). I will outline each of the two foundational propositions in the original version and compare some of their statements to the Lectures of 1811. Since the distinction between "partial" and "absolute dependence" is key in both editions, I will discuss some current interpretations which do not specify clearly enough what their fundamental difference consists in (2.1.3).

2.1.1 Feeling as the location of piety (^{1}§ 8)

Piety is defined in two steps: ^{1}§ 8 investigates its place among the other basic functions of the human spirit and finds it in feeling; ^{1}§ 9 analyses its specificity, which determination of feeling it is. The lead proposition, the "determination (*Bestimmtheit*) of feeling" (^{1}§ 8. I, 26), is proven in a note and in three sections that are instructive in their sequence. The note explains "feeling" as "immediate self-consciousness" that can either accompany or dominate other functions and can thus also persist on its own. ^{1}§ 8,1 states that the possibility of a fourth basic function which could be the seat of piety can be assumed to be unlikely due to the fact that community formations can only be observed with regard to knowledge, agency and piety. ^{1}§ 8,2 then argues for locating piety in feeling first by rejecting its explanation as a mixture of all three, secondly as a link only between knowing and doing, and finally its identification with one or the other, knowledge or the practice of faith. This argumentation for locating it in feeling that proceeds via negating other possible bases is followed by the description of a pious feeling that accompanies acts of knowing and doing and of the content they gain by it in its third subsection, ^{1}§ 8,3.

What is remarkable about this sequence? Regarding the last section, ^{1}§ 8,3, it explains one mode of pious feeling, namely when it accompanies other functions, even before the specificity of piety has been defined in ^{1}§ 9. The first section does not attempt to show the three basic functions as irreducible, essential pursuits of a subject who is exhaustively described through them. The achievement of community formation is deemed to be sufficient. ^{1}§ 8,2 could have reached its goal to conceive piety "in its beginning and its proper (*eigentlich*) essence" (^{1}§ 8 note. I, 26) as residing in feeling if its independence from knowing and doing had been shown. Yet the section does not begin with elucidating this distinction, but with rejecting its explanation as a mixture of all three. The argument given is that defining their proportion would evidence feeling "as the basic note (*Grundton*)... and the original element (*das ursprüngliche*)" (I, 27). If feeling could be reduced to knowing or doing, then the possibility of one turning into the other would have to be clarified. Again, this third element would turn out to be the "innermost immediate self-consciousness of the knowing and acting person" (I, 27) by which feeling was defined at the start.

On the one hand, the points made in these arguments are not superfluous, as the later critiques of the rationalist Johann Friedrich Röhr and the supernaturalist Johann Christian Friedrich Steudel show, and they are insightful. Thus, in order to exclude defining piety through the known content of faith, it is pointed out as a consequence that then "the best proprietor of the doctrine of faith .... would be considered the most pious Christian" (^{1}§ 8,2. I, 27). Identifying it with pious actions is discredited by the ambivalence and heterogeneity of their contents, such as "human sacrifice, Indian suicides, gestures" (Marg. 95, KGA I/7.3, 27). In the first case, the real measure and essence of piety is the "coherence (*Zusammenstimmung*) of one's own self-consciousness with what has been expressed as doctrine" (I, 28); in the second, it is the motivation, instead of the content or the success, of an action. In each instance feeling is the originating and validating location. Knowing and doing relate to feeling "like the outer circumference to the inner centre and radiating hearth (*Heerd*) of life" (I, 29). With this description and the metaphor chosen to illustrate it, feeling has not only been exposed as the location of piety. It has also been identified as the condition of the possibility of the transition between thought and action as well as of the unity of the subject in the changes between these functions.

On the other hand, the proof that "everything leads back to this point", namely the "innermost immediate self-consciousness of the knowing and acting person" (I, 27) does not proceed in a strict, methodologically reflected sequence. What piety is at its core, is already presupposed, rather than identified by distinct steps. ¹§ 8,3 in particular is an example of already using an understanding that will only be specified in ¹§ 9.[42] At the same time, the description leaves the impression that ¹§ 8 not only achieves more than it set out to, namely a definition of the location of piety, but also that it intends more than simply uncovering the equal place of feeling besides knowing and doing: In the final analysis the non-religious basic functions are shown to be dependent on the pious determination of feeling. The actual result is not the independence of the three functions but the dependence of the other two from piety which gives them their guiding direction. To theoretical reason, piety adds "the relation of every circle of knowledge to the whole and the highest unity of all knowing" (I, 29); regarding practical reason, piety orients it towards "the totality of action and its highest unity" (I, 29). This unity is apparently more than just the summarising construction of the idea of totality of the other two functions: it is the "highest and most general order and coherence". This teleological relation of all individual acts of knowing and willing to an ultimate order in which their meaning is accomplished is brought about by the accompanying pious feeling that "appropriates" them (I, 30).

A confirmation of this conclusion can be found in a document that cannot be dated but that is regarded as the "birth certificate" of the epistemic principle of

---

[42] Cf. already Georg Wehrung's judgement in *Die philosophisch-theologische Methode Schleiermachers. Eine Einführung in die Kurze Darstellung und in die Glaubenslehre* (Göttingen: Vandenhoeck & Ruprecht, 1911) that the specification of the "accompanying pious feeling" at this place in the argumentation constitutes a question which can "only be answered by the subsequent deduction. This section is, so to speak (*gleichsam*), an anticipation of the later result" (34).

Schleiermacher's dogmatics.[43] It expresses the basic evidences from which the *Glaubenslehre* was conceived:

> There is only *feeling, knowing* and *doing*, these three types (*Arten*) through which the existence (*Dasein*) of the Human Spirit manifests itself.
> Piety has its source, its seat in *feeling*.
> Feeling is also the original element in knowing and doing, all beginning of thinking or acting, or all transition from one to the other can only take place in self-consciousness which at its most originary (*dessen Ursprünglichstes*) is only a determination of *feeling*.
> True knowledge is only what is being thought in relation to a highest being.
> Only that doing (*Thun*) is perfect and only then true doing when it has its relation to the *highest* being.
> Piety which has its seat in *feeling* is in itself something entirely different from morality (*Sittlichkeit*) and speculation which are to do with doing and knowing. –
> If with the perfection of piety also all philosophy had to die down (*erlöschen*), or vice versa, if in the highest philosophy all piety were to die down, as it has been claimed, then also all morality would have to end, and perish (*untergehen*) in it, something nobody will want to claim –.

Key motives can be found in this document: the independence of piety as an original human capability for receptivity, first articulated in the *Speeches*; the co-existence of a theoretical-philosophical approach to the highest being with a religious outreach; the orientation of morality beyond the recognition of autonomous freedom to a truth which it receives from its divine *telos*; the strong premise of meaning implied in this orientation of the core manifestations of the "Human Spirit"; and the mediating role of feeling for the other two functions, namely, theoretical and practical reason. By uncovering an irreducible third function at the core of human self-consciousness which allows for a basic certitude within the self, Schleiermacher offers a defence of the rationality of faith in a period of prolonged suspicion as well as functionalisation of religion. How the following step, determining the specific difference of piety in the function of feeling, is carried out, will be examined next.

2.1.2 The feeling of absolute dependence as a consciousness of God (¹§ 9)

After securing the independence of piety of both the theoretical and the practical functions of human nature by locating it in the realm of feeling, Schleiermacher specifies its essence in the subsequent proposition with a thesis and an explanation: "that we are conscious of ourselves as utterly dependent, i.e., that we feel

---

43 It is printed in KGA I/7.3, 656–657 in a facsimile copy as well as in transcription.

ourselves dependent upon God" (¹§ 9 LS. I, 31). The two parts of this thesis are proven by an analysis of actual self-consciousness that takes the following steps. It begins with the claim that we always experience ourselves as existing in changing determinations, that is, each time as a specific way of being, or a certain "*Sosein*". The changing states of our self-consciousness on the one hand point to the existence of a "co-determining cause" (*mitwirkende Ursache*). Yet since, on the other hand, it remains self-consciousness, it conceives two moments in itself, "the being-for-itself of the individual" (*das für sich sein des Einzelnen*) and its "being-together-with-others" (*das Zusammensein desselben mit anderen* (I, 31). On the basis of these observations Schleiermacher distinguishes two kinds of feelings: one remaining the same, and one turning to new activity. The first indicates a relationship of dependence, the other one of reciprocity (¹§ 9,2. I, 31–32). The next step in explaining temporal self-consciousness as God-consciousness consists in distinguishing the co-determining cause (*das Mitbestimmende*) in each respective feeling. Here he shows that even vis-à-vis the world as a whole, the self is in a position of reciprocity and thus experiences a feeling of freedom. If, therefore, piety is characterised by a "perfect, steady dependence that in no way is limited or pervaded (*durchschnitten*) by reciprocity", then this cannot point to the world with its "interdivided (*in sich geteilt*) and finitely composed infinity" but implies an equally "simple and absolute infinity" of the co-determining cause. The final step in which the latter is identified with "God" is not argued for, but simply claimed: "And this is the meaning of the above expression that to feel utterly dependent and to feel dependent upon God is one and the same" (¹§ 9,3. I, 32).

The result of analysing self-consciousness in its determination as a feeling of absolute dependence is that in it, God "is given in an inner way as the originating power (*hervorbringende Kraft*) itself" (¹§ 9,4. I, 33). Thus, the "highest being" must be "regarded as innate (*eingeboren*) and as always co-habiting (*mitlebend*)". The first edition leaves it open which one is prior, the feeling of God, or the idea of God, pointing out that the idea of God would arise in any case as a consequence of reflecting on the pious stirrings.

What is shared by the first and the second editions, is the clear-cut distinction between two types of dependence, one partial and limited, and thus subject to be acted upon by human freedom, and the other absolute with no possibility for humans to enact change. The Lectures of 1811 only had two sentences following the location in feeling which give a similarly straightforward connection to God, but no mention of any type of dependence: "3. The religious consists in the consciousness of the relationship of the human person to God. 4. Religion is thus the feeling of the relationship to God, or self-consciousness, modified by the consciousness of the relationship to God".[44]

By 1821/22, an internal analysis of self-consciousness has been added in which the reason for the feeling of a relationship to God is further substantiated. It is reached by making a crucial distinction between two types of feeling of dependence: the everyday awareness of being co-determined by what is one's given context and by the limits of human agency, which are now expressed as "partial dependence"; and a feeling of "absolute dependence" which is identified as being in relation to God.

2.1.3 The need to keep "partial" and "absolute" dependence distinct in the interpretation of both editions

This decisive difference is not always stated clearly enough by commentators on the argumentation in either edition. Since this point is crucial already in 1821/22, I will discuss it here; missing it would mean not only to misrepresent the approach taken originally, but also deprive one of the building blocks to the second argumentation which presupposes this distinction. The "dependence" on the world is clearly set off from "absolute" dependence. The world is marked as a sphere where the freedom to modify what is given is emphasised.

On the one hand, Christian Berner accounts clearly for the difference in the scope of action between the feeling of a partial and that of an absolute dependence; on the other hand, by linking the distinction between "spontaneity" and "receptivity" with Kant's distinction between "*Verstand*" (understanding, or purposive rationality) and "*Sinnlichkeit*" (sensitivity as the capability of being affected by the world through one's senses), the level of Schleiermacher's analysis risks being misconstrued. In his analysis of the second edition, Berner relates the element of "not-having-posited-oneself-in this way (*Sichselbstnichtsogesetzthaben*), or of "Sosein", to the "receptivity" through the senses and identifies this element with "necessity":

> Il y a donc dans toute conscience de soi deux éléments qui correspondent à la liberté et à la nécessité ... On notera qu'il s'agit là d'une transposition dans le sujet des deux pôles de toute activité de connaissance que sont la réceptivité de la sensibilité ("être avec un autre" signifie "être affecté") et la spontanéité de l'entendement. Dans toute conscience

---

[44] Wolfes, "Einleitung 1811", 86.

de soi, en vertu de son être avec autre chose, l'activité se rapporte à une réceptivité première.⁴⁵

It would be important, however, to note the change of levels when Schleiermacher steps back from these two co-existing modes in human self-consciousness to that of a structural analysis where "spontaneity" and "receptivity" are predicated of the "subject". "Spontaneity" is not just that of "understanding" (*entendement, Verstand*) but of the unity of the subject, its reflection on itself as principally able to be a centre of reflection and action. Similarly, "sensitivity" as the ability to take in and relate to the outside world through one's senses is not to be confused with the reflection on the givenness (or sheer existence) of the world and with the insight this allows into the status of human freedom. If the mere fact of being endowed with senses already pointed to God, by interpreting it as showing that receptivity is more basic than the spontaneity of human freedom, this could easily be challenged – as Schleiermacher's argument does – with the counteraction by humans on the material circumstances surrounding them.

While Kevin Vander Schel's discussion of these propositions identifies "contingency" as the key argument, it is not always distinguished sufficiently from "finitude". The continuously held, principled distinction between dependence from the world and dependence from God seems at first to be conflated when he explains the point in the second edition only in terms of finitude and being bound to the world:

> This awareness of absolute dependence marks for Schleiermacher the fullest development of immediate self-consciousness. It is the awareness of one's own finitude and of one's existence as inextricably bound to and contingent upon a world that is itself finite. Notably, however, he also designates this level of self-consciousness as the domain in which the human subject can be said to be conscious of God, for it is in this feeling of absolute dependence that the relation to God finds its echo in human self-consciousness."⁴⁶

Referring to "this level of self-consciousness" as "the domain in which the human subject can be said to be conscious of God" is misleading, since this level is that of partial dependence from and partial freedom towards the totality of the world. Instead, it is the self's consciousness of itself and of the world together as being in a state of absolute dependence from where the connection to God is made. It is

---

45 Christian Berner, "Religion et rationalité chez Schleiermacher", in *Revue de Théologie et de Philosophie* 149 (2017) 153–168, 165.
46 Kevin Vander Schel, *Embedded Grace. Christ, History, and the Reign of God in Schleiermacher's Dogmatics* (Minneapolis: Fortress Press, 2013), 90.

not being "contingent upon a world that is itself finite", but *with* a world that gives rise to the feeling of absolute dependence. This ability of the subject to include the world, too, into a "general consciousness of finitude", as the second edition clarifies (²§ 8,2. I, 67) is decisive for the analysis. Vander Schel's conclusion, that Schleiermacher's analysis is about the "inescapable awareness of the utter contingency of one's existence",[47] is perceptive. But this is not the term Schleiermacher uses himself. He names it "dependence". Vander Schel thus clearly states that the substance of the argument is the ultimate philosophical insight into one's contingency. But this insight is about more than the mere "awareness of one's own finitude", namely about the utter facticity of one's own existence and that of the world. This realisation is the core of the argument in both editions. For the reconstruction to be accurate, it is crucial to elucidate the demarcation between partial dependence, and "absolute" or "utter" dependence.

2.2 The transcendental turn in defining the essence of piety in ²§§ 3 and 4

In his response to the objections of his critics,[48] Schleiermacher revised his theory of religion on two points. First, he clarified how his concept of absolute dependence was compatible with the notion of human freedom. Second, he showed this feeling to be the hermeneutical basis for developing the philosophical concept of God. When this self-consciousness comes to be expressed, it generates the word "God". This latter point is emphasised in the new formulation of the proposition. Now the essence of piety is described as "the consciousness of being absolutely dependent, or, which is the same thing, of being in relation with God" (²§ 4; ET 1928, 12). Unlike the first edition, the second does not refer to the word "God" as to something already known but sets out to explain that the second clause "is the same thing" (*dasselbe sagen will*) as the first. What it means to be "in relation with God", is made clear by "the consciousness of being absolutely dependent".[49]

---

47 Vander Schel, *Embedded Grace*, 91.
48 For an account of the key objections, see his "Letters", 10–21, and Chapter 4 below.
49 In "Die subjektivitätstheoretischen Prämissen von Schleiermachers Bestimmung des religiösen Bewußtseins", in Dietz Lange (ed.), *Friedrich Schleiermacher 1768–1834. Theologe – Philosoph – Pädagoge* (Göttingen: Vandenhoeck & Ruprecht, 1985), 129–162, 137, the philosopher Konrad Cramer sums up the change: "In this correction one must see the decisive progress in the articulation of the basic concept. ... The vagueness of the formulation of the second edition against the un-equivocal determination (*eindeutige Bestimmtheit*) of the formulation of the

2.2 The transcendental turn in defining the essence of piety in ²§§ 3 and 4 — 37

It is this consciousness that is expounded in ²§ 4 and which elicits the expression "God", instead of it being interpreted by a concept of God established elsewhere. The first edition had described the feeling of absolute dependence and linked it to the concept of God known from Schleiermacher's philosophical theory of knowledge, the *Dialectic*. The second derives the meaning of the term "God" from this feeling as its genuine location, supported by a structural theory of the subject. Thus, the priority and independence of feeling is established as the original avenue to God as the "Whence" of the human being's existence in its dual constitution as active and receptive.

Following in this dense argumentation the sequence of steps identified by Thomas Pröpper, I shall chart the starting point and the key turns his revised theory of subjectivity takes. Three moves are constitutive to arrive at this designation: first, the description of temporal self-consciousness as comprising two elements, and reaching a transcendental level of analysis by anchoring these in the structure of the subject (2.2.1); second, the exclusion of the possibility of an absolute human freedom (2.2.2); and third, his concluding interpretation of the "utter dependence" felt by the subject as the indication of being in a relation with God (2.2.3).[50] The final section on questions raised in the history of reception of ²§§ 3 and 4 will discuss alternative readings, including those that object to a transcendental reconstruction, and conclude with a critique (2.3).

2.2.1 The first step: The analysis of actual self-consciousness in its dual constitution

The second edition's analysis of the essential constitution of self-consciousness as the unity of receptivity and activity will be outlined in the following steps: Firstly, changes in argumentation from ¹§ 8 treating the place of "feeling" in relation to thinking and acting (²§ 3) will be discussed in their contribution to the

---

first edition is not to be seen as obscuring, but as making more precise the matter to be highlighted." Duke and Fiorenza also see the difference between the two propositions in that feeling no longer relates "to God as an independent 'object'" ("Letters", 19), though this formulation can be interpreted in different ways.

50 Pröpper's reconstruction of the argumentation of the two foundational paragraphs as constituting three steps is carried out in *Theologische Anthropologie*, vol. I, 475–476, based on his 1988 article. His systematising interpretation of Schleiermacher's complex and at times terse analysis agrees with the equally transcendental philosophical approach of Konrad Cramer on key points of his seminal article of 1985, quoted in the previous footnote.

new aim of offering a complete account that has the status of necessity (2.2.1.1). Secondly, the new subject theoretical terms of "positing" and "posited" and their distinct levels are treated (2.2.1.2), before examining the conclusion drawn regarding the essential structure of the subject (2.2.1.3).

2.2.1.1 The deepened account of ²§ 3 for the place of "feeling" in relation to thinking and acting

The changes reflect the intention to offer a stricter line of argumentation in order to make the results philosophically stringent. By elaborating the underlying theory of subjectivity in greater depth, Schleiermacher seeks to give both the location of piety and the uncovering of actual self-consciousness as a God-consciousness the status of necessary insights that are accessible in self-analysis rather than as evidences that could only be appealed to. The revised ²§ 3, which opens the "Propositions borrowed from Ethics" that specify piety as the basis of a general concept of religious community or church, begins with a new explanation of how the term "feeling" is being used, namely in the sense of an "immediate self-consciousness". Unlike its use in the first edition which understood "immediate" only as "original" in the sense that it was not "attached to a knowing or doing" (Marg. 80, p. 24), the two terms now elucidate each other in the following way: feeling is not "unconscious"; but the type of self-consciousness it constitutes is not "a representation of oneself" that is "mediated by self-contemplation", in other words, generated by reflection on oneself as an object, which is therefore characterised as "more like an objective consciousness" (²§ 3,2. ET 1928, 6). Feeling can either "accompany" thinking and acting, or persist on its own. A quote reinforces the level at which it functions: "the immediate presence of one's whole undivided being".[51] In order to argue for the as-

---

[51] The 1928 ET translates this quote from the philosopher of nature Henrich Steffens, die "*unmittelbare Gegenwart des ganzen ungeteilten Daseins*" as "the immediate presence of whole undivided Being" (7), in which no reference to the subject's individual existence appears. In line with the remainder of the sentence, it should be clear that "feeling" relates to the being of the individual. Also the 2016 ET, while accurate, does not relate "the immediate presence of undivided existence in its entirety" (I, 12, n. 5) to the self's *Dasein* even though the complete quote from Steffens is: "the immediate presence of the whole, undivided, both sensible (*sinnlich*) and spiritual (*geistig*) existence (*Dasein*), of the unity of the person and her sensible and spiritual world" (²§ 3,2 Anm, a. Redeker, I, 17). For a closer analysis of the conceptions of philosophy and the division of labour between "ethics" and "physics" since their appointments at the University of Halle, cf. Sarah Schmidt, "Analogie versus Wechselwirkung – Zur 'Symphilosophie' zwischen Schleiermacher und Steffens", in Andreas Arndt (ed.), *Schleiermacher in Halle 1804–1807* (Berlin/Boston: de Gruyter, 2013), 91–114.

2.2 The transcendental turn in defining the essence of piety in ²§§ 3 and 4 — 39

sumption that knowing, doing and feeling constitute an exhaustive analysis of the basic functions of the human spirit, a new distinction is introduced. They are now explored from the two modes predicated of "life": "a subject's remaining-within-oneself" (*Insichbleiben*) and "stepping-out-of-oneself" (ET 2016, I, 12) or "passing-beyond-self" (*Aussichheraustreten*) (ET 1928, 8). With this subject-theoretical addition, the previous reference to the external evidence of community formation around these functions is no longer needed. Instead, a concise analysis of the subject shows that the three functions offer a complete account. It would be misleading to see the "unity of the subject" as a fourth, coordinated level, rather than as their "common foundation" (²§ 3,3. ET 1928, 8) or "the common ground" (ET 2016, 12). "Feeling" is shown to be the unique occupant of "a remaining-within-oneself": not only "in its duration as having-been-stimulated, but also in its being-stimulated it is not effected by the subject but comes to pass only in the subject" (²§ 3,3. ET 2016, I, 13). It thus "belongs to receptivity in every respect whatsoever", while "doing" and also "knowing", when they are taken not as a result but as an act, are instances of "stepping-out-of-oneself". These two functions that relate to the outside world are anchored in the immediate self-consciousness which "is always the mediating link" (²§ 3,3. ET 1928, 8–9), or, in the new translation, "always functions as a mediating factor in the transition between instances where knowing is predominant and those in which doing is predominant" (ET 2016, I, 13). On the background of these clarifications of the concepts of feeling and of the subject, the final two sections (²§ 3,4 and ²§ 3,5) discuss the possible allocations of piety to knowing and doing, and can now revert to the arguments made in the first edition against it being identified with either of them, and against it comprising a mixture of all three.

The effect of first defining – rather than just alluding to – the terms and factors operative in consciousness is that the new argumentation successfully establishes the starting point of the enquiry into the essence of piety – feeling – as belonging to the essence of the human person. The thesis that piety is located in feeling is thus shown to have the status of general validity. The independence of a religious certitude of God from metaphysics and morality can only be vindicated if the analysis fulfils the claim of necessity: "To these propositions assent can be unconditionally demanded; and no one will deny them who is capable of a little introspection and can find interest in the real (*eigentlichen*) subject of our present inquiries" (²§4,1. ET 1928, 13).[52]

---

[52] "Assent to these statements can be expected without qualification. No one would gainsay them, moreover, who is capable of self-observation to any degree and who can deem the distinctive object of our investigations to be of interest" (ET 2016, I, 20). Peter Grove, *Deutungen des*

2.2.1.2 Actual self-consciousness as marked by the distinction between "positing" and "posited"

Having shown the unity of the subject as the foundation of the three functions and the role of immediate self-consciousness in ensuring the transition between them, the second edition redevelops the terms in which the two elements found in temporal self-consciousness are cast: previously distinguished as "the being for itself of the individual" (*das für sich sein des Einzelnen*) and its "being-together-with others" (*Zusammensein desselben mit anderen*) (¹§ 9,1. I, 31), they are now renamed as "positing-of-the-self-by-the-self" (*Sichselbstsetzen*) and "having-been posited-in-a-particular-way", or, more precisely, "not-having-posited-oneself-in-this-particular-way" (*Sichselbstnichtsogesetzthaben*).[53] The shift that is indicated in these new designations is confirmed in the revised characterisation of the function of the first element. In the original version both the consciousness of ourselves as "always remaining the same" and the consciousness of ourselves as "variable" were considered "only elements of each determined self-consciousness, because each of them is the human person's immediate consciousness of herself as changed" (¹§ 9,1. I, 31). In the corrected version the human person's consciousness of herself as "remaining the same" is not just set at the same level as the second element of determined self-consciousness, but as the condition of continuity in identifying the changing conditions of consciousness as one's own. Thus, the first element can be identified with the "Being" (*Sein*) of the self-identical subject, and the second as its "Having-come-to-be-in-some-way" (*Irgendwiegewordensein*), with the emphasis not on existence as such, as the ET 2016 suggests: "a somehow-having-come-to be" (I, 19), but on factors not of one's own making that have shaped one. The fact that the spontaneous,

---

Subjekts. Schleiermachers Philosophie der Religion (Berlin/New York: De Gruyter, 2004), 556, n. 113, points out that this claim has been linked to that of Fichte's *Wissenschaftslehre* in Georg Wehrung's 1911 study (*Methode*, 43).

53 Instead of following either the 1928 or the 2016 ET, I am using, but also specifying, the translation of Richard R. Niebuhr, *Schleiermacher on Christ and Religion*, 122. Compared with the 1928 ET which names the first "a self-caused" and the second "a non-self-caused element" (13), it keeps closer to the verbal (and therefore "process" rather than "object" oriented) character of Schleiermacher's terms. The contrast is between "self-positing" (*Sichselbstsetzen*) and "not-having-posited-oneself-in-a-particular-way" (*Sichselbstnichtsogesetzthaben*), in other words, finding oneself determined prior to and without one's own doing. The second concept could also be translated as "not-having-posited-oneself-in-this-particular-way". The 2016 ET changes the meaning by rendering the first, active self-positing of the subject as a passive experience, as "a being positioned-as-a-self" over against "a not-having-been-positioned-as-such" (²§ 4,1. I, 19). The problem of the translation of these precise new subject theoretical terms at distinct levels and of the explanation in Ed. note 3 (I, 19) will be taken up in 2.2.2.1 below.

unifying character of the self is the premise for Schleiermacher's further analysis of self-consciousness is evident in the changed expressions and additions in ²§ 4,1, which are in accordance with this insight. An explanation added to this section highlights the newly discovered function of the first element along with the inescapability of being determined by external factors: "every consciousness of self is at the same time the consciousness of a variable state of being. But in this *act of distinguishing* (*in diesem Unterscheiden*, italics mine (MJK); ET 1928, 12: "in this distinction") of the latter from the former, it is implied that the variable does not proceed purely from the self-identical, for in that case it could not be distinguished from it" (²§ 4,1. I,24). Konrad Cramer interprets the crucial highlighting of the subject in its ability to distinguish itself from outside factors in this passage as follows: "By being conscious of these given contents of consciousness as its own, the subject recognises that the consciousness of its identity implied in it is not given, but is based on an act of the spontaneity of the subject, a 'positing-of-the-self-by-the-self', as Schleiermacher says here following Fichte".[54]

On the one hand, the active role of the Ego in relating the outside impressions to itself is being stressed, on the other hand the fact that their effects, resulting in "not-having-posited-oneself-in-this-particular-way", have not been produced by it. The conclusion drawn regarding the structure of the subject moves the enquiry to a new level, from a description of the two components of self-consciousness to a transcendental philosophical analysis.

2.2.1.3 The essential structure of the subject as the functional unity of activity and receptivity

The concluding insight of the first stage of the project of analysing temporal self-consciousness is a claim about the structure of the subject. It is marked by a "double constitution" consisting of two co-equal factors, "activity" and "receptivity" (²§ 4,1. ET 1928, 13). It is an insight into the invariant structure that makes these pursuits possible.[55] To identify the new status reached by the enquiry as "transcendental", however, is a contested interpretation. How the two factors,

---

[54] Cramer, "Die subjektivitätstheoretischen Prämissen", 140.
[55] In her comprehensive study, *Die Freiheit des Subjekts bei Schleiermacher. Eine Analyse im Horizont der Debatte um die Willensfreiheit in der analytischen Philosophie* (TBT 185) (Berlin/Boston: de Gruyter, 2018), 191, Katharina Gutekunst equally takes this finding as having been reached by way of a transcendental method of enquiry: "Feeling is therefore the cipher for the basic transcendental structure of consciousness and thus as such the condition of the possibility of knowledge and action."

"activity" and "receptivity" are understood, depends on it. Regarding their relationship, Katharina Gutekunst states clearly that the consciousness of having been determined by outside realities "does not mean that activity is being derived from receptivity; it only means that the equally original spontaneity receives its direction through receptivity."[56] Yet by proposing to designate them as "attitudes (*Haltungen*) of the subject" (rather than, for example, as "functions"),[57] a crucial insight risks being lost: "Attitudes" implies the possibility of choice, while the discovery made is exactly that the "duplicity" or "double constitution" is an invariant structure over which the subject has no choice. The following second step, to be treated in section 2.2.2, asks about the origin of this structure.

2.2.2 The second step: The impossibility of founding the structure of finite freedom either on itself or on the world

Before examining the second step, the question about the origin of this enabling structure, in greater detail (2.2.2.2), it is important to compare how the argumentations are conveyed in English, especially in the new, in many ways exemplary and elegant 2016 translation; it allows readers to check how these translations make Schleiermacher's concepts accessible and to assess their place in a structural theory of subjectivity (2.2.2.1).

2.2.2.1 Comparing the key terms of the second edition with their English translations

Despite his insightful translation of the key concepts, R. R. Niebuhr subsequently loses Schleiermacher's distinction between the underived original spontaneity of "positing" and the factual determination of "not-having-posited-itself-in-a-particular-way" in his account. After explaining the term "immediate self-consciousness" as referring to "the self that is not qualified by or determined by specific objects and energies located in the world", Niebuhr continues: "It is the self in its original identity, in its being-in-such-and-such-a-way (*Sosein*). This is the identity that the self has to discover and actualize in the world but that it

---

[56] Gutekunst, *Die Freiheit des Subjekts*, 195, also with reference to Grove, *Deutungen des Subjekts*, 558.
[57] Gutekunst, *Die Freiheit des Subjekts*, 192, n. 34, where she also discusses "modes of life" (*Lebensgenera*, one of the terms suggested by Gerhard Ebeling).

2.2 The transcendental turn in defining the essence of piety in ²§§ 3 and 4 — 43

does not derive from the world."[58] Also Terrence Tice, long before engaging in co-producing the eminent work of retranslating the *Glaubenslehre*, has explained the element of "*Irgendwiegewordensein*" as being

> aware that what one now is, at any given moment, is the product of not merely one's self-assertion but more fundamentally still of another factor, a relatively external factor which has enabled any given determination of the self to come to be what it is and which has made self-consciousness itself possible. These two elements elicit the attempt to find objective correlates: both an objectivizing of the self and of the "other" that causes us to be.[59]

In ²§ 4, however, the second element of self-consciousness expressing its state of having always already been determined points to the world and not yet to the cause of personal existence towards which no counterinfluence would be possible. The "Whence" of all being is only disclosed from the feeling of utter dependence which in turn is reached by having moved to a transcendental analysis that discovers the "double constitution" of the subject.

In ²§ 4.1, the active nature of "self-positing" (*Sichselbstsetzen*) which is possible due to the unity of the self that enables the self-activity and the accompanying self-reflection is obscured by its new translation as a passive, constituted factor. It evokes the impression that Schleiermacher is construing a straight line between finding oneself not only as self-positing but also as "*Sosein*", and God, who seems to be assumed to have posited each person in their specificity. In the 2016 ET, each of the two elements in self-consciousness are translated as passive events: "a being positioned-as-a-self" (instead of a "self-positing"), and "a not-having-been-posited-as-such, so to speak, or a being and a somehow-having-come-to-be." The second element as well is rendered without the referent included by Schleiermacher, namely the active self which becomes aware of a crucial limit. Even if the term he creates for this aspect, "*Sichselbstnichtsogesetzthaben*", contains a negation, it is stated in the active mode, which should be translated as "Not-having-posited-oneself-in-this-particular-way". Similarly, the translation of the following sentence changes the meaning by rendering "*setzt ... außer dem Ich noch etwas anderes voraus, woher die Bestimmtheit desselben ist*" ("presupposes apart from the I still something else from which its character of being determined arises") as follows: "Thus, for every instance of self-consciousness, something other than one's 'I' is presupposed, something whence its determinate nature exists and without which a given self-consciousness would not be

---

58 Richard R. Niebuhr, *Schleiermacher on Christ and Religion*, 182–183.
59 Terrence N. Tice, "Schleiermacher's Conception of Religion: 1799 to 1831", in *Archivio di Filosofia* 52 (1984) 333–356, esp. 355–356.

precisely what it is. Still this 'other' would never be objectively depicted in immediate self-consciousness". While the decision is to be welcomed not to follow the 1928 translation which capitalises "Other" (^{2}§ 4,1. ET, 13), the quotation marks added to "other" by the new translation are not in Schleiermacher's text. The editors' comments in notes 3 and 5 corroborate that they read and translate these sentences as pointing to "some agency outside oneself" which through the added term "agency" is more likely to be understood as referring to God than to the world:

> The pairs of concepts here are ein *Sichselbstsetzen* and ein *Sichselbstnichtsogesezthaben* [sic], then ein *Sein* and ein *Irgendwiegewordensein*. The first of each pair refers to an awareness of oneself simply as an existing being, the second to an awareness of one's having come into being and being changeably sustained in a process of being and becoming by some agency outside oneself. [60]

"Sustain" and "agency outside oneself" seem to me to be theologising additions to what is a highly precise analysis of the capability and the internal limits of self-consciousness in ^{2}§ 4,1.[61] From a translation that replaces the key term "self-positing" that stands for the unity of the I which conducts the analysis, with "a being positioned-as-a-self", it is not possible to reconstruct the content and depth of Schleiermacher's argument. Subsections ^{2}§ 4,1–3 deal with partial dependence from the world and the insight into the inescapable double structure of self-consciousness; "being in relation with God" (^{2}§ 4 LS and ^{2}§ 4,4), by contrast, is Schleiermacher's thesis that the immediate self-consciousness of absolute dependence is verbalised as a God-consciousness. The notes make it clear, however, that the editors do not distinguish between the concise philosophical analysis in ^{2}§ 4,1–3 and its theological interpretation in ^{2}§ 4,4.

The danger is that the translation itself already takes sides regarding the interpretation of this sequence and therefore risks misrepresenting Schleiermacher's argument. Having reached the insight into its own double constitution, the decisive question as to the origin of this structure is posed.

---

[60] ET 2016, I, 19, text and notes 3 and 5. Regarding the 19th century spelling Schleiermacher used, which the 2008 German edition by Rolf Schäfer reproduces, the "t" in "setzen" is left out both times, so it should also be *"Sichselbstsezen"* instead of *" Sichselbstsetzen"*.

[61] In his review in *Modern Theology* 33 (2017) 692–697, 695, also Peter Hodgson criticises the addition of the term "agency": "it seems to me misleading to speak of 'some agency outside oneself'."

2.2 The transcendental turn in defining the essence of piety in ²§§ 3 and 4 — 45

2.2.2.2 Enquiring into the origin of the subject's structure

To sum up the results of the first step in the task to establish piety as a necessary function of the human subject: its consciousness has been analysed as containing two factors, finding itself always already as posited in specific ways, and self-positing as the ability to unify and own these diverse impressions. They point to two faculties, "receptivity" and "self-activity" that are always functioning jointly to enable the pursuits of the subject. But where does the structure itself come from? Two possibilities are tested, namely human freedom itself, and the outside world. While the function of the I as the unifying centre of action and reflection is indisputable, its freedom is recognised as only "partial" because it depends on material from outside itself of which it is not the origin. On the other hand, neither is the world suitable as the origin of this structure since it is the recipient of the subject's action and cannot have the status of a co-equal. That leaves the enquiry without a positive answer apart from the insight that freedom finds itself as given to itself in its existence and in its structure, "given" in the sense of not having caused it by itself. As little as its active counterinfluence on the world in its "feeling of partial freedom" amounts to power over the existence of objects, as little can it dispose over its own invariable constitution which it did not give to itself.

The conclusion from the limits of what is at its disposition is instantaneous – the consciousness of partial freedom is interpreted in and of itself as a feeling of "absolute dependence:

> precisely this self-consciousness – which both accompanies all our self-initiated activity, thus also our entire existence because this self-initiated activity is never at zero, and also negates absolute freedom... is already in and of itself a consciousness of absolute dependence. This is so because the consciousness that our entire self-initiated activity likewise issues from elsewhere (*von anderwärts her ist*) just as anything in relation to which we would be thought to have a feeling of absolute freedom would have to issue entirely from us (²§ 4,3. ET 2016, 24).

The only critique that can be made of this second step is that it remains at the level of concrete freedom. It fails to account for the formal unconditionality of freedom that enables the subject to take a stance towards everything given. But as an analysis at the level of concrete existence where objects do not "issue entirely from us" it cannot be faulted.

"What Schleiermacher has been able to show is nothing less than the necessary insight (*zwingende Einsicht*) that our freedom (just like our consciousness and our free faculty of reason) in the facticity of their existence can neither be explained from itself nor from the world."[62] Schleiermacher's concluding thesis that the immediate self-consciousness of utter dependence constitutes an innate relation to God represents a step beyond philosophical enquiry into a theological thesis and will now be analysed as the third step (2.2.3).

2.2.3 The third step: The immediate self-consciousness of utter dependence as an innate relation to God

It is in the fourth and final section of ²§ 4 that the third, decisive step is made to identify the feeling of utter dependence with "being in relation with God" (²§ 4 LS. ET 1928, 12; 2016, 18). It becomes a God-consciousness insofar as "the Whence of our receptive and active existence" that is "co-posited" (*mit gesetze Woher*) in it "is to be designated by the word 'God'" as its "really original signification" (²§ 4,4; ET 1928, 16).[63] Thus, the analysis of temporal self-consciousness reaches its goal in disclosing a natural certitude of God implicit in the actualisation of human freedom. It is even termed "an 'original revelation of God' to human beings or in human beings" (2016, 26).[64]

---

[62] Pröpper, *Theologische Anthropologie*, vol. I, 477–478.

[63] The 2016 ET renders "*wahrhaft ursprüngliche Bedeutung desselben*" (²§ 4,4. 2008, 39) as the "most primary notion" (24).

[64] It is not clear to me why quotation marks that are not in the German text (2008, 40) have been added to "'original revelation of God'" in ET 2016, 26. Notes 24 and 26 play down the general, universally valid status Schleiermacher claims for his analysis. First, the claim that this experience is the basic ground from which all positive religions originate is reduced to the "Christian context, the only context to be considered in this work" (26, n. 26). That is true of Parts One and Two of the material dogmatics but not of the Introduction, which, as Chapter 1 has clarified, in elaborating concretely the Philosophical Theology devised in the *Brief Outline*, includes the non-theological disciplines of "ethics" and a comparative "philosophy of religion". On the previous page, note 23 equally obscures the meaning. It is to explain the feeling of absolute dependence as "precisely that feeling which we consider to be the basic form of all piety" (²§ 4,4. 2016, 25). Note 23 states: "In this context the reference to 'all' can only be to 'Christian piety' (see how the next paragraph begins), or at most to any that rests on the feeling of absolute dependence, though Schleiermacher does also claim that all genuine 'piety' is based on feeling, not on 'knowing'" (25).

Secondly, the claim of offering an analysis to which all people capable of self-reflection can agree and that is a "necessary" insight, is undermined when "reflection" is explained in n. 24 as meaning something else entirely: "This word here refers to such phenomena as a mirror reflection of light or of sound (an echo), not to contemplative reflection (*Betrachtung, Contemplation*)." ²§ 4,1 had ended with the statement, already quoted in 2.2.1: "To these propositions assent can be unconditionally demanded; and no one will deny them who is capable of a little introspection"

2.2 The transcendental turn in defining the essence of piety in ²§§ 3 and 4 — 47

Three elements are contained in this argumentation: first, the basis for claiming a "Whence" is a lack of foundation in the finite (2.2.3.1); second, this "Whence" cannot be grasped as an object (2.2.3.2), and thus, in distinction from the first edition, the feeling of absolute dependence becomes the hermeneutical basis for the theoretical concept of God (2.2.3.3). The final point will compare two opposite theological views on the ultimate shape of the argument for a God-consciousness (2.2.3.4).

2.2.3.1 The lack of foundation in the finite as the basis for claiming a "Whence"

The starting point for concluding a God-consciousness is the negative outcome of the enquiry about the origin of the dual structure as which the human subject exists. It leads to the most profoundly relativising insight not just into the limits of what it can concretely dispose over, but into its status in principle. This insight begins with the awareness that it is in need of material existing prior to it in order to act or think and be more than a merely formal "indefinite 'agility' without form or colour" (²§ 4,1. ET 1928, 13). In particular, it is grasping that "we could not come to be in this way except by some other" (²§ 4,2. ET 2016, 21). This leads to the thought that even if all free movements were taken together, there could be no feeling of absolute freedom "because our entire existence does not come into consciousness for us as having arisen from our own self-initiated activity" (²§ 4,3. ET 2016, 24). When the "feeling of absolute dependence" is concluded from this insight, its core is human facticity, as well as the facticity of the world which cannot be the source of absolute dependence since we "exercise a counter-influence" (²§ 4,2. ET 1928, 15) on it.

The line of interpretation I am following is to take Schleiermacher's demonstration as a precise outline of the reasons for concluding a status of utter contingency for human existence and of that of the world. Schleiermacher claims from here in his final section, ²§ 4,4, that this "consciousness of absolute dependence" insinuates a "Whence" (ET 1928, 16) that is "coposited" (ET 2016, 24) in it. The "most immediate reflection" (*unmittelbarste Reflexion*)[65] on it expresses itself through "the word 'God'" (ET 1928, 16), indicating clearly, howev-

---

(ET 1928, 13), or, as in ET 2016, 20: "Assent to these statements can be expected without qualification. No one would gainsay them, moreover, who is capable of self-observation".
65 Both ETs choose "direct" to translate "unmittelbarste", as "the most direct reflection" (ET 1928, 17) or "the most direct possible reflection" (2016, 26).

er, its complete distinction from an approach by the objective function of reason.

2.2.3.2 Immediate and inaccessible as an object?
The feeling of absolute dependence that turns into a consciousness of God is presented as a modification of "immediate" self-consciousness. What is co-posited cannot be grasped as an object. This makes it difficult to understand the "status"[66] of this consciousness of God, and different readings have been ventured. Konrad Cramer judges that "Schleiermacher breaks with the idea of a consciousness-transcendent God".[67] The translators of the *Sendschreiben* come to a similar sounding assessment: Duke and Fiorenza also see the difference between the two propositions in that feeling no longer relates to God as an independent "'object'".[68]

But is this the only possible conclusion from the changes made to the earlier edition? Cramer correctly summarises them as follows:

> While the first edition identifies the consciousness of utter dependence with the feeling of dependence "upon God" and thus assigns a certain intentional object to this feeling, namely God, the second version does not only dispense with such an assignment: as the distinguishing feature of the feeling of piety from all other feelings, it states the consciousness of our absolute dependence as such and identifies this consciousness with the one in which we are conscious of ourselves as "in relation with God". ... the intentional structure of the consciousness of absolute dependence is diminished in so far as its identification with something like a feeling of dependence upon God is no longer allowed.[69]

He draws a comparison to other feelings, such as "pain which is exactly not experienced as something which has substance (*Bestand*) also independently of it coming to one's consciousness". Yet this comment is made in the context of an argument which has a different aim: Schleiermacher attempts to secure the independent basis of piety in feeling, as distinct from knowledge and action, not its reducibility to other functions of consciousness. Regarding the aim of ^{2}§ 4,4, it is equally a question of interpretation whether one assumes an independent instance to correspond to this feeling, even if this feeling as a modification of the "immediate self-consciousness" cannot have the form of intentionality which the objective consciousness has. If one endorses Schleiermacher's

---

66 Pröpper, *Theologische Anthropologie*, vol. I, 473.
67 Cramer, "Die subjektivitätstheoretischen Prämissen", 161.
68 Duke and Fiorenza, "Letters", 19.
69 Cramer, "Die subjektivitätstheoretischen Prämissen", 137.

analysis of the question about the "Whence" of all being, an origin outside of consciousness is required, one that is "transcendent", to use Cramer's term, to the course of the enquiry itself. It is still possible to doubt Schleiermacher's assertion of an immediate givenness of God in the feeling of absolute dependence.[70] But the question is whether an overall reconstruction of his argument as retreating from "the idea of a consciousness-transcendent God" does justice to it. Does the second edition restrict the idea of the presence of God to human consciousness, or is consciousness, on the contrary, taken only as the location of becoming aware of the reality of God as the origin and creator of all?

2.2.3.3 The feeling of absolute dependence as the hermeneutical basis of the concept of God

This claim marks a decisive difference to the method and result of the first edition's line of reasoning. It had imported the concept of God from an external realm, namely theoretical reason, instead of defining the very meaning of this term from its original emergence in the moment when the immediate self-consciousness of utter dependence expresses itself reflectively. It had stopped its enquiry with drawing a distinction within feeling itself between the co-determining factors – the "world" with its finitely constituted infinity, in contrast to the "simple and absolute infinity" (^{1}§ 9,3. I, 31) of God. In the second edition, God is no longer presented as opposed to, but as presupposed by the infinity of the world. God can only be discovered from the "immediate existential relationship"[71] that the subject becomes aware of in the experience of the conditioned nature of its existence that it did not cause and cannot capture. The conclusion that "God is given to us in feeling in an original way" (ET 1928, 17) or "in an originative fashion" (ET 2016, 26) is upheld in the second edition with a qualification that in-

---

70 The claim of "immediacy" has often been challenged. Duke and Fiorenza object: "Granted that the idea of God is 'the most direct reflection' on the feeling of absolute dependence, it nonetheless arises from reflection, and therefore is not immediate. And, insofar as feeling is immediate, it is not yet a clear self-consciousness that carries with it a consciousness of God" ("Letters", 21). In "Schleiermachers Bestimmung des Christentums und der Erlösung" (1988), reprinted in *Evangelium und freie Vernunft. Konturen einer theologischen Hermeneutik* (Freiburg: Herder, 2001), 149–150, n. 45, Pröpper questions the "immediacy" of a self-consciousness "the determination of which can only be deduced by proceeding from the mediated and by negating an absolute consciousness of freedom". Here he refutes this idea in view of the very steps taken in ^{2}§ 4,3 and ^{2}§ 4,4 – absolute dependence is only reached by ruling out an absolute feeling of freedom, thus contradicting the "immediacy" claimed. Cf. also *Theologische Anthropologie*, vol. I, 477.
71 "Letters", 40.

cludes the equal contingency of the world: "that, along with the absolute dependence which characterizes not only man but all temporal existence, there is given to man also the immediate self-consciousness of it, which becomes a consciousness of God" (ET 1928, 18).[72] It becomes realised as piety in the "measure" in which it "actually takes place during the course of a personality through time" (ET 1928, 18) respectively "really arises during the temporal course of one's personal existence" (ET 2016, I, 27). Other previous statements are omitted, such as some that could be misunderstood in the sense of the projection theory worked out later by Feuerbach: that "in the pious stirrings God is given only in an interior way as the productive force itself" ([1]§ 9,4. I, 33) and that "the highest being" is "innate to" and "always co-existing with" the pious self-consciousness ([1]§ 10,4. I, 36). Thus, in comparing the steps of argumentation of both versions, Georg Wehrung's judgement on [1]§ 9 seems justified to me: "After an analysis (*Zergliederung*) of consciousness that is supposed to be epistemological (*erkenntnistheoretisch*) yet falls into an empirical-psychological mode (no. 2), it suddenly steps forward with its definition and prohibits any contradiction (no. 3)".[73] Nine years before, in his 1911 book on Schleiermacher's method, he had put the ironic question:

> Was there not an earlier agreement to derive (*hergeleitet*) piety from the essence of the human person, did it not count as an "unknown factor" ... which first had to be developed from other given elements? Here, however, it counts as well known in its core to all the world from the start, recommends itself at once to be experienced immediately and expounds ... how it is to be judged.[74]

While the case can be made that the analyses of [2]§§ 3 – 4,3 are decisive for justifying as reasonable the option to believe in a creator God, the step taken in [2]§ 4,4 with its location of an "original revelation of God" in an "immediate" human self-consciousness, must be refuted in its general possibility. This, however, can be seen as not being

> a disadvantage. On the contrary, Schleiermacher's dilemma only confirms the suspicion which I harbour and want to state clearly: that there is no immediate God-consciousness – not only none that ... can be philosophically demonstrated, but ... none *at all*. For what could be the meaning of speaking of a God-consciousness if it did not contain any

---

[72] The new translation (2016, I, 26 – 27) chooses the following formulation: "that what is given to human beings, along with the absolute dependence inherent in all finite beings no less than in oneself, is also the immediate self-consciousness of that absolute dependence arising to the point of being God-consciousness."
[73] Wehrung, *Dialektik*, 205.
[74] Wehrung, *Methode Schleiermachers*, 46 – 47.

reflective determinations and could not even deliver the distinction between God, self and world? Every God-consciousness – especially if it is owed to revelation or to the presence of God through God's spirit in us, carries (in more or less explicit and developed ways) reflective determinations that have to be presupposed logically in order to be able at all to perceive the reality encountered as the reality of *God* – just as I can only perceive and recognise someone as an other if I distinguish myself reflectively (or at any rate in consciousness of myself) from that person.[75]

There is no way around – nor should there be, if both counterparts are to be involved as themselves – a mediation that implies self-reflection, and that allows space for the reflective freedom of each side.

2.2.3.4 Self-authenticating claim or a careful identification of the anthropological foundation for the question of God?

Two judgements on the second edition can show the divergence in appreciation of the method used. Ronald Thiemann's critique may be true for the first edition but does not take on board the decisive change of method and claim regarding the analysis of consciousness in the second version. His objection is that "the foundational belief is established by an appeal to religious intuition, a self-authenticating claim to immediate self-consciousness. The immediacy of the feeling of absolute dependence establishes its extra-ordinary character, its divine origin".[76] As I have tried to show in this section, however, the second edition's course of reasoning reaches God as the origin of all being by a philosophical analysis carried out in general terms. Although, as will be further discussed in the final part of the following section (2.3.3), it finally overstates its findings, its basis (human self-consciousness) and the procedure of the analysis are open to verification, fulfilling therefore the conditions Thiemann sets: "Unless we are aware of and in control of all conditions which might introduce discrepancies between the apparent and real nature of an experience, we cannot claim that the experience is indubitable".[77]

In contrast, Gerhard Ebeling's assessment highlights the hermeneutical achievement of the second argumentation. He explains the progress of the sec-

---

[75] Pröpper, *Theologische Anthropologie*, vol. I, 477.
[76] Ronald F. Thiemann, *Revelation and Theology. The Gospel as Narrative Promise* (Notre Dame, Indiana: University of Notre Dame Press, 1985), 29. See also his contribution, "On speaking of God – the divisive issue for Schleiermacher and Barth: A response to Frei and Sykes", in J. O. Duke and R. F. Streetman (eds), *Barth and Schleiermacher: Beyond the Impasse?* (Philadelphia: Fortress Press, 1982), 108–113, 110.
[77] Thiemann, *Revelation and Theology*, 30.

ond edition with its hermeneutically decisive thesis that the concept of God is to be accessed from the anthropological experience of utter dependence as "tracing back" (*Rückführung*) this idea "to its origin in experience": "This movement of immediate self-consciousness towards a God-consciousness is a movement into the linguistic mode (*Sprachlichkeit*). For Schleiermacher, it constitutes the basic procedure to which the verification of speaking about God has to refer."[78]

Ebeling shares the view that the meaning of the concept of God cannot be taken for granted, that it must be determined with reference to the constitution and self-understanding of humans. He makes it clear that in the second edition, the hermeneutical place of this verification is the experience of utter dependence. While doubting whether Schleiermacher was successful in his "far-reaching aim to demonstrate our real relationship to God", also Pröpper recognises as his "valid achievement" in the first two steps "to have provided the philosophical proof (*Nachweis*) for the human *orientation* towards God."[79]

Theological critiques of the Introduction can be divided into those that share Schleiermacher's insistence on the dual reference of theological thinking, and those that only accept the need for an internal elucidation. Then theology's only task is to seek an interpretive consensus within the community, without having to also justify its claims to a general consciousness of truth. For either understanding of the role of theology it is clear that God's revelation cannot be derived from reason. Ebeling and Pröpper belong to those who defend the elliptical structure of Schleiermacher's *Glaubenslehre* with its dual focus. It is part of the theological project to refound the possibility of speaking of God after the proofs for God's existence had been dismantled by Kant, and core teachings had encountered serious questioning that demanded a well-thought-out response.

2.3 Disputes about the interpretation of the analysis and of its results

It was the need to show the compatibility of his analysis with the concept of human freedom that moved Schleiermacher to develop a transcendental mode of argumentation in relation to the first task of the Introduction, the de-

---

[78] Gerhard Ebeling, "Schlechthinniges Abhängigkeitsgefühl als Gottesbewußtsein", in *Wort und Glaube* (Tübingen: Mohr Siebeck, 1975), vol. III, 116–136, 123.
[79] Pröpper, *Theologische Anthropologie*, vol. I, 479.

termination of the concept of piety. His new enquiry into its nature was carried out through an analysis of the constitution of human subjectivity. As has become evident in the foregoing sections, the progress made compared with the first version can be summarised in two points:

— The feeling of absolute dependence is not only shown to be compatible with human freedom but established as the deepest insight into its constitution: freedom is given to itself. That religion is a necessary feature of humanity is thus not just claimed but inferred as the final step in a general analysis of temporal self-consciousness. Thus, as Pröpper points out, the "definition of the *concept* (of piety) coincides with its demonstration as an *essential* element of the human person."[80]

— The concept of God is not borrowed from the realm of speculative reason but is originally derived from the consciousness of absolute dependence. Only now is the independence of religion from metaphysics and morality really established. Thus, the feeling of absolute dependence serves as the hermeneutical key to the word "God", the term that points to the absolute ground presupposed by the world and not simply opposed to it (as in the first edition). That is, only in the second version is the meaning of the concept of God determined in an original, underived way.

Yet even those who agree on identifying his procedure as "transcendental" disagree on important questions: what this method implies, the content of key terms and what has been established, the starting point and result, whether it can be justified philosophically, and what its consequences are for the relation assumed between God and humans (2.3.1). Secondly, the alternative between a monist and an egological interpretation of the "immediate self-consciousness" will be examined (2.3.2), and thirdly the question of the validity of the philosophical claim of a God-consciousness as the result of the analysis of ^{2}§ 4 will be taken up again (2.3.3).

2.3.1 Questions to a transcendental reconstruction

Different understandings of "transcendental" will be compared first (2.3.1.1) before some alternative proposals resulting from a theological critique will be examined (2.3.1.2).

---

[80] Pröpper, "Bestimmung", in *Evangelium und freie Vernunft*, 136.

2.3.1.1 Different understandings of "transcendental"

In part of his 1994 review article of then recently published Schleiermacher studies, Michael Moxter examines in which sense one can attribute a "transcendental" method to Schleiermacher.[81] In his *Dialectic,* for example of 1814/15, both the terms "transcendental" and "transcendent" are employed in relation to the "ground" from which "knowledge of God" is claimed (§ 15.3); thus, it is a "wide and unspecific" use.[82] Moxter concludes that only that part of transcendental philosophy which is dedicated to developing a "theory of the constitution of subjectivity" can be claimed as a framework for reconstructing his thinking.[83] Even with this perceptive restriction, however, it still needs to be examined how the author of the *Glaubenslehre* has used this mode of analysis. The following quotes from different eras of Schleiermacher scholarship illustrate a variety of perspectives on a "transcendental" line of interpreting the meaning and implications of these passages. The question of whether he oversteps the limits of this type of analysis can only be answered subsequently.

Wilhelm Dilthey's assessment of Schleiermacher's procedure since the *Speeches* as "transcendental" is meant in the sense of discontinuing an "objective" knowledge of God yet explains this in problematic terms. He interprets the *Speeches* as his attempt "in the age of transcendental philosophy to look for the conditions for religious phenomena in our consciousness".[84] He sees also the *Glaubenslehre* as conceived from this standpoint:

> *Schleiermacher is the Kant of theology.* He grasps the transcendental standpoint from which the impossibility of knowing the great objects of religiosity is understood; thus, in the place of these external objects of religiosity their process itself remains as the only object of understanding in the religious realm. An objective knowledge of the attributes of God or the way of our future existence (*Fortleben*) transgresses the limits of our reason. Therefore, religious studies (*Religionswissenschaft*) and theology can only bring to knowledge the proc-

---

81 Michael Moxter, "Neuzeitliche Umformungen der Theologie. Philosophische Aspekte in der neueren Schleiermacherliteratur", in *PhR* 41 (1994) 133–158, especially 134–139.
82 Moxter, "Neuzeitliche Umformungen", 135. Regarding the difference of the *Dialectic* to Kant's critique of the limits of theoretical reason, Horst Stephan observed in 1901: Since Schleiermacher "thinks God and world, the infinite and the finite in a much closer connection than Kant, he extends knowledge in a transcendental way also to factors (*Größen*) which are transcendent for Kant and can thus only be determined in some way by the postulates of practical reason." H. Stephan, *Die Lehre Schleiermachers von der Erlösung* (Tübingen: J.C.B. Mohr, 1901), 162.
83 Moxter, "Neuzeitliche Umformungen", 138.
84 Wilhelm Dilthey, *Leben Schleiermachers,* vol. II, ed. by M. Redeker (Göttingen: Vandenhoeck & Ruprecht, 1966), 6.

ess, the steps and forms in which the deity and the immortality of the soul arise (*aufgehen*).[85]

This would be a correct description of Schleiermacher's method, if the "process of religiosity" itself was retraced to the conditions of its possibility in the essential constitution of the subject. Yet Dilthey's further statements regarding the "content of religion" show that his interpretation of *The Christian Faith* from the position of the *Speeches* does not do justice to the determination of God that is implied in the feeling of absolute dependence; as we have seen, it clearly distinguishes God from what is grounded, the self together with the world. For Dilthey, however, in the *Speeches* and "subsequently" (*späterhin*) it is the case that "always God and world are treated as belonging together and as eternally inseparable". The *Glaubenslehre* "especially in its first edition cannot completely rid itself of the thought of the *Speeches*: Religion is a new extension of self-consciousness to world-consciousness, a feeling of togetherness with everything finite. The *Speeches* only stop at this thought; the *Glaubenslehre* ... adds the thought of *absolute* dependence to it (*hängt daran an*)."[86] This reconstruction in terms of continuity with the *Speeches* is reflected in Dilthey's judgement: "For Schleiermacher, religious life is not a life for itself; the eternal and the divine can only be had with the finite and *with the world*. God cannot be separated from the world not only in speculation, but also not in piety".[87]

Despite the memorable and much-quoted epithet, *Schleiermacher ist der Kant der Theologie*, Dilthey ends up with a judgement that could not be further from what both editions of the Introduction emphasise, the distinction between God and world in the two feelings of dependence. A concise explanation of the key point of the second step of the transcendental analysis is given by Thomas Horst. He identifies as its crucial point not the dependence of self-activity on "material" or on an "object" (which was the reason for having only a partial feeling of freedom, split by the feeling of dependence from the world), but the question of the "being" of the "self-relationship" (*Selbstverhältnis*):

> The point of the argumentation is not that the subject's need (*Angewiesenheit*) for the "material" that is present through its receptivity – a need forced on it by a lack of determination within self-consciousness – would ground the relation to transcendence. For ... the subject compensates its deficit in determination (*Bestimmtheitsdefizit*) under the conditions of its free self-relationship: receptivity for the material of experience presupposes a minimum

---

85 Dilthey, *Leben Schleiermachers*, vol. II, 535.
86 Dilthey, *Leben Schleiermachers*, vol. II, 586.
87 Dilthey, *Leben Schleiermachers*, vol. II, 584.

of self-activity. One could, in Cramer's terminology, say that even the determination through "external factors" is set by the subject under the conditions of determining itself. This is the transcendental moment of an ontology of the subject. The insight, however, that the subject, while it allows itself to be determined by something external, determines itself, leads to the thought about the conditions of the *being* of this dimension.[88]

Thus, the idea of God arises from the subject's insight into the impossibility of grounding the existence of self-consciousness, including the self-relationship inherent in it, on itself. Cramer calls it the insight into the "non-ground (*Ungrund*) of this structure" in self-consciousness.[89]

Thinking about "the conditions of the *being* of this dimension" leads to the realisation that the being of the self-relationship is not necessary, but contingent.

The insight that Cramer and Horst refer to can also be found in a number of English-speaking interpretations which come to similar readings of these passages. John Thiel's definition of "dependence" as "a relation which posits the necessary contributions of the non-self to the constitution of the self"[90] argues on the same, i.e., the transcendental level, of the conditions implied in the functions performed by the self. James Duke and Francis Schüssler Fiorenza explain that the "self-consciousness that unifies these moments" of partial freedom and partial dependence "is present to itself as a given, and thus absolutely dependent".[91] Van A. Harvey identifies the givenness that results from the "analysis of the self-consciousness" as "the feeling of absolute contingency".[92] It is important to retain the active part exercised by self-consciousness in this most radical insight into its constitution. If it was not itself the faculty of uniting the impressions it receives from the world as elements affecting it, this

---

[88] Thomas Horst, "Konfigurationen des unglücklichen Bewusstseins. Zur Theorie der Subjektivität bei Jacobi und Schleiermacher", in H. Bachmair and T. Rentsch (eds), *Poetische Autonomie? Zur Wechselwirkung von Dichtung und Philosophie in der Epoche Goethes und Hölderlins* (Stuttgart: Klett-Cotta, 1987), 185–206, 203–204.
[89] Cramer, "Die subjektivitätstheoretischen Prämissen", 156.
[90] John Thiel, *God and World in Schleiermacher's 'Dialektik' and 'Glaubenslehre'* (Frankfurt/Bern: Peter Lang, 1981), 120.
[91] Duke and Fiorenza, "Letters", 16. Yet when they later refer to "the 'whence' of the feeling of absolute dependence" (26), they risk losing the decisive point of the argument that blocks the road to Feuerbach. If God is claimed as the "whence of ... feeling", no content can be named to assure God's transcendence and prevent the identification of human self-consciousness with God as such. Only as the "Whence" of all existence, i.e., as the absolute ground of all being, is God conceived in a way that makes evident the difference between the human essential constitution and the divine.
[92] Van A. Harvey, "A word in defense of Schleiermacher's theological method", in *Journal of Religion* XLII (1962) 151–170, 161.

insight would not be made. Some reconstructions, however, emphasise the passive aspect without clarifying enough at the same time, as Horst and Cramer do, the Ego as the agent of the insight. It needs to be examined what the reasons for this are, whether they are based on a different philosophical approach or on specific theological premises.

2.3.1.2 Objections to reconstructing Schleiermacher's argument as an analysis of facticity

One of the most recent studies, Gutekunst's treatment of Schleiermacher's concept of freedom from his earliest writings up to *The Christian Faith*, that offers thorough discussions and insightful overviews of lines of interpretation, on the one hand highlights the equal weight of spontaneous activity and of receptivity. It states, as already quoted: being dependent on something given "does not mean that self-activity is to be derived from receptivity but only that the equally original spontaneity receives its direction through receptivity."[93] On the other hand, what should be attributed to self-consciousness which remains the agent of reflection is instead interpreted as an "objective consciousness".[94] Its unifying function risks being underrated by the conclusion of the following statement: the "consciousness of identity requires a reflective achievement (*Reflektionsleistung*), namely the insight into the sameness (*Selbigkeit*) of the Ego in changing states – therefore, it is objective consciousness." This "objective consciousness" seems to acquire the leading role despite the beginning of the sentence which refers to the unifying capability of the Ego. In Cramer's reconstruction (which Gutekunst summarises in its three decisive steps) this capability of the Ego is highlighted as the factor that makes the changing states recognisably "mine". It appears that there is a dividing line between those commentators who stress the active position of the Ego and question Schleiermacher's conclusion of a concretely realised God-consciousness in every human being, and those who accept his result and who focus on the factors determining the self-consciousness. In Gutekunst's study, Schleiermacher's claim in ²§ 4,4 that the immediate self-consciousness constitutes a God-consciousness is accepted, and the explanation of "absolute dependence" as contingency or facticity is rejected: "In my view, Schleiermacher did exactly *not* intend the feeling of absolute dependence to constitute a treatment of the experience of contingency because within his framework of thinking there cannot be factual contingency (cf. his rejection

---

[93] Gutekunst, *Die Freiheit des Subjekts*, 195, referring also to Grove, *Deutungen des Subjekts*, 558.
[94] Gutekunst, *Die Freiheit des Subjekts*, 194.

of factual possibilities for God as for the world in § 54)".⁹⁵ Yet only if facticity is identified as the key argument and taken as the end point of a philosophical analysis, does the possibility become clear that humans in their freedom can take alternative stances to the question of absolute meaning arising from it.

Her reason for ruling out this line of reconstruction is that Schleiermacher himself does not identify his argument in this way. It could also be in keeping with the consciously chosen, self-imposed restrictions of analytical philosophical approaches that facticity cannot come into view as an existential question. Yet there is also a theological reason for not taking up the concept of formally unconditioned freedom presupposed by the transcendental method:

> If God as the ground of freedom makes freedom possible, freedom does not have to ground itself incurring the danger of entangling itself in the aporias connected to this. If, on the other hand, freedom had no ground – something that is not conceivable for Schleiermacher in any case – it would be the product of chance and would thus lose its essence as freedom.⁹⁶

Gutekunst refers to Susanne Schaefer as holding a "similar" view,⁹⁷ but seems to underestimate the difference between their theological stances. Schaefer critiques the premature closure of the question of facticity by Schleiermacher and sees his doctrines of God and of creation as affected by the failure to admit the "radicality" of this experience⁹⁸, as will be seen in Chapter 7.

Ulrich Barth's critical engagement with Konrad Cramer's philosophical analysis is also centred on a point that is relevant for a concept of facticity: the premise that existence can be comprehended as a unity and not only as a sequence of distinct moments. His objection is that Cramer takes Schleiermacher's reference to "our whole existence" in a "structural" sense, while it should be understood instead as an "additive-relational" concept pointing to the series of affected states experienced by the individual. Clearly, with this alternative interpretation, the argumentation can no longer be reconstructed as relating to the contingency of oneself and the world. Ulrich Barth's reading correspondingly only references the world as the sphere of dependence, thus restricting absolute dependence to the scope of immanence:

---

95 Gutekunst, *Die Freiheit des Subjekts*, 214, n. 104.
96 Gutekunst, *Die Freiheit des Subjekts*, 219.
97 Gutekunst, *Die Freiheit des Subjekts*, 219, n. 122.
98 Susanne Schaefer, *Gottes Sein zur Welt. Schleiermachers Subjektanalyse in ihrer Prinzipienfunktion für Glaubenslehre und Dialektik* (ratio fidei 12), Regensburg: Pustet, 2002, for example, 100. 134.

The consciousness of standing in an ultimate basic relationship with the world as a part of it and the consciousness of the finitude of world-related (*welthaft*) freedom implied in it are thus the two forms in which the feeling of absolute dependence attains its religious concretisation. Only due to this reason was Schleiermacher able to understand his doctrine of creation as the indispensable (*unentbehrlichen*) commentary on the subject-theoretical concept of the religious consciousness.[99]

With "consciousness of finitude" as the "most contracted (*verdichtetster*) expression",[100] Schleiermacher's insistence that even towards the world as a whole, as distinct from God, humans can engage in some degree of counteraction is not recognised. While Peter Grove critiques this part of Ulrich Barth's argumentation,[101] he equally distances himself from an approach to Schleiermacher in transcendental philosophical terms. He rejects the line of interpretation that the first and the second editions differ on these grounds and that there is a move from a descriptive account of the feelings to a transcendental analysis.[102] The question to Ulrich Barth's reading of Schleiermacher is whether it points to a reluctance to theorise religion (in the sense of a human relationship to a God who is distinct from the self and the world) at all, or only to the use of a transcendental analysis.

Where transcendental thinking identifies the role of the I or Ego as the subject conscious of being modified in its concrete existence by impressions from others and the material world, the term "consciousness of differences" (*Differenzbewusstsein*) is used but the uniting function of the I is left out.[103] Where Cramer identifies the abiding character of the I through all changes, required to make the incoming exterior effects its own, Ulrich Barth just sees a sequence of changes affecting an individual's lived existence. Schleiermacher does not allow his theory of subjectivity to reach the thought of unconditional formal freedom, as authors in the tradition of Kant do. Yet, there can be no doubt that the steps he takes to demonstrate an innate God-consciousness are formulated with concepts of transcendental philosophy, such as "self-positing", and not in the language of

---

99 Ulrich Barth, "Die subjektivitätstheoretischen Prämissen der 'Glaubenslehre'. Eine Replik auf K. Cramers Schleiermacher-Studie", repr. in Ulrich Barth, *Aufgeklärter Protestantismus* (Tübingen: Mohr Siebeck, 2004), 329–351, 349.
100 Barth, "Replik", 349.
101 Grove, *Deutungen des Subjekts*, especially 572–574.
102 Grove, *Deutungen des Subjekts*, 545.
103 Gutekunst also uses the concept of *Differenzbewusstsein* in *Die Freiheit des Subjekts*, for example, 194.

psychology, even if his 1830 Lectures on this discipline reflect his theory of self.[104]

A further example of a psychological approach to the immediate self-consciousness is Catherine Kelsey's interpretation of ²§ 4,4 which she takes as a concrete relationship of God to every human being. She specifies that this is a statement at the psychological level:

> So in our immediate awareness in every moment of being stirred by something, before thought about what has stirred us, we sense a relationship with God who influences us but whom we do not influence in return. God's influence is upon that immediate awareness that precedes every thought or action. What we have just said describes the psychological make-up of every human being, according to Schleiermacher."[105]

While it is legitimate and insightful to follow the transcendental analysis provided in the second edition into the concrete psychological expressions, it should be clear that this is a second, concrete level, after the philosophical justification which must be valid on its own. Attempts to link the two distinct approaches as, for example, in the term "transcendental-psychological", only reveal the many diverse uses of the term "transcendental". It loses its specifically philosophical meaning and methodical precision when it is applied to any relationship between a condition and a real appearance, almost equivalent to cause and effect. There is only a seeming agreement in the interpretation of the most central thesis of Schleiermacher when the method by which he arrives at his claim is filled with such opposing understandings.

The more clearly an interpretation decodes what Schleiermacher calls "dependence" as facticity, the more unavoidable does the question about its explanation as an immediate consciousness of God become. Before turning to this final assessment of the philosophical claim raised, a further controversy will be examined: the alternative between a monist and an egological reading of the immediate self-consciousness.

---

104 Cf. Sabine Schmidtke, "'Lebendige Empfänglichkeit' als anthropologische Grundbedingung der Frömmigkeit", in Jörg Dierken, Arnulf v. Scheliha and Sarah Schmidt (eds), *Reformation und Moderne. Pluralität – Subjektivität – Kritik. Akten des Internationalen Kongresses der Schleiermacher-Gesellschaft in Halle (Saale), März 2017* (Boston/Berlin: de Gruyter, 2018), 343–360.
105 Catherine L. Kelsey, *Thinking about Christ with Schleiermacher* (Louisville/London: Westminster John Knox Press, 2003), 72–73.

2.3.2 The immediate self-consciousness as pre-reflective, and its divergent interpretations as monist or as egological

Schleiermacher's thesis of an "immediate self-consciousness" has received renewed attention together with the different attempts in German Idealism to enquire into the basis of knowledge and agency within the subject. A crucial problem is what has been called the "reflection trap" which led Johann Gottlieb Fichte to propose other solutions to the crux of an inescapable circle: reflecting on itself, the subject encounters itself as an object and cannot capture itself as the spontaneous self who is conducting the reflection. It is always "too late".[106] One of the solutions proposed for achieving the unity it misses in each act of reflection on itself is to presuppose a prior "ground" in which the subject is founded; another is to maintain the leading perspective of the Ego but to avoid the subject-object dilemma by explaining the constitution of self-consciousness in different terms. The alternative between a subject-theoretical approach and one that interprets it from the "ground" that founds its existence will also be relevant for the relationship assumed between God, humans and the world that will be elaborated in the material dogmatics. Which type of link is conceived between God and world is a question which has, as already evident with Dilthey, received different and incompatible interpretations. Does the concept of an "immediate self-consciousness" in the *Glaubenslehre* follow an "egological" approach or a "monist" one in which the world and humans are comprised in God?

The joint starting point of both positions is a philosophy of the subject. What is contested is whether a prior, ontological foundation between God and the human subject must be assumed, or whether, as the biblical narrative in Genesis and the theological concept of creation state, God remains distinct from humans and the world as the absolute initiator of all out of nothing, *ex nihilo*.[107] What is

---

106 Cf., for example, Georg Essen, *Die Freiheit Jesu. Der neuchalkedonische Enhypostasiebegriff in neuzeitlicher Subjekt- und Personphilosophie* (ratio fidei 5) (Regensburg: Pustet, 2001), 161–173, 163. Cf. 169, n. 134, where the organisers and participants in the original research seminars on Schleiermacher's *Glaubenslehre*, and on Dieter Henrich's and Hermann Krings's analytics of freedom included Thomas Pröpper, Klaus Müller, Magnus Striet and Saskia Wendel. Cf. Magnus Lerch, *All-Einheit und Freiheit. Subjektphilosophische Klärungsversuche in der Monismus-Debatte zwischen Klaus Müller und Magnus Striet* (Würzburg: Echter, 2009), for an analysis of the background positions to this debate.
107 In "Einheit ja – aber welche?", in Klaus Müller and Magnus Striet (eds), *Dogma und Denkform. Strittiges in der Grundlegung von Offenbarungsbegriff und Gottesgedanke* (Regensburg: Pustet, 2005), 85–100, Michael Bongardt outlines the validity of both starting points for philosophical and religious interpretations of the relationship between unity and multiplicity, each of

under dispute is the content of the "immediate self-consciousness" in which the idea of God arises as the "most immediate reflection" (²§ 4,4). In order to explain the opposing philosophical and theological stances, I will outline the comparison drawn by the authors engaged in this debate: between Schleiermacher's argumentation and the philosopher Dieter Henrich's who argues for a "pre-reflective" consciousness that provides a "prior familiarity"[108] with oneself (2.3.2.1). Secondly, the counterarguments to Henrich's interpretation of the pre-reflective level are presented (2.3.2.2).

---

which are part of human experience. He questions each side's objection to the other as not being able to ground ethical responsibility. Monistic religious traditions based on "life in God" call for equal care by each part of the unity for the others, while monotheistic religions based on life "in front of" God (*coram Deo*) include the obligation to respect and foster the freedom of the other (90–91). Since each direction arises from one of two equally possible basic experiences, one prioritising unity, the other difference, and develop positions that are coherent in themselves, the two thought forms cannot be presented as being "internally contradictory" (90). He quotes Dieter Henrich's judgement that "two self-interpretations of self-consciousness can be deduced with equal justification (*mit gleichem Recht*) from the basic relationship" (Henrich, "Das Selbstbewusstsein und seine Selbstdeutungen", in Henrich, *Fluchtlinien. Philosophische Essays* (Frankfurt: Suhrkamp, 1982), 99–124, 117). Each side therefore is called to reflect on how it relates to the elementary view which the other side has developed primarily. For biblical monotheism, Bongardt sees the "unity" perspective that goes beyond individual freedom as reconfigured in the recognition of the freedom of the other in three decisive elements: in the first Covenant concluded by God without conditions with Noah; in human beings freely responding to God through which "the unity between God and humans is realised"; and in a human community where individuality is protected and completed (95).

108 Dieter Henrich has defended the ineluctable role of self-reflection also in his debate with Jürgen Habermas in the 1980s, insisting against his proposal of "postmetaphysical thinking" that also in modernity, metaphysics has an irreplaceable function – not in its antique and medieval forms, but as relating to human subjectivity: Dieter Henrich, "What is metaphysics – what modernity?", in Peter Dews (ed.), *Habermas: A Critical Reader* (Oxford: Blackwell, 1999), 291–319. Henrich's key point in this exchange is not to reduce "reflexivity" to "intersubjectivity" but to keep the two poles in tension. In this series of responses, the concept of a "prior familiarity" with oneself was crucial to show that a self-relation is presupposed even in preverbal children without which the act of learning to speak and eventually to be able to refer to themselves as "I" would not be possible. While it may seem that learning their first language from adults is a prime example of the priority and maybe even exclusivity of intersubjectivity, he shows that a self-relation must be presupposed already for basic actions like pointing. This is a matter on which Schleiermacher would agree at the concrete level of lived freedom. In his Hermeneutics, he highlights himself the astounding achievement of children in their first two years of life to develop the divinatory inventiveness to determine two things at once: the "unity of meaning" of each word, and its local determination (*Localwerth*). Thus, a pre-reflective familiarity with oneself is foundational for the relationship to others and the world; reflexivity and intersubjectivity are equally original.

2.3.2.1 Comparing Schleiermacher and Dieter Henrich on an immediate or "pre-reflective" consciousness

As we have seen, ²§§ 3 and 4 distinguish "feeling" or "immediate self-consciousness" from an object-related use. On the one hand, by using the Fichtean term, "self-positing", and by identifying the subject as the centre of unity in making the changing impressions it receives by being affected from the world its own, Schleiermacher's analysis remains centred on the subject as the principle of the reconstruction. It is the subject's immediate self-consciousness in which the consciousness of God arises to whom the individual is said to be in an "immediate existential relationship".[109] On the other hand, ²§§ 3 and 4 have been claimed for a "non-egological theory of consciousness" that the philosopher Manfred Frank traces back to Hölderlin, Novalis, Schleiermacher and up to Sartre. It conceives of "self-consciousness as 'ego-less' (*ich-los*), as an anonymous familiarity with oneself (*Mit-sich-Bekanntsein*) or feeling".[110] Thus, as Saskia Wendel summarises this approach, "an ego-less being is postulated as the immanent ground of self-consciousness".[111] This anonymous ground is at the same time differentiated, comprising others as moments within it. At this stage of analysing the Introduction, the alternative cannot yet be decided; but especially the general treatment of the God-world relationship in the First Part of the dogmatics will have to be examined for clues in one or the other direction.

One conclusion, however, can already be drawn here: by laying claim to an "immediate" self-consciousness, one that is prior to the division between acting and thinking, Schleiermacher has moved the analysis to a pre-reflective level. This "pre-reflective familiarity of the Ego with itself" can be interpreted, as Henrich does, as arising from an encompassing ground. But it can equally be taken as the first principle of a theory of subjectivity which seeks to solve the subject-object dilemma of a circularity that never achieves its goal of capturing the Ego in its spontaneity. The reasons for this position can now be outlined.

---

109 Schleiermacher, "Letters", 40.
110 Manfred Frank, "Fragmente einer Geschichte der Selbstbewusstseins-Theorie von Kant bis Sartre", in Frank, *Selbstbewusstseinstheorien von Fichte bis Sartre* (Frankfurt: Suhrkamp, ²1993, 413–599, 508, quoted by Lerch, *All-Einheit*, 15, n. 25. In his study, *Gott am Grund des Bewusstseins? Skizzen zu einer präreflexiven Interpretation von Kierkegaards Selbst* (ratio fidei 61) (Regensburg: Pustet, 2017), Klaus Viertbauer outlines the "trap of reflection" but does not discuss the ongoing post-idealist debate on an understanding of autonomy and a concept of the Ego that is not assumed to be *causa sui*, although he refers to the authors who make this point (such as Pröpper and Striet) in a footnote, 105–106, n. 215.
111 Lerch, *All-Einheit*, 175.

2.3.2.2 The "pre-reflective familiarity of the Ego with itself" as the first principle of a theory of subjectivity

The reconstruction of the core of Schleiermacher's argument by Pröpper as constituting an egological theory of subjectivity has been further developed by Catholic systematic theologians like Georg Essen, Magnus Striet, Saskia Wendel, Susanne Schäfer, Bernhard Nitsche and Magnus Lerch. The first point they make is that the much-quoted "reflection trap" is not the necessary fate of this approach. Lerch takes up Wendel's thesis that "the egological theory does not *per se* and automatically lead into the reflection trap; it is only the circular assumption that the free ego respectively its consciousness of itself is the *result* of reflection that does so."[112] Thus, by anchoring the Ego in its familiarity or pre-reflective awareness of itself at a level prior to thinking, a new understanding of the unity of self-consciousness becomes possible. It is a position that is compatible with a religious solution to the abyss of its contingency, namely the personal decision to believe in God as the Creator who founded the world and all its inhabitants. For the advocates of this position in the debate, this is the direction to choose because it avoids a gap between what was to be explained – the Ego in its free capacity for self-reflection – and an anonymous ground which is assumed to be differentiated in itself by including all the instances of otherness as its moments. Wendel makes it clear that this would be a "heteronomous understanding of self-consciousness because ... it is not I who thinks, feels, experiences, but an ego-less ground of which I am a moment, thus, ultimately an anonymous *Id* to which my feeling is owed: but then it is not at all my feeling (*je meines*)."[113]

What has been gained is an "intuitive perception of oneself" which is "the condition of the possibility of having experiences";[114] Fichte called it "intellectual intuition", a formal awareness that the Ego exists. Wendel takes Schleiermacher's claim of experiencing the immediate consciousness of self as being in relation with God as a verbalisation that includes distinct steps which

---

112 Lerch, *All-Einheit*, 178, n. 875, with reference to Saskia Wendel, *Affektiv und inkarniert. Ansätze Deutscher Mystik als subjekttheoretische Herausforderung* (ratio fidei 15) (Regensburg: Pustet, 2002), 274, n. 117. Here she expresses her doubts about stalling further enquiry by stopping at the insight that this understanding of self-consciousness had been discovered to be unsuccessful by Fichte himself. In order to "escape from the fear of the reflection trap one goes for a radical solution and gets rid of the entire problem by eliminating the Ego, since where there is no Ego, there is also no self-consciousness."
113 Wendel, *Affektiv und inkarniert*, 275, quoted by Lerch, *All-Einheit*, 175.
114 Saskia Wendel, "Die Wurzel der Religionen", in *Freiburger Zeitschrift für Philosophie und Theologie* 53 (2006) 21–38.

must be laid open. For her, the feeling of owing one's existence to an other as an interpretation of the conditionedness of self-consciousness belongs to "religiosity" as a human endowment which is then specified in each "religion" in different ways; not being the author and therefore "owing" one's existence, however, can also lead to a non-religious response. For other participants in the debate such as Georg Essen, designating the result of the analysis as the feeling of "owing one's existence" (*Verdanktheit*), a sense of a gracious givenness, is already claiming too much since the feeling is only one of facticity, in other words, the experience of a lack of ground in oneself. They agree with Pröpper that in Schleiermacher's argumentation a decisive step is being presupposed which is not identified as such: the capacity to take a stance to one's partially determined, partially free being. It can result in different responses, including agnostic and atheist ones. In naming this finding a "God-consciousness", an unrecognised act of the will is implied: the decision to opt for absolute meaning.

2.3.3 Questions to the result of the analysis of ²§ 4

Schleiermacher's theory of religion as a constitutive part of human personhood uncovers piety as the determination of feeling or "immediate self-consciousness" by the feeling of utter dependence. He interprets this as constituting a "God-consciousness". Questions arise to three components. A first choice of interpretation is to name facticity an "absolute dependence" from God (2.3.3.1). A second claim is that this God-consciousness arises as an "immediate self-consciousness" (2.3.3.2). The third point to be examined is the extent of the claim that this is present in every human being: is it about the possibility of a relation to God as a decision made by individuals for their self-understanding, or does it claim an inescapable actual connection to God (2.3.3.3)?

2.3.3.1 Distinguishing between the key findings and the choices made in their interpretation: facticity as "absolute dependence" from God

The distinction of partial from absolute dependence which Schleiermacher's precise analysis arrives at is a necessary one, and the level of the enquiry, a worked-out theory of subjectivity that can take up the challenge of the alternative contemporary approaches, is convincing.

Claus Dierksmeier summarises that "religiosity should by no means be represented by a relation of dependence in objective consciousness which would negate human freedom. In Schleiermacher, the feeling of utter dependence does not lie at the level of subjective consciousness where freedom and dependence oppose each other; it grounds this level."¹¹⁵ Yet the term chosen to interpret the absolute contingency of existence, "dependence", is not neutral. Its implication is that there must be a ground from which it depends. The term "dependence" thus acts as a bridge from the end point of the analysis, the most radical experience of freedom with itself, towards a ground beyond it. Schleiermacher takes the step to a reality distinct from the subject by allowing the word "God" arise as the expression of its "most direct" (²§ 4,4. ET 1928, 7) or "most direct possible reflection" (ET 2016, 26) (*unmittelbarste Reflexion*). It would have been equally possible to conclude the philosophical enquiry into piety as an essential human function with the insight into the bottomless facticity of human existence. It is true that the claimed "consciousness" of God is contrasted clearly with the "idea" of God that stems from the objective function of reason; yet in the reflection on its immediate modification, self-consciousness becomes aware of this relational – even if not intentional – counterpart in feeling as "the truly primary meaning of the term 'God'" (²§ 4,4. ET 2016, 24) (*wahrhaft ursprüngliche Bedeutung*). Which unthematised premises are at work here, and what can the epistemological status of a source posited in this way be?

The insight that could be reached by reflecting on the constitution of freedom was the "consciousness of an origin of its structure that was not at the disposition of the subject, together with the utter inability to determine this origin itself"; or, as Cramer summarises, "the self's consciousness of itself in which it becomes aware, due to the knowledge of its structure, of the lack of ground (*Ungrund*) of this structure in itself and in everything it is capable of doing because of it".¹¹⁶ When Schleiermacher moves from the negative finding of the lack of ground in ourselves to the positive conclusion of an absolute ground, he is following the need of reason beyond the actual realisation of freedom to seek an absolute foundation which justifies its existence. This option is reasonable, since it allows the fulfilment of its meaning, but it is not a default solution. It would be equally possible to remain on the standpoint of freedom in the antinomy of its constitution as materially conditioned, yet formally unconditional, and embrace conclusions such as those of

---

115 In his instructive comparison of Kant, Schleiermacher, Rudolf Otto and others on "feeling", Claus Dierksmeier first notes this insight as a core point. Yet he adds that "Schleiermacher can be asked whether the term dependence can express this basic relation adequately; with equal right one could then speak of a feeling of absolute freedom". C. Dierksmeier, "Zum Begriff des religiösen Gefühls im Anschluss an Kant", in *Zeitschrift für Neuere Theologiegeschichte/Journal for the History of Modern Theology* 8 (2001) 201–207, 214–215. He quotes from the 1901 study by Eugen Huber, *Die Entwicklung des Religionsbegriffs bei Schleiermacher* (Leipzig: T. Weicher, 1901, repr. Aalen 1972), 243: Schleiermacher's analysis is not about "the source from which one depends (wovon *man abhänge*), but from where it arises that one depends from anything at all" (woher *es komme, dass man überhaupt von etwas abhänge*) (215, n. 48).
116 Cramer, "Die subjektivitätstheoretischen Prämissen", 156.

Sartre,[117] that the human person is a "useless passion". The fact that the subject can interpret the insight into its absolute contingency in alternative ways is not admitted by Schleiermacher; nor is the participation of the will recognised in this most personal decision for one's self-understanding, having discovered the utter facticity of one's existence. By failing to highlight the involvement of free reflection and self-determination in this existential issue, the freedom in deciding how to respond to the offer of faith in God is played down. How this affects the relationship of human beings to God is a matter to be followed up later in the theological anthropology of the material dogmatics. The premise of meaning that Schleiermacher is privileging here by assuming a "Whence" of existence is one of practical reason.

2.3.3.2 Questions to the "immediacy" of the self-consciousness as a God-consciousness

The fact that the decision for absolute meaning is not the only option available remains hidden also because Schleiermacher declares it to be an "immediate" certitude in feeling. The first critique, turning a negative finding, the lack of foundation, into a positive one, that is, into the dependence from a "Whence" of human existence, can thus be connected to the second objection, against the claim to "immediacy" in the argumentation of ^{2}§ 4. Wolfhart Pannenberg points out that

> the assertion of absolute dependence in § 4,3, is not introduced as "conditioned by some previous knowledge about God" (§ 4,4), but is based solely on the consciousness of the negation of absolute freedom. Nonetheless the *interpretation* of this negation through the positive idea of a dependence remains an entry of finite relations into the book of "immediate self-consciousness" (*Eintragung endlicher Verhältnisse und Vorstellungen in das "unmittelbare Selbstbewusstsein"*); when the latter is also conceived as consciousness of God it can hardly be called "immediate" any longer in view of the extensive effort of reflection required for this.[118]

Having identified that it is "the need for an *absolute foundation* that causes Schleiermacher to posit God", Pröpper observes:

> The contribution of freedom in opting for the positing of God is, however, obscured by Schleiermacher's reference to it as immediate consciousness, thus insinuating its inevitability. Yet what is merely veiled in this way is that it is indeed (also in his own argumentation) a *mediated* one: namely mediated through the negation of absolute freedom, thus, through the insight of freedom or free reason itself into the abysmal contingency of its existence.

---

117 Cf. Pröpper, *Theologische Anthropologie*, vol. I, 478.
118 Wolfhart Pannenberg, *Anthropology in Theological Perspective*, trans. M. J. O'Connell (Philadelphia: Westminster, 1985), 253, n. 33.

This, however, remains a highly ambivalent finding which still very much permits opposite interpretations.[119]

Any claim to immediacy, as already outlined above, is doomed to fail in principle. Pröpper's question, quoted above, is worth repeating: Would it make sense to "speak of God-consciousness if it did not contain any reflective determinations and were not even able to realise the difference between God, self and world? Into every God-consciousness ... reflective determinations enter which already have to be presupposed logically in order to be able to perceive the reality we encounter as the reality of *God*".[120]

At the same time, while the claim to a presence of God given in a modification of immediate self-consciousness must be refuted, Schleiermacher's attention to this level in subjectivity finds support. It is important to distinguish the epistemological status of the two: a pre-reflective familiarity with oneself which Schleiermacher expresses with the term "immediate self-consciousness", and the practical option to believe in an unconditioned, perfect ground of all being, which cannot be put at the same level of certainty. Reminding us of the limits of knowledge "after the Kantian turn in philosophy of religion and theology", Saskia Wendel clarifies that the existence of this ground can only be postulated as a matter of hope but cannot be "known" in the sense that Kant has distinguished from "thinking". Having argued first for defining "religiosity" as the anthropological formal basis of the individual religions with their distinct, linguistically mediated religious experiences, through the sense of owing one's existence to the "unconditioned", she distinguishes the two claims on the basis of the immediacy of their certainty:

> Is the feeling of owing one's existence to an unconditioned source equivalent to the certitude that this unconditioned instance also exists? ... I can know in thinking that in my pre-reflexive knowledge about myself a feeling of absolute dependence and, linked to it, the idea of an unconditioned instance can arise. But I can never know whether existence can be attributed to this idea, neither in the sense of an immediate experience of certitude (*Gewissheitserlebnis*) nor in the sense of a conceptually mediated reflexive act. ... (After Kant) the existence of the unconditioned can only be believed and hoped for, it can be trusted in as a postulate of practical reason from the perspective of agency. On closer examination, the feeling of absolute dependence reveals itself ... as a "feeling of faith" (*Glaubensgefühl*), a feeling of trust which imparts hope but not certitude.[121]

---

119 Pröpper, *Theologische Anthropologie*, vol. I, 478.
120 Pröpper, *Theologische Anthropologie*, vol. I, 477.
121 Saskia Wendel, "Die Renaissance des Religiösen und der Glaube an Gott", in Gregor M. Hoff (ed.), *Gott im Kommen (Salzburger Hochschulwochen 2006)* (Graz: Tyrolia, 2006), 201–238, 218–219.

2.3.3.3 The issue of what is being claimed: the possibility or the actuality of a God-consciousness in all humans?

Reflecting on Schleiermacher's intentions in his step of providing a positive foundation for human existence in its facticity, "knowing full well that he is aiming beyond anything that can be secured by any kind of knowledge", Pröpper distinguishes two possibilities of what ²§ 4,4 is arguing for. How likely is it that Schleiermacher only intended to demonstrate the "anthropological location" from which the "possibility" of a relation to God arises, rather than an *actual* God-consciousness as the endowment of every human being? While it is clear that no "proof" of God's existence is intended, and that "God's reality remains presupposed" in uncovering this relation,[122] Pröpper ultimately rejects the former reading, on the evidence of statements such as those which classify the option of an atheist response to human contingency as misled and erroneous. Thus, an actual, not just a possible relationship with God is what ²§ 4,4 is trying to establish: "Everything speaks for the view that Schleiermacher claimed for this subject-theoretical demonstration (*Aufweis*) of the feeling of absolute dependence to have established the *consciousness of a real relationship to God as belonging to the essence of the human person*".[123]

In view of this far-reaching claim, at first sight it is hard to understand how early reviewers were able to judge that in this book, he had turned "the Christian faith into a philosophy".[124] Yet it is true that this theological result of a philosophical enquiry will affect all the subsequent propositions. What is to be examined in the material dogmatics includes at least the following three consequences: First, since the possibility of taking a stance to God is lacking if God is immediately present in every person's pre-reflective self-consciousness, how will it affect the relationship to God that a free decision either for or against faith in God, or for an agnostic position has been ruled out? Secondly, with the consciousness of facticity already muted to one of "absolute dependence", what will be the effects on the understanding of God as Creator? Thirdly, how

---

[122] Pröpper, *Theologische Anthropologie*, vol. I, 478. "Already the finding that the "Whence" ... escapes any objectivising thematisation, forbids fixing him to such intentions. In addition, Schleiermacher assures again and again that he only wants to uncover the certitude of our original relation to God the reality of which is already presupposed. As a matter of fact, however, this uncovering happens in the framework of comprehensive subject-theoretical reflections which almost inevitably create the impression of also very much meaning to *prove* (*nachweisen*) the presupposed fact of the God-consciousness." (474)
[123] Pröpper, *Theologische Anthropologie*, vol. I, 475.
[124] Karl Gottlieb Bretschneider, Ferdinand Christian Baur and Johann Christian Friedrich Steudel do so in different ways.

does the assumption of an actual God-consciousness given in every person predetermine the role of the Redeemer?

Next to be investigated is the definition of the distinctiveness of Christianity, with the subsequent determination of the content of "redemption" by which its essence is characterised, in Chapter 3. The responses to both essence definitions by his contemporaries from different theological starting points will be followed up in Chapter 4.

3 The Definition of the Essence of Christianity

The general concept of piety has been set out in order to establish religion as one of the essential pursuits of the human spirit, preventing the Christian and other religious traditions from being regarded as "mere aberrations" (BO ²§ 22. 12). The next step of the Introduction is to gain access to the *differentia specifica* of Christianity as one of the concretisations of religion. In sections 3.2, 3.3 and 3.4, I shall compare the Introductions of 1811, 1821/22 and 1830/31 regarding three elements: the individuating factors provided to map the differentiation of the concept of piety into historical religions; the "formula" chosen for Christianity;[125] and its consequences as a criterium for the adequacy of the Christian doctrines. These are to express the Christian pious self-consciousness in a reflected, coherent way. First, however, the functions which this essence definition is to fulfil will be outlined.

3.1 The functions of the essence definition of Christianity

The new enquiry into the essence of Christianity is important for three reasons: it establishes the theological principle of the dogmatics (3.1.1); it replaces the previous method of Protestant doctrinal systems, proofs from the Bible (3.1.2); and it names a point of consensus in the midst of not only contemporary but also historical disagreements about the core of the Christian message (3.1.3).

3.1.1 Establishing the theological principle of the dogmatics

The definition of the essence of Christianity constitutes the theological principle of the *Glaubenslehre* which is to work out in coherent doctrines what is specific

---

[125] The reason for calling it a "formula" rather than a "definition" although it relates to the realm of history is explained in a lecture of the *Theological Encyclopedia* in a comment on ²§ 44 of the BO: "The term (*Ausdruck*) formula is originally located in mathematics. The term definition was to be expected here. But what is individual cannot be defined, and it is only seemingly the case when one calls a statement that is to represent something individual a definition; it can only yield something general, nothing individual. Yet if one is to keep in mind this explanation whenever one speaks of Christianity, the term formula is the most suitable since it expresses the same point." *Theologische Enzyklopädie* (1831/32), Nachschrift David Friedrich Strauß, ed. by Walter Sachs (Schleiermacher-Archiv 4) (Berlin/New York: de Gruyter, 1987), 50.

for the Christian religion.¹²⁶ But how is it possible to move from the level of a theory of the subject at which piety was anchored as an essential function of the human person, to the historical level of concrete religions? Having defined the essence of piety which all historical religions actualise in different concretisations, the Introduction's procedure to single out the essence of Christianity begins by drawing up a system of classification. It then identifies two individualising factors of religions at the highest, i.e., the monotheistic level. The outer unity is characterised by the "definite commencement", that is, the historical beginning of a religion. The inner unity is determined by a principle of the "peculiar modification" of the religious material common to the same kind and level (²§ 10; ET 1928, 44). They are not deducible from the differentiations of the concept of piety but are historically contingent and thus account for the singular essence of each concrete religion. Christianity, having been categorised as "monotheistic" and "teleological", is distinguished by the fact that everything in it is "related to the consciousness of redemption through the person Jesus of Nazareth" (¹§ 18. I, 61). It is decisive both for its content and structure. The way in which this definition of the Christian essence determines the contents of the dogmatics will depend on how the term "redemption" is explicated in its constituent parts. It also bestows a structure on what is to be treated: containing an inherent contrast between a prior, non-redeemed and a new, redeemed state, a two-part layout will belong to its configuration, but equally a space where the underlying general possibility of both concrete states is expounded. Thus, a differentiated sequence of discourses on these constitutive aspects emerges. It can take, as discussed in Chapter 1, one of two possible orders. It could either treat the "redeemed" human person first. It is only from the end point of the self-understanding of having been liberated to be in community with God that she can reconstruct her previous existence as a sinful one, but also as having been able to be addressed by God. This first order would follow the *ordo cognoscendi*. The second possible sequence would not reflect the temporal sequence of insights but begin with an analysis of the human person in general, the logical order which spells out the basic assumptions about the human person, the world, and God first. It would move on from what is claimed as general foundations to the experience of the specific contrast inherent in Christianity's distinctiveness, redemption, that is, of "sin" against "grace". In both cases, however, it is the specific difference

---

126 Pröpper, *Theologische Anthropologie*, vol. I, 461–462, points out the link between the particularity of Christianity as being "non-deducible philosophically" and "defending against the contemporary speculative tendencies the independence of theology as not being able to be sublated (*unaufhebbar*)".

of Christianity from the other historical religions and from the concept of piety that will be spelt out in the material dogmatics. How its elements are defined and justified will therefore be influential. The definition of the essence of Christianity will be able to indicate both the limits of this religious community, that is, determine which heresies are essence-defying, and the internal relationships between revelation, nature, and reason. Beyond a factual consensus, there is a normative element to what is identical and claimed to be continuous in the tradition.[127]

3.1.2 Replacing the method of proofs from the Bible

A clear account of the change of method from the *dicta probantia* of Protestant orthodoxy is given by Christine Helmer. It inaugurates a different starting point than the Bible and responds to the need to identify the guiding theological perspective for interpreting the Bible also in response to changing cultural contexts. Helmer makes it clear which process of corroborating the adequacy of the guiding perspective is being put in place.[128]

The method used previously was built on the authority of the Bible, but it was controlled by the dogmatic agendas through which the Bible was read and for which it was used as proof: "Schleiermacher configures the relation between exegetical and dogmatic theology in a way differing from the *dicta probantia* method of Protestant orthodoxy" which "assumed that discursive articulation did not introduce historical difference into those [spiritual] realities. The methodological result was to semantically flatten the referents of biblical texts to ac-

---

[127] In *Die kritische Identität des neuzeitlichen Christentums. Schleiermachers Wesensbestimmung der christlichen Religion* (Tübingen: Mohr Siebeck, 1996), 43, Markus Schröder highlights the descriptive element of this consensus: "The ascription of the redemptive activity as the determining factor to the person of Jesus can be stated descriptively as a factual consensus within Christianity – the entire plurality of the descriptions notwithstanding." As with any consensus, however, the question of its status arises. Is it a case of an "overlapping consensus" in the sense of Rawls, as seen from above by an observer, or is it a claim about an actually shared and not merely overlapping identical element, from the perspective of the participants? Or is it a regulative statement claiming that persons outside of the circle of those professing "redemption" cannot be counted as Christian believers?

[128] In view of the diverse positions in the history of reception of the New Testament, it is important to specify what exactly "replaces" the previous method. Is it, for example, the Christian consciousness of redemption *tout court*, or is it this consciousness as pointing to a prior historical event that is "given", and not constructed?

cord with doctrinal claims."[129] The new departure of Schleiermacher is to read the Bible as a document that testifies to what is "'behind the text'",[130] which is the "total impression of Jesus".[131] This opens up the possibility of critiquing biblical expressions as well, by distinguishing the message itself from some of the terms in which it was spelt out, and of offering a consistent interpretation. It also allows a more appreciative view of the transformations accomplished in new eras by formulating the core of the message anew in concepts relevant to changed cultural horizons: "The object of empirical study is the essence's discursive manifestation changing through time, differing in linguistic articulation, and situated in particular cultural-historically determined sites."[132]

But is there any way of controlling the adequacy of these new conceptual actualisations, as Early Christianity did, faced, for example, with the challenge of Gnosticism? Schleiermacher's answer establishes a middle ground between a biblical objectivism that is no longer convincing, and a plurality of interpretations that has no internal standard for judging their relation to the original message of Christ. This means on the one hand: "The consequence of this position is that, for Schleiermacher, dogmatic theology must be verified (*bewährt*) but can never be proven by Scripture (BO, § 210). This means that historical and linguistic difference need not be reduced to transculturally identical terms and then collapsed into an eternal truth."[133] But the requirement of "truth" still plays a role: "Constituting identity through time is the 'certainty of each person's own immediate religious self-consciousness' (BO, § 209). This transcultural sameness of feeling, not the identity of a religious object or theological words, provides the content for dogmatic propositions that are to be tested in view of the parameters stipulated by the canon" which is itself an "endless" project.[134]

Thus, changes in subsequent re-articulations and new explications in other languages and cultures are recognised but need to be related back to the one shared feeling of redemption which is attributed to the Redeemer as its originator and abiding cause. For Schleiermacher, the Bible loses its position of being the counterpart to all new interpretations in its history of effects. It is reclassified as the "first member" (but also as "the norm for all succeeding presentations")

---

129 Christine Helmer, "Schleiermacher's exegetical theology and the New Testament", in Jacqueline Mariña (ed.), *The Cambridge Companion to Friedrich Schleiermacher* (Cambridge: CUP, 2005), 229–247, 244.
130 Helmer, "Schleiermacher's exegetical theology", 232 and 245.
131 Helmer, "Schleiermacher's exegetical theology", 241.
132 Helmer, "Schleiermacher's exegetical theology", 244.
133 Helmer, "Schleiermacher's exegetical theology", 244,
134 Helmer, "Schleiermacher's exegetical theology", 244.

(²§ 129. ET 2016, II, 837) of this history of effects of the person of Jesus. With both exegesis and dogmatics as parts of "historical theology", one could be afraid of a different type of renewed domination by dogmatics. But the key systematic point made is the lasting anchorage in the "total impression" of Jesus Christ which links his own lifetime with its effect on the disciples to all subsequent ages where believers can access the same experience of this historical person.[135] Their personal impressions of Christ, as Helmer clarifies, then have to be verified by comparing them to the New Testament's account of him.

The solution proposed by Schleiermacher at the threshold of a modern era marked by an acute historical consciousness, his premise of continuity and the evidence claimed for the "total impression", would need to be discussed systematically and historically.[136] But what Helmer's reconstruction makes clear is that the reference back is meant to be to the figure of Jesus Christ himself, and not merely to the current consciousness of the Christian community on its own. This is important since replacing one kind of warrant (such as the Bible) with another (the Christian pious consciousness) can lead to collapsing what should remain distinguished as counterpoints also within the new method. Examples of such mergers can be found in lines of interpretation for which what is "given" and what therefore requires an "inductive" method – as opposed to a deduction from the concept of piety, as in the steps and types of religion – is simply the "factual self-understanding of the Christian church"; this is the "inductive" counterpart for Schröder, quoting ¹§ 18,3. I. 64.[137] What is clear for

---

[135] Osthövener, "Dogmatik II: Materiale Entfaltung der 'Glaubenslehre'", 362–383, 363–364, equally highlights the relevance of the "Christologically significant conception of the 'total impression'" which "cannot be proved (*demonstriren*) by any single element on its own (¹§ 119 Postscript 3. II, 62). This means that another layer must be distinguished from the reciprocal critique and correction of the dogmatic analysis and the critically appreciated ecclesial tradition. This layer safeguards, so to speak, a connection from the time of the Apostles to the present day ... a religious layer in an emphatic sense which (mediated by the total impression) opens up access to Jesus Christ as Redeemer for each individual believer."

[136] Understanding the "total impression" of Jesus as a unique encounter with God implies an evidence claim. In *Selbstmitteilung Gottes. Herausforderungen einer freiheitstheoretischen Offenbarungstheologie* (ratio fidei 56) (Regensburg: Pustet, 2015), 183–214, Lerch discusses the criteria of this perception as debated in the last two decades. At the level of historical research into the transition from Jesus' own proclamation to key themes expressing this "total impression" in early Christianity, three motives in the New Testament accounts of his ministry have been identified by the Historical Jesus scholar Seán Freyne: Messiahship, openness to Gentiles, and the role of wisdom teacher ("The Galilean Jesus and a Contemporary Christology", in *Theological Studies* 70 (2009) 281–297).

[137] Schröder, *Die kritische Identität*, 48.

Schleiermacher but needs to be added in view of the early and subsequent critiques is that this self-understanding sees itself as constituted by the Redeemer, who in his existence is the "given" and non-deducible element. This point will be further developed in the subsection on the revised edition where the distinction between an "ideal" and a "historical" Redeemer is the key point of correction, and in Chapter 4.

3.1.3 Striving for a consensus in the face of inevitable disagreements

The third function of the essence definition is, indeed, to provide a principle on which all can agree as being central for Christianity. Stephen Sykes explains the need for the uniting capacity of the essence concept as being caused by two factors: the inevitable conflicts due to the internal variety of the New Testament sources, and to a feature typical for Christianity. The first cause lies in the "different, and to some extent conflicting, versions of the Christian gospel but also the very preaching of these versions", as evident already in St Paul's letters to the Galatians and the Corinthians.[138] With the second factor, the religious emphasis on the role of "interiority", quite divergent understandings arise from the start. The significance of individual, personal reflection is contrasted by Sykes to exterior, institutional markers of adherence to a religion and is traced back to the very contrast implied in the term "redemption". An inner change is indicated, and this will be different from one person to the other: "The reason that this conflict cannot, in principle, be eliminated has to do ... with the *problem of the Christian account of the human person*".[139] Summarising it as "interiority" does not mean a turn inwards at the expense of agency in the real world.[140] It denotes an interior motivation based on the self-reflection of a person respond-

---

138 Stephen Sykes, "Schleiermacher and Barth on the essence of Christianity – an instructive disagreement", in Duke and Streetman (eds), *Barth and Schleiermacher: Beyond the Impasse?*, 88–107, 90–91.
139 Sykes, "Schleiermacher and Barth", 91.
140 The key role of this heritage in the Patristic age for turning European thinking from the cosmos to the human subject is spelt out succinctly by Theo Kobusch in *Christliche Philosophie. Die Entdeckung der Subjektivität* (Darmstadt: Wissenschaftliche Buchgesellschaft, 2006). Karl Jaspers's analysis of the unprecedented factors surfacing in the paradigm-changing "axial age" of the joint origins of the world religions and the great philosophical systems could also be added here: Karl Jaspers, *The Origin and Goal of History* (London: Routledge, 1953). Their emphasis on ethical self-reflection is greatly developed in biblical monotheism, in particular by the prophets, and is part of the "heritage" Sykes is invoking under the "Christian account of the human person".

ing to the divine call, expressed especially by the prophets, to transform their hearts and be compassionate and just:

> The longstanding tradition of emphasis upon interiority which Jesus ... inherited from deeply laid strands in Judaism guaranteed that no resolution ... would ever be permanently protected against the outbreak of further conflict. By interiority I mean that the disposition of each member of the church is governed by an interior transformation, the work of the Holy Spirit in the heart. No participation in an external ritual, no formal repetition of orthodox belief or performance of prescribed duties could be proof against false or distorted intentions. Orthodoxy always insisted upon the necessary dispositional accompaniment of rites, professed belief, and good works. But in doing so it proclaimed from within the inherent limitations of its solutions to conflict.[141]

Thus, to engage in a process of seeking agreement on the essence of the message was a "problem-solving requirement essential to the preservation of its coherence as a movement"[142]. Highlighting the "diagnosis of the controversial character" of this definition, Claus-Dieter Osthövener similarly sees the Christian church and theology as marked by the "dynamic elements of a culture of discursive disagreement (*Streitkultur*)" in which "plurality and the capability for error (*Irrtumsfähigkeit*)" are recognised "not as an obstacle but as a life element of the church".[143]

Under the umbrella of the essence definition, diverse understandings are called to engage with each other. Yet two observations are relevant, one, regarding the biblical sources, the other regarding doctrinal limits. It will turn out that the "redemptive activity" is seen as happening through Jesus' life and through the effect it had on the disciples and the origin of the church; his death and the testimony to his resurrection are not needed to accomplish redemption. The second point is that the limits designated by the "natural heresies" will be a further weight-bearing part of the edifice that requires close scrutiny. They may relegate what could be important theological alternatives to the precincts beyond Christianity. The critical decisions made under the titles of "Manicheism" and "Pelagianism" refer to what is considered as being contrary to the Christian faith in the Redeemer. But at least one instance, namely how "sin" is interpreted under one of these signposts for limits not to be transgressed, has called forth theological critiques from his own time to the present day: Schleiermacher's decision that "sin" has to be included under God's causality since it cannot have an independent standing over against God, which would be "Mani-

---

141 Sykes, "Schleiermacher and Barth", 91.
142 Sykes, "Schleiermacher and Barth", 91.
143 Osthövener, "Dogmatik II: Materiale Entfaltung der 'Glaubenslehre'", 370. 369.

chean". Thus, while a "formula" for the essence is necessary to deliver these three functions, the way in which its elements are determined will be a matter for further analysis. The changes they undergo from 1811 to 1821/22 and to 1830/31 are the subject matter enquired to in the following three subsections.

3.2 Methodological reflections and key terms for defining the essence of Christianity in the Lectures of 1811

Key steps and insights of the two published versions are already present in the lecture transcript of 1811 (3.2). It can draw on the *Brief Outline*'s consistent organisation of the disciplines of theology to justify in greater detail the position taken against natural religion already in the *Speeches*. The nuanced argumentation on the relationship between reason and revelation it develops will be maintained as the basis of a middle course between rationalism and supernaturalism; its view on an eventual translation of theology into philosophy will be discarded and replaced with a contrasting position that stresses their independence and continuing co-existence. As will be shown in subsection 3.3, the first edition succeeds in combining the ongoing critique of an extrinsicist understanding of revelation with the counterweight of a theology that finds the core which permeates and shapes Christianity throughout its periods and subdivisions in the confession of redemption by Jesus Christ.

In order to access what is "characteristic in Christianity" in §§ 5–10, already the Lectures mention both general principles, examining first what is due to the "ways in which the feeling of the relationship to God enters consciousness",[144] and then what is particular, concerning the basis for the intrinsic differences between the religions. The first explains the possibility of different relationships between self-consciousness and its modification by the relation to God which give rise to "diverging conceptions of the human person". This "relative difference" consists in some religions being more "affected by freedom", and others more by "nature" which leads to the distinction between "ethical" and "physical religions",[145] the precursor of the later contrast between "teleological" and "aesthetic" modes of faith. The particular character of a religion is "linked necessarily to the fact of its first origin".[146] There is no way of anticipating this factor since it originates in history. The example Schleiermacher gives his students in his lec-

---

[144] Wolfes, "Einleitung 1811", 88, n. 33, quoting from Twesten's diary entry of April 17, 1811.
[145] Wolfes, "Einleitung 1811", 87, on § 8. Cf. Wolfes, "Gegensatz", 651.
[146] Wolfes, "Einleitung 1811", 88 (§ 14).

ture for the link that is missing in principle between the order of reason and the level of history, for "never being able to deduce the specific and individual (*das Besondere und Individuelle*) from the general" (*Allgemeinen*) is that one cannot deduce "the concept of a dog from the general concept of an animal".[147] Therefore, the status of particularity is such that reason can only find it. One could say that there is a dignity to historical individuality which is not in the gift of reason. The differences between religions are internal, based on an "inner, pervasive principle" of each: "Otherwise, the difference could only be external; Christianity could develop anywhere; what Socrates would be lacking to be Christ would only be the conditions of place and time."[148] The differentiating moment in Christianity that "modifies all other feelings" is named in the Introduction, as it was in the *Speeches*, as the "idea of reconciliation".[149]

The positive content of a religion indicates its ground in history. It "cannot be deduced purely a priori, but its existence can only be known in history" (§ 15. 89). For Schleiermacher, this means: "All religion is revealed" (§ 13. 88) in the sense that it could not be deduced in its historically individualised constitution. He rejects the contrast between natural and revealed religion because they are all "positive", affected by their "particular principle" (§ 13. 88). An understanding of revelation as an "external authority", imposing itself from the outside, is not possible if "the consciousness of God is given immediately with reason" (§ 23. 91).

In the doctrine of grace in the Lectures' material dogmatics, divine revelation is discussed in relation to human nature. It is identified on the one hand, as "an act of proclamation (*Kundmachung*) of the infinite in consciousness… which is in no organic connection with what went before" (§ 12). Yet this does not mean that the finite is negated when the "higher principle enters". For Schleiermacher, the task of dogmatics involves keeping a balance between two equally important points: not to "deny the difference between the divine revealing itself in the finite, and the finite", yet "never wanting to find the divine in a way that abolishes (*aufhebt*) the natural" (§§ 13 and 14).[150]

Thus, against a supernaturalist insistence on the purely external nature of revelation, "originating by an affection from outside, caused immediately by God, revealed" (§ 16. 89), he questions the implicit assumption that the "natural" could ever appear purely, not "in a particular form, positively", and resolves that

---

147 Wolfes, "Einleitung 1811", 89 (§ 17).
148 Wolfes, "Einleitung 1811", 87 (§ 7).
149 Wolfes, "Einleitung 1811", 87 (§ 9). Cf. Wolfes, "Gegensatz", 643. The material dogmatics of 1811 also speaks of "redemption", e.g., Wolfes, "Gegensatz", 658–659.
150 Wolfes, "Gegensatz", 659.

they are "both given in consciousness" (§ 16. 89). Against a rationalist disregard for the unique, underivable character of the historical, the principle that limits reason's ability to construct encounters in history is stated clearly. This longstanding insight of Romanticism against an Enlightenment-typical privileging of the universal is again endorsed, well before the critics of the first edition accused the *Glaubenslehre* of replacing the historical person of Jesus Christ with an idea of redemption.

In its formal, terse propositions, the *Brief Outline* had indicated the unsubstitutable function of the historically given by placing the systematic discipline of dogmatics into "historical theology". The Lectures specify the critical task of dogmatics "as an analysis of religious feeling" (§ 49. 96) further: It consists in demonstrating for every dogma that it contains "the particular principle of Christianity", as ascertained in "a reflection on our feeling" (§ 63. 98), by first relating it back to the Bible: not "literally", but in the "spirit and coherence of the whole", when it is "really contained in the Bible", or else "by a procedure of combination" (§ 66. 98). Secondly, the ecclesial character of a dogma must be judged by distinguishing in the symbolic writings what is "regulative" in them, in the sense of "having passed into the view (*Ansicht*) of the church", as opposed to what is the expression of "a private opinion" (§§ 67 and 68. 98).[151] Thus, the treatment of the dogmatic tradition as a "natural evolution of what is contained in Scripture" is tied back to Scripture "as containing what has to be called revelation *per eminentiam* as the first and therefore also the purest appearance of a religious consciousness" (§ 50. 96).[152] What is rejected, however, is a "mere withdrawal to biblical or symbolic teaching" that avoids the "competing claim of explanation of philosophical 'speculation'".[153] To this can be added, as the *Brief Outline*, *The Christian Faith* and the *Sendschreiben* show, the competing claims also of the natural and the historical sciences. Thus, the self-understanding of the dogmatic theologian is to do justice to the biblical testimony, to the internal coherence of the Christian doctrines, and to the challenges of new insights of reason and of the progress of knowledge. How is the second task of the Introduction, after determining the core of religion, to define the essence of Christianity by setting in place an interactive procedure between a constructive and a historical quest, approached ten years later?

---

[151] Cf. Wolfes, "Gegensatz", 659.
[152] Cf. Wolfes, "Gegensatz", 648.
[153] Wolfes, "Gegensatz", 655.

3.3 Steps, explication and implications of the definition of the essence of Christianity in the first edition

By the time of preparing the original publication of the *Glaubenslehre*, the need had become clear to give an account of the Christian faith that showed its contents as remaining independent from speculative reason. The 1811 description of the relationship of theology to philosophy subjected doctrines to the "laws of scientific intuition (*Gesetze ... der wissenschaftlichen Anschauung*)". This was explained as entailing the "dissolution" of feeling in knowledge and the transformation ("*hinüberzuführen*") of "the individual dogmatic statements into the realm of philosophical theory", in order to show the "identity of the religious and the speculative".[154] This former sublation is now replaced with an insistence on their parallel standing and ongoing complementarity. The methodological reflections are expanded, the concept of "redemption" is prioritised over "reconciliation", and it is expounded in a way that underscores the need for a Redeemer. I will examine its account of the principles used for defining historical religions (3.3.1), the combination of methods (3.3.2) and the formula itself (3.3.3), as well as its consequences for delineating the difference between anthropology and Christology (3.3.4).

3.3.1 The general and the individualising principles for capturing historical religions

The general principles of the realisation of piety can be deduced from the elements of self-consciousness. They lead to the stage and the type of a historical religion, which, however, are only "intermediate factors" (^{1}§ 16,3. I, 57) for defining its essence; they are themselves shaped by the difference principle that the second, specific set of factors contributes.

Thus, it is not possible to deduce the real formations appearing in the history of religions from the definition of piety; all one can do is designate their location by developing a system of classification that is not founded on empirical differences but on "the most inner relationships of self-consciousness" (^{1}§ 16,3. I, 57). In order to become explicit and concrete, the God-consciousness that is invariant in itself has to unite with the modifications of the sensible self-conscious-

---

154 Wolfes, "Gegensatz", 646. While marked by "*Congruenz*", "particular laws of individualisation and combination (*besondere Gesetze der Vereinzelung und Combination*)" must be taken into account.

ness.¹⁵⁵ Since it is the highest stage that encompasses finite being as a whole, it gives direction to sensibility and qualifies its contents in a new way. Depending on the porousness of its moments for the relation to God, the result of what is named their "fusion" is "a pleasant (or a painful) pious stirring" (¹§ 11,2. I, 39). Through the "communicative power of the expression" (¹§ 12,2. I, 42) communities are formed which are designated "churches" if they can be clearly distinguished by the similarity of their concrete pious feelings and the ordered form of their on-going transmission. They are classified according to the stage of development that determines which conception of God is possible. It is measured by the clarity of the distinction between the purely sensible and the "higher" consciousness, that is, the realised God-consciousness. In the period before they become differentiated, fetishism reigns with idols which represent only finite realms. When the difference between the two levels has been made and the dependency of everything finite has been recognised, yet the multiplicity of the sensible contents of feeling dominates, the stage of polytheism emerges. The goal of spiritual development is attained when the higher self-consciousness has separated itself so clearly from the sensible that it can relate the feeling of absolute dependency to "One highest and infinite" divinity (¹§ 15 LS. I, 49). This is the case only in monotheism. The possibility to cross-divide the development scale into two opposite kinds is established by the two ways in which the active and the receptive states can be subordinated to each other. The experiences of modification of the sensible self-consciousness can be united with the relation to God in a way that gives rise to new activity; then, the "consciousness of ethical purposes" leads beyond the factual stage, which is the case in the type of goal-oriented, "teleological" piety (¹§ 16,2. I, 56). When the sensible self-consciousness can only unite with the God-consciousness if the states of spontaneous activity themselves are conceived as the result of external conditions and submission to them, thus, if the existing order of things beyond and within the human person appears as a fate ordained by the divine, it is the "aesthetic" kind of piety. Schleiermacher sees it realised in religions oriented towards the "beautiful soul" and fate, such as Greek polytheism and Islam, while Judaism and Christianity belong to the teleological kind.¹⁵⁶

---

155 Regarding the major debate focusing on this point which includes the problem of how the verbalisation of the modification of the immediate self-consciousness is envisaged, cf. Michael Moxter's outline of relevant aspects in "Gefühl und Ausdruck. Nicht nur ein Problem der Schleiermacherinterpretation", in Roderich Barth and Christopher Zarnow (eds), *Theologie der Gefühle* (Berlin/Boston: de Gruyter, 2014), 111–126.
156 In *Bildung und Christentum. Der Bildungsgedanke Schleiermachers* (Göttingen: Vandenhoeck & Ruprecht, 1989), 285, Matthias Riemer sees the difference between the "aesthetic" and the "tel-

To complement the scaffold of concepts established so far which show the location, but not the individual essence of historical religions, principles that determine individuality are needed. Apart from their stage and kind, the monotheistic religions are not just different due to diverse elements picked up by chance but are shaped to their core by the manner in which the (teleological or aesthetic) moments are organised into one positive, characteristic configuration. Since this individuating principle deeply affects a religion's stage and kind, principles of particularity are sought in order to be able to engage in this subsequent enquiry.

Two features constitute a religion's particularity that cannot be anticipated: its own historical beginning, and an internal principle of individuation of the material that is shared by other religions of the same stage and kind. However, the first, external difference of the foundation that is marked by space, time and founder is not sufficient to justify the ongoing distinction and progressive differentiation of a religion. Since the inner cause of particularity affects the God-consciousness, it must be based in the immediate self-consciousness. This individual essential law is founded on an elementary "relation" that has "such a dominating position" that "all other (pious stirrings) are subordinated to it, and it communicates its colour and tone to them" (^{1}§ 17,3. I, 60).

A consequence of this approach to capturing the essence of historical religions is the way in which their perfection is measured. They do not merely count as *realisations* of the general God-consciousness of a certain kind and stage but as *concretisations* that are each modified by an unforeseeable factor in an entirely different way. This is why Schleiermacher had announced at the beginning of his course of enquiry into defining the essence of Christianity that the way in which "what is given historically fits into this (division of the general concept), can only be discovered" (^{1}§ 6,3. I, 21). Since every historical religion "has everything the others have, but all differently" (^{1}§ 17,3. I, 60), each is suitable to be placed, yet remains unified and inexhaustible in its individuality – an irreducibly particular concrete universal that is at the same time open to understanding. Thus, the measure of its perfection does not simply consist in realising the highest stage and its respective kind in the purest and most decisive way, thereby merely fulfilling what is posited in the concept of monotheism. Its perfection is to be found in the measure in which the external and the internal unity (^{1}§ 17,1. I, 58), origin and content, permeate each other in one singular essence.

---

eological" type of piety as first of all relating to the polarity between an orientation towards the "beautiful soul" and the "kingdom of God".

3.3.2 The relation between a constructive and a comparative, historical-critical approach in the first edition

If therefore Christianity, like every other historical religion, is approached as a completely particular entity, where is the key to its basic relation that is formative for its monotheistic stage and its teleological orientation? Through which steps of enquiry does Schleiermacher plan to reach the formula of its essence?

The process takes its starting point with a feature that is beyond doubt: the external unity which begins with the historical person Jesus of Nazareth and continues in the tradition arising from him. It then recognises the key to its inner particularity by observing that Christianity has a different relationship to its founder than Judaism and Islam have to theirs. Not only the foundation of a community is taken to be Jesus' historical achievement but his work of "complete redemption" (^{1}§ 18,1. I, 61). Thus, the enquiry seems to have already attained its goal: the searched-for principal element that "gives everything Christian its particular (*eigenthümlich*) colour and tone" is the "relation of all religious stirrings to redemption". Since redemption is identified immediately with the founder himself, he is the only historical founder of a religion who unites the external and the internal distinguishing feature in his person: The fact that "redemption itself is posited in the person of Jesus is the complete bond (*Band*) between the inner and outer unity of Christianity" (^{1}§ 18 LS. n. I, 61).

This result, however, according to the argumentation of 1821/22, still requires confirmation. Thus, the investigation into the inner unity recommences "from another point" (^{1}§ 18,2. I, 63). The method of beginning from the ground of Christian doctrine in order to find the common denominator for the multiple Christian states of feeling encounters difficulties. The search for the essence of Christianity in the first edition is motivated by the insight that there is no consensus on them. Its subject matter is the enquiry into the pious stirrings, not, as in the second edition, the framework of a "church".[157] The feelings and the doctrines do not only diverge from each other but are also controversial in whether they can count as Christian. This is why the "location" of the investigation matters:

> For if we pick one of these multifarious determinations of the same feeling and the same doctrine in order to get to know from it the essence of what is Christian, but overlook or even reject the others: we would then assume the controversies as decided in advance while we still lack any basis on which to decide them; and we would be accused not without reason to be partial. ... But if we had no such predilection: we could then just as well

---

[157] The effects of this difference are outlined by Martin Rössler, *Schleiermachers Programm der Philosophischen Theologie*, 155–158.

also pick what is really unchristian instead of what is Christian and could spoil our whole enterprise with such an erroneous path (I, 63–64).

What Schleiermacher is alluding to in describing the dilemma that arises between an internal and an external standpoint for identifying a doctrine as essential, is the problem of the hermeneutical circle. Any attempt of determining the concept of something historically given of which the extension is unknown or "very controversial in different respects" (^{1}§ 18,2. I, 63) ends up in such a circle. In order to be able to name the inner specificity of Christianity, it is necessary to take a standpoint that is both empirical and critical, or, at the same time within it and above it: in it, in order to be able to include the extent (*Bestand*) that the formula is to cover; above it, in order to delimit the circumference of the material to be considered, for which, however, the definition is already needed. In view of the inevitability of the hermeneutical circle between the empirical and the critical perspectives on its essence Schleiermacher returns to the first result and determines the particular function of Jesus as its centre. Insofar as "it is already likely in itself and in advance that what is only attributed to the founder of Christianity, the bond between the external and internal unity, does not lie at an uncertain periphery (*Umkreis*) but instead at the centre" (I, 64), he can encompass the essence of Christianity in the formula: "Christianity is a distinctive [*eigenthümlich*] formation of piety in its teleological direction which is distinguished from all others by the fact that in it every individual thing is related to the consciousness of redemption by Jesus of Nazareth" (^{1}§ 18 LS. I, 61).

The dogmatic principle that the Introduction thus proposes can claim for itself to be the testimony of "the general voice of the Christian church" (^{1}§ 18,3. I, 64), its central self-understanding through the ages. It will be decisive how the critical concept, "redemption", is determined, since, as we have seen, it is normative for the design and the elaboration of the dogmatics. It will be expounded on the basis of the insights already established, namely, the God-consciousness shown inherent in human self-consciousness. The explanation of Christ's redeeming activity that is to establish his distinctiveness will have to stand the test of whether it is able to secure the essential and unsurpassable bond of the Christian faith to his person.

3.3.3 The explication of the concept of redemption

^{1}§ 18,3 first explains its general religious meaning, then its specifically Christian use. ^{1}§ 18,4 draws the consequences for the position of the person of Jesus and the place of Christianity among the other religions. The final section examines whether there would have been a methodological alternative to the "historical consideration (*Betrachtung*)" (¹§ 18,5. I, 68) taken: a purely constructive one, based only on the distinctions made at the level of philosophy of religion.

The general meaning of "redemption" is given as "taking away a constraint (*Hemmung*) of life and bringing about a better condition" (¹§ 1,3. I, 64). In the context of teleological monotheism, the "constraint" in question applies to the "unification of the sensible consciousness and the pious feeling of dependence" (¹§ 18,3. I, 65). This presupposes a "relative opposition" between them, since a "complete inability" (I, 65) would require a total "re-creation" (*Umschaffung*) of the subject and would exclude any consciousness of the need for redemption. This is why the "constraint" is described as a "lack of ease (*Leichtigkeit*) in elevating the sensible to the pious self-consciousness" (I, 65). This is attributed to the "relative opposition between the human person's being posited-for-itself" and the "co-positing of God" in pious consciousness. Redemption in the general monotheistic sense is precisely the removal (*Aufhebung*) of this constraint.

Concerning the use of this term in Christianity, its specificity is that it is limited solely to its founder. Redemption is seen as the "immediate and personal" (I, 65) activity of Jesus. The difference between one person causing the redemption of all others, and a reciprocal redemption among fellow humans is shown to be a principal one. While mutual support can reduce, but not abolish, the opposition between the sensible and the higher self-consciousness, it is superseded once and for all in Jesus Christ. From this result the first version draws conclusions concerning the consciousness of the Redeemer. As someone who is able to take away the constraint in the God-consciousness for all, and to reconcile the opposition contained in the concept of redemption, the person of Jesus must be free of this duality and thus be the only human being who does not need redemption. The first edition explains the finding that in Jesus Christ no hindrance can be found between the sensible and the higher consciousness with the assumption that in him both must be "totally the same" (*völlig dasselbe*).[158] Thus, he is characterised by an "absolutely perfect" (*schlechthin vollendete*) piety (¹§ 18,4. I, 66).

These statements about Jesus' inner being, developed as implications of the testimony of redemption, are further elaborated with regard to his position in the history of religions and of humanity. Since Jesus brings the reversal from a uni-

---

158 The reason given in the first edition is that "where there is difference, there still is also reciprocal hindrance" (1§ 18,4. I,66). The second edition, in contrast, explains the absolute strength of the God-consciousness as giving the "impulse to every moment" of the sensible self-consciousness which retains its independent status.

versal need to the effective realisation of redemption, he is the "turning-point for the whole human race" (I, 67). Christianity is correspondingly the most perfect religion and the ultimate goal for the other religions which still require redemption in their concretisations of the God-consciousness.

In summary, the function of Jesus Christ, as it is laid out in ¹§ 18, can be characterised as follows: The definition of Christianity is clearly oriented towards Christology. The historical founder is absolutely decisive for its essence, since inner and outer factor coincide in him. He incorporates the principle of the inner difference, and the principle of outer unity is completely absorbed into the inner one. He thus represents the singular factor from which it is impossible to abstract. The essential content that first came into existence with him is introduced as "redemption" and explained in a way that Jesus as Redeemer is set apart from humanity which is the recipient of redemption. These determinations will come to fruition in the following paragraphs which construct the proper, that is, the essence-defying heresies, as well as clarify the relationship of divine revelation to human nature. I will analyse them in two respects:

First, the historical beginning and content of Christianity coincide completely in the person of the founder. This shows that, in the case of the Christian religion, the task to capture the historical has concluded with a finding which could not be more concrete: The inner specificity of Christianity cannot be separated from his person; insofar as it only appeared with him, it is as little deducible as the fact of his historical existence. How will the following determinations of the implications of the concept of redemption safeguard the essential binding of this content to the person of Jesus? It will depend on the specifications still to be made whether the historical Redeemer will indeed assume the ongoing validity that the Christian faith attributes to him in Schleiermacher's outline.

Second, in order to answer this question, it is necessary to illuminate the inner structure of the consciousness of redemption. Its two poles are the need for redemption, which was explained as a "relative opposition" between the sensible and the higher self-consciousness, and the awareness of this need, that distinguished the hindrance or constraint from a "complete inability" (¹§ 18,3. I, 65). Which relationship between the two – the need, and the awareness of this need, or the relative opposition, and the relative inability – will surface in the following considerations on the distinction between anthropology and Christology?

3.3.4 Implications of the essence formula for drawing limits

With the essence definition, a guideline has been established for delineating the controversial outer borders of Christianity; now basic types of missing or contravening it can be constructed. Analytically, there are only two places that come into question as the tipping points from the Christian into the heretical: the two poles between which the realisation of redemption takes place, namely, specifics pertaining to the person of Jesus, or to the humans who are to be redeemed (3.3.4.1). The way in which these factors are set to interact will then be reflected in the relationship of revelation to nature (3.3.4.2) and reason (3.3.4.3), expounded in ¹§§ 19 and 20.

3.3.4.1 Deriving "natural heresies" from the concept of redemption

What the Introduction develops regarding the limits of what can count as Christian, is a construction of possible heresies. It cannot offer an overview of the doctrines that have been considered heretical in the course of the history of Christian thinking; it can only delimit in advance to all actual doctrinal rulings in principle how the realm of what is Christian can be transgressed and at what point this is likely to be the case. In Schleiermacher's view, this always happens when the elements which are implied in the concept of redemption are coordinated in a way that renders its realisation unthinkable. Real heresies that affect the core of the Christian faith originate from a thwarted balance between the moments that have to be related: of the need, and the receptivity for redemption on the anthropological side, and of the difference and the identity of Jesus on the Christological side. Since they arise from the concept of redemption by accentuating one of its complementary moments in a one-sided way, Schleiermacher entitles them "natural heresies" (¹§ 25. I, 93–98). When he labels them with the names of historically active movements, it is in the interest of the typical, not of the actual counter-positions which they represent.[159]

Thus, it is termed "Manichean" to exaggerate the need for redemption at the cost of the capability to be redeemed, requiring a "complete re-creation" (*Umschaffung*) (¹§ 25. I, 94) into a new subject. The contrasting possibility consists in absolu-

---

[159] Klaus-Martin Beckmann, *Der Begriff der Häresie bei Schleiermacher* (Munich: Chr. Kaiser, 1959), 103, n. 143. Equally, in "Christology and Anthropology in Friedrich Schleiermacher", in Mariña (ed.), *The Cambridge Companion to Friedrich Schleiermacher*, 151–170, 152, Jacqueline Mariña points out the interest in the typical, not the historical when she describes the four natural heresies as "ways in which the fundamentals of Christian doctrine can be contradicted" and as what "must be avoided if the concept of redemption is to be properly understood".

tising the other pole, the capability for redemption. Then deliverance comes about through the mutual support (*Aufrichtung*) and confirmation of those in need of redemption; the opposition is not reconciled, but gradually reduced. This error which overemphasises the inherent power of human nature, thus making redemption superfluous, is qualified as "Pelagian". The Christological distortions are constructed analogously: When Jesus' participation in human nature is denied, redemption becomes impossible, since it destroys the condition for "removing (*aufheben*) the opposition in us" which must be "found in the similarity with him". The common ground for the striving "for a gradual approximation (*Annäherung*) to him" would be taken away. The counterposition to such "Docetism" is the "Nazorean" or "Ebionite" heresy which subordinates Jesus' "peculiar quality (*Vorzug*)" so much to the sameness with human nature that in him "the same difference between the sensible and the higher consciousness reigns as in all others" (^{1}§ 25. I, 95), and he is himself in need of redemption. Thus, it is obvious that a connection exists between the tendencies of the anthropological and the Christological heresies: the "Pelagian" distortion is matched by the "Ebionite", and a "Manichean" anthropology of eternal evil does not allow to conceive of a participation of the Redeemer in a human essence qualified in this way and falls into "Docetism".

A first résumé of the relationship between anthropology and Christology as developed in ^{1}§§ 18 and 25 can be given now that the essence definition has acquired more specific contours by marking its extremes. Even if the first edition's account of the basic types of heresy barely goes beyond what has been stated in the essence formula, the border lines have now been drawn: redemption is the complete overcoming of the opposition between sensible and higher consciousness, which has been set in explicit opposition to a gradual progression of piety. Such a new beginning that definitively ends the chapter of being in need of redemption in the history of the human species cannot be initiated by humanity's own forces. It is therefore dependent on a "proper point of beginning" (*eigentlicher Anfangspunkt*) in the form of an "absolute Redeemer" (^{1}§ 25,4. I, 94) as its counterpart. The definitive distinction of Jesus from all others is to have fundamentally reconciled the opposition between the higher and the lower consciousness. On the other hand, the human capability for redemption has emerged as a systematic pillar of the argumentation as well. If redemption is not to entail "re-creation", then some identity in human nature must be preserved in both eras. Further insights on this aspect can be gained from Schleiermacher's discussion of the term "revelation" for denoting a communication initiated by God.

3.3.4.2 The "natural" and the "supernatural" regarding revelation

In his redefinition of what the "supernatural" and the "supra-rational" character of the divine revelation in Jesus Christ consist in, Schleiermacher offers the most differentiated account so far of the summit and of the limits of the human potential to realise the relation to God. His first move is to incorporate the concepts of the "positive" and of "revelation" into his reconstruction of historical religions by connecting them with the two individualising factors. "Positive" in a religion is the generating principle of its inner particularity which pervades all of its aspects. Since therefore a religion as a whole is "positive", the former counter-concept, what the Enlightenment referred to as "natural", has lost its previous significance. This term can now only relate to the level of generality that is attained by abstracting from the thorough specificity of a religion, an abstraction to which no real religious community corresponds. This conceptual clarification shows again how much Schleiermacher is invested in the radically individual essence of historical religions which undermines the assumption that there are "general" shared aspects, and additional "individual" ones. What is decisive for his understanding of the essence of Christian piety, however, is how the concept of revelation is explicated. It is attached to the remaining individuating factor, the first one, namely its historical beginning. The first edition relates it to "the original coming into being of the essential of the pious community" (^{1}§ 19,2. I, 73), and specifies further that this community "in its first origin cannot be grasped as resulting from a natural development by way of mutual influence of humans on each other" (^{1}§ 19,3. I, 76). Thus it seems that the concept, although only determined negatively at this stage, is to exclude a Pelagian drift of the understanding of revelation. In order to give it a positive determination, Schleiermacher conceives finely adjusted differentiations in the concepts of "nature" and "reason". They are to mediate what is divine in this origin with the contribution of humanity's power of development which is equally seen to be at work.

His thesis that revelation can only be regarded as "relatively supernatural" is founded on a specific concept of human nature. The fact that the content of revelation cannot be explained from the immediate historical context in which it appears does not exclude that it could not stem from the "power of development of human nature in general" (cf. ^{1}§ 20,1. I, 78). To fix this nature to a given state would mean to ignore what is proper to it: its productivity by which it transcends each stage. This power comes to exemplary evidence in those human beings who count as "heroes" or "excellent promoters" of humanity due to the new developments that they initiated in different intellectual or political realms. The "idea of human nature" is thus only captured sufficiently when these leaps of development are included. Viewed in relation to the present stage, these new beginnings are "relatively supernatural" phenomena and are analogous to revelation. They are departures which are conditioned by their historical context yet are not taken as continuations of an already existing level but as the beginning of a new line of development. They emerge in an original way, apart from the series of historically observable tendencies and thus, if one looks for their origin, "in an immediate way from the general source of life" (*allgemeiner Lebensquell*) (¹§ 20,1. I, 78).¹⁶⁰

Having noted the genuine human capability for self-transcending development, the next task is to identify what is special about the revelation in the person of Jesus. It consists in two features: First, it concerns progress in God-consciousness, a realm "in which productivity is not originary" (Marg. 313, p. 63); second, the claim of Christian revelation is not to be limited to specific cultural formations or eras; it is destined to "illuminate (*erleuchten*) the whole human race" (I, 78). At the same time, Schleiermacher insists on understanding even its most principled designation, to attain the point of the "incarnation of the Son of God" (I, 79), as an expression of the original capability of human nature for new beginnings. As "certainly as Christ was a human being, there must reside in human nature the capability of taking up the divine into itself" (¹§ 20,1. I, 79. Cf. ²§ 13,1. ET 1928, 63). Even in the moment in which the mere possibility becomes the reality of the Redeemer, both sides are contributing, the primordial initiative of God and the spiritual nature of the human which reaches its most extensive realisation in this event:

> Even if only the possibility of this resides in human nature, so that the actual implanting therein of the divine element must be purely a divine and therefore an eternal act, nevertheless the temporal appearance of this act in one particular Person must be at the same time regarded as an action of human nature, grounded in its original constitution and prepared for by all its past history, and accordingly by the highest development of its spiritual power (even if we grant that we could never penetrate so deep into those innermost secrets of the universal spiritual life as to be able to develop this general conviction into a definite perception) (¹§ 20,1. I, 79. Cf. ²§ 13,1. ET 1928, 64).

The explanations of the essence definition set the framework for Christology. On the one hand, the argument must be granted that to avoid Docetism, the real humanity of Jesus Christ must be accounted for in a conception of Christology. Yet, as Friedrich Kantzenbach observes, this point can be stretched.¹⁶¹ It is also formulated,

---

160 In the second edition, it is translated as "universal fountain of life" (²§ 13,1. ET 1928, 63).
161 In *Programme der Theologie, Denker, Schulen, Wirkungen. Von Schleiermacher bis Moltmann* (Munich: Claudius, 1978), 29, Friedrich Kantzenbach comments that "the justification contains characteristic deviations (*Abweichungen*) in relation to the ecclesial dogma of Christ. ... Despite these objections against his justification the right of Schleiermacher's thesis does not seem to be able to be doubted insofar as Christ's real humanity (*Menschsein*) is being taken as the point of departure."

in line with the Christological doctrines themselves, at the level of human nature, not examining in which relation the capacity for freedom – both that of Jesus and of human beings in general – stands to human nature. The final pair of terms to be linked to what has been clarified so far is the relation between reason and revelation.

3.3.4.3 "Inner experience" as supra-rational, its secondary dogmatic conceptualisation as "rational"

What is still missing from a complete determination of the concept of revelation issuing from the essence definition is its relationship to reason. The first edition orientates the supra-rational character of revelation towards the question of how the dogmatic teachings relate to the Christian self-consciousness whose content they are to represent. They are "supra-rational" in that they did not *generate* what they present in reason-led speech as the medium of the universal, but in that they *discovered* it: namely "a purely inner experience" (^{1}§ 20,2. I, 80). It is distinct from other experiences in the form of its appropriation which is based on personal involvement. In contrast to the "merely logical direction of natural science" for which "the individual is a matter of chance" (Marg. 373, p. 71–72), it is a question of something "singular and particular (*eigenthümlich*) which cannot be "grasped by reason but only perceived by love" (^{1}§ 20,2. I, 80). This is elucidated further as a contrast to the essence of reason: it corresponds to the essence of love which is defined by "wanting to perceive (*anschauen*)" (Marg. 373, p. 71). In this sense, regarding the wish to get involved with something individual, "the whole Christian doctrine is in everybody not through reason" (^{1}§ 20,2. I, 80).

Christian doctrines are thus "supra-rational" because they emerge from such an inner experience. The Lectures formulate more clearly in what way the receptivity of the faithful is activated by this effect:

> Christ, Christianity is evidently something given in experience; the impression is precisely what produces the concept, not the givenness of the person alone, but the givenness of an experience, that is, receptivity in highest potency. It is clear that at the origin, revelation in Christ was perceived through such an inner experience, in that the disciples said, we have found the Messiah. The need was there, it was satisfied and that is the experience, and thus with all Christians (Marg. 372, *Nachschrift Heegewald* 77, KGA I/7.3, 71).

The original version's demarcation between revelation and reason thus aims at limiting the role of reason to a descriptive rendering of the experience. It clarifies that the Christian doctrines owe their origin not to a "deduction or combination from generally acknowledged and communicable statements" of reason, since then "one would have to be able to turn every human being into a Christian by demonstration and teaching" (¹§ 20,2. I, 80). The task of dogmatics is to express the stirrings of the immediate self-consciousness in conceptual thinking. The contribution of reason that belongs to this task is not further developed or problematised by Schleiermacher at this stage. From the brief justification with which he rejects an understanding of the supra-rational as "counter-rational (*widervernünftig*)", it becomes clear, however, that reason is not alien to the Christian content it has to mediate: "because the self-consciousness and the objective consciousness, that is, the totality of everything rational completely encompass each other (*rein ineinander aufgehn*)" (I, 81).

3.4 The corrections and the new emphases of the second edition

The corrections to the original outline apply, firstly, to the hermeneutical steps and the realm of validity of the essence definition itself (3.4.1); secondly, to foundational definitions that are significant for the elaboration of the dogmatic anthropology and Christology: the evaluation of the sensible in relation to the higher self-consciousness (3.4.2), and the question whether redemption could be constructed a priori as a possible principal feature of a religion (3.4.3). It is not surprising that Schleiermacher reformulates his previous statements on the interaction of the divine and the human after F. C. Baur had objected that the *Glaubenslehre* had constructed an "ideal" Redeemer from the pious self-consciousness at the expense of the historical Redeemer.

3.4.1 Clarifications of the hermeneutical procedure

The second edition indicates the transition to a new discipline and method already by the title chosen for the propositions (²§§ 11–14) which state and explain the essence definition. While the preceding ²§§ 7–10, entitled "Propositions Borrowed from the Philosophy of Religion" developed the grid for locating the different religions, now the "Propositions Borrowed from Apologetics" are to present Christianity "in its peculiar essence" (ET 1928, 52).

Martin Rössler has clarified in which relationship the disciplines of "ethics", "philosophy of religion" and "apologetics" stand to each other. It is true that with Stephen Sykes's warning that they are "oddly named", it is worth investigating how each is defined and what their functions are. Both philosophy of religion and apologetics relate to historical manifestations of religion, whereas "ethics" deals with the fundamental philosophical concepts, such as self-consciousness, reflection, history, community, sciences, or religion. Thus, as Rössler specifies against the impression that it is only "apologetics" which deals with empirical historical formations, this is also the task of what Schleiermacher entitles "philosophy of religion". Their relationship is one of partial overlap (*Teilmengenverhältnis*), since "apologetics" carries out in relation to Christianity what "philosophy of religion" does with regard to the history of religions: "It intends a demonstration of the congruence (*Übereinstimmung*) of the conceptual divisions of the ethical term 'religion' with their historical diversity."[162] The foundational discipline of "ethics", however, "cannot be taken over directly even only partially into 'apologetics' but merely puts the conceptual-speculative ancillary tools (*Hilfsmittel*) at its disposition." These concepts must be "filled with historical material so that a 'critical' comparison can take place at all".[163] These methodological considerations serve the interest of marking out the distinct location of the positive religions which cannot be deduced from the philosophical concept of religion.

According to the definition of apologetics put forward in Schleiermacher's *Brief Outline*, the aim after the general classification of the Christian religion is to "gain external recognition for its inner validity" (BO ^{1}§ 14; ed. Tice, 23), or, as its second edition states, to "communicate... the truth of the mode of faith propagated here ... so that it can be clearly recognised" (BO ^{2}§ 39; ed. Tice, 22–23). Since the *Glaubenslehre* does not complete the task described here itself, but refers to the *Brief Outline*, I will include points from its reworked edition of 1830 and the corresponding lectures on Theological Encyclopedia to develop the necessary background.

According to the propositions of the *Brief Outline*, apologetics takes its standpoint within Christianity and justifies its content as one that can be recognised by reason. This is accomplished through the determination of its essence which grasps what is specific for Christianity, and not deducible; it sets forth "a formula for the distinctive nature of Christianity" and shows "its relation to the special character of other religious communities ... (r)eferring back (*subsumiert*) to the concept of the 'positive'" (BO ^{2}§ 44; ed. Tice, 27).

---

[162] Rössler, *Schleiermachers Programm der philosophischen Theologie*, 158–159. This corrects the distinction made in Doris Offermann's pioneering study, *Schleiermachers Einleitung in die Glaubenslehre. Eine Untersuchung der 'Lehnsätze'* (Berlin: de Gruyter, 1969), 239, that "apologetics" treats what is "empirically given" and thus has a stronger connection to history as opposed to the more general constructions of philosophy of religion. Rössler points out that as "critical disciplines" both use the same method (159).
[163] Rössler, *Schleiermachers Programm der philosophischen Theologie*, 158.

The methodological difference to the previous definition of the essence of piety in general is that it could be attained in a reflection by human subjectivity on itself. Now, instead of a subject-theoretical method, a "critical method" (BO ²§ 44; ed. Tice, 27) that mediates between general concept and historically given material (*Bestand*) is needed in order to determine the essence of a historical individuality. This happens "by comparing (*Gegeneinanderhalten*) what is historically given in Christianity with those contrasts in virtue of which various kinds of religious communities can be different from each other" (BO ²§ 32; ed. Tice, 19). The procedure of critically contrasting what is "posed beside each other" (*Gegeneinanderhalten*) moves in the hermeneutical circle of a conceptual determination of the content and an empirical determination of its outer boundaries; this was already clear in the first edition of the *Glaubenslehre*. On the one hand, the concept has to do justice to what is historically given, a concretisation of the general essence of religion that cannot be constructed in advance; on the other hand, as the concept of something empirical, it still remains a concept, a guiding category that has to be verified on the historical ground but has been conceived in advance.

In view of the problematic of this enquiry, the second edition takes its point of departure directly with the historical testimony of the Christian church which summarises its essence in the "basic category" of redemption (²§ 11,2. I, 76). The new formula refers no longer to the "consciousness of redemption" but to its historical accomplishment: "Christianity is a monotheistic faith, belonging to the teleological type of religion, and is essentially distinguished from other such faiths by the fact that in it everything is related to the redemption accomplished by Jesus of Nazareth" (²§ 11 LS. ET 1928, 52). It does not repeat the attempt of the first edition in view of the splits within the Christian doctrinal tradition (¹§ 18,2), to examine in a second approach whether the inner unity could be grasped independently of the outer, historical unity (¹§ 18,3 and ¹§ 18,5). Beyond the principled difference of Jesus Christ already stated in ¹§ 18,3. I, 66, the second edition now also distinguishes between a "passive" and an "active" side of redemption, in order to rule out a rationalist relativising of his position as the definitive counterpart:

> The term itself is in this realm merely figurative (*bildlich*) and signifies in general a passage from an evil (*schlechten*) condition, which is represented as a state of captivity or constraint (*Gebundensein*), into a better condition – this is the passive side of it. But it also signifies the help given in that process by some other person, and this is the active side of it" (²§ 11,2. ET 1928, 54).

The methodological self-control of the second edition is also noticeable in the explanation of the implications of the concept of redemption which no longer anticipates contents that belong to the dogmatics proper. It thus respects the difference between the Introduction and the material dogmatics which had not become clear to the first reviewers. By drawing conclusions from the concept of redemption for the self-consciousness of Jesus (¹§ 18,4), the first version had transgressed the limits to the material part. The second edition limits itself to the points that "Christ is distinguished from all others as Redeemer alone and for all, and is in no wise regarded as having been at any time in need of redemption Himself, ... separated from the beginning from all men, and endowed with redeeming power from His birth" (²§ 11,2. ET 1928, 58). These statements about the person of Jesus can be traced back strictly to the two features of redemption in Christianity: the "incapacity and the redemption ... as the principal thing", and that it "has been universally and completely accomplished by Jesus of Nazareth" (²§ 11,3. ET 1928, 55–56).

3.4.2 The relation between the sensible and the higher self-consciousness

A major correction results from the important objection of the early critics that the *Glaubenslehre* considers the sensible self-consciousness itself already as sin. In response, Schleiermacher changes the theory of how the two unite. Originally, he had stated as its goal the "fusion (*Verschmelzung*) of the higher (direction towards becoming conscious of God) with the given or incipient sensible determination" (¹§ 11,2. I, 39). The second version distances itself from this description: It treats it as a "co-existence of the two in the same moment. ... Of course, this conjunction cannot be regarded as a fusion (*Verschmelzen*) of the two: that would be entirely opposed to the conception of both of them" (²§ 5,3. ET 1928, 21). The aim is now, "as a person determined for this moment in a particular manner within the realm of the antithesis that he is conscious of his absolute dependence. This relatedness of the sensibly determined self-consciousness in the unity of the moment is the consummating point of the self-consciousness" (²§ 5,3. ET 1928, 21).[164] The second edition thus marks the relation between the two clearly as one of relative preponderance, not fusion.

The fact that Schleiermacher abandons the theory of fusion has important consequences both for the concept of redemption and for the question whether it is possible to construct Christianity a priori. The two versions have each demonstrated one of the two possibilities of relating both levels of self-consciousness to each other. *Either* the goal is the disappearance of the sensible self-conscious-

---

164 The 2016 ET (I, 32) translates "moment" with "element": "This being-referred of what is sensorially determined to higher self-consciousness in the unity of the given element is the consummatory apex of self-consciousness."

ness in the pious one. This seems to be the case in the original outline when it is said that "in Christ ... no hindrance can be found" and that therefore the sensible and the higher consciousness "must be totally the same" (*völlig dasselbe*). This is his "absolutely perfect" (*schlechthin vollendete*) piety. The reason given is that "where there is difference, there still is also reciprocal hindrance" (¹§ 18,4. I, 66). Or, as the second version proposes, the sensible self-consciousness that mediates the relationship to the world keeps its own standing and only allows its contents to be determined by the pious self-consciousness.

The question, however, whether the abiding difference of both levels is recognised, is also decisive for the problem of whether redemption can be constructed. If the difference is acknowledged, then the possibility of a sinless development exists, since the sensible level is neutral; the constraint to which redemption relates, and redemption itself then must be factual-historical events. The first version, in contrast, with its goal of fusion has determined a priori that the difference is to be abolished. This is the ideal, despite the contradiction it constitutes for the anthropological finding that human beings inevitably have the sensible function in order to be able to relate to the world. At the same time it restricts what should be the unique, non-deducible individual character of Christianity, redemption, to the occurrence of a feature that could be constructed a priori. The new theory of a unification based on the dominance of either the sensible or the higher self-consciousness has two effects: On the one hand, it gets rid of the contradiction latent in the anthropological theory, and it safeguards on the other hand with the factual character of sin also the historical character of redemption. If these observations are correct, the corresponding differences should surface in the concepts of sin in both editions.

3.4.3 Redemption – historical event or construction of reason?

The suspicion that the concept of the essence of Christianity is owed not to historical experience but to an a priori construction, is counteracted by Schleiermacher with two further changes: in his account of the procedure of the essence definition which now stresses the limits of construction by a philosophy of religion (3.4.3.1), and in a new, history-oriented conceptualisation of the relationship between reason and revelation (3.4.3.2).

3.4.3.1 The limits of construction by a philosophy of religion
The justification that Schleiermacher had given in the first edition for moving from the comparative philosophy of religion approach to a historical one could

be seen to undermine, rather than defend, the position that the historical cannot be deduced from the a priori, or, in F. C. Baur's terminology, from the "ideal". The 1821/22 inaugural version had admitted the feasibility of a further systematisation of the possible relationships between historical religions; it had anticipated that "the inner character of Christianity could be presented in such a way that its specific location is secured", by carrying out the following steps:

> the principal moments of any pious consciousness could be systematised and it could be shown from their relationship which ones among them are such above all (*vorzüglich*) that the others can be related to them; and if it emerges that the feeling of the contrast (*Gegensaz*) and its removal (*Aufhebung*) belong to these, then Christianity is securely positioned besides all the others, and one could say that it is in a certain sense, constructed (¹§18,5. I, 68).

The second edition, however, clarifies in its formulation that the construction of redemption as a possible basic element can only be carried out a posteriori, by replacing the formula that sounds like a projection, "the contrast and its removal", with a description that gives it a time index: Christianity could be "vindicated (*konstruiert*)" if it could be shown that "the element which we call 'redemption' becomes such a moment as soon as a liberating fact enters where the God-consciousness was in a state of constraint" (²§ 11,5. I, ET 1928, 59). This phrasing retains the contingent character of the historical beginning, and with it the concrete character of the essential feature founded by it, which cannot be deduced. The first version had not excluded that such an event could be constructed at least in principle: "By presenting this inner character in a necessary connection with its historical beginning, we renounce to achieve as much in this way as could perhaps be achieved. For dates of great historical turning-points cannot, at least not at the present state of human knowing, be constructed in this sense" (¹§18,5. I, 68). The second edition omits this sentence and merely states as the principal limit of the procedure of philosophy of religion that it "remains problematic" (²§ 11,5. n. (Th). 2008, 101), in other words, that it cannot make any assertion regarding the existence of what has been constructed. Whether this actually comes to pass, cannot be anticipated.[165]

---

165 Karl Barth's comment on ²§ 11,5 is thus only true of the corresponding section of the first edition, but not of the position of the final version which presupposes explicitly that the liberating fact has indeed occurred historically: "§ 11,5 takes another look at the task of the philosophy of religion from the standpoint of the nature of Christianity as it has just been established. It envisages a structure of the discipline in which the definition of Christianity achieved by the theological apologetics is presupposed, and in which the concept of redemption, and the coming of a liberating fact that is necessary to accomplish it, are seen to be basic in a system of the

In view of the second edition's correction that the Christian consciousness of redemption points to a prior historical event that is "given" and not constructed, it is notable that Markus Schröder finds it regrettable that "redemption" has not been put forward as deducible from the monotheistic-teleological stage in general. He regards it as possible from Schleiermacher's "premises", however, to correct this: "The lifting of the incapability, can be concluded from Schleiermacher's theory of religion. ... the difference between being redeemed (*Erlöstheit*) and being unredeemed (*Unerlöstheit*) is a constitutive element of religious consciousness in general".[166] Yet the revised essence definition was at pains to exclude exactly this conclusion that independently from the Redeemer, redemption could be construed a priori. After the response to the first edition, Schleiermacher himself realises that this is a test case for doing justice to the status of a genuine historical breakthrough which Jesus Christ constitutes in his person. To go back to deducing the event from the concept of redemption would confirm F. C. Baur's suspicion that the *Glaubenslehre* disregards history and posits a projected Redeemer.

3.4.3.2 Changes regarding the relationship of reason to revelation

The second area of specific editing to clarify his position in response to the critics is the relationship of human reason to revelation. Two tendencies can be observed in the changes to the text. On the one hand, the statements about the relationship between the self-transcending human person and divine revelation are developed to produce Schleiermacher's general thesis on the coincidence of human reason and the historically mediated divine spirit.

> Inasmuch then, as the reason is completely one with the divine Spirit, the divine Spirit can itself be conceived as the highest enhancement of the human reason so that the difference between the two is made to disappear. ... If then, the human reason itself in a sense contains that which is produced by the divine Spirit, the latter does not in this connexion, at least, go beyond the former (^{2}§ 13,2; ET 1928, 65).

On the other hand, it is made clear that the "purely inner experience" (^{1}§ 20,2. I, 80) of Christians does not refer to an a priori certain idea but to a historically mediated fact. The corresponding dogmatic doctrines are now said to "rest upon

---

chief moments in the pious self-consciousness, so that 'Christianity is established and in some sense constructed as a distinctive form of faith.'" Karl Barth, *The Theology of Schleiermacher: Lectures at Göttingen, Winter Semester of 1923/24*, ed. Dietrich Ritschl, trans. Geoffrey W. Bromiley (Grand Rapids: Eerdmans, 1982), 237.
166 Schröder, *Die kritische Identität*, 44.

a given" (²§ 13 Postscript; ET 1928, 67). The concept of divine revelation and its supernatural and supra-rational implications are consequently linked to the "appearance of the Redeemer in history" (²§ 13 LS; ET 1928, 62). They pertain to the relationship of the "peculiar being of the Redeemer and of the redeemed" (²§ 13 Postscript. ET 1928, 66). With this revision, the concept of the supra-rational has been redirected to the relationship between Christology and anthropology, and only in the second instance to that of the Christian basic experience to its dogmatic reflection. The new key theses on how divine spirit and human reason are ordered towards each other are justified as follows.

In order to safeguard the absolute priority of Christ and of Christianity not just as a transitional step but as an abiding phenomenon, it is still maintained that the redeeming power of Christ and its effect on the pious self-consciousness of the Christians cannot have been caused by reason. Yet neither are they absolutely supra-rational. The human consciousness of the need for redemption and the fact that redemption really fulfils this longing are the basis for the thesis just quoted, that "the human reason itself in a sense contains that which is produced by the divine Spirit" and that "the latter does not in this connexion at least, go beyond the former" (²§ 13,2; ET 1928, 65). The effects of the divine Spirit and of human reason cannot be distinguished in the individual Christian. In view of this clearly stated identity in content, the only remaining difference is the initiating function of the divine Spirit.[167] Thus, the distinction between them is to be maintained not in their end result, but in their origin. Although "the reason that has dwelt in them from their birth ... does play an indispensably necessary part" in redemption "since such states can never exist in a soul devoid of reason" (ET 1928, 65), they do not originate in it but in the way in which the pious self-consciousness is "affected by the Redeemer" (²§ 13 Postscript, ET 1928, 66). Therefore also the dogmatic propositions that emerge from the "inner experience" continue to be marked by the fact that "they rest upon a *given*; and apart from this, they could not have arisen, by deduction or synthesis, from universally recognised and communicable propositions" (ET 1928, 67). At the same time, also the second edition highlights that being affected presupposes a motivated openness. In contrast to the experience of the natural world, the Christian experience only comes to be if it is appropriated. It "occurs only inasmuch as each individual has actually wanted to have the experience involved" (ET 2016, 101).

---

167 This is noted clearly by Theodor H. Jørgensen, *Das religionsphilosophische Offenbarungsverständnis des späteren Schleiermacher* (Tübingen: Mohr Siebeck, 1977), 327.

The propositions on the interaction between divine and human causality in the process of redemption are the most extended statements that can be made within the limits of the essence definition of Christianity; they need to be filled in by the dogmatics.

Schleiermacher justifies theologically his new determination of revelation as an expression of the human power of development: he invokes the one eternal divine decree to invest human nature with this capacity from the start. To qualify it as "absolutely supernatural" instead, in the sense "that human nature is somehow incapable of taking up into itself the restorative divine element and that the power to do so must first be introduced into it (*hineingeschaffen*)" (^{1}§ 20,1. I, 79. Cf. ^{2}§ 13,1. ET 1928, 64), is seen as engendering contradictions in the idea of God. It is portrayed as a problem to split the one decree of creation and redemption in two, and to set what are only two aspects of the same subject at odds with each other. The second difficulty stated is the "arbitrary divine act" that would result if a particular decree of God was deemed necessary so "that the restorative divine element made its appearance precisely in Jesus, and not in some other person" (^{1}§ 20,1. I, 79. Cf. ^{2}§ 13,1. ET 1928, 64). Schleiermacher's conception seeks to avoid both by taking revelation as having been planned since eternity in a general decision of God for human beings. It was realised, "when the time was fulfilled" (^{1}§ 20,1. I, 79), by the person of Jesus as "human nature's own deed". The point in time of its actualisation is attributed to its dynamics of development.

In summary, according to both editions, divine and human causality complement each other in the appearance of the Redeemer: Human nature is accorded the capability of receiving the divine, with the argument that this must be the case if Jesus Christ's humanity is to be taken seriously. The human side is invested with bearing the continuity in the process of salvation that consists of creation *and* redemption. For the actual "implantation" of the divine into it, however, a pre-temporal act of God is necessary; without it, there would not be anything that it could cause to appear in the course of human history.

In order to conclude the analysis of the Introduction in the first part of this study, two avenues of evaluation will be pursued: the original reception of the first edition will be sketched in the basic critiques of his contemporaries (4.1), before taking stock of the prior, pre-structuring decisions made so far for the dogmatics (4.2).

4 Critiques of the First Edition and Evaluation of the Changes to the Introduction as a Framework for the Dogmatics

It was the reception of the first edition in which Schleiermacher struggled to recognise his work that made an in-depth revision necessary.[168] The following brief sketch of the main questions and counterarguments will be structured by the contemporary theological fault lines mirrored in them. Many of them questioned the anthropological turn performed by *The Christian Faith* in its Introduction and its two main parts. On some points, similar objections came from opposite theological directions, making it even more compelling to clarify the themes under dispute. Those typical of the different basic approaches had to be of special interest to Schleiermacher since he had tried to mediate between rationalism and supernaturalism, honouring the causes of each side, on a higher level. He had also insisted against a speculative theology inspired by Hegel that religion could not be sublated into knowledge. He was aware that his work was written in an anticipative response to intellectual movements that were only emerging. These included the new roles of history and of the natural sciences, and their effects on a general consciousness of truth that had so far been represented only by philosophy. At the same time, he had to be concerned about the reception which his attempt at mediation had found. It was a test case for the clarity with which he had been able to present to the opposed schools of contemporary theology a Christian dogmatics that had taken the anthropological turn on board.

After presenting specific rationalist (4.1.1) and supernaturalist (4.1.2) responses, I will examine in greater detail F. C. Baur's criticism which Schleiermacher classifies together with the older Protestant Tübingen School as supernaturalist. Baur's objection to the "ideal Christ" he found to have been promoted at the expense of the historical person of Jesus led, as we have seen, to major re-

---

[168] Cf. the critical edition of the *"Sendschreiben"* in KGA I/10, *Theologisch-dogmatische Abhandlungen und Gelegenheitsschriften*, ed. Hans-Friedrich Traulsen, with Martin Ohst (Berlin/New York: de Gruyter, 1990), 307–394, 315, and Hans-Friedrich Traulsen, "Historische Einführung", LXIX–LXXXVIII. For an English summary of the main points of criticism, see "Translators' Introduction" by James Duke and Francis Fiorenza in *"Letters"*, 1–32, 4–11 and their notes to both letters, 95–130. For the "Reception and Critique" in five eras up until today, cf. the chapters by Martin Ohst (within Schleiermacher's lifetime), Friedemann Voigt (1834–1889 and 1890–1923) and Hermann Fischer (1918–1960 and 1960 ff.) in Martin Ohst (ed.), *Schleiermacher – Handbuch*, 427–487.

visions in the sequence and the formulations of the Introduction that were to refute this reading (4.2). The chapter concludes with an evaluation of directions surfacing in the revision and with questions to be pursued in Part Two (4.3).

4.1 The reception of the first edition among rationalists and supernaturalists

Despite marking the opposite ends of the spectrum, the two approaches have some presuppositions in common. Sergio Sorrentino identifies the cognitivist understanding of revelation they share to which already the *Speeches* inaugurated a decisive counterproposal:

> Eighteenth-century debates among deists, skeptics, and rational theists ... presupposed ... that religion is a system of factual beliefs with immense moral significance. ... The Christian apologist was expected to show that Christian beliefs are essential and true, or at least that they could not be rationally refuted, and that civic virtue would collapse without them. Kant's critical philosophy transformed this debate by moving the idea of God out of the domain of theoretical knowledge and giving it the status of a moral postulate. Schleiermacher ... introduced two theoretical shifts to these traditional paradigms (the rationalistic and the supernaturalistic) for understanding religion.
> The first shift contests the supernaturalistic paradigm by contending that religion is essentially ... a lived experience that involves the whole of the subject in her innermost being. Religion, therefore, cannot be reduced to external or extrinsic motivations and factors, such as the transmission of information (e. g., a *notitia Dei*) or a body of doctrine, moral and social customs, or the practices of particular traditions and communities. ... its primary content is neither a conceptual ordering of our mind nor human projections of moral striving. ... The second shift ... contests the rationalistic stance of much enlightenment thinking about religion. ... In this alternative to rationalism, one must seek religion within an original connection set up by our existence, that is, within a fundamental, existential relation, in which two existing subjects or terms relate to each other asymmetrically. Here again, religion is conceived as an experience that de-centers the human subject engaged in it.[169]

Both contemporary schools display general premises of the age, some of which Schleiermacher shares, but neither of them justifies their argumentation for faith in God through analyses that only a theory of subjectivity can provide.

---

[169] Sergio Sorrentino, "Feeling as a key notion in a transcendental conception of religion", in Sockness and Gräb (eds), *Schleiermacher, the Study of Religion, and the Future of Theology. A Transatlantic Dialogue*, 97–108, 97–98.

4.1.1 Rationalist objections

The variety of positions in the approach of the Rationalists becomes evident in the opposite conclusions which two of its representatives draw in their reviews on how the *Glaubenslehre* differs from how they think philosophy and Christian theology should interact. In Johann Friedrich Röhr's review of the first edition, the typical position of Enlightenment rationalism is the backdrop of his negative assessment.[170] For him, already the Introduction shows "the tendency to disconnect the Christian (religion) as *specifically*-different from the natural connectedness (*Naturzusammenhang*) of all other historical phenomena".[171] This was a judgement that Schleiermacher had to regard as a complete misunderstanding of the fundamental approach and the basic propositions of his work. By enquiring into the specific difference that marks a religion as a positive, that is, a thoroughly individualised historical formation, far from removing it from the history of religions, he intended to identify its location within it. For Röhr, however, a dividing line runs between a "free-philosophical" and a "positive-theological view (*Ansicht*)"; the latter is characterised by profiling a specific "religious history against all similarity and all connection with the other historical appearances" and regarding its founder as "distinct from all other humans not as a matter of *grade*, but of *kind* or as *specifically* different".[172] In Röhr's eyes, Schleiermacher's mistake lies already in the attempt as such to give a specific role to the person of Jesus. Thus, his definition of his particularity as essential sinlessness and as the unity of the archetypal and the historical which Schleiermacher does intend to be more than a gradual difference, cannot find his agreement. The fundamental conflict between the two views becomes completely evident in Röhr's statement that the question whether "one can go beyond Christ ... should best be left undecided".[173] With this, the attempted bridging of the divide has been rejected

---

170 In *Programme der Theologie*, 38–43, Kantzenbach portrays the position of the editor of the journal *Kritische Prediger-Bibliothek* and general superintendent of the principality of Weimar as remaining fundamentally the same since his 1813 "Letters on Rationalism". Marked by the "heritage of an eclectic Wolffianism" (41), he sees God's providence as working through the intermediate causes of the nexus of nature. The person of Jesus appears as the teacher of a universal religion in which God is the Father of all human beings. A concept of revelation is not required since these truths can be attained by reason, and besides a doctrine of God and an anthropology no Christology is needed in his system of rational faith (cf. 40).
171 Johann Friedrich Röhr, "Rezension", in *Kritische Prediger-Bibliothek* 4 (1823) 371–394. 555–579, repr. in KGA I/7.3, 505–533.
172 Röhr, "Rezension", 555; KGA I/7.3, 507.
173 Röhr, "Rezension", 563; KGA I/7.3, 523.

by an uncompromising rationalism as an attempt that, "however strongly it diverts in many doctrines from the norm held as orthodox, tries to establish *its own orthodox restrictive norm* all too obviously".[174]

Equally negative, but for different reasons and with opposite conclusions, is the assessment of the moderate rationalist Karl Gottlieb Bretschneider.[175] For Röhr, the *Glaubenslehre*, although "inspired by a deep philosophical spirit, in its deepest foundation is of a kind that ... *any* philosophical system that does not allow itself to be captive to a *positive faith*, has to oppose".[176] Bretschneider, in contrast, rejects it with the argument that the *Glaubenslehre* is "actually no dogmatics but a philosophy about Christianity or a processing *[Verarbeitung]* of the Christian faith into a philosophy".[177] He concludes his review with the hope "to have made it clear that the author has not, as he himself judges his system, separated philosophy from Christianity but, on the contrary, has turned Christianity completely into a philosophy".[178] In his view, this philosophy "starts out from an analysis of the sensible and moral consciousness" and thus seems to "rest completely on a psychological foundation".[179] The cause for this transformation of Christianity into philosophy is attributed to its "basic principle" that is inadequate for religion and for Christianity, the "feeling of dependence ... from God".[180] Bretschneider's detailed review of this principle concludes with the judgement that "the feeling of dependence can neither be the essence of

---

174 Röhr, "Rezension", 374; KGA I/7.3, 506–507.
175 The position of the Lutheran superintendent of Gotha, Karl Gottlieb Bretschneider, is outlined by Kantzenbach in *Programme der Theologie*, 44–55, as combining a historical-critical approach to the biblical worldview with an understanding of the effects of divine agency that cannot be "deduced from and seamlessly incorporated into the causal nexus" (45) of nature. This supernatural element is linked to a view of the education of humanity built on Clement of Alexandria and Lessing which yields a progressive understanding of revelation (cf. 46–47). It is rationalist in that it accepts reason, specified as "*Vernunft*" over against "*Verstand*", as the authority for interpreting Scripture (cf. 48). His opposition to the doctrines of original sin and of the vicarious atonement of Christ challenges the heritage of Augustine and Anselm's soteriology (cf. 49) and is evident in Schleiermacher's response in 1819 to his writing on "Election". In *Das Christusbild Sören Kierkegaards, verglichen mit der Christologie Hegels und Schleiermachers* (Düsseldorf: Diederichs, ²1974), Hayo Gerdes notes that in Bretschneider, "the greatest expert on the old Protestant orthodoxy" (99), the "particular Christian experience of justification was missing"; immortality was seen to "make ethical improvement easier" (101).
176 Röhr, "Rezension", 374; KGA I/7.3, 506.
177 Karl Gottlieb Bretschneider, "Ueber das Princip", KGA I/7.3, 369.
178 Bretschneider, "Ueber das Princip", 28; KGA I/7.3, 383.
179 Bretschneider, "Ueber das Princip", 1; KGA I/7.3, 369.
180 Bretschneider, "Ueber das Princip", 2; KGA I/7.3, 370.

religion or of piety nor the first and the basic note (*Grundton*) of piety" and that it "has wrongly been taken as a basis of a system of religious truths".[181]

The two rationalist reviews agree on two points regarding the definition of the essence of piety: first, that an exclusive attribution of piety to feeling is not possible and that it plays down its cognitive and practical features;[182] second, that it is only by relating piety to the theoretical idea of God that it becomes a God-consciousness, and the terrifying element of absolute dependence is contained:

> Even if I were to concede that piety is a feeling, and moreover (*zwar*) a feeling of dependence from a simple, absolute infinity; I cannot grasp what else this feeling could consist in but fear and terror (*Furcht und Grauen*) of such a power, and sadness (*Trauer*) about being completely dependent on it. For in order to love it as being good, and to trust it as being wise, I have to know first from reason that it is good and wise, that is, the idea of divinity has to be first developed by reason if I am to love it and trust it. Apart from this, the absolute infinity is either an *empty* thought, or a *terrifying* entity (*Etwas*)".[183]

Thus, the characterisation of religion as a feeling of absolute dependence is critiqued by both already in the name of religion, not specifically in the name of Christianity. Bretschneider additionally sees the problematic basic principle, which in his view is taken from psychology, as affecting the conception of Christianity. The reason is the concept of redemption which is elucidated in reference to the controversial God-consciousness. He especially rejects the theory of unification of the sensible and the higher consciousness, pinpointing the demand of an "uninterrupted series of pious stirrings", as which he takes this union, as "contrary to nature".[184] Thus, also the definition of re-

---

[181] Bretschneider, "Ueber das Princip", 22–23; KGA I/7.3, 380.
[182] Cf. Röhr, "Rezension", 380; KGA I/7.3, 510. Bretschneider, "Ueber das Princip", 12; KGA I/7.3, 375.
[183] Bretschneider, "Ueber das Princip", 22–23; KGA I/7.3, 379–380. A similar position had been taken by Röhr, "Rezension", 393; KGA I/7.3, 517–518: "The absolute feeling of dependence can in no way be recognized as *religious* by the reviewer, since it is connected to *fear* which drives love away and thus is even opposed to the religious. For the essence of the religious does not consist in being *depressed (Niedergedrücktseyn)* but on the contrary in being *elevated* and *vivified*."
[184] Bretschneider, "Ueber das Princip", 25; KGA I/7.3, 381. In the second part of his review which translates as, "On the Concept of Redemption and the Connected Ideas of Sin and Original Sin in the Christian Glaubenslehre of Prof. Dr. Schleiermacher", he remarks that "the demand that the God-consciousness is to determine every moment is impossible and cannot be made, by which of course also the need for redemption or of the production (*Herstellung*) of a state that has been recognised to be impossible, and redemption itself collapse" (*Journal für Prediger* 67 (1825) 1–33, 6).

demption as the lifting of what constrains this unification is seen as misplaced. The rationalistic school in the wider sense therefore rejects the Introduction's concept of redemption on the one hand as too narrow, as a "restrictive, orthodox norm",[185] and on the other hand, as resulting from a philosophical-psychological basic principle that distorts the true content of religion and then also of Christianity.

4.1.2 A supernaturalist critique

On the supernaturalist side, based on the criterium whether the authority of divine revelation is validated sufficiently, the Tübingen theologian Johann Christian Friedrich Steudel considers the *Glaubenslehre* as rationalist. In order to show the incompatibility of both standpoints, he begins with outlining the following alternative as the decisive benchmark:

> Do you recognize beyond what human beings are endowed with, what resides in them, and what can be developed from them, a historically offered, trustworthy source of instruction about divine things: so that the content of this instruction is accepted as true – not because it belongs to the truths that human reason can find through itself, but because it is sufficiently believed about God as the object of faith – supernaturalist is, who affirms this question; rationalist, who negates it.[186]

Schleiermacher is seen to reveal himself as a rationalist when he describes "Christ and Christianity only as a stimulation (*Anregung*) of the life represented in Christ which is to be appropriated by the others, but not as an institution for the *instruction* about divine things".[187] Steudel takes the fact that Schleiermacher portrays Jesus' belief in angels not as a truth to be believed but as Jesus' time-bound view as a confirmation that his position "*sets itself as higher* than the way in which history gives us Jesus Christ".[188] From this Steudel concludes, as does Baur, that Schleiermacher's approach "creates a Christ *out of itself*, according to which the historical Christ has to reshape himself if he is to

---

[185] Röhr, "Rezension", 374; KGA I/7.3, 507.
[186] Johann Christian Friedrich Steudel, "Die Frage über die Ausführbarkeit einer Annäherung zwischen der rationalistischen und supranaturalistischen Ansicht, mit besonderer Rücksicht auf den Standpunkt der Schleiermacher'schen Glaubenslehre", in *Tübinger Zeitschrift für Theologie* 1 (1828), I. Stück, 74–199, 78; 1 (1828), II. Stück, 74–120. "Negates" (*verneint*) is a correction of the misspelling in German, "vereint", instead of "verneint". Further page numbers in the text.
[187] Steudel, "Frage", I, 108–109.
[188] Steudel, "Frage", I, 113.

count as the revealer of the divinity". With this assessment, the initial question has been answered:

> Thus, also this presentation of faith, however much it turns away from the cold reasoning of rationalism, coincides in an essential point with it, – namely, that it resists recognising a reputation (*Ansehen*) through which something trustworthy is additionally given to the human being – besides what they are to give to themselves, what they are to source from their reason or their spiritual essence.[189]

These quotes illustrate the lengths that separate the two approaches: an instruction-theoretical understanding of revelation versus the "total impression" the Redeemer makes on his followers; the evaluation of what is "historical", which includes the New Testament's account of miracles and angels for Steudel; and the question of whether it is permissible, even necessary, to justify the core terms of the dogmatics philosophically, in order to establish piety as equally essential as, and compatible with, human reason and agency. Schleiermacher's turn against using the authority of divine revelation as an argument in the 1811 Lectures already indicated the alternative route to supernaturalism that he is proposing. Nevertheless, despite the unbridgeable differences between their points of departure and methods, Steudel offers perceptive comments that are taken on board in the revisions of the second edition.

Steudel's further critique of the definition of piety as a feeling of absolute dependence adds some new objections to the rationalist ones: the question about the freedom and the moral imputability of the "utterly dependent" human person; the necessity to draw on the idea of God for determining the God-consciousness more exactly; the significance of the mutual relationship between God and the human person, as well as the element of decision that human beings have regarding faith in God. Consequently, for Steudel to be absolutely dependent is equivalent to "relinquishing the consciousness of oneself as a person".[190] He points out the necessity of "being able to perceive ourselves as being in a relationship of reciprocity (*Wechselwirkung*) with the

---

[189] Steudel, "Frage", I, 113.
[190] Steudel, "Frage", I, 103. While Steudel admits that "certain limits are set for our being and acting and becoming", indeed, that our being "is something that is *given* to us with ourselves and with everything that is" (I, 97), he rejects the concept of utter dependence. If this was the case, "the consciousness of self could not arise any longer, since the *self* points exactly to something that stands on its own", that is, it does not merely exist in relation to an Other. This is why it could not "only be aware of itself as absolutely dependent" (I, 102). In response to this argument, in the second edition Schleiermacher elaborates precisely in what way the feeling of absolute dependence does not extinguish, but presupposes the self's consciousness of itself.

governor of that order" insofar as we "as *free* beings are to make his order real". For this to happen, the concept of God had to precede feeling so that it could become a religious feeling at all: Without "the idea of God having been made resident (*niedergelegt*) in the spiritual being of the human being, no religious feeling whatsoever can be stirred".[191] Steudel's new and fundamental criticism, however, consists in the finding that we ourselves determine the feeling of absolute dependence to become our religious orientation. It only turns into piety through our appropriation:

> The consciousness of ourselves as dependent ... is not yet piety at all; but it belongs to religion, to piety to *recognize the validity* of this dependence. Exactly for this reason, piety is not merely finding ourselves, but *determining* ourselves – a *direction* which we give to ourselves based on our self-activity.[192]

With this religious emphasis on the will, rather than on cognitive reason, Schleiermacher was challenged to explicate an understanding of freedom that, though finite, offers space for decision and self-determination. The third approach to be discussed as part of the early reception starts out from the supernaturalist origins of the Protestant Tübingen School. Yet the principled exposition of its genuine cause, namely the superiority of historical revelation to human reason that Ferdinand Christian Baur develops in his early responses ends up with its subordination to reason. It needs to be treated in a separate section because of the systematic weight of his pioneering perception of the core problem of the Introduction, and in view of the history of reception of his early and his final positions.

4.2 F. C. Baur's interpretation of the *Glaubenslehre* as an "ideal rationalism"

Baur's core objection comes in two versions. The first, to which Schleiermacher responded,[193] arose from supernaturalist premises (4.2.1). In the second, the di-

---

[191] Steudel, "Frage", I, 106.
[192] Steudel, "Frage", I, 99. In KGA I/10, LXXXVI, the editor of volume, Hans-Friedrich Traulsen mentions in his "Introduction" the "cordial personal relationship to Steudel" that "developed when Schleiermacher visited Tübingen in September 1830" despite their opposing starting points.
[193] Schleiermacher summarises Baur's critiques published in 1827 and 1828 in "Letters", 76, as having attempted to "demonstrate Christianity a priori". The fact that Baur's perceptive analysis

rection of the critique is reversed in line with Baur's new Hegelian understanding of the relationship between philosophy, theology, and history (4.2.2). Only by tracing his turn to a radically transformed interest and justification while the formulations are repeated or remain similar, is it possible to understand its history of reception that encompasses positions as opposite as those of David Friedrich Strauß and Karl Barth. I will conclude the analysis of this early and fundamental critique by examining its renewal by Alister McGrath who invokes Baur's observations to make a case against Schleiermacher's anthropological turn from a Barthian standpoint (4.2.3).

4.2.1 F. C. Baur's early critique

Baur sees the *Glaubenslehre* as an example of an emerging theological position between supernaturalism and ordinary rationalism: an "ideal rationalism", or "Gnosticism", which "transposes the historical form proper to supernaturalism to the facts of consciousness and the ideas of reason so that ... they cannot be thought without the historical form".[194] In spite of the supernaturalist element in the "historical form" of this new approach, Baur classifies it as a rationalism with a view to its contents:

> Despite apparently stating the historical reality of Christianity, it can think of Christ only as of an idea of reason. The historical Christ becomes the ideal Christ ... The idea expressed in Christ is the highest stage of the development of human consciousness which can only be reached after all the preceding steps. In this respect the historical or properly temporal form (Gal 4:4) in which ordinary rationalism has no interest is also specific to this system of rationalism.[195]

He finds the proofs for this reading, firstly, in the essence definition of Christianity which in establishing the concept of a Redeemer does not take its starting point in the New Testament. Secondly, the priority of the basic, anthropological

---

also contained reinterpretations that seriously misrepresented his line of reasoning, led to his response in the "Letters" which focused on refuting those misleading assumptions.

194 Ferdinand Christian Baur, "Anzeige der beiden academischen Schriften" in *Tübinger Zeitschrift für Theologie* 1 (1828) 220–264, 223; reprinted partly in KGA I/7.3, 256–277, 258 (= "Selbstanzeige"). This is the German summary he published a year after the Latin "Tübingen Easter Programme" entitled *Primae Rationalismi et Supranaturalismi historia capita potiora*, Pars II: *Comparatur Gnosticismus cum Schleiermacherianae theologiae indole* (Tübinger Osterprogramm) (Tübingen: Hopferi de l'Orme, 1827); reprinted partly in KGA I/7.3, 243–256.
195 Baur, "Selbstanzeige", 224; KGA I/7.3, 258.

4.2 F. C. Baur's interpretation of the *Glaubenslehre* as an "ideal rationalism" —— 111

form of the dogmatic propositions is seen as revealing: being drawn from the "immediate self-consciousness"[196] in Baur's view, they seem to miss any reference to history.

On the one hand, from his first detailed comment in a letter to his brother in 1823 onwards, Baur ignores the internal structure of the work in coming to this result.[197] He seeks in the Introduction, as Schleiermacher comments correctly, what only belongs in the material dogmatics, as well as misunderstanding or redefining the three forms of the dogmatic propositions: descriptions of human states of mind, doctrines on divine attributes, and assertions on the constitution of the world (¹§ 34; cf. ²§ 30. ET 2016, I, 182). On the other hand, what is at stake is a fundamental disagreement on the standing of the person of Jesus: Does he appear as a real historical person, or as a creation of reason? The impression Baur took away from his first reading moved the author of *The Christian Faith* to carry out in-depth interventions into the sequence and detail of the original edition's Introduction and Christology. Sergio Sorrentino identifies the reasons behind accusing the *Glaubenslehre* of being "gnostic": According to Baur, the historical ground

> is absent from the deepest structure of Schleiermacher's theology. This absence accounts for the fact that Schleiermacher's dogmatics is included in the "gnosis" typology. Its theological substance, precisely because the historical element is lacking (in the background there is probably the antinomy formulated by Lessing between a truth of fact, i.e., historical truth, and a truth of reason), is ultimately led back to a cognitive content qualified by reason, not by revelation. Indeed, revelation is irreducibly constituted by a *factual event*. That is why Baur maintains that Schleiermacher's dogmatics belongs to the typology of rationalism … defined as "that system that presents human reason as the highest cognitive principle in religion" and as "that system which, as concerns divine things, never exceeds the sphere, enclosed in itself, of human reason and consciousness."[198]

Thus, the crucial question which Baur puts to Schleiermacher's *Glaubenslehre*, and which determines whether the analogy to Gnosticism is valid, concerns the foundation of its Christology. Does "the concept of the Redeemer coincide

---

[196] Baur, "Selbstanzeige", 246; KGA I/7.3, 269.
[197] The first outline of his critique in a letter to his brother Friedrich August from July 27, 1823, has been edited by Heinz Liebing, "Ferdinand Christian Baurs Kritik an Schleiermachers Glaubenslehre", in *Zeitschrift für Theologie und Kirche* 54 (1957) 225–243.
[198] Sergio Sorrentino, "History and temporality in the debate between F. Ch. Baur and Schleiermacher", in S. Sorrentino (ed.), *Schleiermacher's Philosophy and the Philosophical Tradition* (Schleiermacher: Studies and Translations Vol. 11) (Lewiston, N.Y.: Edwin Mellen Press, 1992), 111–132, 112, with reference to the "Selbstanzeige", KGA I/7.3, 257 and 259.

fully with the concept of redemption so that he is actually only the idea of redemption conceived personally", or is the concept of the Redeemer itself "historically given in the true sense"?[199] The result of Baur's inquiry is that the historical Jesus of the *Glaubenslehre* can "only be the one who expressed the idea of redemption that originated with the ideal Christ as it develops by itself in a certain way from the religious consciousness of the human person, and who thus founded a religious community".[200]

What makes Baur's critique exemplary is that he was the first to point to a decisive problem of the new dogmatics that responded to the anthropological turn: It lies in the lack of a new historical content of a Christology that corresponds to the universal claim made in the Introduction that every human being already finds herself in relation to God. The core point of an "ideal Christ" remains the same from his early to his late critique, yet the evaluation changes. Heinz Liebing, the editor of the letter to his brother, commented that Baur's "taking over of the Hegelian scheme of history did not affect his assessment of the *Glaubenslehre*", since his critique "in its material content ... was directed consistently against the very same points".[201] This judgement has been questioned with good reasons by Dietz Lange who notes correctly that Baur turned "the tendency of his objection against Schleiermacher into its exact opposite".[202] Baur's original critique was not that Schleiermacher "retained ... but that he relinquished the person of Jesus" by subordinating the historical Jesus, as he could be known from Scripture, to the ideal Christ whom the Christian self-consciousness found in itself. Lange identifies in the first orientation of the critique "a residue

---

199 Baur, "Selbstanzeige", 241; KGA I/7.3, 266.
200 Baur, "Selbstanzeige", 251; KGA I/7.3, 272.
201 Liebing, "Baurs Kritik", 229.
202 Dietz Lange, *Historischer Jesus oder mythischer Christus. Untersuchungen zu dem Gegensatz zwischen F. Schleiermacher und D. F. Strauß* (Gütersloh: Gütersloher Verlagshaus, 1975), 200. Lange pursues the question (196–205) which of the two, Baur or Strauß, was the first to put forward "the decisive objections ... that Schleiermacher's Christ is nothing but an idea acquired through a subjective inference (*Rückschluss*) and that the claimed unity of the archetypal Christ and the historical Jesus is scientifically untenable" (197). He comes to the judgement that even if Baur's Gnosis (1835) had an effect on the criticism of Schleiermacher in the concluding part of Strauß's *The Life of Jesus* (1836), Baur himself could have received "the final push" to revise his evaluation of the historical Jesus through Strauß who would thus not depend on Baur after all in the basic ideas of his *Life of Jesus* (204). He could have understood the objections of the *Osterprogramm* and more so, of its German summary, already in the sense of the later critique of 1835. If this hypothesis is true, it would have been a productive misunderstanding by Strauß, which convinced Baur in his further contact with him; the least one can say is that the later reversal of his critique is parallel to the position of Strauß.

4.2 F. C. Baur's interpretation of the *Glaubenslehre* as an "ideal rationalism" — 113

of Baur's earlier supernaturalist position".²⁰³ So how does Baur originally reconstruct the argumentation that in his view contains such a deficit regarding historical revelation? His first comment on the *Glaubenslehre* in the letter of 1823 summarises its course of reasoning as follows:

> The self-consciousness expresses itself as a pious feeling of dependence in general, but then more precisely with the opposition between nature and grace, an inability of one's own and a communicated ability, sin and redemption. From the concept of a natural inability of the human being to redeem himself from sin the concept of a supernatural divine redemption emerges immediately, and the person of the Redeemer is posited with all the qualities through which an essential dignity that distinguishes him from all humans must be attributed to him. From this point everything else is developed in a consistent sequence. In this manner all the main elements of Christianity are established as development and facts of the religious self-consciousness; the historical as it is given in the N.T. continues to stand in its full validity, only what is Christian is not to be proven (*bewiesen*) from it but only shown (*nachgewiesen*) in it.²⁰⁴.

The problematic status of Christology is traced back to a starting point that is not distinguished as to its location in either the Introduction or the dogmatics:

> If the principal elements that refer to the person of the Redeemer are themselves also deduced from the religious self-consciousness, thus, if the external history of Jesus is taken as a history of the inner developments of the religious self-consciousness, then I can conceive of the person of Christ as the Redeemer only as a specific form and potency of self-consciousness which appeared in external history just because the natural development of self-consciousness in its highest perfection necessarily had to manifest itself one day in this way. Christ is therefore in every human being, and the external appearance of Jesus is not the original element here, but the archetypal, ideal element is only to be shown (*nachgewiesen*) in what is historical, and the inner consciousness is to be brought to clear representation (*Anschauung*).²⁰⁵

In these statements, Baur's enduring basic misunderstanding of the *Glaubenslehre* becomes evident: What Schleiermacher distinguishes, the as yet unspecific God-consciousness of the feeling of absolute dependence, and its real determination in a concrete, positive religion – in the case of the religious individuality of Christianity its determination through the historical person

---

203 Lange, *Historischer Jesus*, 201. A programmatic sentence in the concluding part of the *Osterprogramm* that advocates a supernaturalist foundation of the Christian religion in favour of "faith" (*pístei*) rather than "knowledge" (*gnosei*) is weakened in the German summary. Cf. also 202–203.
204 Liebing, "Baurs Kritik", 240–241.
205 Liebing, "Baurs Kritik", 242–243.

Jesus of Nazareth – is taken by Baur from the beginning as *one single* level: that of the "religious self-consciousness the development of which yields the principal elements of Christianity".[206] Thus, for Baur, the pious self-consciousness – that in Schleiermacher's account would only become the *principium cognoscendi* of Christian dogmatics after being specified through this historical determination – comes into competition with the historical source of Christology, the New Testament. From his supernatural position, all that counts is historical revelation. Schleiermacher's intentions to clarify both the concept of religion and the location of Christianity among other positive religions are not specifically registered. Baur's reconstruction in his letter and in the two articles does not take into account that the general, invariable, self-same God-consciousness can only be known through its different historical concretisations. For him, it is piety as such which as "religious self-consciousness" already carries the concept of redemption in itself and posits a Redeemer, independently of all external reality. This conclusion can be traced back to two elements: the first resides in the first edition which had indicated the possibility of a direction of the God-consciousness where the inability to redeem oneself could become the decisive factor; the second is Baur's own identification of *"Urbild"* (archetype) as only an "ideal"[207] and not also, as Schleiermacher claims and justifies already in ¹§114,1 (II, 20), as a historical breakthrough.

In the thesis of the essence definition of Christianity, Baur had admitted, the historical existence of the Redeemer seems to be decisive; yet in the further development of its implications he sees the historical Jesus abandoned in favour of an ideal Christ of absolutely perfect piety.[208] The conclusions for Jesus' own self-consciousness that the first edition draws already from the consciousness of redemption represent for Baur the surfacing of the archetypal in the historical; from this proposition onwards both levels are merged throughout the remainder of the Introduction and the dogmatics. The definition of the essence of Christianity should have used the documents of the New Testament to verify its concept of

---

206 Liebing, "Baurs Kritik", 240.
207 Sorrentino observes in "History and temporality", 118: "So the ideal Christ (symptomatically, Baur renders *Urbild* and *urbildlich* ... as 'ideal') is understood as the supreme evolutionary level of human consciousness that can be achieved only on the premise of passing through the preceding levels of evolution. In this way, Schleiermacher is attributed with a Gnostic model of the comprehension of Christ."
208 Liebing, "Baurs Kritik", 242.

4.2 F. C. Baur's interpretation of the *Glaubenslehre* as an "ideal rationalism" — 115

the Redeemer.[209] Since they do not play the expected role of source of knowledge, it remains unclear to Baur which significance the "specific historical starting point" of the Christian consciousness of redemption has for Schleiermacher.[210]

The ultimate proof for the ideality of the Redeemer, however, is found in a different location of the system. In his published review in German, Baur regards it as having been constructed from two elements, which he calls "the two basic forms of the religious feeling":[211] the empirical-objective one of the Christian religious community, and the merely subjective form of the feeling of absolute dependence. From which of the two the dogmatics is developed, is seen as the key indicator for the question whether the origin of the person of Jesus has been sourced from reason or has been given in history. Due to the priority of the first of the three forms of dogmatic propositions, Baur regards it as proven that the person of the Redeemer has been deduced from the immediate self-consciousness. If this form, which he interprets as taking the doctrinal contents "from the immediate self-consciousness",[212] is to count as the basic form of Christian dogmatics, then it is evident that history which would be relevant in the second form,[213] does not play any role: "If only those propositions which de-

---

209 Between the Latin and the German versions one can spot a critical difference. Cf. Lange, *Historischer Jesus*, 202–203: "Concerning the question whether the qualities attributed by Schleiermacher to the historical Jesus are true features, he no longer refers to the '*vera religionis christianae, qualis ex sacris literis cognoscitur, historia*', but – nuanced slightly – to a historical examination of the documents of the New Testament. Quite confidently, he expects positive results from it for the dogmatics, since the contrasting of *pístis* and *gnosis* certainly has to be understood as taking also here the side of *pístis*".
210 Liebing, "Baurs Kritik", 242.
211 Baur, "Selbstanzeige", 243; KGA I/7.3, 267.
212 Baur, "Selbstanzeige", 246; KGA I/7.3, 269.
213 Baur's depiction of the relationship between the first two forms in his "Selbstanzeige" misconstrues the first, anthropological form that relates to the God-consciousness as determined by the Christian experience of redemption as something completely internal or a priori. The second form which abstracts from the determination by sin and grace when it speaks of God and the divine relationship to the world is, quite on the contrary, taken to thematise the concrete external experience of the world, and with it, the church, which for Schleiermacher belongs in the third form which deals with the world: "Under the first dogmatic form Christ can be spoken of only under the condition that in him an internal state of mind, an idea that belongs to the immediate consciousness is described. The proper historical Christ belongs into the sentences of the second form, in which a determining factor outside consciousness is referred to, thus in this case to the second section about the quality of the world in relation to redemption, or the doctrine of the church, that is, of that religious community which Christ founded as a historical person" (253; KGA I/7,3, 273). The concluding sentence drawn from this erroneous reconstruction shows that it really constitutes a prior assumption, preceding the analysis as a *petitio*

scribe the internal states of mind and are taken from the immediate self-consciousness furnish the proper content of Christian dogmatics, then the historical and ecclesial character is at least not a necessary and essential feature of the *Glaubenslehre*".²¹⁴ The investigation into which source it is committed to, history or reason, has thus in his view achieved an unequivocal result. In the alternative between divine revelation and an ideal produced by human reason, the *Glaubenslehre* has taken the idealist route.

In 1827 and 1828 Baur still uses this insight to defend the authority of Scripture, and with it the historical testimonies about the events of Jesus' life: "The more is attributed to the feeling innate in human nature, the less is retained for the authority of Scripture".²¹⁵ This is the stage and the direction of critique which Schleiermacher relates to explicitly in the *Sendschreiben* and implicitly in the corrections of the second edition.

Thus, on the one hand, the objection that apparently "the person of Christ is a specific form and potency of self-consciousness"²¹⁶ is based on incorrect presuppositions: it overlooks the difference between a priori and historical-empirical God-consciousness that is decisive for the Introduction and the structure of the doctrinal treatment. He does not distinguish in his exposition between the essence definitions of piety and of Christianity, and the material dogmatics. When he states that in fact "the external appearance of Jesus is not the original element" and that this "connects exactly with the pantheistic-idealistic basic view of the whole system",²¹⁷ he is not comparing two separate locations with distinct methodologies but is formulating an overarching verdict.

On the other hand, despite imprecise reconstructions, misunderstandings and errors on the way to his conclusion, Baur's observation itself that the assumption of a natural God-consciousness turns the Christian experience of God into an a priori element of the human spirit must be credited with being incisive. Its effects will have to be examined in the material Christology.

This main objection, however, is also the location where the tendency of the critique is reversed: If in his 1828 defence of the Bible Baur sees the significance of the historical revelation of God in the person of Jesus endangered, he regrets

---

principii: "Thus either the historical Christ separates himself from the archetypal one, and the historical Christ belongs in the second section, or the historical one has in his link to the archetypal one no real historical significance" (246; KGA I/7.3, 269).
214 Baur, "Selbstanzeige", 246; KGA I/7.3, 269.
215 Baur, *Primae*, 21–22; KGA I/7.3, 252.
216 Liebing, "Baurs Kritik", 242.
217 Liebing, "Baurs Kritik", 243.

in 1835 that believers have an ongoing relationship to him. If the content of revelation already resides in humans in an original way, why confront them with another subject who is to communicate to them what they already possess? The dissolution of the historical Jesus into the Redeemer as an idea of reason is now no longer a matter of accusation, but of demand. The fact that Schleiermacher does not draw this conclusion himself, now earns him the objection of being inconsequent.

4.2.2 The final shape of the critique since Baur's turn to Hegel

From 1833 onwards, Baur seeks to decode *The Christian Faith* through Hegelian categories.[218] I will first summarise his new reconstruction, then outline his three main concerns, and finally assess the relevance of his insights beyond the Hegelian framework.

His analysis begins with Schleiermacher's concept of God which – in contrast, for example, to Schelling's – does not allow any distinction of particular features in God's being itself.[219] Thus, it is the human subjective consciousness of God, the feeling of absolute dependence, that "mediates itself to itself" and realises itself through differences of stages, kinds, founder, sin and redemption which are taken as its "moments".[220] Although with regard to the essence of God, the *Glaubenslehre* remains on the standpoint of subjectivity, its consciousness of God is still mediated objectively through the historical community of the church. The question to Christology now is: can it justify cogently that the communication of a perfect God-consciousness to the Christian community could only take place historically, in the shape of its archetypal founder Jesus? Or has this communication been constituted by human consciousness as the idea of redemption

---

218 The presentation of the *Glaubenslehre* in *Die christliche Gnosis oder die christliche Religions-Philosophie in ihrer geschichtlichen Entwicklung* (Tübingen: Osiander, 1835), 626–668, is also the foundation for his account in 1843, in *Die christliche Lehre von der Dreieinigkeit und Menschwerdung Gottes in ihrer geschichtlichen Entwicklung*, vol. III (Tübingen: Osiander, 1843), 842–886. His *Lehrbuch der christlichen Dogmengeschichte* (Tübingen: Fues, 1847, Leipzig 3rd ed. 1867, repr. Darmstadt: Wissenschaftliche Buchgesellschaft, 1979) was translated as *History of Dogma*, ed. P.C. Hodgson, trans. R. F. Brown and P. C. Hodgson (Oxford: OUP, 2014).
219 For Schleiermacher, this is due to human finitude which can only grasp the effects of God's activity, and due to the constraint imposed by him that the perfection of God would be diminished if changes were assumed, since they would introduce categories of temporality to the divine. To prevent this categorical mistake, he insists, as will be further examined in Chapter 7, on the one pre-temporal divine decree of both creation and redemption.
220 Baur, *Die christliche Gnosis*, 634. 633–637.

and must be attributed to its spiritual productivity? Three main critiques can be identified in Baur's discussion:[221] the method of inferring (*Rückschluss*) from the Christian determination of the self-consciousness to the historical person of Jesus (4.2.2.1), the intertwining of the archetypal and the historical in his person (4.2.2.2), and the way in which the content of what is being communicated, redemption, has been determined (4.2.2.3).

4.2.2.1 The method of inferring backwards from the effect to the cause

Baur offers the following counterarguments to the method of concluding backwards "from the effect (*Wirkung*) to the efficacity (*Wirksamkeit*)" and from it "to the person of Christ".[222] As the cause of this effect, only the "existence of a new principle of life implanted in humanity" could be assumed, an "idea, but not at all an archetypal personality".[223]. The fact that the consciousness of redemption "is mediated in some way through Christ" does not yet imply that "the person of Christ" had to be "the concrete representation of the absolute sinlessness and perfection" mediated by him:[224] "With which justification is it assumed that what is only in a relative way in all individuals who belong to the Christian community is given in its founder in an absolute way?"[225]

The retroactive conclusion does not reach as far as it presumes: it does not lead to an unequivocal historical cause. The archetypal nature attributed to the person of Jesus due to its effect cannot be proven historically. And this is even more the case since Schleiermacher himself differentiates between essence and appearance of Jesus, that is, allows for differences of evidence in the historical impression of the archetype: "If this essence was the historical essence of Christ, then it would have to be able to be known from his appearance, that is, his teachings and deeds; it would have to be what is enduring and determining in the appearances or individual moments of Christ's life." Yet, as Baur states

---

[221] In "Der Mittelpunkt der Glaubenslehre Schleiermachers", in *Neue Zeitschrift für Systematische Theologie und Religionsphilosophie* 10 (1968) 289–309, 294, Wolfgang Trillhaas distinguishes three aspects: the "unthinkability" of the joining of the archetypal and the historical, the concept of the archetype, and the method of inferring from a mental effect back to a cause in history. On the Hegelian background, cf. also Pröpper, "Bestimmung", in *Evangelium und freie Vernunft*, 140–142.
[222] Baur, *Kirchengeschichte des 19. Jahrhunderts* (= *Geschichte der christlichen Kirche V*), ed. by E. Zeller (after Baur's death in 1860) (Tübingen: Fues, 1862), 209.
[223] Baur, *Die christliche Lehre von der Versöhnung in ihrer geschichtlichen Entwicklung von der ältesten Zeit bis auf die neueste* (Tübingen: Osiander, 1838), 624.
[224] Baur, *Die christliche Lehre von der Dreieinigkeit*, vol. III, 863.
[225] Baur, *Kirchengeschichte des 19. Jahrhunderts*, 210.

in an overdrawn critique, "here the essence is to be something that cannot be known in the appearance, it is to be more than his appearance, therefore it cannot be the essence of the historical Christ but a concept or an ideal that is independent of his appearance, therefore, beyond history, made up by thinking or imagination".[226]

Consequently, for Baur everything that is stated about the person of Jesus beyond his existence constitutes a projection of ideas or postulates onto him. Since his own coverage of the history of dogma can rest assured of the meaning of history based on his Hegelian foundations, he can afford to dismiss other interpretive approaches to historical persons and their actions in their contingency and particularity. In a different framework, they may nevertheless be recognised as appearances of the absolute within the parameters of finitude – a thought, however, that is unlikely to be shared from his new Hegelian standpoint. In addition, it must be asked what "history" can prove. Already in his early supernaturalist critique an instructive disparity surfaced about what confirmation can be sought from the New Testament. Karl-Heinz Menke clarifies that Schleiermacher's goal was not

> a response to the question in what way Jesus de facto did or did not understand himself. Schleiermacher employs the term "self-consciousness" in a quest for the ontological singularity of the Redeemer and therefore not in the sense of a historicising psychology. Even if there are good reasons to entitle Schleiermacher's Christology a "consciousness Christology", its basic intention cannot be mistaken. On the ground of contemporary philosophy – especially Immanuel Kant's – he wants to locate the significance of Jesus not in the contingent facts of history but in the being of the Redeemer. One has misunderstood him from the start if one measures him exclusively ... by the question of what he has contributed to the historical question about the Jesus of history.[227]

4.2.2.2 The intertwining of the archetypal and the historical

In addition to what he regards as questionable in the method of Schleiermacher's Christology, of tracing finite and fragmentary effects back to an unconditioned cause, it is problematic for Baur to recognise an individual person as archetypal. The Christology of the *Glaubenslehre* cannot reach its goal, the unity of the historical and the archetypal, that is, the realisation of the idea in an individual, for a further, a priori set reason: Since Baur has accepted Hegel's

---

226 Baur, *Kirchengeschichte des 19. Jahrhunderts*, 208.
227 Karl-Heinz Menke, *Jesus ist Gott der Sohn. Denkformen und Brennpunkte der Christologie* (Regensburg: Pustet, 2008), 334–335. 621, n. 1.

distancing of the idea from a merely individual history, the incompatibility of what Schleiermacher seeks to force together is evident from the start.

The unity claimed for both elements had been questionable for Baur already in his early supernaturalist comments in view of the missing validation by the New Testament, and of the priority of the first, "ideal" form of dogmatic propositions over the second, "historical" one.

After 1833, however, Baur posits the "incongruity of the archetypal and the historical in Schleiermacher's Christology ... for the reason that in general, between idea and reality, due to the nature of the matter, a relationship of incongruity obtains". He comes to this judgement by relating "the idea, or the archetypal nature" not to the absolute power of the God-consciousness, but by taking it "in its purely absolute sense" as "equated (*gleichgesetzt*) with the absolute essence of God's self".[228] For Baur, the relationship between the archetypal and the historical no longer refers to the possibility of an absolutely powerful relation to God, but to the human realisation of the whole essence of God. It is due to this identification of absolute God-consciousness with God, that Baur must refute the possibility of a coincidence of idea and reality in an individual.

From the fact that from now onwards the "idea" coincides with the absolute, a hitherto unthinkable move becomes possible: his unprecedented renunciation to its historical existence. While Schleiermacher insists that the perfection of the God-consciousness first had to be witnessed in a human individual life, before it could be grasped as a mediated possibility of one's own, it no longer needs this historical origin for Baur. He thus tries to prove from Schleiermacher's own justification for the necessity of the historical existence of the Redeemer the independence of the idea from history. Schleiermacher's argument that the existence of a perfect God-consciousness either happens in one real person or is never realised, is taken almost as a proof for the self-sufficiency of the idea. In Baur's view, if the necessity of a historical Redeemer is claimed, then this implies the necessity of a perfection of creation. If, however, it belongs to its idea that it must be perfected, then the reality of this perfection has already been proven conceptually which makes it superfluous in reality. The historical existence of an archetypal Redeemer is thus not only not reached,[229] but made expendable:

> The archetypal human person, the God-man, has his objective reality in himself, in his concept; yet if it is posited in the historical existence of a specific single individual, it is subjectively tied to a finite, perishable being with the natural consequence that the archetypal continues to separate itself from it again and again, because it can never enter into a perfect

---

228 Baur, *Die christliche Lehre von der Versöhnung*, 621, n. 1.
229 Baur, *Die christliche Lehre von der Dreieinigkeit*, 864.

unity with it, without having to claim for this reason that the archetypal loses its objective reality, only that its reality is not this sensible empirical existence. Thus, also here we only get as far as the idea, in the archetypal, as it is in itself, but that it also must be a historically existing one, has not been proven.[230]

Whether the second point of critique is considered valid, depends, on the one hand, on whether it offers a correct reconstruction; on the other hand, it depends on whether one judges the prior Hegelian decisions that it brings into the assessment as convincing. The validity of the third argument, however, which supports the other two and often appears entwined with them, must be judged differently.

4.2.2.3 The determination of the content of redemption

Regarding the question of how the content of what is being communicated – redemption – is defined, the starting point of Baur's objection is the same as in his pre-Hegelian phase: The only element in Schleiermacher's Christology that has been caused historically, in his view, is the mediatedness of the consciousness of redemption through the Christian community.[231] On this basis he can attribute the further determination of the unspecific God-consciousness into the concrete Christian consciousness of redemption (which for Schleiermacher was only possible through an external determining cause) to the native potency of human self-consciousness. The *Glaubenslehre* "contemplates the content of Christianity as the immediate statement of the pious consciousness ... which becomes Christian of its own accord by reflecting deeply on itself (*sich in sich selbst vertiefend*).[232] The "whole contents of the Christian faith" is thus "its original property".[233] It is seen to represent a step forward from supernaturalism that the "positive in its abstract supernatural and external character is grasped as an essential modification of consciousness itself".[234] Even against rationalism he concedes that Schleiermacher aims to present the "essence of faith as a content that is independent of thinking and essentially different".[235] Yet his final assessment still is that he "dissolves the contents of Christianity that is historically given into

---

230 Baur, *Die christliche Lehre von der Dreieinigkeit*, 864–865; cf. *Die christliche Gnosis*, 646.
231 Cf. Baur, *Lehrbuch der christlichen Dogmengeschichte*, 353.
232 Baur, *Lehrbuch der christlichen Dogmengeschichte*, 353.
233 Baur, *Die christliche Lehre von der Dreieinigkeit*, 856–857.
234 Baur, *Lehrbuch der christlichen Dogmengeschichte*, 355.
235 Baur, *Die christliche Lehre von der Dreieinigkeit*, 872.

facts of self-consciousness"[236] since what is allegedly "received and communicated" is actually "self-produced".[237]

The missing difference in content between possible and mediated power of the God-consciousness can also not be compensated for by emphasising the sinful nature of humans: Since the relationship to God is admittedly never zero, the content of the revelation received is only gradually superior to the disposition shared by all:

> If it belongs to the original perfection of humans to attain those states of self-consciousness in which the God-consciousness can realise itself, then it is founded upon the human person's own nature that the God-consciousness surfaces (*hervortritt*) in its strength (*Kraeftigkeit*); and it is only a consequence of human development that the God-consciousness ... must be liberated first. But just because of this, one cannot claim that this becoming free ... or this ease ... can only be something that is communicated, ... since the outer facts of the redemption that happened through Jesus cannot communicate anything that has not been founded originally in the nature of humans, thus, that is only awakened through it and brought to effective expression.[238]

Baur's examination thus comes to a judgement that will be much quoted in the controversy's history of reception: "It is a mere illusion if the subject of self-consciousness that is placed in the contrast of the God-consciousness and the sensible consciousness is confronted with another, different subject through whose activity it is to be communicated to him solely what already belongs to the nature of self-consciousness as such".[239]

How should these three points of critique be judged? Baur's reconstructions had already shown that his critique was not for the most part based on a precise grasp of Schleiermacher's argumentation and intentions. His objections to the method of inference, for example, demonstrated that he expected something different from what had been intended: Schleiermacher sought to explicate the Christian experience of redemption regarding its foundation in the person of Jesus, while Baur was looking for proofs for the coincidence of the historical and the archetypal in him. The presupposition of faith to which Schleiermacher refers and which he merely aims to unfold, is exactly in question for Baur. Where the historian of the Christian doctrinal development wants to see proofs, the systematic theologian does not consider demonstrability to be possible. Also regarding the way in which the method of retroactive conclusion is put into prac-

---

[236] Baur, *Die christliche Lehre von der Dreieinigkeit*, 872.
[237] Baur, *Die christliche Lehre von der Dreieinigkeit*, 860.
[238] Baur, *Kirchengeschichte des 19. Jahrhunderts*, 204.
[239] Baur, *Kirchengeschichte des 19. Jahrhunderts*, 203.

4.2 F. C. Baur's interpretation of the *Glaubenslehre* as an "ideal rationalism"

tice, Baur's critique is not adequate: Schleiermacher "not only distinguished the reality of Jesus as the foundation from what had been founded, the consciousness of redemption, but also – however insufficiently – attempted to 'verify' (*nachzuweisen*) his Christology in the New Testament."[240]

In addition to the lack of precision in his analyses, it is due to Baur's concept of idea that the proof of its historical existence has no chance of succeeding. Already the critique of the method is immediately directed towards the argument that the idea can in no way be realised in an individual. This is so because on the one hand its "essence consists in realising itself empirically only when it has expressed itself earlier in its power and significance independently from any empirical origin";[241] on the other hand, this is the case since, even if it realises itself, in view of its content

> there is no reason ... for the assumption that the arch-strength of the God-consciousness has exhausted itself in him, the one person, so much that he is completely identical with it. ... If the God-consciousness can only be thought as a power and disposition implanted in human nature as such, then it belongs to its nature that it develops in the greatest multiplicity of forms and stages. ... it is thus only an unjustified identification of a specific individual with humanity as a whole or of its spiritual disposition when it is stated that the strength of the God-consciousness that is relative in all other humans is absolute in Christ".[242]

The first two points of critique thus appear justified only under Hegelian premises.[243] What is still under debate, however, is Baur's third objection. While it can also be reversed in its direction and end up replacing Jesus with the human species, the observation on which it is based is irrefutable: The communication of something already known and possessed cannot found the principled priority that Schleiermacher intends to secure for Jesus. It cannot safeguard an enduring significance, since "the personality in which such a principle resided at first loses its significance as soon as it has begun to implant itself in others".[244]

---

240 Pröpper, "Bestimmung", in *Evangelium und freie Vernunft*, 142.
241 Baur, *Die christliche Lehre von der Dreieinigkeit*, 867.
242 Baur, *Kirchengeschichte des 19. Jahrhunderts*, 210–211.
243 For Trillhaas, Baur's and Hegelian theology is the fourth type of critique, after Yorick Spiegel's, Karl Barth's, and Wilhelm Dilthey's, in "Mittelpunkt", 293–294. Similarly Pröpper, "Bestimmung", 204: "When Ferdinand Christian Baur declared any individual realisation of the idea to be impossible and David Friedrich Strauß drew the conclusion that only the human species could come into question as the subject of the Christological predicates, this only made sense under Hegelian presuppositions."
244 Baur, *Die christliche Lehre von der Versöhnung*, 625.

Baur must also be credited with having noted the reason why the content of redemption has been determined in such a problematic way: A concept of God that does not allow for differentiations (*Besonderungen*) in itself remains bound to the sphere of the eternal divine decree. Whether his diagnosis of pantheism is true, will have to be debated in Part Two's treatment of the doctrine of God in its general and its specifically Christian attributes. Yet, the impression of pantheism is linked to Schleiermacher's rejection of conceiving beyond God's general absolute self-activity a specific agency in which God could first communicate the divine self. In his later publications, Baur does not seem to have noticed the changes in introducing the God-consciousness in the second edition; in his view, God and world continue to be distinguished in the *Glaubenslehre* only as *natura naturans* and *natura naturata*.[245] It may be asking too much to expect any appreciation for an argumentation that uncovers human contingency from him after his turn to Hegel. Yet what he was correct to identify was the connection between an anthropology of absolute dependency and a concept of God as absolute causality that only allows for general, but not for qualified relationships. In keeping with the entire relation of God to the world, also God's bond to Jesus cannot represent a new determination, and his God-consciousness can only be "absolutely strong (*kräftig*)" but nothing specific in its content: "The divine in Christ is nothing specific (*Besonderes*) in God but the absolute divine causality itself. ... also in him [Christ] only a specific relationship of the feeling of absolute dependence to divine causality is represented".[246] Schleiermacher himself may not have found his view misrepresented in this characterisation of the relationship between Jesus and God and may not have found anything missing in it. His concept of a God of absolute causality is already mediated with a God of love insofar as he optimises the uncertainty of the experience of facticity with the certitude of God in feeling. If the unity of the historical and the archetypal in Jesus is to be determined in a way that prevents it both from being deducible and from the risk of being sublated, then a different framework is required. It must be able to unfold a relationship between the Redeemer and God in which the essence of the divine initiator could only be known through Jesus' free acceptance of God's calling in the history of a humanity which was created by God in the hope of such a response. The correspondence of the content of revelation, God's essence as love, to the form of revelation,

---

245 Cf., e.g., Baur, "Letter" (1823), 239; *Die christliche Lehre von der Dreieinigkeit* (1843), 850; *Kirchengeschichte des 19. Jahrhunderts* (1862), 194.
246 Baur, *Die christliche Gnosis*, 630–631.

the human history of Jesus,[247] needs to be elucidated in a different way: one that highlights its particularities, rather than letting it be absorbed into one singular pre-temporal divine decree.

4.2.3 The renewal of Baur's critique by Alister McGrath

Having compared the core points of criticism from the early supernaturalist to the subsequent idealist premises of Baur's work, it will be instructive to examine which elements are highlighted in the endorsement it receives by the Oxford theologian Alister McGrath. He quotes the conclusion of 1862, which, as we have seen, can also be read without taking over Hegel's position that no individual can ever fulfil what is posited in the "idea". The angle of his critique comes close to the perspective of the early Baur that human reason can only receive from history, that is, God's action in it, what fulfils its quest. I will begin with McGrath's diagnosis that the approach will succumb to Feuerbach's critique (4.2.3.1), and then analyse the alternative he opens up between "history" and the "subjectivism" he sees as inherent Schleiermacher's method of inference (4.2.3.2).

4.2.3.1 On the road to Feuerbach?

Writing after Feuerbach's *The Essence of Christianity* of 1841, the heirs of the supernaturalist school in particular have accused the *Glaubenslehre* to have paved the way to his projection theory. From McGrath's systematic theological position, this is the key danger for a modern theology that makes the anthropological turn its own: it is on a straight path of descent to the post-Hegelian critique of religion. For McGrath, the alternative is to begin with the Word of God: "Feuerbach's critique of religion may indeed lose much of its force when dealing with non-theistic religions, or theologies (such as that of Karl Barth) which claim to deal with a divine encounter with man from outside him; when applied to a theistic construction or interpretation of man's emotional or psychological states, however, it is in its element."[248]

---

[247] An approach to Christology based on the thesis of this correspondence has been elaborated by Pröpper in *Der Jesus der Philosophen und der Jesus des Glaubens. Ein theologisches Gespräch mit Jaspers – Bloch – Kolakowski – Gardavsky – Machovec – Fromm – Ben-Chorin* (Mainz: Grünewald, 1976), 97–148, esp. 110–125, and subsequently. It has been further developed, e.g., by Georg Essen in *Die Freiheit Jesu* (2001) and Magnus Lerch, *Selbstmitteilung Gottes* (2015).
[248] McGrath, *The Making of Modern German Christology*, 45–46.

This is an important warning to consider by those interpreters of the Introduction who take ¹§§ 8 and 9 and ²§§ 3 and 4 as a psychological description.[249] It is true that an appeal to "man's emotional or psychological states" to justify religion would indeed be defenceless against the view that this could just be a human projection. Feuerbach's theory claims more, namely certitude that God is "nothing but" a projection. This is more than can be stated within the limits of human reason as delineated by Kant. But the question to McGrath is whether he does not misinterpret Schleiermacher's justification of faith in God as being based on a "feeling" at the same level as other concrete psychological states; emotions, such as fascination or helplessness, come and go. Yet what Schleiermacher develops in the second edition of the *Glaubenslehre* is a justification of faith in God to the general consciousness of truth, as represented by philosophy, now turned into a critical analysis of the capacity of reason. He achieves this through a transcendental analysis of the structures of human subjectivity, as distinct from psychological or religious introspection into changing affections in the believer's soul that cannot be ascertained by non-believers.

McGrath does not offer a step-by-step reconstruction of Schleiermacher's analysis of human self-consciousness in the Introduction of *The Christian Faith* but fast-forwards to the two specifically Christian parts of the material dogmatics, the consciousness of sin and that of redemption by Jesus Christ. Taking over F. C. Baur's reading of "*Urbild*" as only an "ideal", McGrath concludes that the presentation of Jesus Christ as "archetype" (*Urbild*) or "ideal" of the general human God-consciousness falls victim to Feuerbach's critique of God. It is a figure that seems external, yet owes its existence to human projection:

> Feuerbach's critique of religion called into question the propriety of inferring the existence or nature of "God" from religious feeling, in that this feeling could only be interpreted anthropologically, and not theologically. The possibility that the putative relation between the "archetypal Christ" and the Jesus of history was purely illusory, resulting from the erroneous objectification and externalisation of man's aspirations, could no longer be ignored. The unsatisfactory foundation which Schleiermacher established for this relation was thus cruelly exposed, its inadequacy obvious to all.[250]

---

249 In "Feeling as a key notion in a transcendental conception of religion", 108, Sorrentino already identifies the theory of religion put forward in the *Speeches* as based on a philosophy of subjectivity: "By 'intuition and feeling' he meant the prereflective self-consciousness that cannot be confined to any single aspect of human selfhood, but underlies the whole of it. Nor did Schleiermacher fall into a psychologism that would enclose the religious subject in the sphere of its own subjectivity."

250 McGrath, *The Making of Modern German Christology*, 47, in the second chapter dedicated to "The Hegelian Critique of Schleiermacher: Strauss, Baur, and Feuerbach."

4.2 F. C. Baur's interpretation of the *Glaubenslehre* as an "ideal rationalism"

It should be clear from Chapter 2 that in order to give substance to this objection, it would be necessary to analyse the concept of piety as a modification of "feeling" or "immediate self-consciousness" on its own, before turning to Christology. Especially in the revised Introduction, the necessary clarifications could be found: the "original meaning" of the term "God" that Schleiermacher wants to establish from "feeling" or the "immediate self-consciousness" of the human subject, and independently of the philosophical analysis of his *Dialectic*, is reached as the "Whence of our receptive and active existence" (^{2}§4,4. ET 1928, 16), not of emotion or feeling. It therefore constitutes an analysis of human facticity which is not vulnerable to Feuerbach's theory that God is "nothing but" a projection. Human contingency poses a question that cannot be ignored or explained away; while it does not have to lead to a religious answer, but can be sustained as an open question, an analysis built on it does not fall under Feuerbach's verdict. A theology which begins with the anthropological conditions for understanding God's revelation is not automatically compromised by theories of projection which it, instead, can uncover as naturalising. The intention to clarify this presumes, however, the wish to enter into dialogue with diverse starting points in contemporary culture, based on shared concepts. It is then necessary to justify faith in God as a possibility that does not contradict human reason and freedom.

Here a concept would be useful that Schleiermacher does not use but that is implicit in his argumentation. To argue for faith in God in response to the existential question of meaning which is made more urgent by the Kantian insight into to the limits of knowledge and agency, requires drawing a distinction between the "unconditioned" and the "infinite."[251] It states precisely, against a naturalising interpretation of "infinite" in terms of the human species' ongoing generations, that humans owe their existence to the "unconditioned". Schleiermacher argues explicitly in his Christology that the endlessness of the human race is not a candidate that could acquire the perfection of the God-consciousness in the place of Christ. If the complete response of a human person to the God who is reached in immediate self-consciousness as the unconditioned origin distinct from the relative infinity of the world and of humanity had not been given by Jesus, the hope of such a fulfilment would just have to be abandoned. Instead of falling prey to the consequences of Feuerbach, he offers conceptually precise arguments both on the absolute dependence of human existence – not

---

[251] Wendel, "Die Renaissance des Religiösen und der Glaube an Gott", 214. Cf. also Claus Dierksmeier, "Zum Begriff des religiösen Gefühls im Anschluss an Kant", 214, quoted in Chapter 2, where religion is identified as "symbolisation of the unconditioned", instead of as "schematisation of the infinite".

feeling – from God, and against replacing Christ by the progress of the human race.

McGrath's judgement that an anthropological approach cannot defend itself against the suspicion of projection and is "cruelly exposed" to Feuerbach thus must be refuted. The consistent changes made in the second edition in response to Baur's critique to rebut the impression that the redeeming effect of Christ was conjured up in the believers' own mind are not analysed. They offer differentiations which counteract McGrath's view that his work is discredited by Feuerbach and that a different approach is needed to "salvage" it "from the ashes".[252]

4.2.3.2 Lacking a historical foundation? The method of inference in the dogmatics

Taking over both the inaccurate term, "general consciousness of redemption", and the oppositional pair, "subjective" versus "historical", Baur's diagnosis of an "ideal rationalism" is summed up by McGrath as follows:

> Nowhere, he argues, does Schleiermacher explain how he moves from the general consciousness of redemption to a specific historical individual as the ground of that consciousness. In fact, Schleiermacher appears to make the archetypal Christ (that is, the Christological interpretation of the subjective experience of redemption) prior to the historical Jesus, so that the person and work of Christ may only be treated as derivative functions of the religious consciousness. Baur therefore developed a penetrating critique of the Christology of Schleiermacher's *Glaubenslehre* on the basis of its perceived failure to mediate between the archetypal Christ and the historical Jesus. Unless theology begins with the historical Jesus, in terms of a critical analysis of the Gospel accounts (in which alone he may be encountered), he will never be found.[253]

Like Baur, McGrath interprets the method of the material dogmatics, to justify each proposition (*Leitsatz*) and their exposition by tracing them back to the Christian self-consciousness, as a clear indication of neglecting the historical proclamation of Jesus contained in the New Testament. Since this constitutes Schleiermacher's principled, deliberate approach to the material of the dogmatics – the history of Christian thinking that must be brought into a new systematic coherence –, it is beyond the possibility of individual correction:

---

[252] McGrath, *The Making of Modern German Christology*, 46: "Although Schleiermacher's original Christological method now appeared to be seriously inadequate, it was not totally beyond salvage ... from the ashes of the old."

[253] McGrath, *The Making of Modern German Christology*, 38–39.

4.2 F. C. Baur's interpretation of the *Glaubenslehre* as an "ideal rationalism"

> Baur is particularly critical of the manner in which Schleiermacher infers his Christology from religious consciousness. The experience of pious consciousness within the Christian community is treated as the effect of the influence of a single individual, whose identity may be inferred by arguing backwards from effect to cause. For Baur, this is illegitimate: to understand a historical process, it is necessary to begin with the cause.[254]

Schleiermacher's procedure is seen to be part of a more fundamental failure. The subordinated role of history in Schleiermacher's theory of Christ as archetype which Baur has shown up is judged to be part of an encompassing deficit: "Much more serious, however was the apparent disinclination of Schleiermacher to come to terms with the irreversible trend towards historicisation initiated by the *Aufklärung*."[255]

This is a far-reaching and comprehensive accusation to make, after a long history of exchanges on this symptomatic controversy. McGrath seems to misrecognise that one of the key reasons for Schleiermacher's new departure in dogmatic theology was the rise of the historical and the natural sciences which he wanted theology to take on board and not contradict. The author of the *Brief Outline* and of *The Christian Faith* and lecturer in New Testament Studies already in Halle and in Berlin shares the unquestionable insight into the necessity of historical and text-critical investigations into the New Testament. The undisputed findings from the exegetical part of his teaching have been listed by Christine Helmer:

> Schleiermacher was considered to be at the forefront of New Testament scholarship in his time. In conversation with the nascent early nineteenth-century research on the Synoptics, Schleiermacher proposed a theory of Synoptic dependence resting on orally transmitted stories about Jesus prior to their redaction by the New Testament authors. In regard to 1 Timothy, Schleiermacher showed that the apostle Paul was not its author, thereby paving the way for critical deuteropauline scholarship. Similarly, Schleiermacher's research on the parallel structure of Colossians 1:15–20 set the literary parameters for research on this text well into the late twentieth century. Furthermore, he was the first theologian to offer public lectures on the life of Jesus, lectures that were unfortunately published in 1864, right before D. F. Strauss' devastating critique the following year. Last but not least, for the English-speaking world, Schleiermacher's *Commentary on Luke* was his first work to be translated into English.[256]

While in the meantime Biblical Studies as a historical subject has discarded many of his reconstructions, the "irreversible trend towards historicisation initi-

---

254 McGrath, *The Making of Modern German Christology*, 39.
255 McGrath, *The Making of Modern German Christology*, 31, n. 55.
256 Helmer, "Schleiermacher's exegetical theology and the New Testament", 229.

ated by the *Aufklärung*" is well represented in his work. McGrath, however, presents it as an alternative in an analysis which extends the issue to Troeltsch:

> "The rise in historical thinking particularly associated with the Tübingen school led to an emphasis being placed upon the methodological priority of the *origins of Christianity* over its present-day manifestations. ... the question of the significance of Jesus of Nazareth, and particularly his relation to the 'archetypal Christ' had to be answered by seeking that significance in his history, and not by inferring such significance from the present-day pious consciousness of the community of faith."[257]

The Christological criterium McGrath gives can be completely supported: that "the question of the significance of Jesus of Nazareth ... had to be answered by seeking that significance in his history". Yet the negative judgement on the *Glaubenslehre* in this respect just repeats Baur's view and fails to provide a critical reconstruction of Baur's own premises with which he accesses its first edition. McGrath, too, overlooks specific contents that are treated in a different location than where he expects them to appear. Since along with Baur, he does not distinguish between the general and the historically determined, concrete God-consciousness, he interprets the method of tracing doctrines back to this basis as taking recourse to the "idea" of a Redeemer. This idea is seen not only as being powerless against historically untenable projections but also as turning Christ into a property of the Christian community. If this was Schleiermacher's position, it would indeed not be far to the next step of appropriating the archetype as a principle of the self-description of God's creatures who are then no longer in need of a Redeemer.

What is surprising for a critique which is theologically motivated is that McGrath does not mention the decisive theological reason which led Schleiermacher to this argumentation: his view of the necessary unity of the two divine decrees of creation and redemption. As Jacqueline Mariña has pointed out, it is nothing less than "the guiding perspective".[258] Whether the justification for this strict link, to avoid attributing "arbitrariness" to God,[259] can be defended is another question.[260] But it needs to be noted that the reason is to be found in the

---

257 McGrath, *The Making of Modern German Christology*, 47.
258 Mariña, "Christology and Anthropology in Friedrich Schleiermacher", 159–62.
259 Both editions of *The Christian Faith*, in ¹§ 20, 1. I, 79 and ²§ 13, 1. ET 1928, 64, insist on this view: "Otherwise it could only be explained as an arbitrary divine act that the restorative divine element made its appearance precisely in Jesus, and not in some other person."
260 Critiques such as those of Thomas Pröpper and Susanne Schaefer, objecting that this rules out a relationship of freedom between God and human beings in which God is willing to be moved by individuals, and continues to act in new historical responses, will be discussed in

doctrine of God, and not in a desire to please the educated among the despisers of religion. Certainly the direct connection made between Feuerbach's projection theory and modern theology's turn to examine the anthropological presuppositions of revelation – not as an alternative to God's revelation but as part of the human creature's potential for listening to it – is a jump to unwarranted conclusions. As Schleiermacher had already clarified in advance to these objections: there are other ways than resorting to an extrinsicist position to prove Feuerbach's conclusions as not necessary, as themselves naturalising, and as eminently refutable by an anthropological approach to God's self-communication.

4.3 Evaluation: The Introduction as a framework for the dogmatics. Directions of the revision, ongoing debates, and questions to Part Two

Which tendencies can be recognised in the many revisions of the text and of the order of the first Introduction (4.3.1)? How can they be judged in view of the professed intention of Schleiermacher's recasting of dogmatics after the anthropological turn to safeguard the independence of its contents from philosophy? It seems appropriate to use the dogmatic principle of the *Glaubenslehre* as a test case, since it was the main task of the Introduction to develop it. Is the explication of the concept of redemption successful in putting forward the essential link of redemption to the person of Jesus (4.3.2)? From comparing the purposes and the effects of the changes to the Introduction, questions will arise regarding their implementation in the material dogmatics (4.3.3).

4.3.1 Key orientations in the revision of the first Introduction

The main concerns and the misunderstandings of the reviewers as well as Schleiermacher's own reasoning regarding his revisions have been presented. It is time to assess which new lines of argumentation he has taken to strengthen his pioneering proposal of a doctrine of faith that can be vindicated to a general consciousness of truth which respects the limits of reason. Two main tendencies can be identified: a conscious connection to the thematic of freedom, and a thor-

---

Chapter 7. Cf. Pröpper, *Theologische Anthropologie*, vol. I, 480, n. 176. Schaefer, *Gottes Sein zur Welt*, 134–135 and 237–262.

ough-going emphasis on the historical character of the Christian experience of redemption.

Challenged by the doubts of the critics whether the basic concept of his theory of religion, the feeling of absolute dependence, could be reconciled with human freedom, he had to take a stance to this key idea of the era. The main result is the transition to a transcendental philosophical argumentation which demonstrates in ^{2}§ 4 the connection between concrete freedom and absolute dependence. It thus vindicates in its content as well as in its method, by way of self-reflection, that freedom must be actualised if one is to be able to experience oneself as utterly dependent and relate this consciousness to a creator God. The recognition of human freedom is accompanied by a more consistent conception of the relationship between the sensible and the higher consciousness that acknowledges the enduring validity of sensibility which mediates the possibility of interacting with the world. On the one hand, the mode of argumentation is stricter: it claims necessity for its findings based on the systematic and scientific character of its subject-theoretical statements. On the other hand, this also leads to a different relationship of the Introduction to the dogmatics which is in tension with the second major tendency of the revisions: the essential relation of the Christian self-consciousness to history.

The second version elaborates in new formulations and material corrections that the Christian faith which is to be outlined in the dogmatics in a reflected and coherent way is constituted by history. The changes are meant to clarify that the concept of the Redeemer relates to a historical person and does not actually owe itself as the "personally conceived idea of redemption"[261] to a projection of the pious self-consciousness of Christians. All statements that could be interpreted as constructing redemption, such as above all ^{1}§ 18,5, have been eliminated. Its new emphasis on the "one source from which all Christian doctrine is derived, namely, the self-proclamation of Christ" (^{2}§ 19 Postscript; ET 1928, 92) equally serves this purpose.

The same reason is behind the new sequence of the Introduction which is to make the separation between it and the material dogmatics more distinct. It relates it immediately to the historical community of the Christian church; the definition of its essence is the presupposition for the explanation of the dogmatics. Changing the order of the paragraphs and organising the first section of the Introduction into a system of *Lehnsätze* is also part of the effort to present Christianity as a historical fact. By making the steps of his enquiry more visible, it becomes easier to test the avenues of comprehension through general categories from different disciplines. It

---

[261] Cf. Baur, "Selbstanzeige", 241; KGA I/7,3, 266.

4.3 Evaluation: The Introduction as a framework for the dogmatics

allows for a better control of the methods and concepts when their adequacy is judged against the historical phenomenon they are examining. As elucidated in Chapter 1.3.1, instead of beginning with the definition of Christian dogmatics, everything needed for it in its new position as ²§ 19 is carefully developed along the way – a general concept of piety (²§§ 3 and 4) and its diversifications (²§§ 5–9), the principles of individualisation of the real religions (²§ 10), and the proposition of the essence of Christianity (²§ 11), as well as an account of the relationship between the Christian pious self-consciousness and the system of doctrines (²§§ 15–18).

Yet, while the clear separation of the Introduction helps to underscore the character of dogmatics as a historical discipline, there is a side effect of the new argumentation which is at cross-purposes with its explicit intention, affecting the material unfolding of this historically given faith in the two main parts. When Schleiermacher elaborated the different disciplines from which the first part of the Introduction "borrows" ("Ethics", "Philosophy of Religion", and "Apologetics"), and then also claimed necessity for his theory of subjectivity (culminating in the thesis of a natural God-consciousness), he made the whole Introduction more scholarly. But the result, unforeseen by him, was also to change its format and its relative standing compared to the dogmatics. Although he only wanted to give the Introduction an instrumental character, it then became a self-sufficient whole which required to be judged on its own, as distinct from the Christian faith conviction. The second version of the Introduction thus stands in greater competition with the material dogmatics than the first. While the first edition merely expounded piety, a determination of "feeling", as the basic element presupposed by the Christian religion, the second tries to justify it with cogent philosophical reasons in the framework of a theory of concrete freedom. This change affects the relationship between the a priori relationship to God and its historical determination. When Schleiermacher attempted to establish a natural God-consciousness with transcendental necessity within the framework of a theory of temporal self-consciousness, the status of its historical determination by Jesus Christ changed. For if the relationship to God is not only demonstrated to be a feeling which in fact exists but rather is grounded transcendentally, then the historical embodiment of this certainty in the person of a Redeemer can spur and confirm it, but it can hardly count as its unrelinquishable historical origin. The intention of the revision is thus in conflict with its effects. The Introduction acquires a foundational significance that any type of Christology can scarcely counterbalance; if every human being is already marked by an actualised God-consciousness, the revelation of God through the person of Jesus risks being only a confirmation. Which determinations of the concept of redemption are still open after this foundation? It will have to be examined both in the difference of the genuinely Christian to the general attributes of God and in Christology whether the categories introduced in the

Introduction pre-determine the contents of the dogmatics and possibly counteract its key intention, the bond to Christ.

4.3.2 The enduring bond of redemption to the person of Jesus Christ

There is a criterium by which it can be assessed whether Schleiermacher's unfolding of the concept of redemption does justice to the religious content which it is to express: the essential and ongoing relatedness of the Christian pious self-consciousness to the person of Jesus Christ. It will be crucial how it is justified that the process of redemption cannot be disconnected from him, and how the status that distinguishes him from the rest of humanity is explicated.

The following points of intersection between Christology and anthropology have become evident: A basic theological argument appeared in the position that the decrees of creation and redemption cannot diverge from each other and that the reality of redemption in Jesus Christ cannot be founded on an arbitrary choice of God's; it must be based in a plan of salvation that encompasses all of human history. With this assumption, the decisive Christological difference between divine and human spirit has been principally conceived as one between possibility and reality: "Everything real", that is, "the divine as it has been conceived of (*gedacht wird*) in Christ ... must be possible" (^{1}§ 20,1, I, 79). Insofar as the reality of a reconciled God-consciousness in the people redeemed is one that has been communicated to them, this possibility is restricted to the human capacity of receptivity. This is true in a temporal-historical perspective. From the complete perspective of creation, however, it is also possible to classify the appearance of the Redeemer as part of the process of a "supernatural" self-transcendence of human nature.

According to God's eternal decree, human nature has been ordered in such a way that it can realise its God-consciousness as a deed that has been pre-established as part of its structure. The temporal causality for this possibility breaking through in the person of Jesus is assigned to human nature. The critical anthropological feature in this proposal seems to be the element that remains identical before and after redemption and that excludes its understanding as complete re-creation, but which is not explained any further.[262]

---

[262] The point made in ^{2}§ 11,2 in the context of explaining the essence of Christianity as redemption that a complete re-creation is not necessary has been met with objections. Schleiermacher's view that this is not contained in the concept of redemption is rejected forcefully by Karl Barth in *The Theology of Schleiermacher*, 238–239: "only now do we have the full outbreak of the sickness

4.3 Evaluation: The Introduction as a framework for the dogmatics — 135

Although no specification is given as to what it consists in, it is reasonable to assume that it must be the pious modification of the immediate self-consciousness that is a feature of every human being. This, however, would then have to be unable to actualise itself as a possibility. If this is true, then the question arises what a transcendental analysis refers to if not a possibility that, if it is essential, must be able to be realised at least in principle. In this case, the two cornerstones of anthropology – the capability, and the need for redemption – turn out to mark the difference between the transcendental disposition of the God-consciousness and its real, diminished form of existence.

It looks as if the Introduction is able to establish and protect the superior status of Jesus Christ only at the cost of introducing a tension between philosophical and theological anthropology. In order to underline the unprecedented new element that enters history through him, it must admit a factual curtailment of the God-consciousness that has earlier been disclosed as a general human feature. The reason for all the problems in relating Christology and anthropology seems to lie in the determination of redemption. Consisting in the "absolutely perfect piety of Christ" (^{1}§ 18,4. I, 66), it does not offer a content that could not have been anticipated and that would be able to determine anthropology in a new way; it is only the first complete realisation of God-consciousness in general.

As the discussion above of the contemporary responses to the first edition have already shown, the observation that the content of redemption is determined only as the (absolutely perfect) reality of the possibility of the God-consciousness that is implanted in everyone was made early on in the history of reception. Apart from F. C. Baur, Georg Weissenborn's analysis of 1849 also makes it clear that the philosophical and the dogmatic principles of the dogmatics – the definitions of piety and of the essence of Christianity – differ from each other merely as possibility and reality. Since Schleiermacher has shown that the feeling of absolute dependence "belongs to the essence of the human being and constitutes its highest stage of development", Weissenborn concludes that "what belongs to the human essence, must be able to become real. In the concept of the feeling of absolute dependence its re-

---

of the feeling of absolute dependence presupposed as a basic systematic concept. ... Schleiermacher ... transferred the ambiguity of his basic concept to the concept of Christianity which is normative for all that follows. ... it is the dreadful heresy of § 11,2, which is enough by itself to make the whole of Schleiermacher's Christian faith completely unacceptable." His critique of the apologetic that "as soon as it opens its mouth to utter the first borrowed statement" ends in such heresy concludes with the much-quoted question: "Where is the originality of the *founder* if the *foundation* is not original?" It is evident from the context that for Barth at this stage of his engagement with Schleiermacher, an "original foundation" would require a concept of redemption that does not give any validity to human nature or freedom.

ality is thus immediately included".[263] This leads to his conclusion, not unlike Baur's, that the principle of dogmatics is the "redeemed feeling of absolute dependence" (328). The consequences for the difference between the redeemer and the redeemed are pointed out with equal clarity: While his "redeeming causality" is "external", there must be a

> point of contact (*Anknüpfungspunkt*), of ignition (*Zündstoff*) in human self-consciousness. Indeed, the relationship of possibility to reality is, even if it comes from the outside, the most internal (*allerinnigste*). As soon as the reality of the feeling of absolute dependence enters into human self-consciousness and encounters the possibility that is founded internally, the two combine so closely that one can no longer distinguish whether the reality was mediated from the outside or whether it emerged from the internal possibility as its foundation".[264]

Thus, already the early reception identifies the modification of the immediate self-consciousness that is the feeling of utter dependence as the linking anthropological element before and after redemption. Having taken stock of the main directions of the changes in the Introduction, it is now possible to formulate the questions that need to be tracked in the two parts of the dogmatics.

4.3.3 Questions for the dogmatics

On the basis of the revisions followed so far, analogous differences in the material elaboration of theological anthropology and Christology are to be expected. The enquiries relating to Schleiermacher's *theological anthropology* concern the capability and the need for redemption. The capability consists in the human receptivity for the divine and in the willingness for a redemption which is only experienced by those who allow themselves to be captured by the impression of Jesus. Since this point of contact can only be the God-consciousness, the claim of a pure receptivity must be examined. The formulation, "receptivity in highest potency" (Marg. 372, Nachschrift Heegewaldt 77, KGA I/7.3, 71) seems to be indicative of the problem because on closer examination it seems to point to an alternative. *Either* it is an openness that can be fulfilled only from beyond its own resources, *or* a potentiality that has enough substance to be able to ac-

---

[263] Georg Weissenborn, *Darstellung und Kritik der Schleiermacherschen Dogmatik* (Leipzig: T. O. Weigel, 1849), 327.
[264] Weissenborn, *Darstellung und Kritik*, 336.

4.3 Evaluation: The Introduction as a framework for the dogmatics — 137

tivate itself, that is, an incipient God-consciousness that can invigorate itself of its own accord to a point of complete realisation.

Regarding the need for redemption that is prior to the God-consciousness in its active capacity for reception and that explains the need for an absolute Redeemer, the following question arises: How does the dogmatics explain the reversal from a potency to a factual inability, from an essential element to one that cannot be actualised? What is the content and what systematic standing has sin in both versions of Schleiermacher's model of salvation history?

Christology, as we have seen, is to secure the enduring bond of redemption to Jesus Christ. One critical question will be whether both Introductions have programmed it as restitutive so that Jesus' role can only consist in repairing or reviving the constrained or underdeveloped God-consciousness and to restore the previous original state. In that case, the significance of the person of Jesus for humanity would have been made dependent on the factual occurrence of sin. If, however, the dogmatic elaboration identifies other elements in him beyond being a Redeemer in the restorative sense, how will it relate them to each other?

At this stage, the following insights can be summed up that are to flag problems to be followed up in Part Two. Based on the argumentation developed so far, Schleiermacher has succeeded in stating incontrovertibly the *factual* significance of Jesus concerning the need for redemption (however this will turn out to be elucidated in detail). Yet an ongoing significance and enduring validity of the redeemer cannot be established in this way. If his distinction to all other humans really only consists in being the first to have realised in full strength the relationship to God which is oppressed in all others, then his primacy would only be a temporal priority, and not of a principal and unreachable kind, but factual and passing. He would be ahead of humanity as an initial point of ignition, but would not, as Schleiermacher claims as essential for the Christian faith, have an ongoing function and different status. For his perfect realisation of the higher self-consciousness only differs in a quantitative way from an incipient one. The highest form of piety is not a new qualitative determination.

If the content of divine revelation merely consists in the unhindered reality of what is a structural disposition of human nature, then nothing can ward off the sublation of Christianity into religion as such. After this strength (*Kräftigkeit*) has been appropriated, there would be no content that could still justify the necessity of relating back to the historical person of Jesus. Then its validity does not rest on a content that is given only with his person, determining human existence in a new way, but on the fulfilment of an already established ideal of human nature, a religiously anchored realisation of reason.²⁶⁵ The singular fact that God's self-commitment to humans was realised in a particular human life would then be absorbed without remainder into the course of development of humanity.

The reason for reconceiving anthropology and Christology in these directions in his new proposal of a dogmatics that is able to hold its own in the exchange with a general consciousness of truth lies, as already Baur observed, in the doctrine of God. In order not to contradict the discoveries of the natural sciences and of history in their emerging new roles, theology is to steer clear of areas of possible competition. It is to engage in the different approaches within the history of Christian thinking to the Bible, the Councils and creeds in relation to their cultural and philosophical contexts. The proposal to be made is one that can be validated by Christian believers on the basis of their tradition, but also by the power of human reason that is open to the divine. In any case one can look forward with some expectation to the categories in which the *Glaubenslehre* will move forward on the tightrope walk between pantheist, deist and tradition-vindicated concepts of God as well as between a rationalist Christology of moral exemplar and a supernaturalist extrinsicism of revelation.

---

265 In *Selbstmitteilung Gottes*, 143, Lerch points out that "Jesus' *sinlessness* becomes the decisive criterium of his singularity" and that his "constitutive and lasting significance is ultimately only secured hamartiologically".

II Schleiermacher's Reworking of Christian Doctrine in his Material Dogmatics

Introduction

The ways in which the principles developed in the Introduction are elaborated in both parts of the system of doctrine is the theme of Part Two of this study, to be examined in three specified areas: theological anthropology (Chapter 5), Christology (Chapter 6), and doctrine of God (Chapter 7). Again, relevant differences between the two editions – which already testify to the scope opened up by the basic principles – will be highlighted. One of the perspectives pursued in comparing the two editions will be the question of what is owed to the essence definition of religion in its further determination by the consciousness of redemption through the person of Jesus Christ, and what is owed to other sources.[266]

The three dogmatic treatises are examined in the order which Schleiermacher considered for his revision but did not implement: beginning with the specifically Christian self-consciousness under the contrast of sin and grace in Chapters 5 and 6, and only then examining the concept of God in its general monotheistic propositions (Part One) and its Christian specification (Part Two of his material dogmatics). The difference in obtaining the two types of doctrines will be exemplified at the start of Chapter 5. The reason for me to conclude with the doctrine of God is that it holds the key to the prior decisions made in the outlines of the human person in her possible perfection and actual sinfulness, and of Christology; in order to assess its keynote function, these provisions have to be studied first. This means that much of what is developed in the "abstracted" statements deliberated in Part One of *The Christian Faith* will be treated only in Chapter 7. The only elements of its First Part that are considered before Chapter 7, namely in Chapter 5, relate to what the human person has been endowed with from creation onwards. The features of her "original perfection" lay the ground for a Christology that overcomes an extrinsicist model by clarifying in detail the relationship between anthropology, Christology and soteriology.

---

[266] This is the model Susanne Schaefer's study, *Gottes Sein zur Welt*, provides. It traces, on the one hand, the steps of the actual argumentation, and outlines on the other hand the alternative options which could have been taken, distinguishing critically between the directions Schleiermacher's approach opened up for the first time, and those which he chose himself in its implementation. By keeping these two aspects apart, it becomes possible to maintain the basis of justification but not to accept the decisive turns which the *Glaubenslehre* takes especially in the doctrine of God.

In view of the possibilities which Schleiermacher's approach contains, the concluding eighth chapter will include a contrasting model, that of Duns Scotus, which would have been open to him from his anthropological starting point. It will show that the direction he took was not the only, necessary way of working out his pioneering classical realisation of a dogmatics in response to the intellectual premises of modernity (Chapter 8).

5 The Theological Anthropology of the *Glaubenslehre:* Original Perfection, Sinfulness and Receptivity for Redemption

The task which Schleiermacher's anthropology has to fulfil is to mediate a Christology which gives equal weight to the divine and the human in the person of Jesus to the general First Part through a conception of the human person in her perfection and sinfulness. This complex, dialectical task will be investigated in five sections: First, the location and double task will be highlighted (5.1). Second, some elementary assumptions regarding original perfection that are operative in both editions will be uncovered (5.2). The third section will examine how the basic line of argument that becomes visible in 1821/22 is subsequently both secured and corrected by linking it to the revised theory of subjectivity worked out in the second Introduction (5.3). What platform the final shape of the doctrines of perfection and sin offers for Christology will be assessed (5.4) before taking stock of the foundations laid down so far (5.5).

5.1 Theological anthropology in its role of mediating in two directions: to the doctrine of God and to soteriology

As we have seen, the Introduction had deduced a tripartite scheme for the treatment of the material dogmatics from its *principium cognoscendi*, the essence definition of Christianity. All of the dogmatic system expresses in its doctrinal propositions the content of the God-consciousness in its Christian *specification.* Yet before reaching its two sides, sin and redemption, to be considered separately in its second main part, the moments that are already *presupposed* in the Christian modification are analysed. These are the dogmatic statements that remain when one abstracts from the real, historical-individual realisation of the God-consciousness. But exactly in the generality that exposes their content to be rudimentary and artificially isolated, they form the framework for every possible determination. Since the doctrine of God is only completed once the Christian modifications of the general divine attributes have been specified, also its general part will be treated only in the penultimate chapter of this second part (Chapter 7); by then, through the elaboration of the *Glaubenslehre*'s theological anthropology in this chapter and through the corresponding Christology in Chapter 6, we will have seen how the categories in which the Introduction's definition of the essence of Christianity has been explicated have been put into service.

Insofar as the need for redemption has been shown to be the identity-defining borderline against Pelagianism, the theological anthropology must be carried out as a doctrine of certain incapacities, or of "sin". On the one hand, it must be compatible with the subsequent unfolding of the consciousness of redemption in Christology; on the other, both of these concretised Christian parts will be subject to the general premises of the First Part of the dogmatics. How are these premises founded, and which conditions do they set for both parts of the doctrine of redemption?

The First Part of the dogmatics elaborates the feeling of absolute dependence by screening off its particular Christian determinations of the attributes of God, of the human person and of the world that are implied in it. In their quality of being divine creations, human beings and the world can only be approached in this general part as "originally perfect" (^{1}§§ 72–74, ^{2}§§ 59 and 60). Whatever will have to be said about sin, will not be able to contradict these conclusions, but can merely determine them further. But how can the givenness of sin originate from the divine all-causality, derived from the feeling of absolute dependence, and from the original perfection of the human creature? Schleiermacher solves the problem of connecting to the first main part in the following way: what seems to contradict itself at the abstract level, still undeniably exists together in the fact of the Christian self-consciousness. Its doctrinal reflection therefore cannot stop at the direct opposition but needs to attempt to order both contents in relation to each other. Then, however, sin, seen in itself as contradicting God, cannot have the same validity as the foundational divine causality; seen in relation to this causality, it is not independent, but part of an overall divine plan which accords it only a conditional validity in relation to redemption. Sin thus appears in two perspectives: looking back to the general part as "that what would not be if there was not redemption"; looking ahead to Christology as "that what can only disappear through redemption" (^{1}§ 85,2. I, 263). The *Glaubenslehre* eliminates the danger of a contradiction between the statements drawn from the general God-consciousness and from its Christian concretisation by taking recourse to the divine order in which the development towards actual sin and from sin to redemption was always already intended.

The ways in which the general doctrine of God and the abstracted anthropology imprint the doctrine of sin with their provisions, will become clear in the details of its material elaboration. One thing should, however, be clear from the beginning: The more plausible sin is made due to this framework and the more it is integrated into God's plan of salvation as a pre-ordained step, the more difficult will it become to explain what is different, specific and unprecedented in the new beginning in Christ. The problem that Schleiermacher's conception of sin solves regarding the relation of Christian anthropology to the first main part's definition of God as all-causality, will return at the other end: as problems of the independence and the nondeducible status of the content of the Christological part, and of the absorption of God's salvific action into God's pre-temporal decree.

5.2 The basic conception of a humanity receptive for redemption

Which features do the first, "abstracted" part and the Christian specification in the second part establish as elementary assumptions about human individuality and sociability, about the human relationship to the world and to the divine cause of its being? The first subsection will deal with the overall designation of the conditions, context and character of human life as the "nexus of nature" (5.2.1), while the second relates this foundational concept to the coordination envisaged by Leibniz between independent centres of action.[267] The third subsection treats the careful delineation of sinfulness as one pole of the "contrast" typical for the Christian religion but equally as the connecting point for its complement, divine grace (5.2.3).

5.2.1 Original perfection as the world's openness to enquiry

While the second edition relates the perfection of the world specifically to its ability to call forth moments of pious self-consciousness,[268] the first determines it more generally as the suitability of the world for human knowing and effective agency. What is foundational in both versions, however, is, firstly, that it is derived from the divine causality that becomes clear in the feeling of absolute dependence. Both share, secondly, Schleiermacher's determination to prise this

---

[267] Among the scholars who follow up traces of Leibniz in Schleiermacher's *Dialectic*, dogmatics and ethics are Michael Moxter (1992), Susanne Schaefer (2002), Eilert Herms, who in *Menschsein im Werden. Studien zu Schleiermacher* (Tübingen: Mohr Siebeck, 2003), 79. 93, emphasises the distinction of the Leibniz-Wolffian epistemology from Kant, Fichte and Schelling, Jacqueline Mariña (2008), Andrew Dole (2010), and Katharina Gutekunst (2018).
[268] The "totality of finite being as it influences us – including human influences on the rest of being that arise from our position within it as well – harmonizes (*zusammenstimmt*) in such a way as to make possible the continuity of [1928: the] religious self-consciousness within that totality" (²§ 57,1. ET 2016, I, 337). The 1928 ET uses "works together" for "*zusammenstimmt*" (233).

treatise of theological anthropology away from the grip of a misinterpretation of the Genesis narrative as historical, where an originally innocent human nature was changed forever by the Fall. Thirdly, the theological ideas of the human creature as being made in the image of God, of creation out of nothing, and of direct interaction between God and humans are critiqued as being either too anthropomorphic, or as containing other problematic implications which reduce God's all-causality. The goal of the revision of this traditional treatise is to validate only such doctrinal statements that are in keeping with the stringent systematic outline of a God who is distinct from the world and is its absolute cause, but to whom no change, no temporal action and no particular relationships can be attributed. These results from the abstracted, general but nevertheless Christian first part[269] will influence the second part of the material dogmatics which, as we know, spells out the pious affections under the contrast of sin and grace. So, under what model are the human centres of agency living in this world conceived? A subsequent question will be what type of relationship of the world's human inhabitants to God remains possible if individual communications are ruled out. This can only be pursued in Chapter 7 when the distinct kinds of presence and effect of divine and human agency are considered.

In keeping with the primacy of the absolute causality of God, Schleiermacher first outlines the overarching context for human activity: the so-called "*Naturzusammenhang*" which comprises the whole realm of natural processes and finite interactions within it. It is to this "nexus of nature" that "original perfection" is first attributed. What are the premises of a concept that includes both nature and history as comprised of the interactions of humans?[270] John Thiel observes a dual function: the term indicates "not only the sensible realm as a whole designating the unity of self-consciousness, nature and history, but rather an epistemological concept that includes the possibility of coherent human experience and interac-

---

269 This is correctly emphasised by Matthias Gockel, *Election*, 57 n. 71, with reference to ²§ 62,3, in his own translation: "in the reality of the Christian life, there is neither a general God-consciousness without a co-posited relation to Christ nor a relationship with the redeemer which would not be related to the general God-consciousness" (cf. ET 1928, 261). Thus, Gockel concludes, "this is an indication that the first part of the *Christian Faith* is not merely a description of the 'form' of a general God-consciousness, in abstraction from its particular Christian 'content'. The distinction between form and content ... fails to take into account that the content of the Christian pious self-consciousness is described not only in Part II but also in Part I, since piety never exists apart from its historical actualization."
270 The complete meaning of "nature" as the realm of reciprocal effects also includes culture. Hermann Fischer, *F. D. E. Schleiermacher*, 106–107, highlights the action of human reason on nature, as treated in his philosophical ethics.

5.2 The basic conception of a humanity receptive for redemption — 147

tion with the world and each other."²⁷¹ What is implied in this quest for "coherence"? The decision not to start with human individuality as the bearer of original perfection but with the encompassing framework takes on board several philosophical insights: it reflects the need for a totalising outreach, relating to the concept of the "world" as an idea, not as a given. This insight, examined by Kant in the antinomies of pure reason, that the totality of the world can only ever be anticipated and constitutes a regulatory idea, is at the level of epistemology. But it has consequences for the theoretical and the practical relationships of the human subject to his or her contexts. The ability to locate oneself as a centre of thinking and action requires a world that is open to research and transparent enough to establish some degree of predictability through the specification of natural laws. "Coherence" or harmony thus comprises something that cannot be taken for granted: that the "world" provides spheres and scope for action that match human competences.²⁷² Beyond the assumption that nature is accessible for human insight and agency, intersubjective relations equally give rise to the question of what makes human co-existence and coordination possible. The definition of original perfection names the precondition for the human possibility of achieving goals in a world that is open to productive endeavour: that "all lasting forms of being (*beharrlichen Gestaltungen des Seins*) and all its opposite functions belong together (*Zusammengehörigkeit*)" (¹§ 70,3 I, 227–228). Perfection is given in the "unity and completeness of the harmony of the posited in itself (*Einheit und Vollständigkeit der Zusammenstimmung des gesezten in sich*)" (¹§ 70 LS Note. I, 226).

In the first edition, the idea of the world as being open to human knowing is pushed as far as being able to perceive things in their "essence". The original perfection is claimed for correct insights into the structures themselves, not, as specified in the second version, in their ability to offer fitting occasions to combine world- and God-consciousness. "Self-activity" consists in

---

271 Thiel, *God and World in Schleiermacher's 'Dialektik' and 'Glaubenslehre'*, 174–188, quoted by Gockel, *Election*, 50.
272 In *The Eternal Covenant. Schleiermacher on God and Natural Science* (Berlin/Boston: de Gruyter, 2017), Daniel J. Pedersen emphasises the significance both of Leibniz and Spinoza for Schleiermacher's conception of nature. Yet if Spinoza's point of departure, the necessity of natural processes, is taken as the basis for scientific research, the epistemological insight that coherence has to be assumed as a regulative idea for any piece of individual research to be undertaken is turned into its opposite: into the position that the materially given processes of nature enable scientific research because they are fully determined. The sequence identified by Kant is reversed, misrecognising the logic of enquiry which needs to cast a prior assumption of regularity over the phenomena so that they can be researched. For a review of the book, see Anne Käfer, in *Theologische Revue* 144 (2019) 491–492.

> noticing and summarising in such a way that the result corresponds to what is at the basis of the effects (*Einwirkungen*) of things on our senses. Concerning the matching (*Zusammentreffen*) of our conceptions (*Vorstellungen*) with the essence of things (*Wesen der Dinge*), we must regard our disposition (*Anlage*) as complete, at least in reference to the earthly world ... thus we can regard the complete depiction (*Aufgehen*) of our world in our knowing (*Erkenntnis*) as the goal of this striving (¹§ 74. I, 237).

In 1830/31, this earlier, in effect pre-critical confidence in attaining more than the appearance of things by human understanding is pared back to a position in keeping with the Kantian critique of the scope of theoretical reason. The revised version makes it clear in its more circumspect formulations that dogmatic theology respects the lines drawn by a philosophical critique of the faculty of knowing, and that it claims something quite different to knowledge of things in themselves:

> everything rests on some agreement of these notions – and judgements made regarding them – with the nature and circumstances of things. ... God-consciousness, once evoked, would not be imperiled at all if particular notions were not in conformity with the nature of whatever object were to be depicted by them. ... so long as less than all of being is represented in our thinking, every act of thinking would also still continue to have something erroneous admixed in it (²§ 60, 1. ET 2016, 358–359).

The second edition still maintains that a fit is needed: "Upon all the agreement of these ideas and judgements with the being and relations (ET 2016, 359: nature and circumstances) of things depends all the influence of man on external nature which is more than simply instinctive, and also the connexion between knowledge and practical life" (ET 1928, 246). Yet the claim of error-free objective knowledge is dropped as no longer tenable, but also as unimportant from a religious perspective. A different concern becomes key, that of coordinating the self-active centres whose "impulse" it is to "express God-consciousness", thus connecting "species-consciousness with personal self-consciousness" (²§ 60 LS. ET 2016, 355).

5.2.2 A model for combining natural determination with receptive and self-active individuality: Leibniz's theory of monads

In the "nexus of nature", two aspects are kept in balance: the embeddedness and determination of the individual within the web of natural reciprocal influences, and the significance of his own perspective. Against conceptions of conscious finite life that view it as determined by overarching forces, Schleiermacher resists a view that would turn the human subject into a "point of transition" (*Durch-

gangspunkt) for other forces with no input of his own.²⁷³ To secure the irreducible standing of the individual, yet within a conception that does justice to the network of relations which is infinite in principle, he employs the concepts of a thinker who developed an alternative framework to Spinoza's pantheism: Leibniz with his insistence on the self-active power of the elementary units of any system, the "monads" whose unique contribution to the world are their own, never repeated perspectives.

Before discussing which differences to Leibniz the first edition notes as part of the propositions on original perfection, the points it takes over need to be highlighted first. Among them are Leibniz's idea launched against Descartes's mechanistic account of *res extensae* to "think nature as a whole, as a system of living forces"; the unprecedented "metaphysical rank attributed to the individual, prepared in his theory of force (*Kraft*)" which opened up the possibility of a "social model of nature of human beings as a union of persons (*Personalunion*), a reign founded on freedom".²⁷⁴ This provided an alternative to traditional visions of God's agency, by making it possible not to conceive of "God's manner of acting (*Wirkungsweise Gottes*) as a sudden impact from outside (or even from 'above') that comes down on us."²⁷⁵. God's way of governing is by creating entities which have their own driving force and that are coordinated by God in their locations in a productive way.²⁷⁶ While this may appear like a top-down approach to managing units marked by divergent spins, it is justified in Leibniz's

---

273 Schleiermacher's repeated refusal to think of the human individual as a "point of transition" (*Durchgangspunkt*), for example in ²§ 49,1. ET 2016, I, 274, is the basis for opposing readings that also see his *Glaubenslehre* as affected by Spinozism. In my view, his defence of the individual as its own centre of action amounts to a sustained critique of the Spinozist position which can be traced back to the critical alternative to monism put forward by Leibniz.

274 Herta Nagl-Docekal, in her overview and summary of the different contributions, "Leibniz heute lesen. Eine Einführung", in Nagl-Docekal (ed.), *Leibniz heute lesen. Wissenschaft, Geschichte, Religion* (Berlin/Boston: De Gruyter, 2018), 1–21, 14.

275 Nagl-Docekal, "Einführung", 14 (*"niemals schlagartig von außen (oder gar von 'oben') auf uns niedergeht"*).

276 In the ongoing dispute about the interpretation of the *Speeches*, it would be worth discussing whether Leibniz's theory of nature as interconnected individual units fitted with Schleiermacher's insights from the pantheism, atheism and theism controversies in early Romanticism and idealism For a background of these disputes, cf. C. Danz and G. Essen (eds), *Philosophisch-theologische Streitsachen. Pantheismusstreit, Atheismusstreit, Theismusstreit* (Darmstadt: Wissenschaftliche Buchgesellschaft, 2012), and Danz's chapter, "Der Atheismusstreit um Fichte", in this volume 135–213, which locates Schleiermacher's agreement with Fichte in the position that the concept of God is a secondary reflection (198–201).

rationalist argumentation by attributing to the monads, as Susanne Schaefer points out, the issuing of a "demand" to God:[277] regarding the

> influence of one monad over another ... it can have its effect only through the intervention of God, inasmuch as in the ideas of God a monad rightly demands that God have consideration for it when organising the others from the beginning of things. For since a created monad cannot have a physical influence on the interior of another, this is the only way that one can be dependent on another.[278]

Schaefer sees Leibniz's combination of "self-determined action" with envisaging for the monads that they "step into exactly those relations that have been foreseen for them" as "quite similar" to the way in which "Schleiermacher's *Christian Faith* conceives of the creatures' joint existence (*Zusammensein*) within the nexus of nature".[279] A system that could hold individuality and natural determination together suited Schleiermacher's dialectical understanding of self-active/receptive human life and of the process of knowledge.

He does not follow the lead of Leibniz, however, on three other points: the status of the purported "harmony", the conception of this world as the "best of all possible worlds", nor Leibniz's philosophical use of the biblical understanding of the human person as made in the image of God. In both editions, Schleiermacher relates the "original perfection" of the world to a state of harmoniously fitting together not at the empirical, but at an underlying primordial level. He does not subscribe to optimism as a worldview at the level of concrete outcomes. The harmony pre-established by God refers to the conditions of possibility of bringing forth resonance between different centres of action. For Schleiermacher, it refers concisely to "what lies internally at the basis of the appearance, that is, to the living forces in their relative way of being posited for themselves and conditioned through each other" (^{1}§ 70,1. I, 227).

---

277 Schaefer, *Gottes Sein zur Welt*, 188.
278 Cf. Leibniz, Monadology § 51, in L. Strickland, *Leibniz's Monadology. A New Translation and Guide* (Edinburgh: Edinburgh University Press, 2014), 24. The translator and editor comments on § 51: "Here Leibniz explains the relation of monads in terms of the correspondence that holds between them. Or rather, their coordination, since he holds that God has actively accommodated monads to each other so that they mutually correspond. Because his understanding is the realm of all possibles, God is able to inspect monads prior to creation. ... Thus every monad is so adjusted from the outset that its perceptions will always accord with those of every other created monad, despite there being no influence or interaction between them. Nevertheless the mutual adjustment is so precise that it creates the impression of mutual causal interaction between substances" (114–115).
279 Schaefer, *Gottes Sein zur Welt*, 188–189.

5.2 The basic conception of a humanity receptive for redemption

Secondly, the reason for rejecting the "doctrine of the best world as it has been put forward since Leibniz in the so-called natural theology" is that it is seen to reduce God to a deliberating and choosing role which for Schleiermacher is not in keeping with the implications of all-causality. He notes a partial agreement on the one hand, indicating that Leibniz's view "partly amounts to the same thing" (*besagt eines theils dasselbe*); yet, it is judged to differ in another respect, in that "not only the perfection of the living forces but also the entirety of their development is contained in it as well" (¹§ 70 Postscript. I, 228).[280] In contrast, Schleiermacher wants to keep the attribution of perfection to the foundational level, instead of subsuming the development of the units as well as the forces within and between them in the course of history also under this label. What may result from original perfection as concrete developments is not part of his theological use of Leibniz's conception of reality as a field made up by interrelated forces and singular perspectives.

A further difference can be observed in their relation to the biblical and theological concept of being made in the image of God. Leibniz uses it without hesitation in an argumentation that attributes a crucial capacity to humans: to "imitate" God. It is linked, as Herta Nagl-Docekal points out, to a key issue that connects Leibniz and Kant, a "question that is still irrefutable today about the totality of the cosmos – presupposed in empirical research but never given empirically as such". In order to conceive this totality as "founded and as holding together", a philosophical concept of God as the ultimate foundation stone is constructed. It affects how the human person is "situated", as becomes evident from the appendix to a letter of Leibniz to Nicolas Rémond, written in July 1714: "each simple substance is an image of the universe, but … each mind is, on top of that, an image of God, having knowledge not only of facts and of the empirical connections between them, as do non-rational souls, which are only empiricists". This enables the human subject to attain and possess

---

280 This addition to ¹§ 70, "*nur dass nicht allein die Vollkommenheit der lebendigen Kräfte sondern auch die der Gesammtheit ihrer Entwicklung mit darin begriffen ist*" (I, 228), is maintained in its critical edge in ²§ 59,3. It equally distinguishes between primordial structures and actual history, with "original perfection" only applying to the former. This is captured more clearly in ET 1928, 241, of ²§ 59,3: "The doctrine is concerned not only with what lies at the basis of temporal existence but with temporal existence itself." ET 2016 translates "*der Zeiterfüllung zum Grunde liegt*" with "fulfilment over time" instead of "of time", treating the first reference as if it indicated the level of history: "However, this doctrine regarding the best world has to do not only with something that underlies fulfilment over time but also with fulfilment of time itself" (²§ 59,3. ET 2016, I, 351).

knowledge of the necessity of the eternal truths, understanding the reasons of facts and imitating the architecture of God, and thereby also being capable of entering into fellowship with Him and of becoming a member of the city of God, the best governed state that is possible, just as the world is likewise the most perfect of all structures and the best-framed physically, and the best-framed morally.[281]

In his *Monadology* published the same year Leibniz similarly spells out *imago Dei* in terms of cognitive knowing and analogical constructions: that

souls in general are living mirrors or images of the universe of created things, whereas minds are also images of the divinity itself, or of the very author of nature, capable of knowing the system of the universe, and of imitating something of it through their own smaller-scale constructions, each mind being like a little divinity in its own sphere.[282]

In the two following propositions, Leibniz also draws conclusions on how the Creator is inclined towards the human creatures and on their intersubjective connections:

It is for this reason that minds are capable of entering into a kind of society with God, and that his relation to them is not only that of an inventor to his machine (which is God's relation to other created things) but also that of a prince to his subjects, and even of a father to his children. ... From this it is easy to conclude that the assemblage of all minds must make up the City of God, that is, the most perfect possible state under the most perfect of monarchs.[283]

In contrast to such a soaring philosophical appropriation of the biblical designation *imago Dei*, Schleiermacher's reticence against this most significant concept of Christian anthropology is because it has "something uncomfortable. ... Similarity with God has hardly anything to offer for the main elements of original perfection." The main reason for refusing to build his theological anthropology on the foundation of *imago Dei* is the incongruence between the human "relationship of the lower forces of the soul to the higher ones", a constellation to which "nothing similar at all can be found in God" (¹ § 76,2. I, 244).

---

281 Nagl-Docekal quotes this summary of the "leading thought of his writings" in her "Einführung", 7. The letter is translated in Strickland, Leibniz, *Monadology*, Appendix 3, 278–279, 279.
282 Leibniz, *Monadology*, § 83, trans. and ed. Strickland, 31.
283 Leibniz, *Monadology*, §§ 84 and 85, trans. and ed. Strickland, 31. The relationship between the created human subjects and God is important also for God, as § 86 explains: "This City of God, this truly universal monarchy, is a moral world in the natural world, and is the most exalted and the most divine of God's works, and it is in this that God's glory truly consists, since there would be no glory if his greatness and his goodness were not known and admired by minds."

Whether this negation of the appropriateness of the term *imago Dei* is to be accepted, will have to be pursued after examining the attributes of God in Part Two that deals with the specific determination of Christian piety. Some patristic authors had opened up a different avenue when they located the similarity of the *imago* not in a rationality which was attributed both to God and to humans, but in human freedom. Could the human ability to love arising as a possibility of freedom have been identified as a candidate for being in the likeness of God? Is the argument for the dissimilarity claimed as foundational by Schleiermacher, an anthropology of higher and lower forces of the soul which do not find a parallel in God, not itself problematic in its naturalising tendency also for humans? In contrast to Leibniz's philosophical endorsement of the *imago Dei* conception, Schleiermacher prefers not to make use of it but to emphasise Jesus Christ as fulfilling the original perfection of humans instead.

Despite these explicit differences to Leibniz, there are parallels. The problem that is being solved by Schleiermacher's reinterpretation of the biblical narrative of "original perfection" is one which Leibniz had answered with the concept of "pre-established harmony": how human beings in their individuality can be coordinated through meaningful communicability. Both editions agree that this is what the basic perfection of humans consists in: in their capability to orientate themselves and to relate to the natural and social contexts in which they realise their lives from their own unique perspectives. Schleiermacher attributes this basic endowment for a possible harmony to God's causality. The concept of the "best of all possible worlds" is rejected because it is speculative. The biblical judgement by God after completing the creation of the world and of humans, that "everything was good", is deemed sufficient. But apart from steering clear of superlatives beyond the foundational, originary affirmation, there is another motive to reject Leibniz's reasoning: it would have given options to God, a space for choice which for Schleiermacher must be excluded because the realm of divine power is co-extensive with the realm of "nature".[284] It can only be decided in Chapter 7 whether the view of world history that Schleiermacher ends up proposing, a steady course of development towards a fully realised God-consciousness, is something similar to Leibniz's "best of all possible worlds" in which it is not foreseen that God's project could be derailed.[285]

---

284 There can be "no distinction between the potential and the actual", or "between 'can' and 'will'", as ¹§ 68 a, 3. I, 207–208 and ²§ 54,3. ET 1928, 214 state.
285 Having compared the similarities and differences to Leibniz where Schleiermacher's main addition is the reciprocal interaction between the individual units, in contrast to their "windowlessness" in Leibniz's concept of monads, Schaefer concludes with the assessment: "The difference to Leibniz's monads who are not able to take a stand towards the prestabilised order be-

However, Schleiermacher's next step can be seen as a correction of rationalist optimism: portraying the opposite part to "perfection", namely human "sinfulness" and the factors leading to this condition, due to which the original possibility of harmony is always counterbalanced by actual religious and moral failure.

5.2.3 The interpretation of human sinfulness

The biblical narrative of the Fall as a state subsequent to original perfection has been modified to the position of a co-existence of sinfulness and potential for perfection from the beginning of humankind onwards; it is now important to explain what this problematic condition consists in. Both editions locate the possibility of sin at the intersection of the sensible with the higher consciousness and explain it at least in part by the head start which the first enjoyed over the latter. A critical benchmark which received divergent assessments by theologians at the time is the human capability for morality. Schleiermacher frames the problem of sin as the challenge to avoid both "Manicheism" and "Pelagianism". How the two perspectives can be reconciled, explaining human sinfulness from the earlier occurrence of the relationship to the world mediated by the senses, and maintaining an anthropology that does not fall prey to either heresy, is a problem shared by both editions.

In the essence definition of Christianity outlined carefully in the Introduction, the two anthropological "natural heresies" which Christian doctrine had to avoid had been named as "Manicheism" and "Pelagianism". These two extremes constituted the border posts beyond which the essence of Christianity would be missed regarding the human being's dependence on, and receptive ability for redemption. What they consist in is elaborated here, in the material dogmatics' doctrine of sin. One aspect is the relationship of original perfection and sinfulness to morality. This had been one of the points of debate with his Lutheran contemporary Karl Gottlieb Bretschneider in 1819 in an essay on "Election". It was one of the divisive theological themes between the Reformed and the Lutheran confessions which had been united into one church in 1817, a process between the Protestant churches and the Prussian state that Schleiermacher had been engaged in with programmatic writings and negotiations. Noted as a

---

comes minuscule. Also the elements of Schleiermacher's nexus of nature ultimately only fulfil what divine providence has determined for them" (*Gottes Sein zur Welt*, 198).

semi-rationalist,[286] Bretschneider emphasised morality as a human capacity in Kantian terms, a foundational human endowment which, as the general superintendent of Gotha argued, was recognised in the New Testament, in Paul and in Acts. How does Schleiermacher define the two opposite limits, and how do they relate to this intra-Protestant ecumenical debate?

Viewed from the overarching canopy – the doctrine of God as it appears in the general part –, it is termed "Manichean" to conceive of sin as an independent principle and thus "exclude it completely from the realm of dependence from God" (^{1}§ 85,2. I, 263). Yet to explicate sin in a way that it could appear as reconcilable with the original perfection of the human being, would be "Pelagian". In order not to attribute it to a force outside of God, as in Manicheism, sin has to correspond to the original created disposition of human nature; yet in order to exclude a Pelagian ability for self-perfection, it also needs to constitute an effective contradiction. Schleiermacher defines it as an "opposition (*Gegensaz*) between spirit and flesh" in which human sensibility remains below its orientation towards the God-consciousness and seeks to fill the moments of life by itself (^{1}§ 86 Postscript. I, 265). Since it blocks itself off from the inherent possibility of outreach towards God, sin is "a disturbance" of "nature" (^{1}§ 89 LS. I, 268), and such a grievous one that it leaves the human person in a "complete inability to the good" (*vollkomne Unfähigkeit zum Guten*) (^{1}§ 91 LS. I, 273) which can only be lifted by redemption (^{1}§ 93). Even if it can be explained through the course of human development as the result of the "unequal progress of the understanding (*des Verstandes*) and the will" (^{1}§ 88), it can still be imputed to the individual as his or her own "deed" (*That*) (^{1}§ 90,1. I, 270). Schleiermacher reiterates his reserve, already stated in his critique of Bretschneider's position in the essay on "Election", against recognising a capability for morality that is based on the inner freedom of each human being in Kant. By opting for a positive answer to the question of meaning – as also Schleiermacher does in his move from an analysis of facticity to a "Whence" –, Kant was led to the postulate of the existence of God. For him, it had the status of a "reasonable subjective faith" (*Vernunftglaube*), accessed in a similarly compelling analysis that established the idea of God as pertaining to the realm of "hope"; as such, God's existence is not objectifiable, though it is required by the conditions of a moral agency that seeks meaning.[287] From his

---

286 Cf., for example, Kantzenbach, *Programme der Theologie*, 44–50.
287 Cf. Nagl-Docekal, *Innere Freiheit. Grenzen der nachmetaphysischen Moralkonzeptionen (Deutsche Zeitschrift für Philosophie Sonderband 36)* (Berlin/Boston: de Gruyter, 2014), 155–157. I have treated its relevance for the connection between philosophical and theological ethics in "What scope for ethics in the public sphere? Principled autonomy and the antinomy of practical reason", in *Studies in Christian Ethics* 32 (2019) 485–498.

early writings onwards, Schleiermacher had not been convinced by Kant's deontological approach to ethics; he had decidedly appropriated only the epistemological insights of the inaugurator of the anthropological turn. Yet on the backdrop of his theological contemporaries on the rationalist side working out a connection between Kant's moral view and biblical universalism, it is all the more significant that he distances himself from their theological efforts. This becomes clear in his explanation of "Manicheism" in the context of ethics. In the Introduction, it represented the view that there is no point of access in the human person for redemption and that a complete re-creation into something else ("*Umschaffung*") (^{1}§ 25,3. I, 94) was required. This was considered a heresy since its radical dualism made "redemption" in the proper meaning of the term impossible. While this point still holds, it is significant that "Manichean" now stands for evil as an independent principle, that excludes sin "completely from the realm of dependence from God" (^{1}§ 85,2. I, 263). It would have been equally possible to allocate moral evil and sin to human freedom and expound their relation to creation as a risk which was freely accepted by the Creator, allowing the human counterparts to exercise their own free agency. Having conceived of humans as occupying pre-ordained places in their individual historical locations within the nexus of nature, however, such a conception of freedom is not available to Schleiermacher; instead, a different solution had to be sought to square original human perfection and actual sin with God's all-causality. The human condition of sinfulness is explicated in a way that gives space to a receptivity for divine grace. It allows for a reorientation through the redemptive encounter with Jesus Christ that does not have to refute the continuing basic constitution marked by original perfection. By locating the origin of sin in a time lag between sensibility and the emerging clarity of the God-consciousness, two factors have been chosen that are not radically at odds with each other and that can be increasingly aligned towards a more balanced human development. The lead proposition of the "Second Point of Doctrine" (*Zweites Lehrstück*), "Regarding the Original Perfection of Humanity" concludes that it consists in "every state (*Zustand*) being compatible (*Vereinbarkeit*) with the consciousness of the highest being or that the lower and the higher self-consciousness belong together" (^{1}§ 74 LS. I, 236).

5.3 The revised argumentation of the second edition

The corrections of the second edition relate to the theory of subjectivity on which the doctrine of sin is based. In line with the reworked understandings of the essence definitions of piety and of redemption in the Introduction (^{1}§§ 8 and 9, § 18; ^{2}§§ 3 and 4, § 11), Schleiermacher has reconceived in particular two basic points:

the relationship of the sensible and the higher consciousness (5.3.1); and as a consequence, the role of human freedom in the realisation of the God-consciousness (5.3.2). Objections to the naturalising concept of sin also in the ultimate position Schleiermacher arrives at will be treated (5.3.3) before concluding how the new accentuations result in a changed starting point and direction of Christology (5.4).

5.3.1 The relationship of human sensibility to the God-consciousness

Already from comparing the lead propositions on the essence of sin, a reorientation from a naturalistic to an agency-oriented conception becomes evident. At first, sin consisted in the "opposition (*Gegensaz*) between the flesh or that element in us that produces (*hervorbringt*) pleasure and displeasure, and the spirit, or that element in us that produces the God-consciousness" (¹§ 86 LS. I, 264). In its revised form, it consists in a "positive antagonism (*Widerstreit*) of the flesh against the spirit" (²§ 66 LS. ET 1928, 271), that is, of the "totality of the so-called lowly powers of the soul" (²§ 66, 2. ET 1928, 272) against the God-consciousness. Although both editions agree that the sensible function is only sinful when it closes itself off from the spirit and asserts an "independence" (e. g., ¹§ 90,3. I, 271; cf. ²§ 66, 2. ET 1928, 273) that runs counter to its higher orientation, two different models of coordination are implied. They become visible in how "natural perfection" is determined, that is, the ideal state of human nature originally established by God in comparison with the state of sin.

For the first edition it was a given "that, if the consciousness of sin were not a pervasive element of our lives, we would not at all have made that earlier distinction (sc. between flesh and spirit)" (¹§ 86,1. I, 265). For with it, "the possibility of a counteraction (*Gegenwirkung*) was already posited" (I, 264). It is true that also for the first version, the process of their possible union proceeds in the way that "every moment would begin and end in the spirit, and sensibility would everywhere only be an organ and a living mediating element (*Zwischenglied*) (I, 265; cf. ²§ 66,2. I, 357); it is therefore a relationship of determination and not of a complete dissolution of sensibility in the God-consciousness. Yet in the original outline, the difference between spirit and embodiment, God-consciousness and the inevitable relatedness of human pursuits to the senses, has no original validity. While this difference is constitutive of the embodied human being, the doctrine of natural perfection distinguishes flesh and spirit only as possibly competing functions in anticipation of the "possibility of a counteraction" (I, 264) that is then realised in sin.

This portrayal of the anthropological ideal parallels the statement made already in the first Introduction about the structure of the self-consciousness of the

Redeemer. In him, "the being-posited-for-itself or the sensible self-consciousness and the being-co-posited of God or the higher self-consciousness must be totally the same; since where there is difference, there is also still reciprocal hindrance" (*in ihm [muß] das Fürsichgesetztsein oder das sinnliche Selbstbewußtsein und das Mitgeseztsein Gottes oder das höhere Selbstbewußtsein völlig dasselbe sein; denn wo noch Verschiedenheit ist, da ist auch noch gegenseitige Hemmung*) (¹§ 18,4. I, 66). Also in the doctrine of regeneration (*Wiedergeburt*) a denial of the enduring function of the sensible self-consciousness is to be seen. Together with the "creative activity" that is necessary for the "beginning of the new life", a "completely changed relationship of human nature in the individual must happen, in that the sensible unit of life as such is destroyed, and that both the mainly receptive and the mainly active states develop in a different and contrasting direction" (¹§ 128,1. II, 106). These diverging assessments of the constitution of the human self-consciousness from which sin arises will have an effect not only on individual elements, but also on the approach to Christology itself, as will be shown below.

The second edition makes it completely clear that it is a question of which of the two predominates in the "relation of the lower and the higher self-consciousness to each other which occasions the whole process of the excitation of the God-consciousness" (²§ 58,1. ET 1928, 236). The sensible function is seen as having always existed and is recognised as regular. In line with ²§§ 4 and 6 of the Introduction, the original perfection now consists in human nature being "sufficient" for the realisation of the "original demand that the God-consciousness should exist continually and universally", including "its communication from one to the other" (²§ 60,3. ET 1928, 247), or "for the process of transmitting God-consciousness from each individual to others" (*der gegenseitigen Erweckbarkeit*) (ET 2016, I, 361).

Instead of the term "spirit" used mainly in the first edition, the second speaks of "God-consciousness" and reinforces the religious reference also in other places. ²§ 70,2 explains the concept of the "good" (cf. ¹§ 91,1. I, 275) with the addition, "good being understood here solely as that which is determined by the God-consciousness" (ET 1928, 283). It also specifies the "practical interest" (¹§ 102,4. I, 330) in the idea of the purely good in contrast to the evil that characterises Manicheism, as a "practical religious interest" (²§ 80,4. ET 1928, 330). A formulation that expressed the practical interest in terms of the self-governance of practical reason is similarly changed: first, it consisted in "positing in ourselves the idea of the purely good as a principle of guidance and formation in the ethical world" (¹I, 320); subsequently, the practical religious interest is left much more vague: it "postulates somewhere a perfectly pure impulse" (²§ 80,4. ET 1928, 330).

Thus, the second edition, on the one hand, rehabilitates the role of sensibility; on the other, it moves what was attributed to the human spirit into the religious sphere, to the God-consciousness. This is also evident in the systematisation under-

5.3 The revised argumentation of the second edition — 159

gone by the four aspects of the original perfection into two in the revised version. At first, it consisted in

> the capability of the human organisation to be enlivened by the spirit, or in body and soul belonging together; secondly in the excitability of the human capability for knowledge by the world surrounding it, or in reason and nature belonging together; thirdly, in the capability of the personal feeling to be moved by the common feeling (*Gemeingefühl*), or in the individual and the species belonging together; finally in the compatibility of every state with the consciousness of the highest being, or in the lower and the higher self-consciousness belonging together (^{1}§ 74 LS. I, 236).

The new proposition that combines these four elementary, evocative capabilities into two quite abstract features makes up with precision for what it has lost in verbal and visual appeal:

> The predisposition to God-consciousness, as an inner impulse, includes the consciousness of a faculty of attaining, by means of the human organism, to those states of self-consciousness in which the God-consciousness can realize itself; and the impulse inseparable therefore to express the God-consciousness includes in like manner the connexion of the race-consciousness with the personal consciousness; and both together form man's original perfection (^{2}§ 60 LS. ET 1928, 244).

By correcting the position that already the natural division between spirit and flesh is the beginning of sin, the path is now open to put all the weight on the type of relationship the pious individual adopts towards the sensible self-consciousness. The new description highlights more clearly that it is a case of taking a stance to the God-consciousness and thus of sin as a deed: What is sinful now is "the swift movement of a sensuous excitation towards its object without ranging itself with the higher self-consciousness" (*sich dem höheren Selbstbewußtsein zu stellen*) (^{2}§ 69,1. ET 1928, 279). Before, it was "the progression of a sensuous excitation towards its object without unifying with the higher consciousness" (^{1}§ 90,1. I, 270). The new element of a practical option is elaborated in the way in which the relationship between the divine and the human parts in sin (^{1}§ 103; ^{2}§ 81) is explained, and in the closer examination of the factors whose interaction ends in the victory or the defeat of the God-consciousness: of "will" and "understanding" (*Verstand*) (^{1}§ 88). The second version formulates this point less from the perspective of the practical and theoretical faculties than from the process of determination itself, of "willpower" and "insight" (^{2}§ 68). The stronger emphasis on the aspect of action is matched by starting more definitely with human freedom which now, as far as the framework permits, assumes a more significant role.

5.3.2 The content and the standing of human freedom

In both editions, the problem of how the human authorship of sin and divine all-causality can be related to each other is solved through the same distinction. God can only have been the cause of the fact of the sensible drive of nature (*Naturtrieb*) and of the conception (*Vorstellung*) of divine command (*Gebot*) inherent in the God-consciousness, but not of sin itself; it originates only through a "negating combination and unification (*verneinende Zusammenfassung und Ineinsbildung*) of these two elements in our consciousness" (¹§ 103. I, 336), thus, through the way in which the human person takes a stance to her situation determined by natural drive and divine command. There is a considerable difference between the first and the second version, however, in how the freedom involved in taking a position is conceived. In the original outline, it signifies "mainly the wavering (*das schwankende*) and choosing element in the development of our states" (¹§ 103,3. I, 336). It is the "ground" (*Grund*) of sin insofar as "the wavering and choosing element in general has to be posited first, in order for it to exist in a link to the not yet vigorous God-consciousness". Yet also in the first edition, the choice, even if it is wavering, is understood as a kind of self-determination; at least it is not blamed on exterior factors. It is implied in the concept of "freedom of the will" and of the "essence of conscious life itself that … an exterior effect (*Einwirkung*) determines in and of itself also the counter-effect, but that every stirring is first received in the innermost centre of life and the counter-effect arises from this centre". This is why sin can be imputed to the individual: "as certainly as it is founded on the freedom of the human being, as certainly (is sin) his deed" (¹§ 103,3. I, 337).

The reference to a capability of choice given in the "innermost centre of life" is decisive for the question whether sin is avoidable. The first edition suggests but does not elaborate on this presupposition. A location where this could have happened is when the attitudes of the will and of the intellect or understanding (*Verstand*) are treated; but here, the discrepancy between them is interpreted in a clearly naturalistic direction: "The lagging of the will behind understanding occurs mainly in the living together of youths with adults", the reverse "in the living together of uneducated with educated people" (¹§ 88,1. I, 267–68). The pious consciousness is affected by their mismatch mainly in a passive way. Through this "inequality, it is also dimmed and made impure (*getrübt und verunreinigt*) in itself". With a self-consciousness into which the pious feeling is "implanted", it should normally "transfer into the will just as easily as into understanding", but there is a "disparity" in their realisation (¹§ 88,2. I, 268). In the second version, however, Schleiermacher explicates sin no longer just as indecisive and misdirected choosing, but as a practical resistance against the priority of the God-consciousness that has been recognised as posing a demand. He explains the process of self-determination going wrong by recourse to the "immediate self-consciousness" which in its relationship "to the other two factors (intellect and will) … serves as the measure of the disparity in their development" (^{2}§ 68,1. ET 1928, 275). The fundamental recognition of the intellect that the higher self-consciousness is always to be prioritised to the lower must become an actual "insight", by "the individual's appropriating it". This requires an "act of self-consciousness in which the said discernment, as giving approval and recognition, becomes a command". For the concrete realisation of the relation to God, however, a particular impulse is necessary, that attempts to put the higher consciousness in force against the "flesh that has habit on its side" (^{2}§ 68,1. ET 1928, 276). Precisely the fact that each time, a special effort of the will is needed, is judged by Schleiermacher to constitute a "derangement of nature" (*Störung*) (^{2}§ 68 LS. ET 1928, 275) since it contradicts the steadiness of the God-consciousness that had earlier been declared as possible.

Thus, the second analysis of the consciousness of sin unfolds the steps that mediate between the recognition and the realisation of the God-consciousness. Has its description of the – successful or failing – relationship of the human person to God left the level of nature behind and reached the level of freedom? What counts against such an assessment is that the terminology of sin as consisting in an "unequal development of insight and willpower" (^{2}§ 68 LS. ET 1928, 275) and its explanation as a merely temporal discrepancy are maintained: "Now the fact that this excitation of the self-consciousness follows upon the discontentment more rapidly than it is able to determine our volitions, constitutes just that inequality along with which sin and the consciousness of sin are given" (^{2}§ 68,1. ET 1928, 275–276). In view of the far greater subtlety shown in tracing the elements and stages of the decision-making process this constitutes a disappointing return to a naturalising account.

At the same time, new weight is given to the "corporate life" in the habitualisation of sinfulness. This corresponds to the subject theoretical deepening of the doctrine. Original sin is essentially understood as a structural factor, resulting from and being further entrenched by human historical interactions that constitute "real sin": "the strength of the resistance made by the flesh and manifested in the consciousness of sin, is due to the advantage gained by the flesh during the prior time, though again, of course, in association with the corporate life upon which the amount of that advantage depends" (^{2}§ 67,2. ET 1928, 274). Redemption will therefore also be directed to a greater degree towards the corporate life. But ultimately, also in the corrected version it is only the "flesh" that resists. The spirit may be weak, but it is willing. It is due to its constitutive disadvantage, based on the factual course of the development of humanity, that it is always late in relation to the power of the flesh, firmly established antecedently. The question remains if an understanding of sin as a discrepancy belonging to the "necessary conditions of the stage of existence ... on which humanity is located" (²§ 81,4. cf. ET 1928, 162) is compatible with defining sin as a "free deed", as Schleiermacher wishes to.

5.3.3 Objections to a naturalising concept of sin

The factual inevitability of sin – besides the objection against an only gradual contrasting of evil and good – is one of the key critiques that have been advanced in the history of reception against the way in which both editions of the *Glaubenslehre* reshape the doctrine of sin. Erich Schrofner has summarised this point concisely:

> Sin as a derangement of development is a mere negation and is at the same level as limitations that arise from human finitude. Only because it – unlike finitude – represents a disturbance (*Störung*) of nature or an impairment of the even development of the spiritual functions of the human person and thus something that should not be, does it receive the negative qualification of sin and guilt.[288]

Schrofner notes the "impression of a certain naturalism of this theory of sin" which is due to

> the explanation of the material element of sin (as) ... an uneven development of the spiritual functions. ... Only subsequently (*nachträglich*) is this disturbance of nature related back to the responsible deed of the individual and identified as guilt. ... This general sinfulness of the human person formally becomes sin merely on account of the God-consciousness, which is never completely missing, and of the conscience linked to it which registers the deficient state as something that should not be. ... Human freedom in the sense of responsible agency or behaviour plays almost no role.[289]

Richard R. Niebuhr recognises the "inner sense of disproportion between the spirit and the flesh" as the "focus" of Schleiermacher's conception of sin, leaving out the "assertive, catastrophic moments of the will's rebellion".[290] He notes the discrepancy to previous biblical and theological views:

> While Schleiermacher does call sin a "turning away from God", the metaphor of rebellion or disobedience is not significantly present, and its absence is undoubtedly coupled with the

---

[288] E. Schrofner, *Theologie als positive Wissenschaft. Prinzipien und Methoden der Dogmatik bei Schleiermacher* (Frankfurt: P. Lang, 1980), 200.
[289] Schrofner, *Theologie*, 165–166.
[290] R. R. Niebuhr, *Schleiermacher on Christ and Religion*, 201.

unimportance of the role that divine law plays in his theology (cf. Gl. § 68,3) and with the omission, from his view of the divine economy of creation and redemption, of any serious consideration of Israel and its Scriptures.[291]

Thus, the "reader necessarily misses the characterizations of sin as disobedience of God and as infidelity", and the emphasis on "confusion and conflict" constitutes an "obvious impoverishment of the theology and piety Schleiermacher received from his spiritual precursors".[292] Nevertheless, Niebuhr rejects the critique that he has "reduced sin to proportions consonant with an evolutionary naturalism or monism".[293]

From his comparison with Kierkegaard's concept of sin Hermann Fischer comes to the judgement:

> There is no way around stating that Schleiermacher has re-interpreted sin as a necessary element of natural human development. It denotes the not yet fully developed power of the God-consciousness ... a negation ... not a fully responsible antagonism to God of the human person who knows about himself through revelation.[294]

Dietz Lange arrives at a similar result: By "ordering sin into the scheme of the idea of development, its character both as fate (*Verhängnis*) and as responsibility are mediated at a higher level and thus ultimately sublated". This is why, also Lange concludes, "the criticism is correct that he has ultimately robbed sin of its seriousness in favour of the unity of the concept of God".[295]

Reconstructing sin from the perspective of the doctrine of God throws up a further question regarding the implications this interpretation of sin has for the relationship between the anthropology in the first, abstracted part of the dogmatics and its Christian modification in the second. Fischer regards the two perspectives under which sin appears as a duality that is incompatible with the *principium cognoscendi* of the dogmatics, religious self-consciousness in its Christian determination:

> The argument proceeds on two levels, on the level of the feeling of absolute dependence which states God's absolute causality, and on the level of the pious self-consciousness

---

[291] R. R. Niebuhr, *Schleiermacher on Christ and Religion*, 201, n. 34.
[292] R. R. Niebuhr, *Schleiermacher on Christ and Religion*, 201.
[293] R. R. Niebuhr, *Schleiermacher on Christ and Religion*, 201, n. 36, with reference to his subsequent discussion of the concept of Christ as the Second Adam, 214 ff., against its critique as an apriori ideal.
[294] H. Fischer, *Subjektivität und Sünde. Kierkegaards Begriff der Sünde mit ständiger Rücksicht auf Schleiermachers Lehre von der Sünde* (Itzehoe: Verlag "Die Spur", 1963), 116.
[295] Lange, *Historischer Jesus*, 142.

that is determined by the antagonism which cannot transpose the immediately felt antagonism of sin and grace to God. This means: the pious self-consciousness states a contradictory state of the matter. Schleiermacher balances this contradiction by taking recourse to divine thinking, against his principled premise only to argue from the pious self-consciousness. He thus retreats to an argumentation *sub specie dei* and comes to propositions which, strictly speaking, sublate (*aufheben*) at a higher level the propositions of the consciousness that is marked by the antagonism.[296]

Thus, Fischer finds fault not only with the content of the doctrine of sin, that "sin has transformed itself, so to speak, into a speculative concept of development", but also with the method of arriving at this solution. He sees the epistemological principle of the material dogmatics affected as well when the "antagonism of sin and grace experienced in the pious self-consciousness ... is robbed of its depth and seriousness".[297] Dietz Lange evaluates the same move differently: Schleiermacher "here transgressed the limits of human thinking which Kant had drawn irrevocably not by contradicting the demand to start from the religious self-consciousness, but in order to fulfil it, for the sake of the centrality of the consciousness of redemption".[298] For Lange, taking one's starting point in the (Christian) religious consciousness means that all elements necessary to express the experience of redemption are to be accessed, including the perspective of God.

The question raised by Fischer and Lange, on whether Schleiermacher can reach such statements about God from the Christian modification of the self-consciousness as the principle of knowing, points to a symptomatic problem, in my view. Schleiermacher's solution to reconcile the antagonism felt immediately in the Christian self-consciousness by transposing it to the higher level of the eternal divine decree is a key example for how the general level dominates the particular. What is implied in the general consciousness wins out over the second moment, the Christian modification. Precisely those specific descriptions which express the opposition that is constitutive for Christian piety are taken back and are turned into temporal modifications within the divine decree. What risks being left behind is the definition of sin as a deed of freedom, despite the correction in the understanding of human embodiment and a greater emphasis on agency and reflection in response to the critiques of the first edition. It will be a matter for Chapters 6 and 7 to examine the consequences for the significance of the person of Jesus, and for the difference between God's creative and God's salvific action.

---

296 Fischer, *Subjektivität*, 80.
297 Fischer, *Subjektivität*, 81.
298 Lange, *Historischer Jesus*, 143.

But how would Schleiermacher have had to define sin in order to avoid the reduction of its character as deed to an inevitable problem of natural human development? The basic symptom of the difficulties which his doctrine of sin runs into seems to me to be that it posits the conflict between spirit and flesh, and not in the spirit itself. This objection was already put forward by Bretschneider against the first version of the doctrine of sin: "Experience teaches that it is not sensibility that has differences but the spiritual principle in the human person. The reason therefore, why the God-consciousness does not fill all of life's moments unconditionally, surely has to be sought much more in the uneven development and activity of reason, than in sensible nature".[299] Only then would the antagonism be "positive", that is, not only a weakness of willpower against the stubbornness of sensibility, but a choice of one's own, a clear decision, affirmed as a matter of defiance in its misdirection.[300] The differences between Schleiermacher and Kierkegaard that Fischer lists in his comparison of their doctrines of sin are founded on their divergent understandings of freedom. Kierkegaard distinguishes the moment of unconditional freedom from existing freedom, tied to finite mediations. He can therefore grasp sin as a position, as a relationship of the human person to herself, that is, to the synthesis as which she exists. Only in this conception is sin a deed that can be committed or avoided. Yet this possibility is no longer open to Schleiermacher in the framework he has established. His approach does not allow for identifying it as a "sickness in the spirit itself", as the desperate 'willing to be oneself' or 'not willing to be oneself' of "a freedom anxious in the awareness of its contingency and asserting itself in the sphere of the finite".[301] Despite the revisions that recognise the role of freedom more than the first edition does, especially in the gap between intention and realisation, also

---

[299] Bretschneider, "Ueber den Begriff der Erlösung, und die damit zusammenhängenden Vorstellungen von Sünde und Erbsünde in der christlichen Glaubenslehre des Herrn Prof. Dr. Schleiermacher", in *Journal für Prediger* 67 (1825) 1–33, 21.

[300] In *Subjektivität*, 115, Fischer characterises Kierkegaard's model as follows: "This process does not have the shape of a gradually rising line, but that of a broken line. Faith is defiance broken (*zerbrochener Trotz*)." It presupposes an analysis of contingency that leads to despair, and does not already contain a "Whence" of existence, thus resulting either in self-assertion or self-negation which become sin if upheld also against the possibility of the self to be "grounded transparently in the power that posited it". Kierkegaard, *The Sickness unto Death*, trans. with an introduction and notes by A. Hannay (London: Penguin, 1989), 44 (trans. amended). The crucial correction of Schleiermacher's position offered by Kierkegaard in this book is that sin is an attitude of the spirit.

[301] Cf. Pröpper, "Bestimmung", in *Evangelium und freie Vernunft*, 151. On Schleiermacher's understanding of freedom and its effect on his proposal of a philosophical ethics, cf. 148–150, nn. 44. 46. For the explication of a "more radical conception of freedom", cf. 148–152.

the final elaboration of the *Glaubenslehre* still fails to commit to a more radical concept of freedom.[302]

5.4 Consequences of the revised subject theoretical foundations for the approach to Christology

The new statements of the second outline of the doctrine of sin, finely attuned to the revised settings of the framework, engender changes also in Christology as the positive part of the doctrine of redemption. Even if they can only be discussed in detail in the following chapter, it makes sense to indicate the two major new accentuations here, in connection with the model of anthropology to which they are related. One consists in a new emphasis on the historical mediatedness of the Christian experience of redemption (5.4.1), the other in reorienting Christology towards the title of the "Second Adam" (5.4.2).

5.4.1 Can a sinless existence be constructed a priori?

The two different explanations of sin, first attributed to nature as a gap between spirit and flesh, then to historical agency as a recurrent defeat of the God-consciousness, can be expected to result in changes in the approach to redemption. After the Introduction, these revisions appear for the first time when the task arises to show sin to be an avoidable disturbance of the true nature of the human person by indicating the possibility of a sinless development (^{1}§ 89; ^{2}§ 68). Already the first edition's doctrine of sin states the conceptual possibility: We cannot "deny (*abläugnen*) in and of itself the possibility of a completely even

---

302 It can be evaluated as a symptom of this disregard that he downplays the freedom that gives rise to *iustitia civilis*. Gunther Wenz examines Schleiermacher's view of it as an "ambivalent" human property: On the one hand, "even the sharpest highlighting of the human incapability of the good could not avoid the admission 'that there is an opposition (*Gegensaz*) of what can be praised and what can be reprimanded *(des löblichen und tadelnswürdige*n) which does not at all depend on the relationship of the human being to redemption' (§ 70,3)." On the other hand, " according to Schleiermacher's judgement, the *iustitia civilis*, insofar as it emancipates itself from the context of redemption, is a thoroughly ambivalent feature, as becomes evident in one remark among others: 'This is why even what is best in this realm, insofar as it exists independently of the power of the God-consciousness, can only be subsumed under the attitude, wisdom and justice of the flesh (*zur fleischlichen Gesinnung, Weisheit und Gerechtigkeit*). G. Wenz, "Sünde und Schuldbewusstsein. Zur Hamartiologie in Schleiermachers Glaubenslehre", in *Kerygma und Dogma* 63 (2017) 309–337, 325.

development which therefore would also be sinless" (¹§ 89,2. I, 269). Being able to conceive of it in principle is even turned into a presupposition for redemption: "The possibility of a redemption depends on the assumption ... and on the possibility of a completely pure appearance of the consciousness of God in the human soul; and we can become aware of sin as such only in relation to redemption so that the one can only have truth for us together with the other" (¹§ 89,2. I, 269).

The second explication of this crucial junction makes it clear that the "relation to redemption" means a fact of history. Instead of naming the hypotheses which must be presupposed to make redemption thinkable, it refers to the experience – termed *Gewißheit*, translated as "assured belief" and "certainty" in 1928 and as "surety" in 2016 – to which these insights are owed:

> In order to affirm, however, that it is possible to obviate entirely the active resistance of the flesh, we require to have an assured belief (*Gewißheit*) in a development of power of the God-consciousness that has proceeded continuously from its earliest manifestation (*Hervortreten*) to a state of absolute strength, i.e., a condition of human perfection evolved without sin. This certainty (*Gewißheit*) is therefore at once the basis of the full consciousness of sin as a derangement of our nature, and of faith in the possibility of redemption by the communication of the spiritual power so attested (²§ 68,3. ET 1928, 278).[303]

It was necessary, therefore, to have the evidence of a perfect sinlessness in the lived testimony of a human person to be able to form a conception of it subsequently; then, the habitualised sinful state could first be recognised as a disruption of true human nature and as something that can be defeated. This self-recognition arising in view of the existence of Jesus could not have been brought about by a self-legislation made obligatory against sinfulness:

> It is of course true that the consciousness of sin comes from the law, but as the law in the very multitude of its precepts is but an imperfect representation of the good, and even in the unity of an all-embracing maxim does not show how it can be obeyed, the knowledge of sin that arises out of it is ever in some respects incomplete and in some uncertain; and it is only from the absolute sinlessness and the perfect spiritual power of the Redeemer that we

---

[303] The new ET of ²§ 68,3 uses "authenticate" instead of "attested" for "*bewährten*" in relation to "*geistigen Kraft*", and it adds "process of" to "redemption" (*Erlösung*): "In contrast, what would belong to positing the possibility of a total capacity to avoid the actual resistance offered by the flesh is this: surety regarding a constantly advancing dominion of God-consciousness, from its very first emergence up to its reaching an absolute strength – that is, a sinlessly developed human perfection. Two characteristics would thus be equally rooted in this surety: full consciousness of sin, viewed as a distortion of nature, and faith in the possibility of a process of redemption through communication of spiritual force, a process of redemption that would be authenticated by this communication" (ET 2016, 412–413).

gain the full knowledge of sin. And our belief that sin is a derangement of human nature rests solely upon the possibility that, on the assumption of the original perfection described above, the God-consciousness could have developed progressively from the first man to the purity and holiness which it manifests in the Redeemer (²§ 68,3. ET 1928, 279).

The second edition states unequivocally that the real appearance of a sinless redeemer could not be projected by humans, but only given by God. It declares with equal clarity the anthropological relevance of the historical appearance of Jesus: the fulfilment of anthropology in Christology, the possibility of judging sin retrospectively as imperfection. This is the view from the perspective of the one divine decree in which creation and redemption are joined. The bridging element between anthropology and Christology that secures the continuity and excludes the necessity of a completely new creation, is now named: complementing the "initial divine activity which is supernatural" is "a vital human receptivity in virtue of which alone that supernatural can become a natural fact of history. This is the link that connects the corporate life before the appearance of the Redeemer with that which exists in the fellowship with the Redeemer, so as adequately to bring out the identity of human nature in both" (²§ 89,4. ET 1928, 365).[304] Thus, viewed from the whole sequence of events, "in this whole context, the appearance of the Redeemer in the midst of this natural development is no longer a supernatural emergence of a new stage of development, but simply one conditioned by that which precedes – though certainly its connexion with the former is to be found only in the unity of the divine thought" (²§ 89,4. ET 1928, 365).

On the one hand, the second version emphasises the historical character of the Redeemer; on the other, it allows a thought that becomes available only at the highest level of theological conclusion to be the doctrinal expression of the experience of the Christian self-consciousness: the concept of divine ordination or "the unity of the divine thought" which itself is not given in this experience but extrapolated. By elaborating a further conclusion, the direction of the Christology of the second edition is changed: the idea of a singular summit reached in Jesus Christ is now embedded in a continuity from creation that was always intended in the one divine decree.

---

304 At the same time, the second edition is careful not to allow the "vital receptivity" of human nature to develop into self-activity. It eliminates the earlier distinction between receptive human nature as cause and self-active appearance as effect: "Both for the mission of the Redeemer ... and for the linking of the individual into a life fellowship with Him on the one hand only the divine activity is to be posited, in which human nature behaves only as receptive; the result, however, or the side that appears of this divine activity is the highest human self-activity through which a new active element of life arises in human nature and in the individuals" (¹§ 109,4. II, 10).

5.4.2 The completion of the creation of human nature and Jesus as "Second Adam"

What was already expressed in the first edition, is now expounded as the new basic conception: the "appearance of Christ ... would have to be regarded as the completion, only now accomplished, of the creation of human nature" (²§ 89 LS. ET 1928, 365–366); in view of the "effect as a whole" of the divine decree, Christ's appearance as "the beginner and originator of this more perfect human life" is to be encompassed more adequately under the title of "Second Adam" (²§ 89,1. ET 1928, 367).

The right to throw a bright light from the appearance of Christ on sin as a merely intermediate stage is derived from taking into consideration the divine decree. The reticence of the first edition to argue from it is dropped in the second. The original version had marked the interpretation of redemption as "completion of creation" as one of the "elucidating propositions of combination" which "only have their value in the doctrinal edifice (*Lehrgebäude*) and for it, and that can thus never be transferred to any other realm of religious communication" (¹§ 110,1. II, 11). It was a matter of fact for it that the new doctrinal formula "could never be presented as an analysis of the immediate self-consciousness" (¹§ 110,2. II, 12), since it was only to express the "link between the thought that evil cannot be thought in God and thus also nothing can have been ordered for its sake, with the thought that due to the native (*eignen*) inability of the human person the misery (*Unseligkeit*) of sin could only be taken from him by divine contribution (*Zuthun*)" (¹§ 110,1. II, 11). For the final version, however, the new title of Second Adam for the salvific work in its completeness is "when considered more closely ... a more precise and direct expression (*ein ebenso richtiger und unmittelbarer Ausdruck*) of our Christian self-consciousness" (²§ 89,2. ET 1928, 367). Not as a combination of two propositions in need of mediation, but as a genuine feeling, it experiences in its fellowship with Christ the consciousness of sin no longer as a "need of redemption", but as "simply an incapacity for what has only just come to be" (²§ 89,2. ET 1928, 368).[305] This change will be elaborated further in the new emphasis on the receptive activity of the converted in the revised Christol-

---

[305] According to the second edition, the theological statement of the completion of creation can point to being founded on the experience of the Christian self-consciousness. In *Die Entwicklung der Lehre von der Person Christi im 19. Jahrhundert* (Tübingen: J.C.B. Mohr, 1911), 50, Ernst Günther makes this point relevant against Baur's objection of a "double Christ" in the *Glaubenslehre*. The "basis of the postulate (of the union of the archetypal and the historical) is precisely not another idea, but the reality of the new corporate life that can be experienced; thus one can speak of speculative elements, but not of a speculative basic tendency."

5.5 Taking stock of the doctrines of human perfection and sinfulness

Although Schleiermacher strives to accentuate the "completion of the creation of human nature" as a *new* phase, presupposing a prior stage of captivity in sin, the key terms of the second version capture sin retrospectively less as a "derangement" (ET 1928) or as a "distortion" (ET 2016) than as a weakness of the God-consciousness. On the one hand, it insists against the first edition on the necessity of a *historical* new beginning for the God-consciousness to be actually implemented in the process of human development. Yet, on the other, despite this emphasis, the new evaluation of redemption as "completion of creation" fixes the content of Christology all the more definitely to being the realisation of the originally implanted essence of the human person.

It is true that the revised *Glaubenslehre* has saved the unity of the concept of God in view of the fact of sin and of redemption and has avoided the "arbitrariness" it feared. Not God's special act of election constituted the beginning of salvation history, but God's decision for a two-part foundation of creation and redemption which, once begun, unfolds with necessity. Yet this overall framework limits what Christology can outline as its content. It is bound merely to unfold that the human person of Jesus was necessary for the foundation of the second phase, salvation, and that also after it has begun, he is still required for its present and future. He matters as the archetype of the realised unity of God- and self-consciousness. It needs to be examined whether the critique expressed by Armin Sierscyn is accurate: Christ

> cannot interest as a person but only as that point of the whole ethical process through whom the natural event of the new creation realises itself in an archetypal and epoch-making way; in this, this new creation does not appear as the result of his own deed and his own, personal work, but as the result of the causality working through him, that is, as a "deed of nature".[306]

Viewed from the doctrine of God, it is a matter of the "preservation" of the "original perfection" of human nature (¹§ 110,1. II, 11–12; cf. ²§ 89,1 and 2. ET 1928, 366–369).

---

[306] A. Sierscyn, *Das Sünde- und Schuldproblem im dogmatischen Denken Schleiermachers*, Diss. theol. Erlangen-Nürnberg 1973, 159.

5.5 Taking stock of the doctrines of human perfection and sinfulness

One can already assume that the second edition's Christology will also emphasise the aspect of freedom and will explicate what Sierscyn characterises as merely a "deed of nature" in this respect. Both the concrete configuration of the God-consciousness by Jesus, and the willingness of the faithful to be receptive to it will be explicated in terms of freedom. While "receptivity" has now expressly acquired a lynchpin function between anthropology and Christology, the second edition also tries to play it down: it "is, strictly, not a co-operation at all, but a yielding of the self to the operation of grace" (²§ 70,2. ET 1928, 284). Yet it is to be doubted whether this attenuation helps if, to use Baur's formulation, "the exterior facts of the redemption achieved by Christ cannot communicate anything that has not been originally founded in the nature of the human person, thus, that could only be awakened and be brought to effective expression through them".[307] As we have seen in Chapter 3, Kantzenbach points out, on the one hand, the distance of Schleiermacher's explanation of the supernatural becoming natural to the Christological dogma: His

> justification contains characteristic deviations from the Christological dogma of the church insofar as the temporal event (*Eintreten*) of an eternal act of the implantation of the divine (already this conception is completely remote from the dogma of Christ: the Word became flesh) is supposed to be based on the highest development of a spiritual power of human nature, of which neither the New Testament nor ecclesial dogma have any knowledge.

On the other hand, he had conceded that "despite these objections, the legitimacy (*Recht*) of Schleiermacher's thesis cannot be put in doubt that... 'as surely as Christ was human, there has to be the possibility in human nature to receive into itself the divine just as it was in Christ'".[308] Having "taken Jesus Christ's real humanity as his starting point", it will be decisive how this very broad justification will be explicated: as a natural endowment brought to perfection in Jesus, or as a decision of his freedom to realise his God-consciousness fully by putting all his trust in God's love and loyalty.

---

[307] Baur, *Kirchengeschichte des 19. Jahrhunderts*, 204.
[308] Kantzenbach, *Programme der Theologie*, 29.

6 A Christology from Two Perspectives: the Consciousness of Redemption, and the Single Divine Decree

From the key changes analysed so far in the theological anthropology, it has become clear that the defining term for the essence of Christianity, "redemption", has undergone a considerable transformation. The material dogmatics was to present the Christian doctrinal propositions "in their connection".[309] Through the framework of the general doctrine of God and the Christian doctrine of sin as the precursor of the experience of grace, redemption has come to be seen in a new, enlarged perspective: it is only the "beginning" of a whole process of the "imparting of blessedness" (^{2}§ 89,1. ET 1928, 366). What appeared as the "redemption" of the human person from its effect on the Christian self-consciousness, turned out to be the completion of God's creation viewed from the intention of God's action. What needs to be examined now is how the basic outline of Christology develops between the first and the second version. This enquiry will be guided by the following questions: Firstly, through which categories and against which anticipated objections does the original approach seek to articulate the unique significance of Jesus, which was already stated in the essence definition and in the doctrine of sin (6.1)? And secondly, since it was precisely the first realisation of the Christology that could not disprove the suspicion Baur had developed in view of the Introduction, that Schleiermacher's Christ only represented the personified idea of redemption, how is this basic conception revised and justified? One can expect that the new accentuations and corrections made so far will find their most focused formulation here: in the elucidation of the activity of the historical person of Jesus and of his position in God's overall plan marked by an original human perfection which already included an actualised God-consciousness (6.2). Thirdly, how is the final, comprehensively elaborated presentation to be assessed based on Schleiermacher's own criterium, that it must express the unsurpassable and ongoing significance of Jesus Christ? How should the new emphasis on him as the Second Adam, which now reveals itself as the guiding conception of the whole work, be judged in comparison with the first, that of Redeemer? Can it safeguard the essential connectedness of the Christian self-consciousness to him, and his enduring function for the community development arising through him? Examples from the history

---

309 Cf. for example, Fischer, *Subjektivität*, 114, on how coherence implies the need to fit together, balance and attune the different propositions to each other.

of reception and critique of the *Glaubenslehre* will illustrate how this fraught question has been evaluated (6.3). In conclusion, the guiding perspectives for the examination of the doctrine of God as the key to the work will be identified (6.4).

6.1 The basic outline of Christology

The task of Christology is to explicate with regard to the person of the Redeemer the source of the basic Christian experience of redemption, mediated in a new corporate life that is opposed to sin. The sufficient reason for this salvific effect for humankind is found in the unity which Jesus of Nazareth realised between what Schleiermacher terms the "archetypal" and the "historical". "Person" and "work", "dignity" and "activity" of Christ "completely match each other and each is the measure for the other" (^{1}§ 113,1. II, 18). The "spiritual outcome" must have its source in the specificity of the Redeemer; otherwise it would be more accurate to assume "redeeming eras and events than a Redeemer in the proper sense, and see the cause in favourable circumstances owed to chance" (^{1}§ 113,1. II, 17). For the historical fact of the foundation of a new corporate life it is necessary to assume a dignity commensurate with this work. The form of the lead proposition, an inference from effect to cause, is to show the connection to the *principium cognoscendi* of dogmatics, the Christian pious self-consciousness. It states: "Since the promotion (*Förderung*) of the higher life is traced back to the Redeemer in the consciousness of the Christian, this refers to the historical and the archetypal as inseparably united in his person" (^{1}§ 114 LS; II, 19). The justification of this core thesis of Schleiermacher's Christology in which he anticipates some of the subsequent objections will be followed up in detail in subsection 6.1.2; first, however, his trenchant critique of the categories inherited from the early Christian theological disputes and Council decisions, "nature" and "person", has to be analysed for its reasons (6.1.1).

6.1.1 The inconsistencies of the two-natures terminology in Christology

The new concept of "archetype" (*Urbild*) is to replace doctrinal expressions that have become "untenable" (^{1}§ 117,2. II, 36). This is due to three factors: firstly, to changes of meaning in key concepts in the intellectual frameworks subsequent to antiquity and scholasticism, secondly to inconsistencies between them already in the patristic age, and finally to the pastoral need for meaningful expressions of the consciousness of the faithful in relation to the Redeemer.[310] He demonstrates in what ways the traditional concepts have failed to convey the core conviction of the Christian faith in a terminologically defensible way. The conclusion becomes inescapable that the space which the old formulas held with their mainly negative delineations of how the dual constitution of Jesus Christ is to be thought needs to be filled with a description that is accurate and relevant for believers. The short formula Schleiermacher offers is "that God was in Christ and that he wants to be in us through him" (¹§ 117 Postscript. II, 38). Thus,

> the correct designation for the interrelation (*Ineinander*) of the divine and the human in the Redeemer is still to be found. ... a new attempt to elaborate this doctrine is by leaving out both expressions, the divine nature in itself as well as the duality of natures in One Person; this task is all the more urgent as the definitions of the older confessional writings have for quite some time become a completely dead letter (¹§ 117,2. II, 36).

The key conceptual problem for Schleiermacher is that two terms which belong to entirely separate realms, "God", and "nature", are used as if they could be combined. Christ's "divine nature" seems to be at the same level as his (semantically unproblematic) "human nature". The first edition begins its critical exercise of identifying the causes of confusion in ¹§ 117,1 with the point that subsuming both under the term "nature" as if it could equally extend to the divine evokes the impression that both are "completely the same".[311] This, secondly, makes the question of their relationship in the Redeemer look as if it was "a mat-

---

310 The "task" laid out in ¹§ 117,2. II, 37 is "to organise a scholarly expression in which the essence of the Christian faith in the Redeemer is not only mirrored in negative formulas; at the same time, it has to be reconnected to what can be used in religious communications to Christian congregations." Jacqueline Mariña summarises that he "preserves the upshot of the insights of Chalcedon while at the same time rejecting the language in which those insights were framed" (Mariña, "Christology and anthropology", in Mariña (ed.), *The Cambridge Companion to Friedrich Schleiermacher*, 153.
311 The second edition starts its analysis of the problems with a point not mentioned in the first: the equivocation regarding the subject of agency, arising from using the name "Jesus Christ" both for "the subject of union (*Vereinigung*) of the natures ..., but also the divine nature of the Redeemer from all eternity before its union with the human nature, so that this union no longer appears as an element that goes to constitute (*mit konstituierendes Moment*) the person, Jesus Christ, but rather as an act of this person Himself" (²§ 96,1. ET 1928, 391–392). The interpretation that "Jesus Christ" refers to the divine eternal Son before the incarnation is rejected, based on the New Testament's use of the term "Son of God" for the Redeemer as the subject of the union. For an analysis of the systematic treatment of this point in the second edition, cf. Menke, *Jesus ist Gott der Sohn*, 341–343, and Benjamin Dahlke, "Die Christologie in Schleiermachers Glaubenslehre", in *Catholica* 70 (2016) 278–299, 292–294.

ter of chance" (*zufällig*), instead of the human nature "always being subordinated to the divine". More specifically, thirdly, the concept of "nature" is unsuited for serving as a unifying term under which the divine and the human can be subsumed equally because its already existing meaning in the human realm relates to the manifold, internally divided, mutually interlinked totality of the finite (*Inbegriff alles endlichen Seins*) (II, 33); this for him is the very opposite of the simple and undivided totality of God as its absolute cause. The fourth reason for abandoning the traditional concepts is the inconsistent use of "person" and "nature" in the Christological and the Trinitarian doctrines, one speaking of "two natures in one person", the other of "three persons in one essence". To make their treatment consistent with that of the second person of the Trinity would require that each person of the Trinity, too, be attributed an individual nature (II, 34, n. 1 on Reinhard's *Dogmatik*). This would inscribe a term specific for finite beings into the divine essence.[312] A fifth point is the difficulty of visualising (*Anschauung*) (II, 34) and "appropriating" (II, 35) the unity of one person in two natures, a definition which has therefore become a "dead formula". The history of Christological thinking shows how "unproductive" and misleading the attempts to resolve the tension have been, oscillating (*schwanken*) between prioritising the divine or the human, or mixing them into a third that would be "neither human nor divine" (II, 35). Based on these categories, understanding is torn between either expressing one or the other in an insufficient way, or undermining the unity of his person when two wills, minds or centres of action are assumed (II, 35–36). The incongruence of stretching what can only be attributed to the will or mind of God to a finite human being is especially clear; it is "equally unthinkable that a

---

312 In *Jesus ist Gott der Sohn*, 242–243, Menke summarises the discrepancy in the definition of "person" in Christology and in the doctrine of the Trinity as a dilemma in which "either the Christological formula of the *physis* of the *logos* is incorrect; or in the theology of the Trinity the formula of the one divine being in three persons (*mia ousia kai treis hypostaseis*) which are only distinguished relationally has to be replaced through the self-contradictory formula *mia ousia kai treis physeis*. ... With admirable analytic acuity Schleiermacher recognises the inconsistencies of the terminology left by the fathers of the Christological councils. To transpose the concept of nature to God would signify the finitude of God. Already the fathers distinguished between a general nature (*ousia*) and an individual nature (*physis*). But if ... under the premise of the *one* divine essence (*mia ousia*) the second divine person is also attributed an individual nature (*physis*), then the *infinite* God is composed of three *finite* natures (*treis physeis*) – an obvious self-contradiction! If, inversely, Father, Son and Spirit do not signify three finite natures but relations of the one divine essence, then the second divine person cannot be attributed a *physis* of its own."

divine mind thinks the same as a human mind, and that a human will can have the same volition as a divine will" (II, 36).[313]

Since these definitions have only opened up a space of "hair-splitting vacuity" (*spitzfindigen Leerheit*)" ([1]§ 117,3. II, 38), it is evident for Schleiermacher that a different way out of the aporetic of a two-natures Christology has to be found, one in which neither aspect gets short-changed.[314] What is needed is another model in which a Christology from below and one from above can be closely interrelated.[315] His attempt to dove-tail both in one consistent framework begins with the earthly Jesus whose sinlessness is unique but at the same constitutes a conceptual possibility of human nature. On the other hand, his existence cannot be explained from his human context. The element "from above" retains what is divine, without splitting the unity of his self-consciousness in two:

> Once the difference between the Redeemer and all other human beings is stated as having in him a pure being of God under the form of consciousness and conscious activity, instead of our impure and darkened (*verunreinigten und verdunkelten*) God-consciousness: then the divine in the Redeemer is the innermost fundamental power (*Grundkraft*) from which every activity proceeds, and which holds every element together; everything human is in every moment the receiving and representing organism of the former ([1]§ 117,3. II, 37; cf. [2]§ 96,3. ET 1928, 397).

To this definition of what the uniquely divine consists in, the second edition will add the origin of Jesus' "peculiar spiritual content". It is owed to a "creative divine act", as distinct from the "universal (*allgemeine*) source of spiritual life ... in

---

313 In "Christology and anthropology", 155, Mariña quotes the distinction in [2]§ 96,1. ET 1928, 395–396 and sums up the result: "The human will 'always strives for only separate ends and one of the sake of the other'; the object of the divine will, on the other hand, can be 'nothing but the whole world in the totality of its development'. The attributes of both are mutually exclusive."
314 The analysis of the problems of the terminology exposed by Schleiermacher for its lack of consistency and its incompatibility with a modern, subject-theoretical framework has been endorsed and further developed under the heading, the "aporetics of the two-natures doctrine" in 20th and 21st century systematic theologies, for example by Pannenberg, Pröpper, Essen, Schaefer, Menke, and Lerch. It is a symptom of the substance ontological thought form of antique and medieval philosophy and theology which had to be overcome towards an interpretation of Jesus Christ that included his self-understanding and a concept of God's self-revelation in history.
315 The discussion about how this dovetailing can be carried out successfully, avoiding the long-standing division into alternative emphases on the divine (Trinitarian) and human, continues, as the debate about approaches such as those of Pannenberg, Rahner, Kasper and Pröpper shows. Cf. the contributions in Georg Essen and Christian Danz (eds), *Dogmatische Christologie in der Moderne. Problemkonstellationen gegenwärtiger Forschung* (2019).

which, as an absolute maximum, the conception of man as the subject of the God-consciousness comes to completion" (²§ 93,3. ET 1928, 381). As R. R. Niebuhr summarises, the inherited terminology of a "divine nature conjoined to a human nature" is replaced by the "constant potency" of Jesus' God-consciousness[316] in his self-understanding, thoughts and acts. Moving from substance ontological categories to modern concepts of subjectivity and history, however, introduces challenges of a different kind to Christology.

6.1.2 The arguments for the unity of the archetypal and the historical in the person of Jesus

Having explained why the problematic term, "divine nature" in the first "theorem" or "point of doctrine" (*Lehrsaz*)[317] has been replaced with the designation of the historical founder of Christianity as "archetype" in ¹§ 114, a new set of objections emerges that has to be dealt with. A key problem arising across different starting points, from a Kantian to a Hegelian position, is the gap between an "idea" and its realisation.[318] For Kant's critical philosophy, the validating authority lies in reason, which can recognise in Jesus a life of moral goodness from its own premises. As an individual, he illustrates this idea, but its validity does not depend on him. In Hegel's idealist system, no historical individual can be the exhaustive accomplishment of an idea which requires evermore renewed instantiations. If Schleiermacher's use of "archetype" is seen to be more Platonic than Kantian, the element of empowerment which is crucial for the function he stresses in Jesus, the imparting of the strength of his God-consciousness, may be captured more adequately.[319]

---

316 Richard R. Niebuhr, *Schleiermacher on Christ and Religion*, 225.
317 Cf. the translations for "Lehrsatz" in ET 1928, 391 and ET 2016, II, 595.
318 Menke, *Jesus ist Gott der Sohn*, 336: For Kant, "Jesus' significance consists in being merely a mediator of the idea of the perfect human being, ... the greatest possible visual concretisation (*höchstmögliche Veranschaulichung*) of the 'idea of the Son of God'. It was not only said of Jesus that the realisation of the 'idea of a human being morally pleasing to God' (*Gott wohlgefälligen Menschen*) is the destination of all human beings. This truth lies in the reason of humans itself. For Lessing as for Kant or Fichte something finite and contingent can never become the principle of something necessary, unconditional and general (*Allgemeinen*). The specific person of 'Jesus' therefore cannot have a constitutive but only an illustrative and stimulating significance."
319 Menke, *Jesus ist Gott der Sohn*, 340, n. 723: "With the term 'archetype' borrowed from Platonic philosophy, Schleiermacher wants to explain that the Redeemer is not a mere example but that he *enables* the faithful to be representations (*Abbildung*) of the archetype."

But the modern problem of the different standings of "idea" and "history" is an additional factor in Schleiermacher's intellectual setting.

The first point he tackles is close to F. C. Baur's later critique: that the redemptive effect could also be explained without the existence of an archetypal person from its mere "representation", that is, as an imagined ideal or mental construct:

> If one said it was not necessary that such a person ever existed in reality, but that the representation was sufficient – even if also this point is mere fiction because it could not be explained from whence such a representation could have come: the development of such a corporate life as the Christian church provides, being obviously (*offenbar*) older than the existing representations, would remain a complete mystery. The concept of a Redeemer would then also be completely void, since the representation as archetypal would itself be the product of the corporate life that originated, we know not how, independently of such a person (^{1}§ 114,1. II, 20).

The counterarguments of the first edition against denying the archetypal standing of the historical person of Jesus are therefore that it would destroy the concept of a Redeemer in distinction from the church, and that it would leave the New Testament testimony unexplained as to its origins. The second anticipated objection argues from the "imperfect effect that the new corporate life of the Christian church represents" back to the conclusion of "a historical, but not an archetypal founder" (^{1}§ 114,1. II, 20).[320] The first edition rejects these arguments both with reference to the consciousness of Christians and with historical reasons. The origin of the church must have had a real historical foundation that is prior to all representations; and the original testimony of the archetypal nature of Christ would remain as unexplained as the fact that the church founded by him did not move beyond him.

But how can the two moments that have each been shown to be unrelinquishable be united, against the position that what has the status of an "idea"

---

320 This objection is still a core argument for David Friedrich Strauß. In Theodore Vial's summary of this part of his critique, "Strauß makes a logical objection to Schleiermacher's Christology. If one is making inferences from effect back to cause, from the relatively heightened but still imperfect God-consciousness found in the Christian communities back to the God-consciousness of Jesus, one is not allowed to infer a greater cause than is required for the effect. At most one could infer a relatively heightened God-consciousness in Jesus." Vial, *Schleiermacher. A Guide for the Perplexed*, 100. The key difference to Strauß and Baur is that Schleiermacher does not intend to prove the archetypical status of Jesus by means of historical investigation. He presupposes it as the core of the Christian self-consciousness the origin of which calls for an explanation. For him, the burden of proof lies with current researchers to account for the fact of this new movement.

can never be realised fully in an individual instance? Schleiermacher defends his thesis that the unity of both in a singular person is precisely what is "miraculous … in the person of the Redeemer" (^{1}§ 114,2. II, 20) against three other attempted explanations; he then unfolds in the following paragraph how the two interrelate. The first counter-position is a reduction of Jesus to his historical context; the second explains him as the projection of an ideal, and the third is a combination of both which assumes that the imperfect historical beginnings were purified in the passing of time. This explanation comes down to assuming that the corporate life was based "on a series of errors, or well-meaning dissimulations" (^{1}§ 114,2. II, 22). His argument against these alternative interpretations is that they contradict the claim as well as the content of Christianity. Its self-understanding is that it constitutes both an independent form of religion, and its highest realisation. Against Kant's use of the concept of archetype for a self-produced idea of practical reason that has only been transferred to Jesus, he invokes the power of sin; it binds both the will and the intellect and prevents them from being able to conceive self-actively of pure ideas.[321] Thus, both moments, the historical and the archetypal, have been shown to be equally necessary. They are implemented as follows: The "archetypal has to appear in the form of the historical, that is, the Redeemer must have a temporal development; but each historical moment must at the same time have borne within it the essence of the archetypal, that is, of the temporally unconditioned" (^{1}§ 115 LS. II, 23). If the concept of the archetypal is thus able to encompass also the development and the historical conditionedness of the person of Jesus, what is its content? Schleiermacher defines it as the steady, "unstruggling *(kampflos)*" superiority of his God-consciousness over his sensible self-consciousness. Insofar as his appearance represents the "reality of the purely sinless development which was conceived of as only possible before" (^{1}§ 115,2. II, 25), the creation of human nature has been completed in him, as also the first edition states. Since Jesus' sinlessness is understood as "pure activity of God", it is true of Jesus' God-consciousness that it represents a "true" or "veritable *(wahres)* being of God in Him", and that this being of God constitutes "His innermost self" (^{1}§ 116,3–4. II, 29–30).

---

321 Kant, *Religion within the Boundaries of Mere Reason, and Other* Writings, ed. Allen Wood and George di Giovanni, Introduction by Robert M. Adams (Cambridge: Cambridge University Press, 2010), 81–84 (Part Two, Section One, B. The objective reality of this idea).

6.2 The final outline of Christology

In his revisions, Schleiermacher seeks to emphasise especially the necessity of the historical appearance of the Redeemer, to counter F. C. Baur's misreading. The lead propositions which could indeed be misinterpreted as constructions are reformulated accordingly and ¹§§ 114 and 115 are forged together. The lead proposition and the first section of ²§ 93 which state the unity of the historical and the archetypal ("ideal" in ET 1928, "prototypical" in ET 2016) in the person of Jesus refer immediately to the shape of his life in which this unity is expressed:

> If the spontaneity of the new corporate life is original in the Redeemer and proceeds from him alone, then as an historical individual He must have been at the same time ideal (*urbildlich*) (i.e. the ideal must have become completely historical in Him), and each historical moment of His experience must at the same time have borne within it the ideal (²§ 93 LS. ET 1928, 377).[322]

The "true manifestation of His dignity, which is identical with His activity in the founding of a community, lies not in isolated moments, but in the whole course of His life" (²§ 93,1. ET 1928, 377). Against Baur's objection to the dominance of the idea of the Redeemer over his historical person Schleiermacher justifies in a principled way that the existence of the archetype cannot be replaced by its mere idea (6.2.1). He then elaborates in detail the conception of the completion of creation that has now advanced to become an argument for the historical nature of the archetypal Redeemer (6.2.2). How the turn of the whole work to a Second-Adam Christology has been evaluated will be examined subsequently (6.2.3). In keeping with the revisions of ²§§ 3 and 4, the mediation of redemption is now expounded as relating to human freedom (6.2.4).

6.2.1 The historical nature of the archetypal Jesus

In response to the questions raised about the unity of the archetypal and the historical in the person of Jesus, Schleiermacher now offers principled reflections

---

[322] The ET 2016 formulates: "The self-initiated activity (*Selbsttätigkeit*) of the new collective life (*Gesamtleben*) is taken to be original in the Redeemer and to proceed from him alone. Thus, he must, at the same time, have been prototypical (*urbildlich*) as an individual entity in history (*geschichtliches Einzelwesen*). That is, what is prototypical had to have become completely historical in him. At the same time, moreover, every historical element (*Moment*) in him had to have borne (*in sich tragen*) what is prototypical within it" (²§ 93 LS. ET 2016, II, 565).

which replace the reasons of historical plausibility marshalled before: the otherwise unexplained testimony of the archetypal nature of Christ and the simple fact that the church did not seek to surpass him. He first reconstructs the objection that the archetypal nature of Christ cannot really be founded in him. Rather, this predicate is deemed to represent the idea of perfection conceived by the human soul and projected onto the person of Jesus: "a fundamental exaggeration into which believers fall when they regard Christ in the mirror of their own imperfection" (^{2}§ 93,2. ET 1928, 378). This hyperbole must be all the steeper the more deeply its starting point is set in the experience of one's own sinfulness. Against this type of explanation Schleiermacher addresses the clarification that with this statement, the "boundary (*Grenze*) of the Christian faith" (ET 1928, 378) is being transgressed in two ways: on the one hand, the demotion of Jesus from archetype to mere exemplar implies the perfectibility of Christianity beyond Jesus; on the other hand, the completion of creation would then still be outstanding. It would remain hypothetical, "since undoubtedly in progress thus continual perfection remains always only a bare possibility" (ET 1928, 379).

Schleiermacher's justification illustrates the distance between critics like Baur and his own approach. In his review of 1828, Baur had called it "a purely historical question, which can only be answered by a historical examination of the written documents of the history of the gospels (*evangelischen Geschichte*)", whether "the person Jesus of Nazareth really had the qualities that are assumed in the concept of the Redeemer posited (*aufgestellten*) here".[323] For Schleiermacher however, this is the faith-based presupposition with which the members of the Christian community already approach their research on the historical life of Jesus; it is not investigated but accepted as the finite representation of a God-consciousness that is experienced as a "veritable existence of God in Him" (^{1}§116,3. II, 29; ^{2}§ 94 LS. ET 1928, 385).

This part of the argumentation shows the presupposition of the whole dogmatics at work: it is its premise, not something it sets out to prove, that Jesus is the archetype or complete realisation of the God-consciousness. Counter-questions are answered consistently by referring to the content of the Christian experience of redemption which is only represented adequately if the uniqueness of Jesus is portrayed. Despite having taught New Testament since his first appointment as a professor at the university of Halle in 1805, and despite having inaugurated a "Life of Jesus" lecture course, for Schleiermacher it is sufficient here to point out the contours of the Christian self-con-

---

[323] Baur, "Selbstanzeige", 242; KGA I/7.3, 267.

sciousness: doctrines have to be validated by referring back to it as their basis. Even if the New Testament is used as corroboration or as a critical instance, it is how the Christian self-consciousness has been determined that matters for doctrine. It would be going beyond its limits to try to "prove" Jesus' archetypal character directly from the Bible. A further reason for continuing with such stringency on the path chosen in the Introduction, not to begin with Scripture, but with the human ability to be accessed by God's causality and love, is a specific limit of historical research: it can only reach external behaviour but not the source of a person's agency. The second edition makes it clear that perfection cannot be conclusively proven.

Today, after renewed quests of the historical Jesus, it can be doubted whether this reference to the limit of the shared Christian conviction is still adequate as an answer to a history-related question: "It can hardly be denied that this point of information does not sufficiently do justice to the problem of the foundations of Christology, ever since the Bultmann School raised the 'new quest of the historical Jesus' and the discussion about its 'theological relevance'."[324]

Yet it also appears unduly restrictive, mistaken or reductive on the part of F. C. Baur not to point out the documents' character as theologised history, not to link the key motifs in the New Testament's accounts both to their Jewish matrix and to their history of reception,[325] and not to offer some hermeneutical reflections on the process of enquiry, as if it could be free from all presuppositions.

Regarding the second point, the arguments Schleiermacher develops against hypothesising redemption or the completion of creation, are so perceptive and thought-through that they do not only defeat the critique already made; they also disprove in advance the subsequent well-known conclusions drawn by David Friedrich Strauß and Ludwig Feuerbach, anticipating their conceptual mistake. At stake is the thesis that not in an individual person, but "in the totality of individuals which complete each other" the goal of the completion of the creation of human nature could finally be attained. This claim is rebutted with the insight that "perfection cannot be obtained by adding together things that are imperfect" (^{2}§ 93,2. ET 1928, 379). Schleiermacher's sobering analysis is that *if* such a goal is to be reached, it must happen in one individual. For if in such incremental progress "the perfection of one vital

---

[324] Pröpper, "Bestimmung", in *Evangelium und freie Vernunft*, 142, n. 30.
[325] For the Jewish matrix and the variety of the contexts of the first century inculturations of Christianity, see, for example, Seán Freyne, *The Jesus Movement and Its Expansion – Meaning and Mission* (Grand Rapids, MN: Eerdmans, 2014).

6.2 The final outline of Christology — 183

function be posited in the concept but actually found in no individual" (²§ 93,2. ET 1928, 379), then it does not draw nearer but is chronically missed. The human race cannot make up for what the individual lacks. Thus, if creation is to be fulfilled at all, it can only be achieved in one individual, Christ.

In line with this reflection, Schleiermacher does not extend the archetypal nature of Christ to all the functions of human conscious life but focuses it on the singular power of his God-consciousness. This power or "capacity" again is distinguished from its necessarily finite expressions: We are

> not concerned with the multifarious relationships of human life – as though Christ must have been ideal for all knowledge or all art and skill which have been developed in human society – but only with the capacity (*Kräftigkeit*) of the God-consciousness to give the impulse to all life's experiences and to determine them. ... There are those who say it is not only possible but our duty to go beyond much of what Christ taught to his disciples, because He Himself (since human thought is impossible without words) was seriously hindered by the imperfection of language from giving real expression to the innermost content of His spiritual being in clearly defined thoughts; and the same, it may be held, is true in another sense of His actions also, in which the relations by which they were determined, and therefore imperfection, are always reflected. This, however, does not prevent us from attributing to Him absolute ideality (*Urbildlichkeit*) in His inner being, in the sense that that inner being may always transcend its manifestation, and what is manifested be only an ever more perfect presentation of it (ET 1928, 378–379).[326]

What is decisive, is not the conditioned, contextual expression but the underlying "capacity" or power which is either given or lacking. This clarification corresponds to the thought that the addition of imperfect finite entities does not result in a breakthrough to perfection or infinity. Thus, the only way to envisage the completion of creation is if one historical individual has the generative power to "produce every possible advance in the totality" (ET 1928, 379). With this, the definitive character of redemption as a historical turning point is underlined, one that had to be initiated in history, not just conceptually. The principled argumentation that Schleiermacher breaks through to in the second edition seems to me to be anything but a "bottomless metaphysical spec-

---

[326] The ET 2016 contrasts the "myriad relationships of human life" with "the strength of God-consciousness for giving impetus of all the elements of life and for determining them all" (II, 566). The finite expressions of his appearance are distinguished from the internal power: "it can still be the case that an absolutely prototypical character belongs to him in accordance with his inner nature, with the result that the supposed surpassing-of-his-appearance referred to could, at the same time, always become simply a more complete unfolding of his innermost nature" (II, 568).

ulation", as which Dilthey portrays it.[327] It is the one decisive argument against replacing the Redeemer by the idea of a human species that is allegedly able to develop to a stage of perfection by mutually complementing itself.[328] If there is to be a progressive self-attainment of a God-conscious humanity at all, then this can only happen by drawing from the archetypal orientation towards God that was given once, in the existence of Jesus.

By establishing with an irrefutable argument the point that the idea cannot be transferred to any other instance than an individual, the second edition reinforces at the same time the significance of the historical person who realised this pinnacle in his existence. With this principled justification, however, the concept of the completion of creation has taken over the leading role, requiring further elements to anchor it.

6.2.2 Christ as the completion of creation

The major changes made in relation to this point are marked by a double concern that is subject to a latent tension. What would be required from the overall framework is the elaboration of the conception of the completion of creation. Yet

---

327 Dilthey, *Leben Schleiermachers*, vol. II, 489. Lange, *Historischer Jesus*, 153, refers to Dilthey when he judges: "The other argument brought into the equation in this connection that then the creation of the human person would not yet be completed, so that he would rank below the other living organisms (§ 93,2), is to be mentioned here only for the sake of completeness; the critique has justifiably called it scarcely convincing." Also for Horst Stephan "the logical proof that Schleiermacher adduces for the necessity of such a realisation (§ 93,2) ... is of a rather hairsplitting (*spitzfindig*) nature". It "can only convince someone who wants to be convinced" (*Erlösung*, 47, n. 1). If the argument is not taken as a proof, however, but as an explication of what the nature of free human beings implies, the result is different. Cf. Pröpper, "Bestimmung", in *Evangelium und freie Vernunft*, 141, n. 29: "The *Glaubenslehre* has already seen through the senselessness of the proposal to speak about a mutual complementarity of individuals to a stage of perfection with a 'species that develops itself freely' (ET 379) ... an insight that throws a bright light in advance on the aporias and deficits of Feuerbach's anthropology. ... Schleiermacher himself related Jesus' archetypal character not to the finite expressions but to the *power* of his God-consciousness which is real in an individual or not at all ... and thus cut off the path to Strauß (and Feuerbach)."
328 I have developed this point in greater detail in *Urbild*, 178–80. A short English version of the book's argument is contained in "The transcendental turn. Shifts in argumentation between the first and the second editions of the '*Glaubenslehre*'" in *New Athenaeum/Neues Athenaeum* 3 (1992) 21–41, and in "Genetic Perfection, or Fulfillment of Creation in Christ?", in Celia Deane-Drummond and Peter M. Scott (eds), *Future Perfect? God, Medicine and Human Identity* (London: T. & T. Clark, 2006), 155–167.

at the same time, it is necessary to emphasise against Baur the significance of Christ as the historical turning point. In order to underline the discontinuity in the appearance of Christ, the second edition newly accentuates his unique function of mediating the being of God in the world. Since, however, the overall guiding conception is the idea of a two-stage creation of human nature, the particular status of Christ merges into the continuity with the state of creation achieved up to now. Thus,

> the appearance of Christ Himself is to be regarded as a preservation, that is, a preservation of the receptivity, implanted in human nature from the beginning and perpetually developing further, which enables it to take into itself such an absolute potency of the God-consciousness" (^{2}§ 89,3. ET 1928, 368).

This perspective is justified as the more encompassing one. In it, not only the "effect", but also the "purpose" of the divine decree and not only the "beginning", but the "totality" of the salvific plan are seen to be expressed (^{2}§ 89,1. ET 1928, 366).[329] At the same time, Schleiermacher claims, the title of "Second Adam" also contains the arrival of something new:

> Christ Himself is the Second Adam, the beginner and originator of this more perfect human life, or the completion of the creation of man. This at the same time indicates in the most definite way that it was impossible to attain to this higher life out of the natural order which had its beginning in Adam (^{2}§ 89,1. ET 1928, 367).

Against the development-oriented drift of the overall conception, Schleiermacher tries to expound as impressively as possible the appearance of Christ's God-consciousness as a break with what went before. What seemed like an apparently unessential difference or even a weakening in the terminology of the lead propositions, whether Jesus' God-consciousness is referred to as a "true" (*wahres*) (^{1}§ 116 LS. II, 27), or a "veritable (*eigentliches*) existence of God in Him" (^{2}§ 94

---

329 In "Christology and anthropology", 159–62, Mariña uses the anchoring of the appearance of Christ in God's eternal decree as an argument against K. Barth, Brunner and other critics of *The Christian Faith* for having reduced Christology to anthropology and thus lost the vertical dimension of faith in God. "Such judgments cannot be farther from the truth, and can only be the result of a lack of acquaintance with Schleiermacher's *Christian Faith* as a whole. ... the 'completion of the creation of man' (^{2}§ 89) goes back to the undivided eternal decree (^{2}§ 95). Through this decree it was ordained that the first Adam should reach completion in the second" (160). While it is good that this theological argument is highlighted, the reason for insisting on one decree instead of two separate divine decisions would be equally unacceptable to K. Barth as to critics from other starting points, since it undermines any action of God in history.

LS. ET 1928, 385), turns out to be a major change. It implies a completely new conception of the relationship between God and world and of the cosmological standing of Jesus. Even if both editions do not differ in their key statement that the existence of God (*Sein Gottes*) constitutes "His inmost self" (*sein innerstes Selbst*) (¹§ 116,3. II, 30; ²§ 94,3. ET 1928, 388), it is based on a different outline. In the first edition, it is only the relative maximum of the being of God that the Redeemer realises. If

> already every life that is only comparatively and partially new is justifiably called a divine revelation, and every revelation of God in a finite being is nothing else than the being of God announcing itself in this finite being; then undisputedly (*unstreitig*) redemption is the absolute revelation, and thus a perfect being of God is posited in the Redeemer (¹§ 116,3. II, 29).

It is "true" insofar as in contrast to the general human God-consciousness, it is pure and vigorous in its content and its intensity. But even in this maximal realisation it remains a special case of the ever-present being of God. The person of Jesus merely has the status of a particular instance subordinated to the general. The second edition reverses this slant: there is no mention of a being of God in a finite entity prior to the appearance of Jesus, merely of a general-indefinite presence of God which takes place in the world as a whole. Only insofar as an individual being represents the world in itself, a being of God in it becomes thinkable. With this new starting point, a different direction has been opened up: If a specific being of God can only exist in a particular self-consciousness, namely in one that expresses its own relationship and that of everything finite to God without hindrance, then a presence of God in everything and thus also in each individual is no longer conceived in terms of nature. God's presence can now only be thought of as refracted by the self-reflexivity of a particular, historical human being. Instead of being encompassed in latently objectivising terms, the possibility of a specific being of God in the world now depends on subjective freedom. This type of presence is not automatic, it relies on an actual willingness to realise it.[330] If it becomes real, it deserves to be identified as "a being of God in the pro-

---

330 Hans Scheel, *Die Theorie von Christus als dem zweiten Adam bei Schleiermacher* (Naumburg: G. Pätz'sche Buchdruckerei Lippert, 1913), 70, in contrast sees the being of God outside of God realised first in the world and only then in an individual: "What does God's being in a human person signify? God's being is, as counterpart to the feeling of absolute dependence, pure activity. Since, however, each singularised (*vereinzelt*) being consists of activity and suffering, properly speaking there can only be a being of God in the world, not a being of God in an individual being. Now the human person as a rational being is capable through his lively receptivity to represent in himself the world, thus a being of God would be possible in him. Since,

6.2 The final outline of Christology — 187

per sense" (²§ 94,2. ET 1928, 388), as designated in the lead proposition, as "veritable (*eigentliches*)" (ET 1928, 385):

> originally it is found nowhere but in Him, and He is the only 'other' in which there is an existence of God in the proper sense, so far, that is as we posit the God-consciousness in His self-consciousness as continually and exclusively determining every moment, and consequently also this perfect indwelling of the Supreme Being as His peculiar being and His inmost self. Indeed, working backwards we must now say, if it is only through him that the human God-consciousness becomes an existence of God in human nature, and only through the rational nature that the totality of finite powers can become an existence of God in the world, that in truth He alone mediates all existence of God in the world and all revelation of God through the world, in so far as He bears within Himself the whole new creation which contains and develops the potency of the God-consciousness (²§ 94,2. ET 1928, 388).

These new statements underline the historical turning point that has been reached through the person of Jesus, giving an ultimate definition of what the reversal consists in: his singular God-consciousness in its absolute strength is the "only original" place outside of God's self in which there is "an existence of God in the proper sense". Through him, the God-consciousness given in the feeling of absolute dependence is realised as "an existence of God in human nature" which is now being opened up to all humans, and through them is subsequently extended to all other life. The hierarchy has thus been reversed: It now runs from God and the human person of Jesus as the "only other" location of a being of God in the strict sense as the highest point, to the redeemed who themselves becomes mediators to the lowest stage, reason-less being. Since the whole process of introducing the being of God into finite reality is attributed to Jesus, it becomes evident why he embodies the completion of creation in its original content, to be an expression of the activity of God. He advances from being a special case of what has always been present and operative, to being the inaugurator

---

however, he allows his pure God-consciousness to be overcome by his sensible consciousness, thus allowing it to become active, no being of God can be constituted in him. Thus, it is Christ whose God-consciousness is pure activity and whose sensible consciousness, his organism, is pure receptivity, the only one in whom the being of God represents itself."

What speaks against this reconstruction is, first, that according to it, the world as a whole would have to be pure activity. For Schleiermacher, however, it remains a system of reciprocal effects, thus, of the interdependence of activity and receptivity. There is no "being of God" in this realm on the parameter of "pure activity". The world attains a relationship to divine activity in the second edition only through the human self-consciousness which grasps the dependence of its existence and of everything finite from God, the "Whence" of all being. Insofar as Jesus realises this consciousness in its purity, he mediates the active being of God to all humans and through them to nature which is destined to be unified with reason.

and mediator of a self-understanding that is destined to grow: an individual who mediates God's active being by allowing it to be active in him without hindrance. In this new outline Schleiermacher has elaborated his basic definitions in the most extensive way possible; he has secured a function for the historical person of Jesus that is as unsurpassable as his approach allows, having taken his starting point in the Introduction with an already active God-consciousness in every human being.

6.2.3 Evaluations of the turn to a Second-Adam Christology in the history of reception of the second edition

The changeover from the previously guiding category of redemption to the encompassing perspective of the completion of creation has been partly defended, partly relativised in the reception history of the *Glaubenslehre*. The scholarly debate in subsequent eras from a variety of starting points ranges from endorsement for different reasons to an awareness of the tension between a reversal in the history of humanity and a continuity embedded in the one divine decree.

At the beginning of the twentieth century, before the upheavals of the First World War, Hans Scheel seeks to highlight the aspect of newness which he sees founded on a "possession of beatitude" (*Besitz der Seligkeit*) in contrast to an understanding of redemption that is focused negatively on the sin that has been overcome. For him, the new determination goes beyond the concept of redemption in two respects: "Firstly, the concept of the Second Adam or of the completion of creation emphasises the life brought by Christ in its whole extension, and secondly, the concept of the Second Adam or of the new creation is especially appropriate to underline what is new in the person of Christ and in his work".[331] His examination of its particular use in the section on reconciliation concludes that in this new stage, "a completely different standpoint" has been reached to that of redemption, since we are "confronted with something absolutely, unsurpassably new". If the "forgiveness of sins was the beginning of reconciliation, the full state of union with Christ represents reconciliation in its whole fullness, so that Christ is completely the centre of life. The reconciled Christian knows himself to be in the real possession of beatitude".[332]

Here the reversal in the course of human history is connected with the standpoint that the breakthrough to the new condition of beatitude is now effective. It

---

331 Scheel, *Zweiter Adam*, 51.
332 Scheel, *Zweiter Adam*, 75–77.

6.2 The final outline of Christology — 189

is an inner reality that Christ's work has made accessible to all. More than fifty years later, in the mid-1960s, while critical of an overemphasis on reconciliation, Friedrich Jacob accentuates a different aspect. He locates the value of the idea of the perfection of creation in the "objectivity of the salvific work" which it secures:

> by pointing back to the world, it safeguards the objectivity of the salvific work. ... the statement that in Christ the creation of humanity has been completed means at the same time that corresponding to the perfect God-consciousness that issues from him and fills the church and every Christian there is a reality outside us and existing independently from us. The description of the work of Christ as perfection of the world protects the *Glaubenslehre* from the impression that redemption could be a human deed. For we do not redeem ourselves by taking over the Christian consciousness; in Christ redemption has already happened.[333]

Earlier, at the very beginning of the twentieth century, Horst Stephan had also seen the "doctrine of the new possession of salvation as the backbone", but subordinated it again to the basic category of redemption. Here, both of these elements are identified as the main moments of a dogmatics founded on redemption. Schleiermacher is seen to "have indeed delivered the proof how all other sections of the dogmatics develop from redemption. It constitutes the proper point of unity of the *Glaubenslehre*".[334] Stephan also admits that "the name of redemption (in the narrower sense of the 'taking away of sin', thus as a negative goal in the affected self-consciousness ... becomes inappropriate (*unpassend*)" and that Schleiermacher "needs a new goal of redemption which is in no direct logical connection with sin, that serves to rescue (*hinüberretten*) the goals sourced from the analysis of the Christian consciousness". Even if he "elevates in ²§ 89 'the completion of the creation of human nature' to the pinnacle of redemption",[335] Stephan still sees good reasons to "maintain redemption ... everywhere as the key concept and to subordinate those other meanings to it". The reason for keeping redemption as the overarching category is that

> there is no change of substance. ... the same content is only being regarded under different aspects and thus better appreciated. Secondly, redemption remains the dominating concept, indeed, after the conclusion of the proper doctrine of the person and work of Jesus (e.g., in ²§ 113 or at the end, ²§ 166) it is used as much as at the beginning. Christ is called the Redeemer everywhere, also when his reconciling activity or the perfected creation of

---

333 Friedrich Jacob, *Geschichte und Welt in Schleiermachers Theologie* (Berlin: Evangelische Verlagsanstalt, 1967), 108–110.
334 Stephan, *Erlösung*, 95.
335 Stephan, *Erlösung*, 41.

human nature are treated; it is always only the human need for redemption that is invoked, never the need for reconciliation or perfection.[336]

Keeping the key term of the first edition, redemption, in circulation alongside the new significance of attaining the second, always intended final stage of creation, could be interpreted as showing that Schleiermacher trusted the concept to be wide enough to also encompass the new meaning. Wolfhart Pannenberg notes how this enlargement and reorientation fits into the decision to subordinate the concept of creation to the ongoing "preservation" by God, allowing newness to emerge while indicating the continuity with the previous state through the term "preservation": "the new origination (*Neuentstehen*) of individual things could also be regarded as the preservation of the species". Pannenberg sees this assumption exemplified in the key Christological proposition: "How much the appearance of something new and the idea of historical development are co-conceived (*das Auftreten von Neuem und auch der Gedanke der geschichtlichen Entwicklung mitgedacht ist*)", finds expression "in the famous formula of § 89 according to which the appearance of Christ is to be 'regarded as the completion, only now accomplished, of the creation of human nature'. § 89,3 expressly applies the concept of preservation to it."[337]

How far Schleiermacher has moved beyond the anthropology of the first edition becomes visible again in the new way in which the acceptance and continued sharing of Christ's work are described.

6.2.4 The mediation of redemption

The second version has put greater emphasis on expounding the essential feature of Jesus, the designation of his God-consciousness as a "veritable existence of God in Him". It now also explicates from this crucial point in the history of humanity the way in which redemption is transmitted as the "work of Christ". If in general, God's activity in relation to the world consists in creation and preservation, it does so, in particular, in relation to humanity, having become the innermost principle of Jesus' essence. Schleiermacher tries to do justice to either aspect by explicating both the new beginning and the linking up with the existing stage in categories of freedom: "the creative activity of Christ ... is entirely concerned with the sphere of freedom" (^{2}§ 100,2. ET 1928, 426). The first edition

---

336 Stephan, *Erlösung*, 9.
337 Pannenberg, "Schwierigkeiten", 8, and 8, n. 4.

had presented the content of the redeeming effect of Jesus as a "communication of his sinlessness and perfection" (¹§ 121 LS. II, 66), but had elucidated this communication above all negatively, in terms of an opposition between divine and human nature. It is true that also the second edition retains the formulation that "the former personality may be slain (*Ertötung der früheren Persönlichkeit*) and human nature, in vital fellowship with Christ, be formed into persons in the totality of that higher life"; yet it now also explains the "continuation of the person-forming activity of the divine nature in Christ" (¹§ 121,3. II, 69; cf. ²§ 100,2. ET 1928, 427) in a positive way. By taking its lead from the "being of God" from which "(a)ll Christ's activity ... proceeds", it explains how Christians are assumed "into the power of His God-consciousness" in line with the distinction between the creative and the preserving aspect of God's activity. What can claim continuity with the existing human constitution, is "preserving"; what can only be established through a new beginning, is "creative", and this is now specified as being "entirely concerned with the sphere of freedom. For His assumptive activity is a creative one, yet what it produces is altogether free" (ET 1928, 426).

The following description of the interplay between the attraction of the Redeemer and the believer's free response treads a fine line between receptivity and engagement of their free will. Even if it is finally attenuated to merely "assenting", it is the new orientation of the believer's willing, not this will itself, that the Redeemer produces.

> Christ can also influence what is free only in accordance with the way in which what is free enters the sphere of Christ's life (*Lebenskreis*) and only in accordance with the nature of what is free. Christ's activity of taking us up into community with him is thus a free engendering of the desire-to-take-him-up-into-oneself (*ein schöpferisches Hervorbringen des Ihn-in-sich-aufnehmen-Wollens*). Or it is, rather, a creative engendering simply of an acquiescence (*Zustimmung*) to the working of his communicating activity, for this desire (*es*, relating to *Ihn-in-sich-aufnehmen-Wollen*) is simply a receptivity to his activity in the process of his communication (*Mitteilung*) (ET 2016, 623).[338]

---

[338] The 1928 translation keeps the term "will" for "*Wollen*" which in 2016 has been changed to "desire": "It follows that He can influence what is free only in accordance with the manner in which it enters into His sphere of living influence (*Lebenskreis*), and only in accordance with the nature of the free. The activity by which He assumes us into fellowship with Him is, therefore, a creative production in us of the will to assume him into ourselves (*ein schöpferisches Hervorbringen des Ihn-in-sich-aufnehmen-Wollens*), or rather – since it is only receptiveness for His activity involved in the impartation – only our assent to the influence of His activity" (ET 1928, 426). In the context of emphasising the freedom of the redeeming interaction between Christ and the believers, it is important to retain this term, as the 1928 ET does, even if its formulation, "a creative production in us of the will to assume him into ourselves" does not distinguish the will from the

The first edition had portrayed the new orientation as something so abruptly new that it risked championing an unwanted "magical" (²§ 100,3. ET 1928, 429–430) understanding of redemption; the second moves it into a context of continuity in which existing human faculties are turned into a different direction:

> For the pervasive activity of Christ cannot establish itself in an individual without becoming person-forming in him, too, for now all his activities are differently determined through the working of Christ in him, and even all impressions are differently received – which means that the personal self-consciousness, too, becomes ... different (*ein anderes wird*) (ET 1928, 427).[339]

The process of redemption had to be redescribed when the key category, the "being of God" in Jesus, was reconceived and connected in its expression to the "form of human life". It belongs to freedom as the essential mark of finite human life that it is contextualised in a "life sphere" (ET 1928, 426). The statements about how redemption is realised are refocused deliberately as engaging the individual in her self-understanding. It takes the insight seriously that the anthropological turn to the subject is an opportunity for the Christian faith to explicate its contents in categories of freedom. The testimony of redemption cannot be set forth in ways that diminish the consciousness of freedom but only in ways that correspond to such a historically new self-understanding. By choosing as its starting point the self-communication of God in Christ, the revised material dogmatics is able to establish human freedom as its addressee far more clearly than in the first edition. It enriches the mediating function of Jesus to stress the willingness of those ready to be redeemed to accept him. Also the presentation of Jesus' self-communication in teaching, learning and sharing the principle of his life benefits from the new systematic starting point with the "veritable (*eigentliches*) being of God" in him and from the newly accentuated freedom

---

act of willing. Schleiermacher's highlighting of the "*aufnehmen-Wollen*" presupposes the will as an existing, independent faculty to its actual use. The first translation's "assent" for "*Zustimmung*" grasps the element of active decision more than the 2016 passivity-conveying "acquiescence" does.

339 Here the 1928 ET adds a term that is not contained in the German original and that contravenes the overall intention of emphasising continuity, by adding "altogether" to "different": "the personal self-consciousness, too, becomes altogether different (*ein anderes wird*) (ET 1928, 427). The attempt to replace the previous understanding of redemption as disrupting the sinful orientation and imposing a new life is not portrayed adequately in the translation of this passage. Schleiermacher even adds that a consciousness of sinfulness is not a prior condition for redemption and that "it may just as well arise ... as the effect of the Redeemer's self-revelation as indeed it does come to full clarity only as we contemplate His sinless perfection" (ET 1928, 427).

of the motivated recipients. Yet all the revisions in this direction are only more pointed realisations of the basic approach. How can it be judged at this stage with regard to the dignity and unsurpassability of the Redeemer?

6.3 The liberation of human God-consciousness by a sinless redeemer: Enough to secure the ongoing significance of Jesus Christ?

Can this explanation of Jesus' work to liberate the human God-consciousness from sin and to inaugurate a new communal life secure his abiding significance? I will compare and discuss evaluations of four aspects by authors writing in the nineteenth, twentieth and twenty-first centuries: on locating the distinction of Jesus in the unique strength of his God-consciousness (6.3.1) on the effect of neglecting Jesus' revelation of God on the link of faith to culture (6.3.2); circularity at the cost of contingency (6.3.3), and the balance between Christology and ecclesiology (6.3.4).

6.3.1 Jesus' distinction: the unique strength of his God-consciousness

In the second edition, Schleiermacher has been able to show that the historical existence of Jesus, the archetype, is irreplaceable. The content of his particularity has, however, been fixed to be the completion of the creation of the human being. The guiding concept has turned out to be the creation of the human person in two stages. This explanation secures the factual significance of Jesus and enlarges the meaning of salvation history. It is no longer solely defined by overcoming sin. The line in the first edition that restricted it to this horizon has been eliminated: "without sin, however, also redemption would be nothing (*ohne Sünde aber wäre auch die Erlösung nichts*" (^{1}§ 114,2. II, 22). Yet how does the second edition seek to prevent the consequence that the significance of the person of Jesus is exhausted in the breakthrough to the proper realisation of the essence of the human person and is absorbed by the newly founded corporate life?

The revised version underlines with added detail the principal relation of the church to its founder. It replaces, for example, the statement (directed in the first edition against proofs from Scripture and elsewhere for the truth of Christianity) that "faith begins absolutely (*schlechthin*) through the immediate power exerted by its object" (^{1}§ 109,2. II, 8) by the rule to "unfold the way in which this faith originated, along with its content" (^{2}§ 88,2. ET 1928, 362). This new, historically oriented formulation successfully counteracts the suspicion that faith could be a projection from the longing for redemption which might arise if faith is said to begin "absolutely" in view of his person. Faith is an effect of Jesus; it is not faith that generates him as Redeemer, but Jesus who generates faith in him. His sinless perfection is not a projection but an experience. At the same time, the new corporate life is tied evermore closely to him: It develops from the assent to his communication of his perfect God-consciousness and is thus not separable from him. It would undermine the identity of faith if the strengthened God-consciousness present in the new corporate life emancipated itself from its founder. Whatever subsequent theological eras will propose, for Schleiermacher this tie has been established unequivocally. The ultimate statement of Christology appears in the testimony of the Christian self-consciousness not to be able to surpass its founder.

Yet, the course that decides on the enduring or passing validity of Jesus has already been set at a previous juncture. Once an actualised certitude of God has been stated as given with human nature, as ^{2}§ 4,4 does, the content that is to be mediated through the Redeemer is already materially given in those in need of redemption. Since there is no content that could ground the essential difference of Jesus, despite all the effort, his function is after all restricted to stimulating this capacity. Only in comparison with the old corporate life of sin is what he mediates new. Apart from this contrast, its novelty is due to the insight that the connection between the two moments of the "one undivided eternal divine decree" is "unreachable" for human knowledge; the "laws" of development that God founded in human nature, are "unattainable by us" (^{2}§ 94,3. ET 1928, 389).

The objection that no new content is mediated in redemption has been put forward also in eras subsequent to F. C. Baur, based on different readings and leading to diverse conclusions. The following selection of authors is quoted to exemplify the different accentuations of this core finding which some welcome and justify, and others reject.

Martin Schulze's perceptive investigation of 1893 identifies the consequence of locating Jesus' significance only in the absolute strength of his relationship to God: he is not credited with communicating any new insight into God's being and God's interaction with humans. Schulze also notes that an actual relationship to God is attributed to every human being:

> the *revelation* given in Christ is not a matter of a new *content* of the God-consciousness but only of its absolute *strength* and *steadiness* and the resulting complete unification with the changing sensible relations ... What Christ has sought and found is not the communication of a new, ... so far unattained understanding of God and of God's relationship to us that could not have been reached in any other way, but only the imparted capability (*Befähigung*) to really recognise the highest relatedness in every moment that imposes itself (*sich*

aufdrängend) on *every* consciousness ... The communication of Christ consists in the highest possible *increase* (*Steigerung*) of the life of religious feeling (*religiösen Gefühlslebens*).[340]

He then points out that in view of the definition of piety this understanding of redemption is not surprising, but that it short-changes the Redeemer: "It does not need any further proof of how the fact of redemption conceived in this way is compatible with the concept of piety as something inherent in the essence of the human person and able to develop by itself, even if only gradually"; but from this foundation "of a theory of *development*, the assumption that the Redeemer is *absolute* at present still remains a mystery" (25). His concluding comparison is overdrawn and misleading, since it is not true that the difference between God and humans is given up, but it is accurate regarding the role of the Redeemer which is absorbed into human capacity. He sees a correspondence "not unlike Hegel, only that with him, the deity comes to itself in the conceptually thinking spirit, whereas with Schleiermacher it does so in the immediate self-consciousness" (38).

An opposite evaluation of the same finding is given in 1901 by Horst Stephan. He welcomes the fact that "redemption does not consist in an extravagance which some Christians in their marked religious feeling may afford themselves to have", but that it "remains a necessary element in the spiritual unfolding of each human person". He recognises that the content is identical: "Christian redemption merely offers the only effective means to reach the goal of general human development, it does not add anything different. It thus elevates Christianity to its absolute height as pinnacle and fulfilment of all religion."[341]

In this argumentation, it is the validation of what each human being is known to possess already that makes Christianity the complete realisation of religion. A study of the idea of development in Schleiermacher's concept of sin a few years later, by Ernst Flöel, comes to a similar judgement:

> The original God-consciousness and the one that arises in the fellowship with the Redeemer differ not in their content but only in their form, according to the *Glaubenslehre*. The first is always marked by powerlessness (*Ohnmacht*), the latter appears with specific strength. Apart from this, the original God-consciousness and that which is communicated by the Redeemer are the same.[342]

---

[340] Martin Schulze, *Das Wesen und die Bedeutung der besonderen Offenbarung in Schleiermachers Glaubenslehre* (Niesky: P. Jenke, 1893), 29. Further page numbers in the text.
[341] Stephan, *Erlösung* 1901, 106.
[342] Ernst Flöel, *Der Entwicklungsgedanke in Schleiermachers Lehre von der Sünde* (Darmstadt: C.F. Winter, 1913), 48.

Marc Michel's treatment of theological approaches to culture concludes: "Christ is the model of religious consciousness and it is through communion with him that the Christian gains access to salvation by accessing the progressive continuity of the feeling of absolute dependence. But this salvation, strangely, is the exact and perfect realisation of the initial postulate".[343] Friedrich Jacob formulates a similar finding with the following analogy: "What Christ brings to the human person is not something completely new; rather, he activates and perfects what is already implanted in the world and in the human person. In other words, Christ makes the notes resonate to which the human being has always already been tuned".[344]

Having analysed the premises and rejected the principled assumption of an incompatibility between philosophy and theology in Karl Barth's critiques of Schleiermacher, Richard R. Niebuhr spells out the lacuna which Schleiermacher's reconstruction of Christology leaves regarding the understanding of God:

> Schleiermacher makes no attempt, for example, to derive a knowledge of God from the disclosure of God exclusively circumscribed by the figure of Jesus. His doctrine of God has more than one source, and while this fact may be adjudged a weakness by Barthian critics, it nevertheless places Schleiermacher in a substantial theological tradition ... Christ is the reformer of man's knowledge of God and of himself ... On this score, Schleiermacher is closer to, and more faithful to, Calvin than is Barth. Schleiermacher's weakness is that he does not give to Christ, in his thinking about God, nearly the same power of reforming the mode of thought that he allows him, in his thinking about man.[345]

In his reconstruction of God's self-communication in the terms of a theory of freedom, Magnus Lerch points out the

> under-determination of the specificity of Jesus or the figure of Christ as the exclusive location of the self-communication of God ... This is 'balanced' (*abgefedert*) systematically merely by the fact that Jesus' sinlessness is used as the only criterion of his uniqueness. In the logic of justification, the difference between Jesus' humanity and ours lies only in the sinfulness of human nature or correspondingly the sinlessness of Jesus so that the constitutive and lasting significance of Jesus is ultimately secured on *hamartiological* grounds.[346]

---

[343] Marc Michel, *La théologie aux prises avec la culture. De Schleiermacher á Tillich* (Paris: Cerf, 1982), 25–77, 77.
[344] Jacob, *Geschichte und Welt*, 100.
[345] Richard R. Niebuhr, *Schleiermacher on Christ and Religion*, 1964, 212, Fn. 2.
[346] Lerch, *Selbstmitteilung Gottes*, 143.

Even if, as the comparison of the two editions has shown, the link to human sin is played down in the revised version which emphasises the completion of creation by the Second Adam, it remains necessary as a structural counterpart. Lerch is correct in asking: The "question that is posed by connecting anthropology and Christology, philosophy and theology (too) tightly, is whether ... taking recourse to the sinlessness of Jesus is the only protection from sublating the truth of revelation into a truth of reason." It will only be possible in the context of the doctrine of God to outline the alternative to this understanding of the link between the two, namely "to reject inscribing (*Einzeichnung*) what happened in Christ into the general Creator-creature relationship".[347]

6.3.2 The under-determination of Jesus' concrete relationship to God

What appears in Jesus is thus the ideal of the essence of the human person, that is, of human reason comprehensively understood from the pre-reflective consciousness that mediates thinking and acting. Even if it happens only through him as a mediator, what it finally attains in the course of redemption is humanity as it was meant in the original perfection, the higher consciousness expressed without hindrance in the embodied pursuits of humans. Christianity is needed so that history can acquire this quality; but what it acquires is only a state of reason fulfilling itself in its consciousness of God. The process of Christianity flows into the process of culture and founds the trust in a reason that has been affirmed and made accessible to itself by redemption.

Theological approaches which welcome this positive relation to reason underline at the same time the need for a productive tension between the processes of reason and of Christianity. Wilhelm Gräb's study of the concept of history in Schleiermacher's mature work ends with the thesis that this tension is enduring and that collapsing the two is to be avoided: "The dual unfolding of the thematic of history prevents the theory of culture with its anthropological-ethical foundation from being posited in unison (*Ineinssetzung*) with the theology of Christianity".[348] Corresponding to the "restrictive unfolding of the concept of reason" in his philosophical ethics

---

[347] Lerch, *Selbstmitteilung Gottes*, 143.
[348] Wilhelm Gräb, *Humanität und Christentumsgeschichte. Eine Untersuchung zum Geschichtsbegriff im Spätwerk Schleiermachers* (Göttingen: Vandenhoeck & Ruprecht, 1980), 178. In "Feeling and sense, ethics and culture", in Niels Jørgen Cappeløm et al. (eds), *Schleiermacher und Kierkegaard. Subjektivität und Wahrheit/Subjectivity and Truth*, 159–177, 176, Cornelia Richter agrees

is a theory of the history of Christianity which shows that Schleiermacher saw the process of the realisation of reason which the ethical construction describes in the structural interconnection of its general possibilities as only beginning with the advent of Christianity in history.[349]

It seems to me, however, that the question remains what difference or stimulus is driving the ongoing, interminable process of realisation of what began with Christianity. It would have to be founded on a content that reason cannot appropriate to itself without this realisation losing its specificity. A content of this kind, however, cannot consist in the full strength of a God-consciousness that is latent in all. An essence that cannot be secularised without losing its core would have to consist in a specific, unprecedented content: such as, the love of a God who is able to act in history. It is true that Schleiermacher emphasises love as the defining truth of the Christian God when he subsequently develops the attributes of God specific to the consciousness of grace. He adds a new decisive sentence to his Christology: "Now this 'divine' is the divine love in Christ, which, once and for all or in every moment – whichever expression is chosen – gave direction to His feelings (*Wahrnehmungen*) for the spiritual conditions of men. In virtue of these feelings, and in consequence of them, there then arose the impulse to particular helpful acts" (^{2}§ 97,3. ET 1928, 407).

But the framework prohibits him from finding in Jesus' love for his fellow humans the self-revelation of God. It would have called for highlighting Jesus' readiness to invest his life into the proclamation of an unconditionally loving God and his free acceptance of the practical bearings of this unique insight. Schleiermacher does refer to Jesus' "obedience". His approach is meant to offer an alternative to the theory of atonement by Christ for the sins of all humans which had become doubtful both for moral reasons and as part of a supernaturalist theology with "magical" explanations that were unacceptable to the modern era. The objection is not that his argumentation is insufficient on staurological grounds.[350] The isolation of the cross from Jesus' life can be seen to have

---

with Gräb: "as neither Christian theology would become an ethical or cultural theory nor cultural theory would consist of the history of Christianity, both aspects would remain irreconcilable."
349 Gräb, *Humanität*, 175.
350 The theological objections to the central decision not to build his Christology on the memory of the passion, death and resurrection of Jesus Christ have to be examined for their backgrounds. In one of the most recent critiques, in "Christologie Schleiermachers", 288–291, Benjamin Dahlke would like it to be discussed whether the explanation of redemption as the Redeemer's communication of the strength of his own unrestrained God-consciousness to the human beings in need of redemption does not constitute "an under-determination of staurology. ... Thought figures of a soteriology of satisfaction do not play any role in the entire doctrinal

been a highly problematic legacy of major authors in the Latin soteriological tradition which could have equally included Jesus' life into its history-oriented understanding of salvation.[351] The point is rather that Jesus' proclamation and praxis has too little effect on opening up a new understanding of God, even when the attribute of love is specified as God's essence (²§ 166). To determine the core content of redemption as communicating God's love would need to overcome the split observed by Reinhard Slenczka between two modes of referring to Jesus – a soteriology which is cast too much in terms of causality, and a Christology which describes his activity without sufficient attention to his concrete, personal understanding of God:

> There is only a fine line between connecting Christology and soteriology closely, and dissolving the person of Jesus Christ into an anonymous causality ... As to the effect, the causality directed towards the pious consciousness is described on the one hand soteriologically as "consciousness of redemption", "corporate life" ... The relationship to Christ then often appears only as a purely mechanical link between cause and effect. Juxtaposed to it, almost without a connection, are expressions in which this effect is represented as an activity of the person of Christ. Schleiermacher uses concepts like "self-proclamation", "self-communication", "self-representation", "self-revelation" for this. The "activity" is not a deed of the person. It does not consist in a claim to authority (*Vollmachtsanspruch*), in a call to discipleship, a word of proclamation ... The "activity" is rather the effect of the personality in which there can be no "empirical emergence of divine properties" (96,3. ET 1928, 398). In being determined by the being of God, the person of Jesus Christ is ... the seed from which the new creation develops organically.[352]

While the *Glaubenslehre* succeeds in explaining the attraction of the person of Jesus in terms of the "total impression" (*Totaleindruk*) (²§ 14 and ²§ 99, or in the first edition "the person himself and his immediate power", ¹§ 21,1. I, 83) he made on his followers, this is not spelt out any further by highlighting the unique insights his life and proclamation offered into the being of God. Instead, the emphasis is on continuity: between him and the growing new corporate life,

---

section (*Lehrstück*). Rather, Schleiermacher raises concerns in relation to the term 'vicarious atonement' (*stellvertretende Genugthuung*) which he considers to be the central concept (*Inbegriff*) of the ecclesial doctrine. For him, the cross is the place where Jesus' complete obedience to God becomes visible for all human beings. What is redemptive is the communication of the new consciousness".

351 Cf., for example, Th. Pröpper's comparison of the "incarnational soteriology of the East" with the "staurocentric soteriology of the West" in *Erlösungsglaube und Freiheitsgeschichte. Eine Skizze zur Soteriologie* (München: Kösel, ³1991), 69–88.

352 Reinhold Slenczka, *Geschichtlichkeit und Personsein Jesu Christi. Studien zur christologischen Problematik der historischen Jesusfrage* (Göttingen: Vandenhoeck & Ruprecht, 1967), 216.

as Reinhold Slenczka points out, and between his life and his continuing effect to which his death does not pose any real interruption. Schleiermacher's downplaying of the relevance of the passion in the history of Jesus has earned him the critique of Docetism.[353] He excludes from Christology what he calls the "facts of the Resurrection and the Ascension of Christ, and the Prediction of His Return to Judgment" since they "cannot be laid down as properly constituent parts of the doctrine of His Person" (^{2}§ 99 LS. ET 1928, 417). Anything that could point to a singular, unrepeatable relationship between Jesus and the God he testified to and that would contain specific actions of expressing it, is barred from this presentation of the person and work of Christ. The respective critiques of Horst Stephan and Dietz Lange are instructive since both defend many of Schleiermacher's premises but regret his position on this point; it endangers his own intention to present the real, concrete God-consciousness of Jesus Christ. For Stephan it is a missed opportunity that the passion is not recognised as a place where the strength of his God-consciousness was threatened, and where Jesus showed the lengths to which his love was ready to go.

> The passion of the Lord shows more clearly than many other situations of his life the strength of his God-consciousness ... And also the blessedness of Christ only appears in its whole depth by not being overcome even by the fullness of suffering. Schleiermacher thus tries to integrate into his scheme the redeeming power of a love ready to offer itself up ... Yet it is not an independent ethical or religious motif, but only a measure for the strength and blessedness of the God-consciousness.[354]

Dietz Lange indicates the reason for Schleiermacher's unwillingness to consider anything that could take away from the steadiness of Jesus' God-consciousness, which leaves his description "close to a *theologia gloriae*": his doctrine of God. In order to safeguard "Jesus' uninterrupted continuous development", he interprets "death and resurrection as an uninterrupted transition from the bodily to the spiritual presence of Jesus". For him, the "criterion of continuity is problematic insofar as it endangers the reality of the human life of Jesus and even veils his death. Yet for Schleiermacher, it was a necessary criterium in order to make it possible to think the being of the timeless God in an historical human person."

For Lange, the emphasis on continuity threatens the historicity of Jesus "insofar as it becomes the main criterion of his archetypal nature, forcing him to

---

353 Cf., for example Gunther Wenz, *Geschichte der Versöhnungslehre in der evangelischen Theologie der Neuzeit* (Munich: Kaiser, 1984), 385–386, n. 49.
354 Stephan, *Erlösung*, 51.

eliminate Jesus' struggle (*Angefochtenheit*) and to cover up the cross".[355] Already Bretschneider had invoked the "struggle of his soul in Gethsemane" as an argument against attributing a constant, unchallenged strength to Jesus' God-consciousness.[356] For Schleiermacher, it was the key formula which marked his perception of Jesus' life and was the measure under which he subordinated all individual events. He saw it as verified by the New Testament, specifically by the Johannine portrayal of Jesus. Yet he failed to use the chance to interpret "exhaustively the inner life of Christ and to take it as the revelation of God or as principle of knowledge of God. With one stroke, many a lacuna would have been filled: the consciousness of the forgiveness of sins would be explained, ... and the objection of the formal character would fall at least to some degree."[357]

6.3.3 Continuity of natural forces versus contingency of history

The reason why the *Glaubenslehre* fails to expound on the singularity of Jesus was identified early on: it is due to the categories set by the Introduction to which the material Christology was bound and which it could only implement. As Isaac August Dorner observed only a few years after its second publication, they are responsible for the fact that the determination of the soteriological function does not allow enough space for Jesus' own interpretation of his relationship to God:

> the whole significance of Christ's personality is exhausted in the implantation (*Einsenkung*) of a new principle of life in humanity, without noting or proving sufficiently how essential the personality in which it appeared and continues to exist is for its implantation and reproduction. It is clear that this new principle of life, not conceived in a personal way itself, but only as a force, does not guarantee the significance of the personality of Christ ... That the personal effectiveness (*Wirksamkeit*) of Christ is downgraded in Schleiermacher, is connected to the fact that Christ is only the perfected God-consciousness. If Christ's dignity only consists in this, it is true that he can only remain significant as a generative (*fortpflanzendes*) principle, but not as a personality; and his personality is only of value until the strengthened God-consciousness has been implanted into humanity through it as its vehicle ... Yet if we seek for Christ the specific dignity which the Christian consciousness demands and which also Schleiermacher maintains, ... we shall be forced to either state

---

355 Lange, *Historischer Jesus*, 170–172.
356 Bretschneider, "Ueber den Begriff der Erlösung, 28–29.
357 Stephan, *Erlösung*, 156.

less about Christ, or more than Schleiermacher did, when he conceives of him mainly just as a new life principle and as the perfected God-consciousness".[358]

Dorner's contrast between "life principle" or "force", and "personality" points to the two different realms of nature and history: whether Christ is seen in a long-term, potentially naturalising, perspective as incorporating the second stage of creation and completing it through the mere strength of his God-consciousness; *or* whether its concrete contents, his particular, one-of-a-kind, authoritative understanding of God's being and will, is decisive for his significance. This content could have been determined, as also subsequent interpreters propose, as Jesus' embodiment of God's love to all humans, a content that cannot be derived from speculation, but only revealed in the testimony of a life determined by it; it would then have had to be interpreted in categories of history and freedom, rather than those of nature. But this would have required Schleiermacher to completely reconceive his idea of God, in order to allow for a particular identification of God with the person of Jesus; this had been excluded due to his stance that assigning anthropomorphic and arbitrary ways of acting to God was to be avoided. The reasons why Schleiermacher cannot express the relationship between God and human beings in terms of a history between them, will be followed up in the next chapter on his doctrine of God. With regard to the role left to history in this framework, Theodor H. Jørgensen offers the following perceptive explanation:

> Despite the greater weight that is attributed to history in Schleiermacher's understanding of revelation in terms of philosophy of religion, history is not being taken seriously in its contingency and historical concreteness. The history of Jesus as a filled span of time is not the content, but only the medium of the revelation of Christ. The uniqueness of this history consists in its ideal content and not in what God allows to happen through Jesus to humans and for them. That God identifies with this history of Jesus in a special way and becomes historical in it in order to share through it and transform the fate of humans, is a thought that cannot be shared (*unnachvollziehbar*) by Schleiermacher. Such an identification of God with a particular history could, according to Schleiermacher, "only be explained as an arbitrary divine act (*Willkür*)", that is, "an anthropopathic view" (§ 13,1) which is unacceptable. Schleiermacher thinks that the only way to avoid this kind of view of God is to sublate the temporal appearance of Jesus into God's *eternal* decree.[359]

---

[358] Isaak August Dorner, *Entwicklungsgeschichte der Lehre von der Person Christi* (Stuttgart: S. G. Liesching, 1839), 522–525.
[359] Jørgensen, *Das religionsphilosophische Offenbarungsverständnis*, 333–334.

In Chapter 2, when discussing the claim of a natural, actualised God-consciousness in all human beings in ²§4, both a philosophical and a theological critique were put forward: that it overextended the results of the analysis of self-consciousness which should have concluded with human facticity; and that it made a relationship that could only emerge historically into an a priori element.[360]

The authors quoted so far from the history of reception and critique of the *Glaubenslehre* have pointed out the connection between the theory decisions made in the essence definitions of piety and of Christianity, and his Christology. The relationship between anthropology and the doctrine of Christ appears not simply as circular in its method, but as a circle which is closed in such a way that it prevents Christology from having a content of its own. The interpretation of God which Jesus proclaimed in his parables, actions and readiness to suffer death for this vision of God is not specified in its illuminating details. This "closed circularity" is identified by Pröpper as the core problematic of "his hermeneutics of faith … Schleiermacher's doctrine of redemption and Christology only thematise the realisation of what already the anthropology had vindicated as an essential constitution, or – vice versa – the anthropology already contains the content of what was to be given only through Jesus."[361]

Having examined his Christology, there is now increasing evidence that the concept of the God claimed to be reached in the Introduction's analysis of subjectivity may also turn out to be bound by its own restrictive features, which will have to be explored in the following chapter.

6.3.4 The balance between Christology and ecclesiology

The *Glaubenslehre* has performed the modern turn to the subject by finding its starting point in the pious self-consciousness of Christians and taking the ecclesial doctrines as its expressions that had to be reconstructed in their systematic

---

360 In *Embedded Grace*, 147, Kevin Vander Schel accurately sums up the critique about the "relationship between the interconnected natural order of the world and the Reign of God proceeding from the Redeemer", though he does not share it. "For many of his critics, the essential theological content seems to be given already in the work's first part through the general consciousness of God that accompanies our finite experience in the natural world, and when measured against this basis, the specific aspects of Christian doctrine considered in the second part appear only as supplemental and repetitive. The analysis of the present chapter suggests a significantly different understanding of Schleiermacher's dogmatic thought."
361 Pröpper, "Bestimmung", in *Evangelium und freie Vernunft*, 146.

coherence. Dogmatics is thus the reflected *explication* of the contents that are implied in the Christian consciousness of faith which is an experience of redemption. It is based on contemporary Christian practice and reflects its self-understanding in a historically informed account; it is therefore a function of faith in Christ which, being teleological, is oriented towards the realisation of the kingdom of God.

On the one hand, the dogmatics as a reflected expression of the Christian experience of redemption, and the emphasis on its historical character in its orientation to the given consciousness of faith of a specific era (cf. ^{1}§ 1; ^{2}§ 19) are necessary consequences of the anthropological turn. On the other hand, a strong link to the contemporary consciousness of faith also contains the danger that the possible tension between Jesus' own history and its current understanding does not appear. The question remains whether the reference of the Christian self-consciousness back to Jesus can also contain a critique of current faith perspectives on him. If the origin of the faith only becomes accessible through a contemporary consciousness which has been mediated through the corporate life founded by Jesus, it seems unlikely that this origin can exert a counterweight to its current actualisation. By over-emphasising the mediatedness, at the same time Christology risks being subordinated to ecclesiology. The following comment points to this subordination from having analysed Schleiermacher's eschatology: The work of Christ with "all its implications (for the person of Jesus and for the person who believes in him) takes place exclusively within the new corporate life of the church ... Everything that is stated in Christology and in soteriology, must be understood in its subject-matter (*der Sache nach*) as an implication of ecclesiology."[362]

The strong systematic position of the corporate life is also a consequence of the second edition's greater emphasis on history against the reproach that the redeemer was an ideal projected by the pious consciousness of individual believers. But the question is whether a greater curiosity for the historical details, as captured in the different accounts of the four gospels and other New Testament writings, would have called for more caution in situating the historical realisation of Christianity in the current ecclesial consciousness. Taking the New Testament seriously as a counterpart of the church of each era and reconstructing the underlying perspectives of its communities would have offered another basis for appreciating the diversity of subsequent developments and the incompleteness of each.

---

[362] Eilert Herms, "Schleiermachers Eschatologie nach der zweiten Auflage der 'Glaubenslehre'", in *Zeitschrift für Theologie und Kirche* 46 (1990) 97–123, 107. 105.

The seventh chapter will have to investigate the role of the doctrine of God in sealing the tension between what the anthropological turn in theology could have made possible, and the way its new categories were in fact filled: subjectivity and self-consciousness, the unity of the historical beginning and of the internal particularity in the person of Jesus, dogmatics as clarification of the expressions of the pious consciousness, and church as the community of believers engaged in the realisation of the kingdom of God. With the rejection of speculative and objectivising metaphysical foundations of faith in God, it seemed as if theology had found its way back to its own ground: the historical self-disclosure of God in the person of Jesus, something that could not be derived from reason. Yet despite opening up these promising new categories, the way in which the doctrines of the person and the work of Christ have been elaborated was curtailed. A special identification of God with the history of Jesus was excluded as much as the idea that "the proclamation of Jesus in unity with his destiny was God's self-testimony (*Selbstzeugnis*)".[363]

Chapter 7 will examine the reasons for the format of the doctrine of God which prohibits any statements that would portray God as engaging in a more than general way with the world and its creatures. Apart from Christology, it also affects what can be said about the believers' relationship to God and about history as it is shaped by their agency. The key idea that constitutes the bracket linking creation and redemption, God's eternal decree, will have to be scrutinised in its guiding premises and its consequences. Since the complete sequence of the events of salvation is contained in this decree, the danger of this concept is that what should be captured as the unfolding *history* of salvation in its open-endedness is moved back into the pre-temporal realm of divine causality. This retrojection would also explain the supralapsarian standpoint from which the *Glaubenslehre* unfolds its propositions about the human person, the world and history. Especially the second edition can be seen as arguing from a Christian self-consciousness at the stage of being in possession of blessedness. Schleiermacher adopts a position from which "all divine action is under the perspective of what has been accomplished (*Vollbrachten*)".[364] This standpoint is the consequence of an approach in which the real difference between God's action of

---

[363] Jørgensen, *Offenbarungsverständnis*, 345.
[364] In "Die Ausscheidung der Lehre vom Zorn Gottes in der Theologie Schleiermachers und Ritschls", in *Neue Zeitschrift für Systematische Theologie und Religionsphilosophie* 10 (1968) 387–397, Hans-Walter Schütte sees this as a consequence of Schleiermacher's understanding of Christianity. It interprets "divine action with humanity ... as the action of grace in Christ which leads it from a world of being torn (*Gespaltenheit*) to the fulfilled community with God" (391).

creation and that of redemption disappears in the idea of eternal all-causality (*All-Wirksamkeit*). In contrast, it should be exactly the mark of a human capacity for reflection that draws on the heritage of biblical narratives and theological reflections for its construction of meaning, that it is able to perceive the contradictions and failures that make humans suffer. When history is posited as the unfolding of a divinely preconceived plan of salvation, not only are tragedies and faults levelled[365] but also a return to the unrealised hopes of the past, to be recouped by individuals and generations in the present, is blocked.[366] The reasons for the directions taken lie in the parameters Schleiermacher considered to be decisive in developing a doctrine of God that would be in keeping with the insights of contemporary philosophy and science.

6.4 Summary and guiding questions to the doctrine of God

In summary, from the treatment of Christian anthropology, both general and specific, and of Christology in the material dogmatics, questions have arisen that will now be pursued in the doctrine of God. Schleiermacher's intention from his Lectures of 1811 onwards has been to offer an account of the Christian understanding of God that can be justified to a critical contemporary audience by relating it to the general consciousness of truth. The outline of *The Christian Faith* was therefore designed in an elliptical shape.[367] The Introduction offered an anthropological foundation of the concept of religion before expounding the Chris-

---

365 Cf. Lange's conclusion in "Die Kontroverse Hegels und Schleiermachers um das Verständnis der Religion", in *Hegel-Studien* 18 (1983) 201–224, 223: The fact that Schleiermacher "finds himself forced to assume (*unterlegen*) a continuity both of the biography of the individual person and – despite all epoch-making new beginnings – of history as a whole which threatens to level, rather than integrate, the negativity of counter-forces (*Widerständigen*) … can be seen as much from his theory of sin as a mere potentiality of the God-consciousness as from his theory of history which ultimately aims for an *apokatastasis panton*". The question whether negativity can be "integrated" not just conceptually remains controversial, but it is true that the reasons why Schleiermacher interprets "election" in terms of an ultimate reconciliation of all will have to be examined.
366 For an understanding of history in these terms, cf. Paul Ricoeur, for example in *Reflections on the Just*, trans. David Pellauer (Chicago: University of Chicago Press, 2007), 105.
367 While rejecting Karl Barth's critique that Schleiermacher's theology constitutes a circle centred on anthropology, Richard R. Niebuhr does not regard Christology as the second focal point. It "is not the Archimedean point by means of which the *Christian Faith* moves all the other doctrines of theology before the reader's view … Schleiermacher's theology like that of Calvin and others … has more than one center and does not pretend to exhibit the artificial simplicity of the circle" (*Schleiermacher on Christ and Religion*, 212).

6.4 Summary and guiding questions to the doctrine of God

tian particularity based on its type, its historical starting point, and its internal content. The second focal point was developed in the material dogmatics. It was split into a general part, abstracted from the subsequent specific elaboration, and a treatment of Christian doctrines in their particularity. The procedure itself of documenting in the structure of Christian dogmatics the distinction between the necessary philosophical categories, and a Christian determination of these guiding thought forms can be endorsed as an ingenious outline that offers a transparent succession of steps. Yet having followed up the theory decisions made regarding the order and elucidation of the material system of doctrines so far, the following questions arise for its anchor point, the concept of God:

First, how do the propositions reached on these two avenues relate to each other? What are the general attributes of God, developed in keeping with the feeling of absolute dependence, and how will they be further determined through the Christian antithesis of sin and grace? In other words, what space does the framework provide for elements that could only be known historically, through the person of Jesus, such as God's love?

Secondly, do the revisions of the doctrine of sin and of Christology that were made in response to the critiques of the first edition find a counterpart in the doctrine of God?

Thirdly, if the exposition of the conception of God confirms the objection about the closed circle between anthropology and Christology, the concluding question will be: What changes in the understanding of God would be needed that would enable this circle to be opened? For example, if God was not only explicated as absolute causality but as absolute freedom, what new understandings would emerge: of creation, of revelation, and of Jesus' relationship to God as well as of human agency responding to God's self-disclosure?

7 A Doctrine of God Developed from the Feeling of Absolute Dependence

The earlier decision to treat the doctrine of God as the third material chapter in Part Two was taken because the concrete determinations of the human person and of the Redeemer were needed as the backdrop for the way in which Schleiermacher conceptualises God's activity. The chapter will begin with an analysis of the key points established already in the first edition (7.1). An examination of the changes in the revised version in response to questions which beset the first reception of *The Christian Faith* will follow, some of which have their roots in the "abstracted" status of the First Part of the material dogmatics (7.2). The third section will discuss the alternatives arising up until today for assessing the provisions of his concept of God. Also current commentators disagree on whether Schleiermacher abandons all "realist" understandings of God as the transcendent reference point distinct from humanity and the world and puts forward a self-contained, "pantheist" theory instead, thus reading the *Glaubenslehre* on the lines of the *Speeches*. The opposite view is that the distinction between God and world that was crucial in the definition of the essence of piety is also the key to the material doctrine of God.[368] After weighing up the evidence from these necessary conceptual-philosophical clarifications it will be time to sum up the theory decisions Schleiermacher did in fact – but did not have to – take. The criterium guiding the assessment continues to be the freedom of both God and of the human beings created and sustained. Which other perspective could have been developed on the basis of his theological endorsement of the anthropological turn (7.3)?

---

368 Among the representatives of the first view are Andrew Dole and Daniel J. Pedersen, while the second interpretation is held by Jacqueline Mariña, Thomas Pröpper, Susanne Schaefer, Martin Ohst and others. Ohst insists on the need to take account of the vastly different intellectual contexts of Schleiermacher's understanding of the natural sciences from today's, qualifying his view on the "nexus of nature" as teleological-metaphysical. Cf. Martin Ohst, Review of Dole, Andrew, *Schleiermacher on Religion and the Natural Order* (Oxford: OUP, 2010), in *Church History and Religious Culture* 92 (2012) 456–459.

7.1 Foundational points from the first edition onwards: God as absolute causality

The consequence drawn from the Introduction's connection of absolute dependence to a "Whence" is that the only adequate way to determine the concept of God is as absolute causality. This key idea for the difference between God and world is elaborated, however, under the provision that God's omnipotence is "completely represented (*vollkommen dargestellt*) in the totality of finite being (*Gesammtheit des endlichen Seins*)" (¹§ 68.a. LS. I, 204). Aware of the "seeming pantheism" of this innovation, Schleiermacher still argues for understanding the divine omnipotence that follows from this all-causality entirely from God's relationship to the world (7.1.1). A further consequence of taking all-causality as his starting point is that "preservation" trumps "creation" as being more in keeping with the feeling of absolute dependence. It also includes, as we have seen, the appearance of the Redeemer which is considered at the same time as new, and as a "preservation" of human original perfection, depending on the perspective taken. By shifting the vantage point from the experience of the believer to the enabling framework, the thought of the "one divine decree" is reached in which both components have been eternally founded (7.1.2). The third theory decision already taken in the original outline – deriving, among others, from the "theism dispute" that arose from Fichte's critique of a personalist concept of God – is that any restrictive definitions which limit God to terms typical of human finitude must be excluded. The idea of God as engaging in particular actions and relationships to human beings belongs to what must be refuted, as well as the notion of a "self-limitation"[369] of God (7.1.3).

7.1.1 God and the "interconnected process of nature" (*Naturzusammenhang*)

Schleiermacher's position that human agency is embedded in the encompassing "nexus of nature" – an interlinked conception informed by Leibniz's critique of a dead, mechanistic understanding of natural causes – was a key premise explained in Chapter 5. Having reached the doctrine of God, it now turns out that also the Creator is seen as necessarily relating to the world. On the one hand, the idea is underlined as central that God and world are not identical. This point is driven home already by distinguishing God's "omnipotence" from

---

[369] Schleiermacher, "Letters", 43.

creation. Schleiermacher effectively sides with Descartes and Leibniz in restituting the idea of free omnipotence:

> In Descartes' new version of the ontological argument, the idea of the omnipotent God who has power also over God's own existence acquires a momentous function, since with Spinoza's definition of substance as aseity and thus of God as the only substance, the concept of free omnipotence becomes obsolete. Leibniz rehabilitates faith in creation, yet conceives of God's omnipotence, wisdom and goodness in such an interlinked way that the creation of the best of all possible worlds follows with necessity … Schleiermacher whose analysis of the feeling of absolute dependence reformulates the contingency problem in subject theoretical terms nevertheless regards God's omnipotence as "completely represented in the totality of finite being" (^{2}§ 54).[370]

In the first edition, God's distinction from the world becomes clear in Schleiermacher's comment on the usual elucidation of the "simplicity" of God as a negation of materiality: "it goes without saying that when we are to distinguish God and world in any way, then all matter has to belong to the world. But strictly speaking simplicity not only excludes materiality but also the similarity with finite spirit. … the highest being must be as much above the nature of finite spirit as above the physical" (^{1}§ 69,2. I, 224; cf. ^{2}§ 56,2. I, 304). Here, the difference between the divine and the finite is made evident. As absolute causality and founder of the world's existence, God is prior to the totality of the reciprocal effects that make up the web of nature, humans and their history included.

On the other hand, as already indicated in the final line of the previous quote, despite these clearly anti-Spinozist statements, Schleiermacher balances this point with a position which borders on the "heretical", as he admits in the marginal notes to the first edition:[371] that the omnipotence which is derived from God's all-causality is in fact "completely represented" (*vollkommen dargestellt*) in the nexus of nature (^{1}§ 68.a. I, 204; cf. ^{2}§ 54 LS. I, 279).[372] At the same time, the second half of the proposition in the first edition reinforces the distinction between the world and God by explaining God's omniscience in a way that safeguards God's sovereignty in knowing what the omnipotence consists in. The second section, ^{1}§ 68.b., defines the "omniscience" of God as the "absolute spirituality" (*Geistigkeit*) (I, 211) of divine omnipotence, indicating a subject in charge of and not only exhaustingly represented in the nexus of nature.

---

[370] Pröpper, "Art. Allmacht", in *Evangelium und freie Vernunft*, 288–293, 291.
[371] The new ET includes these marginal notes quoted in the Redeker edition. Cf. ET 2016, vol. I, 305, 2. Ed. note.
[372] Instead of "represented", both ETs use "completely presented" for "*vollkommen dargestellt*", the term used both in the first and the second editions.

Schleiermacher's doctrinal innovation of limiting God's omnipotence to the realm of the world leads to the explicit conclusion that there can be no difference between willing and effective capability (*Können*) in God. It is put forward as an implication of the thesis (*Leitsatz*) that "all exists and happens in reality for which there is a productivity in God" (¹§ 68.a. I, 204); or, as the second edition states, "consequently everything for which there is a causality in God happens and becomes real" (²§ 54 LS. ET 1928, 211). Since there can be no "difference between the real and the possible" (¹§ 68.a.,3. I, 207), it is further concluded that no distinction applies between "'will' and 'can'" in God (¹§ 68.a., 4. I, 208). In the context of the anthropology developed in the third section of Part One, regarding the original perfection of the world, the same position is expressed in Schleiermacher's critique of Leibniz's argumentation that the existing world is the "best of all possible worlds".[373] Any such qualification is ruled out based on the argument that assuming a possibility of choice for God would diminish God's "perfection".[374] The reason for tying God's omnipotence to what has been actualised and making this totality synonymous with the complete range of divine power is a certain idea of "perfection" that is not further explained. It is only stated that for God, the difference between the real and the possible does not obtain and that it is only "a truth for us" (¹§ 68.a.,2. I, 206). How this argumentation affects the designation of the divine-human relationship will be analysed in 7.3. Regarding God's relationship to the divinely sustained nexus of nature, Susanne Schaefer enquires: "Is God's action (*Wirken*) entirely exhausted in the world? But what standing does this leave for God's transcendence? In view of the dominance of the causal interrelatedness which is conceived as even tying in the appearance of the Redeemer, is a free historical agency of God in fact still possible?"[375]

---

373 See above, Chapter 5.2.2.
374 In its notes to ²§ 54,3, the ET 2016, I, 309, n. 15, quotes the marginal note: "In God both a difference in willing and being able [*eine Differenz von Wollen und Können*] and a separation [*Trennung*] would be an imperfection [*eine Unvollkommenheit*]". The negative view of attributing freedom of choice to God is based, as Marg. 765 to ¹§ 49 explains, on the judgement that "freedom as choice always points to an imperfect inner production" (KGA I/7,3, 133). Schaefer, *Gottes Sein zur Welt*, 119, notes the "remarkable addition" that in "independent self-activity must and willing are the same" (*In dieser ist müssen und Wollen gleich*) (Marg. 765), which indicates a necessary activity of God, not merely God's ability to do what God wills.
375 Schaefer, *Gottes Sein zur Welt*, 134–135. Cf. 237–262.

7.1.2 The priority of preservation over creation

A further outcome of the hermeneutical principle of the material dogmatics, the feeling of absolute dependence in its Christian specification as redemption, is the reversed sequence of creation and preservation. God's all-causality is first experienced in the continuity of the life of the world and of one's personal existence; its beginning, in contrast, is not accessible for thinkers under the conditions of finitude. While the theological concept of *creatio ex nihilo* is retained from the Christian history of thinking, it is used to underline the sovereignty of a God who is not merely ordering pre-existing matter. The distinction between the Christian God as the creative origin of all that exists and the Greek idea of matter as eternal is upheld.[376] But the emphasis is on continuity, not on the free and unprecedented act of creation. With "preservation" as the lens through which "creation" is viewed,[377] the first becomes a category that also encompasses the historical breakthrough signified by the Redeemer. It joins the two parts of salvation history into one unified decree, making the whole approach supralapsarian. As indicated by the well-chosen title by Edwin Van Driel, *Incarnation Anyway*, this view conceives of redemption as always already intended in the creation of humanity, and not as a new divine initiative in view of the Fall.[378] With the appearance of the Redeemer classified as the "preservation" of original perfection, it can also ultimately be traced to the realisation of "love", understood as the "unification" (*Vereinigung*) or "union" of the divine being with human nature"

---

[376] The first edition calls it a "faultless and necessary" (*tadellos und notwendig*) concept (¹§ 49,1. I, 142), the second leaves out "necessary" after "*tadellos*" (²§ 41,1. I, 200).
[377] Robert J. Sherman, *The Shift to Modernity. Christ and the Doctrine of Creation in the Theologies of Schleiermacher and Barth* (New York/London: T & T Clark, 2005), 121–122.
[378] Edwin Van Driel, *Incarnation Anyway: Arguments for Supralapsarian Christology* (Oxford: OUP, 2008). This worthwhile comparison of three crucial perspectives in the history of modern theology (Schleiermacher, I. A. Dorner and K. Barth), however, comes to judgements that are questionable in the way they ignore distinct levels as well as the need to do justice to Jesus' humanity. His impression that based on Schleiermacher's argumentation, "God did not have to choose Jesus to be the Redeemer. He could have chosen any of us" (28), is drawn from the principled statement that in all of us "reside(s) the possibility of taking up the divine into itself, just as did happen in Christ" (²§ 94,1. ET 1928, 385; ²§ 13,1. ET 1928, 64). Van Driel's verdict, which seems to be close to F. C. Baur's objection against promoting the "ideal" of a Redeemer, fails to take into account the role of the gospel of John for Schleiermacher's image of Jesus and the consistent interest to relate his dogmatic Christology to biblical texts by equally referring back to the Synoptics and to Paul, also in his Sunday sermons. The difference from F. C. Baur regarding research into the historical foundations is that it is not the reason for believing in Jesus as the Redeemer, though it is crucial for tracing the "total impression" he made on his disciples.

(^{1}§ 181,1. II, 344; ^{2}§ 165,1)[379] in the concluding section on the particular attributes of the Christian God.

It is possible to acknowledge the challenges of the intellectual context to which *The Christian Faith* was responding and equally highlight the price paid for this decisive shift in the doctrine of God. Wolfhart Pannenberg respects the "courage" with which Schleiermacher was ready to take up the philosophical critique of unexamined theistic premises and break with established theological thought patterns. Regarding the prominence of "preservation", however, Pannenberg points to an opposite prevalence in the dogmatic tradition: In it, "the creature finds itself not at all as 'continuing' ('*im Fortbestehen*') by its own forces but relies in every moment on the divine creative action ... each moment of her existence is owed to the freedom of the divine action of creation"; in contrast, "Schleiermacher accentuates the continuity of ongoing existence which as such is thought as being dependent from God."[380] An observation Schaefer makes corresponds to the theological tradition's emphasis on the wonder of each new moment which Schleiermacher plays down. He is able to do so on the basis of his analysis of subjectivity in the Introduction. There is a connection between its result, his claim of an absolute dependence from God – thus overdrawing in a philosophically problematic way the finding of an unavoidable contingency – and the reliance on "preservation" as the key to the world relationship. Her examination of ^{2}§ 4 (but no less true already of ^{1}§ 9) ends with the anticipatory question: "And how will it affect the doctrine of God that the human experience of contingency is ultimately one that has always already been appeased (*beruhigte*)? Will Schleiermacher be able to do justice to the radicality of the idea of a *creatio ex nihilo?*"[381] Her subsequent answer after having investigated his doctrine of God, is that the content of *creatio ex nihilo* lacks significance for him because the "basic human experience of existing" is always depicted as being in "continuity" or "process" (^{2}§ 39.1, I, 193–194):

> Yet if the fact of our own existence appears as such a matter of course for us, if we cannot really be astonished about the fact that there is a world, then the idea of a creator God who sustains people in existence suggests itself much more (*näherliegt*) than that of a creator who calls from nothingness into being. The lack of interest in *creatio ex nihilo* is finally owed to the fact that ... the abysmal experience of the non-necessity of one's own being

---

379 The ET 2016 has "union of divine being with human nature" (II, 1004), the ET 1928, "the union of the Divine Essence with human nature" (727).
380 Pannenberg, "Schwierigkeiten", 16. I will come back to the shortcomings Pannenberg identifies in his solution in 7.3.1.
381 Schaefer, *Gottes Sein zur Welt*, 100.

is never brought to complete consciousness but is always pacified through the perspective of its further theological qualification by the Whence of absolute dependence."[382]

The question about the "origin of all finite being" is ruled out by Schleiermacher as "raised not in the interest of piety but in that of curiosity" (*Wißbegierde*) (²§ 39,1. ET 1928, 148–149).[383] The priority of preservation is also consistent with a further feature of doctrinal expressions that he sees as being in need of correction: personalistic concepts which risk reducing God to the level of finite beings.

7.1.3 The view of personalistic concepts as limiting for God

The doctrine of God, a treatise that has offered other theologians a location for flourishing conclusions on their reconstruction of the truth of the Christian faith, is used by Schleiermacher above all as a field of demarcation, dividing permissible from unacceptable statements. Based on the criterium of the infinity of God, the task he has set himself is to impose strict methodological limits on what can be said about God. In his comparison of the doctrines of creation in Schleiermacher and Karl Barth, Robert Sherman identifies the concise sense of method in the procedure especially of Part One:

> The first part sometimes plays a negative role, that is, it seeks to exclude understandings or beliefs that Schleiermacher views as unnecessary or inappropriate to the essence of Christian piety or as incompatible with modern intellectual assumptions. Alternately, it sometimes plays a preliminary role, that is, it seeks to expound certain general presuppositional

---

382 Schaefer, *Gottes Sein zur Welt*, 175.
383 This judgement should be considered surprising in view of the biblical and theological traditions of thinking. By allocating the question of the origin of humanity and the world instead to "knowledge" or "curiosity" (*Wißbegierde*) (¹§ 47,1. I, 139; ²§ 39,1. ET 1928, 148–149), Schleiermacher underestimates the relevance of the problem of meaning which cannot be answered by natural scientific enquiries. Philosophically, the question if the world does or does not have a beginning belongs to the antinomies of pure reason (*Vernunft*) and rules out any resolution by way of the knowledge that is obtainable by the faculty of "understanding" (*Verstand*). Cf. Kant, *Critique of Pure Reason*, trans. Norman Kemp Smith (New York: St. Martin's Press/Toronto: MacMillan, 1965), 364–484, esp. 396–402 (A 426–434; B 455–462). By shifting the religious conviction of meaning to the preserving role of God, the question of the possible groundlessness of all being is bypassed and the only remaining problem is how to think its continued existence. Together with other conclusions such as that personalist terms are to be avoided, and that God must count as the indirect author of sin, the subordination of creation to preservation has been one of the most criticised theory decisions in the doctrine of God.

beliefs that are to be embraced and completed in a specific Christian manner in the second part.³⁸⁴

The first qualification made takes seriously the critical limits of reason as well as the hermeneutical principle of developing the propositions on God derived from the pious stirrings first in the fundamental dogmatic form of anthropological statements; at the same time, it undercuts all naïve assumptions to be speaking about God. Its subject matter is reclassified more modestly as being about impressions of the Christian consciousness: "All attributes which we ascribe to God cannot indicate something special in God, but only something special in the manner in which our feeling of absolute dependence is being related to Him" (¹§ 64 LS. I, 188; cf. ²§ 50 LS. ET 1928, 194). Pannenberg clarifies their status: "When in the feeling of absolute dependence a causal relationship between God as the principle of original activity (§ 37,1) on the one hand, and human receptivity as well as the being of everything finite on the other hand, is expressed, then the attributes ascribed to God are to be taken as modifications of this dependence."³⁸⁵

The propositions obtained on the basis of the Christian determination of the feeling of absolute dependence, however, still need to be explicated in a consistent way that respects the distinction between a finite and an infinite subject. What is rejected as inadequate is to implicitly reduce God to the human "sphere of limitedness". An example of this can be found in the different types of knowledge attributed to God in the history of Christian thinking under the attribute of omniscience which he rejects since they break the "rule that in God there is no change" (²§ 55,2. ET 1928, 222). This conception of God, "derived from the one fundamental religious consciousness that God is the sole immutable determinant of all that is, the all-encompassing 'Whence' in § 4",³⁸⁶ has several consequences. Under these premises, there can be no "relationship of reciprocity" (*Wechselwirkung*) between Creator and creature (²§ 147,2. ET 2016, II, 933); instead of being able to interact in history in specific ways with human beings, only a general, preserving action on the nexus of nature is conceivable. It is equally ruled out as unthinkable that "an act of divine self-limitation" could be attributed to God.³⁸⁷ Robert Sherman resumes accurately: When "divine activity, whether

---

384 Sherman, *The Shift to Modernity*, 120.
385 Pannenberg, "Schwierigkeiten", 12.
386 Sherman, *The Shift to Modernity*, 133.
387 Schleiermacher, "Letters", 43. Such a divine resolution, however, could be conceivable out of respect for human freedom, as Pröpper points out in *Theologische Anthropologie*, vol. I, 480, n. 176.

conceived as creating or sustaining, consists of *a single and uninterrupted act*", human self-activity is located at a different level that does not intersect with the level at which God operates "as the sole determinant of the world, enabling development on the basis of one eternal decree".[388]

But are these only the abstracted, general propositions of Part One which will be further qualified by the particular Christian impressions? For Gunther Wenz, the outlook towards Part Two's second section "under the consciousness of grace" to the insight "that the absolute primordial ground of all Being and of all that exists (*Urgrund allen Seins und allen Seienden*) is nothing else than pure wisdom and love" is decisive: "Without this certainty, Christian hamartiology cannot be meaningfully thought but would end in desolation (*Heillosigkeit*)".[389] In a close examination of Schleiermacher's procedure, Pannenberg, however, comes to the judgement that the critique of personalist conceptions remains dominant:

> It is true that Schleiermacher increasingly recognised the great significance of the conception of God as a free, personal counterpart to the human person in the immediate life of religion. Yet in the treatment of the divine attributes, it remains out of consideration even though many of the attribute concepts like omnipotence and omniscience, and especially God's love imply the conception of the deity as a personal counterpart.

He observes in the very definitions of the Christian concepts the effect of the general framework, also in how

> the divine love revealed in Christ is interpreted, although he said of it that in love as the only attribute of God the very own essence of God communicated itself (§ 166). According to Schleiermacher, we can know also divine love only in the consciousness of redemption as an effect coming from God. Thus, in this case as well, Schleiermacher was able to evade the idea of immediate personal involvement (*Zuwendung*) that is inherent in the concept of love and hold on to the thought of the effects of God's activity as the basis of ascribing attributes instead.[390]

Pannenberg ends with a dual appraisal:

> It was Schleiermacher's achievement as a theologian to be able to reformulate the content of Christian doctrine and thus preserve it under the conditions of the critique of the traditional concept of God. On the other hand, he was probably too quick in conceding ground (*das Feld überlassen*) to the critique of the idea of a freely acting God that arose with Spi-

---

388 Sherman, *The Shift to Modernity*, 122. 133.
389 Wenz, "Sünde und Schuldbewusstsein", 322.
390 Pannenberg, "Schwierigkeiten", 12–13

noza and was sharpened by Fichte in 1798, in contrast to the leading philosophers of the time, especially Schelling and Hegel.[391]

Also for Pröpper, Schleiermacher's investment into the insights drawn from the "theism" dispute in which he sided with Fichte, as already made clear in the *Speeches*, overpowers the contents of a Christian dogmatics. He regards his insistence on driving out personal language on God from the consistent dogmatic exposition he strives for as marked by "an almost zealous (*eifernder*) concern".[392] Most affected for Pröpper is the understanding of human freedom which is diminished in several individual theory decisions to a degree that is odds with the increased effort of the second edition to specify it as the capacity that enables the analysis of human subjectivity in its distinction from God. How important it is to secure human individuality against being sucked into the Spinozist All-One monism, will be followed up under "Ongoing disputes" in section 7.3, after turning next to examining two changes between the two editions that affect the doctrine of God.

7.2 Clarifications in the final elaboration of the doctrine of God

The fundamental lines of the doctrine of God either precede or have been set in the first edition, with the organising concept of the "one decree" of creation and redemption developed already in the "Election" essay of 1819.[393] The corrections carried out for the second edition do not effect changes of direction but they indicate a need for clarification on instructive points. The reviews had shown that the "abstracted" character of the First Part had been mistaken for a natural theology (7.2.1). A further reason for this impression were the references Schleiermacher had included to the concept of God that he had established within his theory of knowing; with these sections deleted or modified in the second edition, crucial propositions are now explained strictly on the basis of the pious consciousness, without support by the *Dialectic* (7.2.2).[394]

---

391 Pannenberg, "Schwierigkeiten", 16.
392 Pröpper, "Bestimmung", in *Evangelium und freie Vernunft*, 146.
393 Regarding the theme of election, Gockel's judgement is that the "doctrine of election in the first edition is identical in content with the slightly enhanced version in the second edition and does not merit a separate discussion." *Election*, 37, n. 1.
394 These differences include replacing general references to the human "spirit" with its direction to the "God-consciousness" and adding "through Christ" to the effects of the Spirit. Many of

7.2.1 The status of Part One: not a natural theology

The inclusion of a new type of doctrinal statements in which "general" features were outlined that would subsequently be concretised in their Christian characteristics gave rise to misunderstandings. Although it was carried out with concise methodological explanations, the innovation of supplying a first general part was affected also by earlier misinterpretations as well as by issues in need of deeper analysis. Some readers had mistaken the material dogmatics as beginning with the Introduction's first proposition. Highlighting the disciplines at the origin of the "borrowed propositions" (*Lehnsätze*) was one measure taken to counteract this false impression. A further opportunity to come to misleading results was the undeveloped argumentation of ¹§ 9. It concluded the "Whence" of absolute dependence not from the dual constitution of human subjectivity but directly from the latter of the two states of being either self-active or passively determined, which the early reviewers questioned on behalf of human freedom. When the "co-determining factor" was captured in Part One by the concept of "absolute causality", it was easy to think that this statement and the components it implied were true of all historical religions, thus mistaking the concepts "abstracted" from the Christian pious impressions for a general philosophical statement of natural theology. Robert Sherman describes clearly Schleiermacher's aims when expounding two specific themes from the Christian stirrings:

> the First Part of the *Glaubenslehre* produces two doctrines in the "fundamental form": divine preservation and creation ... he intends to offer a preliminary understanding of the world as the catalyst for the emergence and continuity of the fundamental feeling of absolute dependence as it is perceived by Christians. Thus, the propositions given will not offer specific data or knowledge about the world, but rather the Christian attitude toward and

---

these changes in the specification of the "common spirit", however, relate more to Christology and ecclesiology than to the doctrine of God. A greater emphasis on sinfulness as a collective and historically embedded condition in the revised version leads to a more communal understanding of redemption. The "Spirit" becomes unmistakeably linked to the Christian church which continues the work of the Redeemer for the Kingdom of God. As Martin Rössler has noted in his treatment of the discipline of "Philosophical theology" and its partial implementation in the Introduction of the *Glaubenslehre*, the "church" acquires a different role from the first paragraphs of the second edition onwards. The argumentation changes from the first edition's method of directly accessing "piety" from the given Christian pious stirrings to a new layout in which the concept of church for which the dogmatics is written is justified. Cf. Rössler, *Schleiermachers Programm der Philosophischen Theologie*, 155–156.

interpretation of that world's ultimate source, meaning and destiny, as revealed by a thorough exposition of the fundamental feeling."[395]

The source of access is Christian piety, not human reason concluding from the existence of the world that there must be a creator God. Instead of such a pre-critical philosophical approach, it is a case of tracing in the different monotheistic traditions the particular path each takes and of exploring how they unite the feeling of absolute dependence with the determinations specific to them. Gockel quotes Schleiermacher's conclusion that a "merely monotheistic piety in which the God-consciousness in and for itself forms the content of pious moments, does not exist". A comparison reveals their particularities: "just as in Christian piety a relation to Christ always appears with the God-consciousness, in Jewish piety a relation always appears to the law-giver and in Islamic piety a relation to the revelation through the Prophet".[396] Sherman chooses an analogy to drive home the same point: "actual pious moments are never generic, but always particular ... just as in the natural realm there are, for example, no actual mammals 'in general'."[397] He concludes that the architecture of the dogmatics, with the second material part under the contrast of sin and grace, allows to relate the two levels in a unifying orientation without which "his Second Part would be nothing more than a Christian addition to a natural theology".[398]

At the same time, when analysing the premises of the concepts used in the doctrines of the First Part, their provenance can be a matter of dispute. Pannenberg draws attention to the dual origin of key terms where especially the feeling of absolute dependence stems both from Schleiermacher's "own view of it as the quintessence (*Inbegriff*) of the religious relationship", and from his "philosophical conception of God's relationship to the world". This explains "the priority of the causal relation for justifying statements on the attributes of God." Otherwise, it would be "curious (*merkwürdig*) that the considerations about the causal link between Creator and creature – as the basis for propositions on the attributes of God – work with a specific philosophical argumentation, while Schleiermacher usually prefers to appeal to the immediate expression of piety as decisive for his theological statements."[399]

Examining the feeling of absolute dependence in its function as principle, Schaefer notes the "far-reaching preliminary decisions made" when "the defini-

---

395 Sherman, *The Shift to Modernity*, 118.
396 Gockel, *Election*, 47, n. 37, with reference to ²§ 32,3. I, 174.
397 Sherman, *The Shift to Modernity*, 39.
398 Sherman, *The Shift to Modernity*, 40.
399 Pannenberg, "Schwierigkeiten", 13–14.

tion of God's relationship to the world is characterised by the category of causality", especially for the Christian concept of revelation.[400] Thus, while interpreting Part One as natural theology clearly runs counter to Schleiermacher's explicit intention and method, it must be examined how concepts he considers to be derived from the specific Christian experience may harbour contents that stem from other sources: such as a concept of divine perfection or of immutability that is part of the philosophical heritage, and may obfuscate a genuinely Christian configuration of the concept of God. This problem reappears in the area to be scrutinised next: the relevance of his philosophical reconstruction of discursive knowledge as equally presupposing an idea of God.

7.2.2 The role of the *Dialectic*

It was evident in ^{1}§§ 8 and 9 of the first line of argumentation for a universal human God-consciousness that the enquiry was conducted at a phenomenological level and then broken off by reaching for the concept of God already known from the *Dialectic*. Why are references to such confirmations from the ground of his theory of knowledge dropped in 1830/31? With the new structural analysis of subjectivity in ^{2}§§ 3 and 4, the human God-consciousness had been reached in the stringent steps of a transcendental enquiry. Schleiermacher had stated his claim that the points made could not be denied by anyone who was "capable of self-observation to any degree" (^{2}§ 4,1. ET 2016, 20). By turning a descriptive approach into a result argued with philosophical necessity, he had established a separate principle which no longer depended on the use of human rationality that is oriented towards conditions of objective knowledge. If he had continued to refer to this function, he would have undermined the newly established independent foundation of religion that he now also claimed to be prior to the objective function. In Schaefer's reconstruction, the three crucial points are concisely identified: (1) securing the original and independent place of religion, by (2) taking the starting point in the consciousness of contingency, and (3) by elevating the Christian pious consciousness to the hermeneutical principle of the dogmatic system:

> Insofar as piety or religion is specified exactly by its originality and non-derivability, theology can and must no longer be anchored in the system of the sciences by deducing it from the highest knowledge. Relying on the revelation of God in history, it represents the type of a positive science ... By determining the proper essence of piety more closely, the human

---

400 Schaefer, *Gottes Sein zur Welt*, 105.

7.2 Clarifications in the final elaboration of the doctrine of God — 221

person's God-consciousness is demonstrated on the basis of the consciousness of contingency.[401]

She resumes: "The specification of the essence of Christianity takes place in fact within the framework of piety as a philosophically demonstrated basic fact that is an essential component of the human person. Insofar as dogmatics depends on the given datum of the Christian pious consciousness, it has a contingent basis and is thus formally distinguished from philosophy."[402] This gives it its independence and signifies that references to the *Dialectic* are now no longer in keeping with the distinct foundation of a piety that stands on its own; it would actually cause confusion on the legitimating reasons and undermine the dogmatics.

Also Pannenberg questions an accompanying use of the *Dialectic* because it becomes more than a parallel avenue to the idea of God. It risks encasing dogmatics within its own framework:

> In the Dialectic, God and world are correlating concepts: No God without world, as correspondingly no world without God ... Could the idea of a correlation between God and world not make the notion of God dependent on the concept of the world – in contrast to Schleiermacher's intention to ascribe dependence only to the totality of the finite in its relationship to God, thinking God moreover as primordial activity (§ 37,1)? The idea of world presupposes the first idea, that of God ... The inseparable connection between the idea of God and the idea of the world as the final condition of knowledge corresponds to the thought in the *Glaubenslehre* that it is only possible to speak of God in relation to the world: whether a being of God without creatures can or cannot be thought is in no way related to the immediate content of the feeling of absolute dependence (§ 41,2) ... it throws a light on the fact that in describing the dependence of the world on God, the aspect of preservation is prioritised over that of creation.[403]

In this interpretation, it is not because of outside influences that key contents of Christian monotheism like the free decision to create are downplayed but due to Schleiermacher's own epistemological system. The restriction of God's free agency and interaction with the world to a correlation that limits divine agency to what is materially given has internal reasons that are evident to the author of the *Glaubenslehre* but that are not declared and discussed.

---

401 Schaefer, *Gottes Sein zur Welt*, 28. 34.
402 Schaefer, *Gottes Sein zur Welt*, 97.
403 Pannenberg, "Schwierigkeiten", 14, n. 12, with reference to the 1822 *Dialektik*, ed. Rudolf Odebrecht (Leipzig 1942, repr. Darmstadt: Wissenschaftliche Buchgesellschaft, 1976), 310 ff, 314.

The impact of the approach and the theory decisions taken in both editions will now be investigated in the final section in relation to the legacy of questions that continue to be debated in current controversies.

7.3 Ongoing disputes in the reception history

Disputes on the doctrine of God arose from the beginning in the reviews of the first and second editions by fellow theologians and philosophers, including, among others, alternative proposals in philosophy of religion to interpret the "Whence" of everything finite,[404] and the charge of pantheism. I will focus on three themes: the relation between the general and the Christian attributes of God (7.3.1), the monism-dualism debate arising from the framework for the God-world relationship (7.3.2), and an assessment of its consequences for the interaction between God and humans in their freedom (7.3.3).

7.3.1 The general and the specifically Christian attributes of God

Before discussing the key example of the traces left by the conceptual framework on the core attribute of God in Christianity, that is, love (7.3.1.2), the difference between attributes and philosophical canons for consistent thinking about God must be clarified (7.3.1.1).

7.3.1.1 The canons of divine unity, simplicity and infinity, and the identity of essence and attributes

The question of how the First and the Second Parts of the dogmatics relate to each other, whether and how the "abstracted" premises studied first preshape what can later be claimed about the specifically Christian understandings of God, self and Christ is linked to the rules for consistency established independently of the Christian pious stirrings. Schaefer draws attention to the fact that they are owed to a change of perspective, which she evaluates as "constituting the very specificity of Schleiermacher's approach".[405] In addition to the three

---

[404] Johann Friedrich Röhr argues for an opposite solution to tying God to the effects of divine causality within the world by invoking Kant's concept of the awesome (*Erhabenes*) which would have captured the distance that is necessary to distinguish Creator and creation at a principled level. Cf. KGA I/7.3, 505–533, 513, and Pannenberg's comment in "Schwierigkeiten", 10–11.
[405] Schaefer, *Gottes Sein zur Welt*, 191.

canons, the rules include the stipulation that "in God no distinction can exist between essence and attributes" (²§ 167,1. ET 2016, II, 1007). She observes that both requirements taken together result in the key statement that God's "attributes" are indeed only ascriptions from the human side to God and cannot be taken as indicating any real single aspects within God, as defined in the lead proposition of ²§ 50: the attributes "are to designate (*sollen bezeichnen*) only something particular in the way in which the feeling of absolute dependence is to be referred (*zu beziehen*) to God" (ET 2016, I, 279).

This critically limiting insight arises when one of the canons, for example, simplicity, in conjunction with the identity stipulated between essence and attributes, encounters the variety of qualities found in God in the Christian faith tradition, such as mercy and justice. A contradiction ensues between the level of the Christian experience and of statements permitted within the premises of methodologically conscious theological designations of God. It can only be resolved by drawing the above conclusion, namely that the seemingly divine qualities are expressions ventured by the finite consciousness. Schaefer concludes: "The variety of divine attributes is stated from the perspective of the believing consciousness. The change of vantage point permits Schleiermacher to keep God's self free of differences",[406] as the canon of simplicity requires.

While the conclusion in what sense the attributes are to be understood is drawn explicitly, the canons themselves are not further argued for. They are in fact owed to the philosophical tradition and are not, as Schaefer notes, expressly "justified in themselves"; yet they are "guiding" for Schleiermacher exactly in the sense that "they cannot be derived from the hermeneutical foundational datum of the *Glaubenslehre*".[407] However, while Schleiermacher's interest in justifying the content of Christian belief to a general consciousness of truth is correct and continues a long line of theological enterprises since the Patristic era, these premises for speaking about God may also be in need of critique. Wolfhart Pannenberg has shown in a detailed study of authors in Early Christianity how the Greek philosophical premises were critiqued and redefined to become adequate to the content they were to express, namely the God of history confessed in biblical monotheism and the Christian testimony to Jesus Christ. For example, "immutability" could no longer be accepted as such.[408] In order to judge which

---

406 Schaefer, *Gottes Sein zur Welt*, 192.
407 Schaefer, *Gottes Sein zur Welt*, 191.
408 Pannenberg, "The appropriation of the philosophical concept of God as a dogmatic problem of early Christian theology", in *Basic Questions in Theology*, Vol. II (London: SCM Press, 1971), 119–184. In this article, written in 1959, he compares the philosophical concept of God in the "inner coherence" it shows "despite differences" of schools with the reshaping it under-

component carries the day, the existing categories of the philosophical tradition, or the portrayal of God presented by Jesus as it appears in the Gospels, Schleiermacher's interpretation of divine "love" will be examined.

7.3.1.2 Love as a complete definition of God's essence, or as a modification of divine causality?

In Sherman's reconstruction, the limits of Part One become clear through the need to find the reason and purpose, intention and motivation for the existence of creation within the statements which only the Second Part with its Christian determination can provide: "the attributes presented in the First Part are ... characteristics of God's *causality,* but not of the divine *essence*. They have form but no content. They describe the basic mode of God's relation to creation, but offer no understanding of God's purpose. They tell us *how* God relates to creation but not *why*".[409]

When discussing the unity of the divine decree with the Christological orientation contained in it from the start, Sherman describes its aim as giving "direction and meaning to creation" which is "intended for development, ... to become 'closer' to God, that they actualize ever more fully the potential for God-consciousness intrinsic to their nature ... They can become the mouthpiece of nature

---

went by early Christian theologians such as Justin, Tatian, and Theophilus. God as "origin", the "unity" of God, the "otherness and unknowability of the origin" are traced to various intellectual streams such as Plato, Aristotle and Stoicism. Some of the differences brought in by Christian reflection to what they found missing in the philosophical concept are similar to what Pannenberg later questions in Schleiermacher as owed to the influence of his *Dialectic:* as "free, creative source", God's "essence is not exhausted by being the invisible ground of present reality"; that God's freedom needs to be thought in terms of "ever new, as yet unheard of works was beyond of scope of Greek philosophy" (138). Since the "philosophical concept of God does not tolerate such supplementation", the way forward was to "remould" it "in the light of the history-shaping freedom of the biblical God" (139). Their "critical assimilation" effected the following changes: from the concept of the "world-ground" to the "personal Lord, out of his otherness effecting the new and contingent"; "immutability" becoming "faithfulness", and "timelessness" becoming "lordship over time (history) as almighty simultaneity". This latter point is captured in Schleiermacher's definition of "eternity" and divine governance, but the element of the unexpected is minimised by abolishing the distinction "between 'can' and 'will'" (^{2}§ 54,3. ET 1928, 214). For Pannenberg, these authors located the "otherness of the freedom of God precisely in his acts, surpassing all expectation and planning", as in the "revelation of the divine essence in Jesus Christ" (180).

409 Sherman, *The Shift to Modernity,* 123–124.

and the agent of God in the development of creation towards its ultimate fulfilment".[410]

Also for Schaefer, it is key how Schleiermacher explains the relation between the two Parts: that only in Part Two the "mode and orientation (*Art und Richtung*)" (²§ 165,1. ET 2016, 1003) of the "one and undivided divine causality" (²§ 165,1. ET 1928, 726) as well as its "motive" (²§ 167,2. ET 2016, 1008) have become evident.[411] Thus, how is this love defined, and how is it known? Its goal is the "union of the Divine Essence with human nature (*Vereinigung des göttlichen Wesens mit der menschlichen Natur*)" (²§ 165.1. ET 1928, 727).[412] God's love is unfolded from the fact of redemption, without which it remains uncertain: "yet, apart from redemption, and taken only in this sense, the divine love must always remain a matter of doubt" (²§ 166,1. ET 1928, 728). Regarding the attributes outlined in Part One, this determination brought by redemption is much needed: "we will always remain unsure as to what the will of God co-posited in the concept 'omnipotent' is, as such" (²§ 166,2. ET 2016, 1008). It alone grants the definitive insight into God's essence: "The recognition of the divine love (²§ 166,2. ET 1928, 729) first arises with the efficaciousness of redemption and from Christ" (²§ 166,2. ET 2016, 1006). Schaefer sums up how the abstracted concepts are filled at the end of Part Two by the determination of God's essence as "love": It consists in the "desire to lead the work that has been accomplished to perfection and to redeem what has been created".[413]

The ultimate determination of God's all-causality by "love" is decisive also for the following ongoing debate, on whether Schleiermacher's theory of religion and doctrine of God in the *Glaubenslehre* are to be read as Spinozist.

7.3.2 The God-world framework: metaphysics of monism or of individuality, Spinoza or Leibniz?

The suspicion or, at times, the unproblematic admission that a Spinozist view of the God-world relationship is being promoted also in Schleiermacher's mature

---

410 Sherman, *The Shift to Modernity*, 182.
411 The new translation relates "mode and orientation" to the "attributes", while the 1928 ET relates "its nature and its aim" to the divine causality" (*um die Art und Richtung derselben zu einem klaren Bewusstsein zu bringen*". "*Derselben*" could relate either to the causality or to the attributes, but in the context of the following sentence on "human causality" the 1928 ET's solution may be more accurate.
412 The ET 2016, 1004, has "divine being" for "*göttlichen Wesens*".
413 Schaefer, *Gottes Sein zur Welt*, 168.

theological work has marked the reception history up until today. It is a view he protested against as unfounded: "It is almost inconceivable how people can have ascribed pantheism to me, since I completely sunder the feeling of absolute dependence from any relation to the world" (^{2}§ 4,4, marginal note Thönes, 1873. ET 2016, 24–25, n. 3). The following two sections will compare the evidence for Spinozism (7.3.2.1) and against it (7.3.2.2); my conclusion will show that the fundamental critique by Leibniz of the Spinozist system, that it erodes the constitutive status of individuality, is being underestimated by the first group of scholars. However, even if Leibniz counts as the counterpart to a monist approach in the history of modern philosophy, an expert on his work has recently declared his God-world distinction as unnecessary, thus making his position compatible with pantheism.[414] This controversial interpretation that turns him into a virtual Spinozist must be left to the ongoing philosophical discourse. For me, the backdrop for clarifying which findings speak for and which against subsuming the *Glaubenslehre* under the Spinozist view will be the premise that in the sequence of philosophical approaches, Leibniz's system represents an alternative to Spinoza's.

7.3.2.1 Arguments for a Spinozist reading

There are three theory decisions which give rise to a pantheist interpretation, at least one of them foreseen by Schleiermacher: (1) reducing creation to an aspect of preservation, (2) complete inclusion into the web of nature, and (3) the deletion of the distinction in God between 'will' and 'can'.[415]

7.3.2.1.1 Subordinating creation to preservation

The reason Schleiermacher gives in Part One for a doctrinal proposition that privileges the ongoing existence of the world over its beginning is that the feeling of

---

[414] Pirmin Stekeler-Weithofer describes the God-world distinction in his presentation, "Das monadologische Strukturmodell der Welt. Leibniz zwischen Descartes und Kant", in Nagl-Docekal (ed.), *Leibniz heute lesen*, 25–53, as the "contrast between the perspective of a finite standpoint and a conceived (*gedachten*) complete view (*Gesamtansicht*) from the end" (46). He concludes with the idea of "God as the super-monad" who is "so-to-speak, the 'unification' ('*Vereinigung*') *of all possible perspectives*. In God and only in God is the contrast between 'my world' and 'the world' conceptually *sublated* (*gedanklich* aufgehoben)" (49).

[415] In "Schwierigkeiten", 14, Pannenberg makes the point that "Schleiermacher's conception of a theory of science was an additional factor in strengthening the pantheistic tendency of the *Glaubenslehre*". He quotes from the *Dialectic* of 1822, "No God without world, as much as no world without God" (*Dialektik*, ed. Odebrecht, 303).

absolute dependence is experienced as continuous and that an absolute beginning is not in the realm of what human reason can reach. While the latter insight corresponds with Kant's analysis of the limits of reason, it does not rule out a faith perspective which attributes the origin of the universe to God's decision to create. In his scrutiny of the argument, Pannenberg suggests that the analysis of subjectivity in ²§§ 3 and 4 would have permitted to interpret the "Whence" as Creator, since creation "in its contingency (*Zufälligkeit*) is the expression of the sovereignty of the omnipotent will of God, not limited by anything". A different reason than the one given is seen as decisive: since the "idea of creative freedom can only be thought as personal ... Schleiermacher's reticence becomes more understandable".[416] It is the lesson taken to heart of Fichte's critique of a personal concept of God as anthropomorphic that motivates his distance from creation as the most adequate expression to be inferred from absolute dependence.

7.3.2.1.2 Tying God to the world

While in creation and preservation, the distinction between God and world is maintained, a further decision – which Schleiermacher correctly predicted to evoke the "appearance (*Schein*) of pantheism" (²§ 46,2. ET 1928, 174) – closes the gap between them by ascribing everything that affects humans to the conditioning and determining (*bedingt und begründet*) totality of the nexus of nature.[417] While this notion on its own could still be interpreted along the lines of Leibniz's reciprocal effects of self-active monads on each other, set in a pre-established harmony by God,[418] the addition that in these effects, God's omnipotence is completely expressed, reduces the difference to naught. It is remarkable, as Schaefer points out, that this position is seen as compatible with divine freedom.[419] For Schleiermacher, the two statements are not in contradiction and

---

416 Pannenberg, "Schwierigkeiten", 11.
417 The ET 1928 speaks of "the unqualified conviction that everything is grounded and established in the universality of the nature-system" coinciding completely with "the inner certainty of the absolute dependence of all finite being on God" (173); in the ET 2016, "the fullest conviction that everything is completely conditioned by and grounded in the totality of the interconnected process of nature and the inner surety regarding the absolute dependence of all that is finite on God ... wholly coincide" (I, 252).
418 Pannenberg does not consider this possible intellectual heritage when he refers to the "agency (*Wirken*) of God in the created world" that is held to be "mediated by creaturely factors and their relationships to each other" ("Schwierigkeiten", 7).
419 Schaefer, *Gottes Sein zur Welt*, 118: "The fact that God cannot be conceived without creation, is completely compatible (*durchaus ... vereinbar*) for him with the idea of God's creative freedom."

the appearance of pantheism can be – correctly, as Pannenberg judges[420] – refuted.

7.3.2.1.3 Declaring 'will' and 'can' as identical in God
The closest clue to Spinozism is the abolishment of a divine capacity of willing beyond what is actually effected, which implies two assumptions. The first comes close to replacing the freedom of God with a premise of necessity;[421] there is no way of distinguishing divine action from the internal necessity of God's nature to produce and sustain the world and its inhabitants, making them similar to emanations which are forever tied to their originator. The second consequence is that any capacity to transform, undo or rescue is taken away from God who excels instead in all that has come to be. In view of the course of history, this means the denial of any eschatological power,[422] and in effect sanctifies the existing world as what God intended. The reason for the identity of reality and possibility in God is once again the fear of personalistic expressions which draw God into the realm of the internally divided causality proper to the conditioned interchange between finite agents.

7.3.2.2 Points incompatible with Spinozism
Which are the reasons to assume that the *Glaubenslehre* is "justified in defending itself against the objection of pantheism"?[423] There are four prominent features that speak against the diagnosis of a Spinozistic framework: (1) the analysis of the concept of piety itself in both editions, but much more clearly in ²§§ 3 and 4; (2) retaining the *ex nihilo* qualification of God's creative action; (3) the explication of the attributes of omniscience and eternity; and (4) Schleiermacher's repeated option for individuality as the opposite of being a transition point, siding with the heritage of Leibniz.

---

420 Pannenberg, "Schwierigkeiten", 12.
421 Cf. Pannenberg, "Schwierigkeiten", 15–16 , Pröpper, "Bestimmung", in *Evangelium und freie Vernunft*, 144–146, and 145–146, n. 37; Schaefer, *Gottes Sein zur Welt*, e. g., 118–119, 184, 192, 195, 209.
422 Pröpper, *Theologische Anthropologie*, vol. I, 602; Schaefer, *Gottes Sein zur Welt*, 261–262.
423 Pannenberg, "Schwierigkeiten", 12.

7.3.2.2.1 The definition of piety itself reached in an analysis of subjectivity

Schleiermacher's protest quoted above, how "inconceivable" a pantheist understanding is on the basis of his approach to religion, is an invitation to understand his dogmatics from the perspective of the opening argumentation in ²§§ 3 and 4. Intended to replace all proofs for the existence of God from the external world, the proposed feeling of absolute dependence is accessed in its exact contrast to the partial freedom and partial dependence which humans experience within and towards the world. This analysis seems to be the reason why he thinks he can afford to enact major modifications of the doctrine of God in its different locations without being misunderstood as denying God's existence as distinct from the world.[424]

7.3.2.2.2 *Creatio ex nihilo* as indicator of the difference between God and world

By retaining the designation of creation as an *ex nihilo* deed of God and elucidating its function as safeguarding the feeling of absolute dependence, Schleiermacher identifies its necessary connection with the paragraphs in the Introduction on which the whole argumentation of the dogmatics is founded:

> The expression "out of nothing" denies that before the emergence of the world anything at all would have been in existence besides God... the assumption that there would have been any material at hand independent of divine activity would destroy the feeling of absolute

---

[424] In his portrayal of the author as a religious naturalist, Andrew Dole examines the claims that conflict with this interpretation but decides to reinterpret Schleiermacher's argumentation as pointing to a theory of religion as a human faculty which does not only leave open the question of the existence of God but answers it in the negative. He is able to arrive at this conclusion as compatible with the position of the *Glaubenslehre* with the help of three moves: one, by reducing the claim of philosophical necessity which the second edition attaches to this analysis to a reading held as "purported" by some; two, by taking the inference to a Whence as a "postulate"; and third, by confining the statements about God at the beginning of the First Part to the dogmatic section which treats what Christians hold to be true. He concludes with the qualified position that Schleiermacher offers an analysis at the level of concepts: "the notion that the feeling of absolute dependence is veridical and thus that there exists a God on whom the universe is absolutely dependent (1) is *not* assumed within the introduction to *The Christian Faith*, (2) *is* assumed as a fundamental postulate in the doctrinal sections, and (3) is *argued for* nowhere in the text." Andrew Dole, *Schleiermacher on Religion and the Natural Order* (Oxford: OUP, 2010), 171.

dependence and would present the world as a mixture made up of what existed by God and of what did not exist by God (²§ 41,1. ET 2016, II, 223).⁴²⁵

7.3.2.2.3 The explication of the attributes of omniscience and of eternity

In the elucidation of some of the First Part's attributes of God, countermeasures to an identification of God and world are taken. In the description of what "omniscience" entails, a clear critique of a certain view of God's causality is issued: It would be incompatible with the feeling of being relation with God to assume "a lifeless and blind necessity" which "would not really be something with which we can stand in relation" (²§ 55 LS. ET 1928, 219). An equally correcting element can be found in the definition of "eternity" as a counterweight to finite causality. As part of the first "assertion" in the determination of God's omnipotence it is clarified that "since it is eternal and omnipresent, (it) is set in contrast to all finite causality". The second assertion, by contrast, sounds monistic: "that divine causality, as expressed in our feeling of absolute dependence, is completely presented in the totality of finite being" (²§ 54 LS. ET 2016, I, 305).⁴²⁶ Sherman explains Schleiermacher's attempts to think of creation as an "eternal", not a "temporal" act with the strictures of doing justice to God's standing beyond categories belonging to the realm of finitude: "it is inappropriate to think of God as making a transition from nonactivity to activity".⁴²⁷ Thus, a polarity between the infinite and the finite is driven home. It offsets or at least qualifies the close connection which the doctrine of God in the First Part draws from the same feeling of absolute dependence that the Introduction clarified as indicating the total contrast between God and world.

7.3.2.2.4 Individuality not as transition point, but as constituted in itself

The Spinozism debate is crucial for the understanding of Schleiermacher's complete enterprise; it is not a matter of indifference which conceptual system he ends up promoting. One must revise one's understanding of key parts of his work if one judges his outline to be pantheistic. The interest in freedom and individuality evident in his hermeneutics and his pedagogics are affected as much

---

425 Thus, as Schaefer points out in *Gottes Sein zur Welt*, 161, two types or levels of causality are distinguished which can co-exist without contradiction: God's absolute causality, and human finite causality within the nexus of nature.
426 In her outline of these objections Schaefer refers to the "badly needed argument of God's freedom" which ensures that creation is not simply necessary (*Gottes Sein zur Welt*, 240).
427 Sherman, *The Shift to Modernity*, 130.

as his theology if his ultimate allegiance is to an approach in which there is only one agent, God, suffusing all of reality with just one irresistible causality. Schleiermacher's opposition to this view is evident from his repeated defense of the individual as more than a "point of transition". He pictures vividly what would ensue if no place was given to individual human freedom as a causality within the world:

> It would take only one further step to restrict causality to divine causality alone – namely, to hold that human beings would also regard themselves to be only part of the mechanisms of nature, and they would treat consciousness of self-initiated activity simply as an irremediable illusion ... this move, however, would annihilate the feeling of absolute dependence and all piety along with it ... by this mode all finite causality would be reduced to mere illusion, thus no reason would be left even for regarding any particular finite being as enduring in and of itself at all ... Rather, everything would be regarded either as indivisibly one or as an unquantifiable mass of isolated points of transition, namely, atoms." (^{2}§ 49,1. ET 2016, I, 274).[428]

Freedom as self-initiated activity is the final theme to be broached before concluding the investigation with a sketch of alternative paths that would have been open to Schleiermacher from his foundation of an approach to religion that takes on board modernity's anthropological turn.

7.3.3 Consequences for the concept of human freedom in relation to the world and towards God

Despite these decisively formulated arguments which separate his position from a Spinozism that swallows up human freedom into modifications of the divine substance, the question remains whether the freedom Schleiermacher claims as a crucial factor is spelt out radically enough to serve this function. I will first trace its key role for dismissing the "nonreligious (*unfromme*) explanation" of the feeling of dependence as resulting from the material world (7.3.3.1). Secondly, places where freedom is downplayed, such as his understanding of evil and the question of freedom in relation to God, will be examined (7.3.3.2). Thirdly, his reasons for endorsing an *apokatastasis panton* as the reconciled outcome of history will supply a test case for judging its role (7.3.3.3).

---

428 Schaefer, *Gottes Sein zur Welt*, 126.

7.3.3.1 Freedom as the backstop against a reduction to materialism

Already in the first edition – before the changes implemented against the impression of its reviewers that human freedom is underrepresented when religion is defined by absolute dependence – freedom is the key argument for seeing off the challenge of a monistic worldview. In the Introduction, the core proposition that established temporal self-consciousness as the feeling of utter dependence from God already underlined the difference from interaction with the world (¹§ 9,3. I, 32), invoking the human subject's awareness of freedom. These foundations are built upon in the opening proposition of Part One when the "nonreligious explanation" of dependence is refuted in principle. Deleting the difference between God and the totality of the world would come at the price of denying human freedom which does exist towards the world. Two types of dependence need to be held apart to account for the feeling of partial freedom. Only towards God "no counter-action" is possible (¹§ 36,2. I, 124). In his review, Bretschneider had queried the possibility of reciprocal influence on the world, giving as examples the facts of gravity and of ageing.[429] The second edition does not respond with an argument at the empirical level but underlines the distinction between dependency from the world and from God with two principled points: "even at the highest level of Christian piety and given the clearest consciousness of having the most unhampered self-initiated activity, the absoluteness of the feeling of dependence would still remain undiminished in relation to God" (²§ 32,2. ET 2016, I, 190). The argument is conducted at a different level than unchangeable conditions of natural and human life, such as the movement of the planets, also cited as proof by Bretschneider: It is about the "Whence" of existence as such. The second extension is that a new group is added to those who "declare all feeling of freedom to be an illusion". The description fits a naturalist position: those who "reject all efforts to keep separate from each other all ideas regarding 'God' and 'world' in that they claim that nothing would exist on which we could feel ourselves to be absolutely dependent" (²§ 32,2. ET 2016, I, 190). The whole point makes it clear that it is a question of choice whether to go with human existence and freedom grounded in God, or with a monist view that collapses the two.

7.3.3.2 Not recognised: the unconditionality of human freedom

With the concise justification that one cannot be "absolutely dependent" on something towards which counteraction is possible, the unmistakeable status of freedom has been established. The ground of freedom cannot be attributed

---

[429] Bretschneider, "Ueber das Princip", KGA I/7.3, 378.

to the world because the latter is also the recipient of self-initiated human acts.[430] Yet, the way in which freedom is spelt out in itself and towards God shows that a decisive dimension has not been reached: its unconditional character, the conditioned nature of its concrete pursuits notwithstanding. This failure to conceive of freedom at the formal level of its spontaneous, self-originating constitution lies at the basis of some crucial problematic turns: the transition, in effect a jump, from conducting an analysis into the facticity of human existence and of the structure of self-consciousness to claiming an absolute ground of being that ensures its meaning; the impossibility to take a stance and possibly say No to God's offer; the prior coordination also of free human subjects by divine omnipotence; and the explanation of sin in terms of a natural lag of the God-consciousness to the world-relation owed to sensibility. In the proposition on God's omnipotence, both sides are emphasised: "What is certain, moreover, about the accompanying self-consciousness is that we are only capable of the feeling of absolute dependence as freely acting agents – that is to say, that we are conscious of our freedom as something which is received and gradually developed in a universal system (*im allgemeinen Zusammenhang*)" (²§ 49,1. ET 1928, 190). But the context of this assertion is exactly the proposition that subsumes the activity of free causes to God: "Whether that which stirs our self-consciousness and, as a consequence influences us is to be traced back to some aspect of the so-called 'mechanism of nature' or to the activity of free causes, either one is completely arranged for by God, each no less than the other" (²§ 49 LS. ET 2016, I, 272).

The thought that humans could cooperate with God is explicitly dismissed not only because God's agency must be kept within the eternal as distinct from the temporal sphere. The idea of divine-human interaction is also ruled out since it would imply that the finite can have "an activity (*Wirksamkeit*) in and for itself and thus independent of the sustaining divine activity' (²§ 46 Postscript. ET 1928, 176). Sherman sums up that this would be an "obvious violation of Schleiermacher's fundamental principle that all finite being is always absolutely dependent on God".[431] It shows how momentous it is that the Introduction qualified its analysis of what amounts to human facticity by the term "dependence", insinuating the connection to an origin that cannot be breached by self-

---

430 Pröpper summarises this point: "The world could never be what founds human freedom … because the essential structure of human freedom as the unity of agency and receptivity cannot be explained from something that is itself the object (*Gegenstand*) of freedom" (*Theologische Anthropologie*, vol. I, 471. Cf. 476). Schaefer points out that "neither the world nor the human subject are necessary, both are utterly contingent in their existence" (*Gottes Sein zur Welt*, 229).
431 Sherman, *The Shift to Modernity*, 138.

activity. The cooperation of free yet finite causes with God would not be a problem in a different framework where human freedom is highlighted both in its unconditionality and in its quest for absolute meaning. It could then also not be assigned a position in a pre-arranged network of centres of self-reflective action, as in the scheme of Leibniz taken over into the *Glaubenslehre*.

The complete attribution of "the activity of free causes" to God includes human sin. The reason for rejecting the Genesis narrative is not only its misinterpretation as a historical event but also its presentation of sin as a conscious human deed. What Schleiermacher misses at the literary, not the historical, level is its symbolic depiction of the origin of evil. His alternative explanation of sin underrates the significance of the "Adamic myth" as the one narrative in the ancient world that squarely places the responsibility for evil on humans.[432] The standing which this central account and its reception history in Christianity has had for a self-image of human agency that has marked European culture is downplayed; with it, the significance of having to give account to God for developing the idea of self-reflective, transcendental freedom is lost: the consciousness of having been able to have acted otherwise.[433]

Sherman makes a case for the view presented in the *Glaubenslehre*, discrediting the judgement that is offers a quietist consent to conditions that could be tackled and transformed. He argues that Schleiermacher's confirmation in ²§ 48,2 that "every evil disappears into the good itself" (cf. ET 1928, 187) and that its "purpose is to be put to use in the service of the developing good" is "more than saying we should take 'the longer view'".[434] He highlights his rejection of "any causal link between human sin ... and evil and death", and comes to a conclusion that is not unlike Kant's in view of the mystery of evil: all we can do is to take it as an "opportunity for some form of moral activity". Thus, it is

> not simply a Christianized Stoicism advocating public service and a modified *apatheia* in the face of an impersonal divine decree ... the failure to respond actively to such opportunities would appear to represent a failure to understand the nature of one's original perfec-

---

432 Cf. the comparison with three other Ancient Near Eastern myths or symbolic narrations of the origin of evil by Paul Ricoeur in *The Symbolism of Evil*, trans. E. Buchanan (Boston: Beacon Press, 1967).
433 The role of such narratives for enabling the realisation that one could have acted differently is highlighted by Friedo Ricken in his contribution to a volume issuing from a public debate with Jürgen Habermas on the role of religion in helping to identify and solve pathologies of rationalisation: "Postmetaphysical Reason and Religion", in Habermas *et al.*, *An Awareness of What is Missing. Faith and Reason in a Postsecular Age*, trans. Ciaran Cronin (Cambridge: Polity Press, 2010), 51–58.
434 Sherman, *The Shift to Modernity*, 159.

tion and one's divinely given role in the world and history, which is to participate in creation's progress toward the good.[435]

This is a necessary correction of typical misrepresentations of Schleiermacher's position which prefer to ground a culture-critical position in an extrinsicist concept of revelation.[436] The real lacuna in the *Glaubenslehre* is not located in an under-qualification of God's significance. The third section will briefly assess with regard to the Last Judgement whether Schleiermacher's endorsement of a final all-encompassing reconciliation equally manifests what is missing in his thought-through system: an unreserved recognition of human freedom.

7.3.3.3 A test case: The reasons for endorsing an *apokatastasis panton*

Schleiermacher's severe critique of double predestination contained in his treatment of the outcome of God's tying God's self to the world regarding the end of history is a controversial position. The reason to query this vision of the endpoint of the process begun by God is not a different view of God's mercy but the basis from which he chooses this hope of ultimate fulfilment. The problem is that the fulfilment of creation happens "without mediating intermittent steps. God attains God's goal … because it was always part of providence (*vorgesehen*). The free actions of humans cannot contradict this because they are ultimately only moments in God's eternal plan".[437] For Schaefer, it would contradict human freedom if "divine providence came to its fulfilment under all circumstances". In view of the history of human cruelty and its victims, this is a problematic assumption because in this scheme, *apokatastasis* becomes

> a necessary implication of the eschatological redemptive action of God. Yet this action cannot be envisaged otherwise than that God – because of the ethical dignity of the victims but

---

435 Sherman, *The Shift to Modernity*, 162.
436 One can even include J. Habermas's classification of the method of Schleiermacher's inauguration of a modern theology in the reception history of Kant as constituting a "turn away from the world" and as an "elegant reconciliation of religion and modernity" under this strand of critique. *Between Naturalism and Religion*, trans. Ciaran Cronin (Cambridge: Polity Press, 2008), 233–234.
437 Schaefer, *Gottes Sein zur Welt*, 260. This interpretation can be linked with Gockel's observation: It is "necessary to understand the concept of predestination in a strict sense as an affirmation of the 'omnipotent and thus irresistible will of God'" (*Election*, 28, with reference to the 1819 Essay on Election, "Ueber die Lehre von der Erwählung", in KGA I/10, 195).

also because of the enduring human dignity of the perpetrators – respects and allows human freedom to participate. A reconciliation that goes ahead over the heads of the victims and perpetrators would mean to yet again cause injustice to the victims.[438]

She concludes with an alternative to Schleiermacher's die-hard belief in progress: "What is lost is the unshakeable certainty with which the ... *Glaubenslehre* could expect a 'good ending' to God's history with humans. What is won, however, and this is worth the stage of only being able to hope – is the freedom which alone enables a real encounter between God and the human person."[439]

---

438 Schaefer, *Gottes Sein zur Welt*, 260–261. In "Fragende und Gefragte zugleich. Notizen zur Theodizee", in *Evangelium und freie Vernunft*, 266–275, 274, Pröpper has insisted on a conception of ultimate reconciliation that takes the prior forgiveness by the victims as its condition.
439 Schaefer, *Gottes Sein zur Welt*, 261.

8 Conclusion: Creation and Redemption in Categories of Freedom

What remains to be sketched is how a theology developed from the starting point of an analysis of freedom can be taken in a different direction. This will be done based on a summary of Schleiermacher's theory decisions and solutions (8.1) and of the problems encountered in his version of a theology that takes up the anthropological turn (8.2). An alternative direction for the concepts of God and of the human person was already opened up in the late Middle Ages by Duns Scotus for whom the reason for creation was God wishing to "have fellow lovers" for the world. Justified, like the second edition of the *Glaubenslehre*, by a transcendental analysis,[440] a different understanding of God is proposed, who creates a free counterpart and risks an open history (8.3).

8.1 Key theory decisions and achievements of Schleiermacher's *Glaubenslehre*

Three of the new paths made possible by Schleiermacher's elaboration of a response – both to Kant's critiques of reason and to the post-Kantian approaches that changed the foundations for reflection on religion – will be visited. First, identifying human freedom as the philosophical principle in the Introduction (8.1.1); second, taking up the challenge of the aporias of the two-natures terminology in Christology (8.1.2), and third, recasting theology as a project of spelling out the core of the Christian message of redemption in ways sensitive to their era's consciousness of truth (8.1.3).

---

[440] In "Erste Philosophie als Transzendentalwissenschaft: Metaphysik bei Johannes Duns Scotus", in *Woher kommen wir? Ursprünge der Moderne im Denken des Mittelalters* (Darmstadt: Wissenschaftliche Buchgesellschaft, 2008), 114–132, Ludger Honnefelder analyses the reasons for the centrality of the question of how metaphysics is possible (115) and the history of reception of key concepts and divisions from Ockham over Suarez and Wolff to Kant (130–132). Cf. also Magnus Striet's chapter on "Ontologie als Transzendentalwissenschaft" in *Offenbares Geheimnis*, 126–146.

8.1.1 The choice of thought form: human freedom

Leaving behind argumentations for the existence of God that started out from the external world to establish its ground in God, Schleiermacher inaugurates the transcendental method of an analysis of subjectivity within theology. Opting for human freedom as the philosophical principle of the *Glaubenslehre* has structural consequences: there is the need for an Introduction that explains why Scripture is not the opening theme, which elucidates the two-part format of the material dogmatics and its method of retroactive conclusion from the Christian determination of the feeling of absolute dependence to the doctrines in their three forms. Before the dogmatic system itself can be expounded, the relationship of the philosophical and the theological principle must be clarified: the essence of Christianity as a contingent, historical foundation is a further determination of the essence of religion as an anthropological given.

Contrary to the view that the anthropological starting point is itself marked by an inevitable slide towards Feuerbach's conclusion that faith in God is "nothing but" a human projection, as stated by Karl Barth, Alister McGrath and other defenders of an extrinsicist concept of revelation, this objection to Schleiermacher is incorrect. His distinction of two types of infinity in the context of arguing for the unique difference of the Redeemer makes sure well in advance of Feuerbach's *The Essence of Christianity* that the concept of the human species results from adding finite entities together and cannot be confused with the infinity of God (^{2}§ 93,2. ET 1928, 379).

8.1.2 Renewing Christology

In his rigorous analysis of the equivocations within the two-natures terminology of the Christological and trinitarian doctrines, a key dissatisfaction of Schleiermacher's had been the inability to convey a portrayal of the person of Jesus as a living unity with the "essential being of God (*das wesentliche Sein Gottes*) in him" (^{1}§ 118. II, 40) or the "veritable existence of God (*eigentliches Sein Gottes*) in Him" (^{2}§ 94 LS. ET 1928, 385). Yet his understanding of the Redeemer as inaugurating the full potency of the God-consciousness which was part of humanity's "original perfection" had been read as turning redemption – the abolition of the discrepancy between a self-enclosed sensuous and the "higher" consciousness of God – into an a priori constructed idea. The second edition makes it even clearer than the first that Jesus is the historical turning point who effects redemption, then and now, by the "total impression" (^{2}§ 14 Postscript. ET 2016, I, 115 and ^{2}§ 99 Postscript. ET 2016, II, 619) of his person which draws believers

8.1 Key theory decisions and achievements of Schleiermacher's *Glaubenslehre*

into the strength of his God-consciousness. Roger Haight's indications, partly quoted already in the Introduction of this study, of the starting point of his Christology and the content of his soteriology are apposite:

> Schleiermacher's is a Christology from below. His *The Life of Jesus* shows that he had an interest in the earthly life and ministry of Jesus. His Christology has Jesus of Nazareth, the earthly figure, as its initial imaginative focus of attention.
> Schleiermacher's theory of salvation bears out his attention to Jesus. Salvation consists in appropriating Jesus' God-consciousness in such a way that people are united with God and receive God's forgiveness of sin and empowerment in their lives. Schleiermacher broke the hold of the mythological views of redemption in which something was accomplished between God and God, or Jesus and God, and then extrinsically received by human beings. By contrast, Christian salvation begins historically in each person who absorbs Jesus' message and person in such a way that this consciousness becomes internalized.[441]

A conception has been reached that does justice to Jesus' humanity and that attributes his coming to the one divine decree. This supralapsarian position is not a diminution of Christology even though it is the consequence of a problematic concept of God whose agency can only be eternal and never within history. Karl Barth's much-quoted critique that this framework turns God into "a prisoner"[442] of his own decree has a point. Yet regarding his Christology, Schleiermacher is justified in claiming that his intention was to work out in systematic connection "that the verse John 1:14 is the basic text for all dogmatics",[443] that "the Word was made flesh".

---

[441] Haight, "Take and Read: The Christian Faith", in *National Catholic Reporter* May 23, 2016, accessed March 1, 2020. https://www.ncronline.org/blogs/ncr-today/take-and-read-christian-faith. He goes on to specify the label of a "consciousness Christology" as being one of the "Spirit": "Schleiermacher's formal Christology, that is, his construal of the humanity and divinity of Jesus, has been called a 'consciousness' Christology. And so it is. But that is often construed in a thin or shallow psychological sense of consciousness. Schleiermacher, however, insists that the cause of Jesus' exalted God-consciousness and consequent sinlessness was the presence of God within him and to him. For this reason, it seems more correct to think of Schleiermacher holding a Spirit Christology, even though in *The Christian Faith* this category is not developed. The phrase 'Spirit Christology,' that is, the 'explanation' of Jesus' divinity through the presence and action of God as Spirit within him, fits his construction of Jesus' divinity."
[442] Karl Barth, *Die kirchliche Dogmatik* (Zürich: Evangelischer Verlag, ⁴1958), vol. II.1, 596: "the prisoner of the world from which to distinguish (*sich abzuheben*) God's self has been forbidden by the theologian!", quoted by Schaefer, *Gottes Sein zur Welt*, 209.
[443] Schleiermacher, "Letters", 59 (2. *Sendschreiben*, KGA I/10, 343).

8.1.3 Recasting theology as a project of elaborating the core truth of Christianity in critical interaction with modernity

The task to give an account of the truth of the Christian faith that is relevant to the contemporary cultural setting presupposes a historically conscious understanding of dogmatic theology, and it requires linking up with the general consciousness of truth of the era. Before examining what the first point assumes about the continuity of the Christian message, the second point needs to be upheld against interpretations which deny this key orientation of Schleiermacher's work. It is visible, for example, in his abolition of a special hermeneutics for biblical texts, and in the way in which the Introduction draws on existing non-theological disciplines for the tasks at hand, to determine the essence of religion, laying the ground for the further determination of historical faith traditions, such as Christianity. The "interest in truth for its own sake" is not "alien" to him but part of the duty of accountability of Christian believers and in particular of professional theologians.[444] But what does the insight that the interpretation of the core message is affected by the cultural horizons of each era mean for the understanding of the faith tradition? Roger Haight sums up this insight:

> the inseparability and mutual influence of world-consciousness and God-consciousness helps to mediate a deep historical consciousness and to explain pluralism in any community sharing common teachings and values ... Schleiermacher's ecclesiology is historically conscious. This is reflected in his view of the doctrines of the church, which are accounts of religious experience set forth in speech at any given time.[445]

The requirement to actively continue the process of the Christian tradition is captured under the category of "heterodoxy" in the *Brief Outline* (§ 203) and claimed for the *Glaubenslehre* at the end of the first *Sendschreiben*.[446] Behind this is the insight explicated by Thomas Pröpper and Georg Essen that

---

444 In *Schleiermacher on Religion and the Natural Order*, 169, Dole states: It is "standard practice to take at face value Schleiermacher's explicit refusal to offer proofs of the 'truth or necessity of Christianity' in both editions of *The Christian Faith* and to understand this refusal as based on his view that the project of metaphysically grounding theology would be an example of the commingling of religious reflection and 'speculation' – in my terms, a recipe for the contamination of religion by an 'alien' interest in truth for its own sake."
445 Haight, "Take and Read: The Christian Faith", in *National Catholic Reporter* May 23, 2016, accessed March 1, 2020. https://www.ncronline.org/blogs/ncr-today/take-and-read-christian-faith.
446 Schleiermacher, "Letters", 53 (*Sendschreiben*, KGA I/10, 334).

the process of tradition, indeed does not follow a schema of explication but takes place as a process of transformation, more precisely, as transformation both of the truth of faith and of the thought forms that have been adapted to it. The proper dynamic of the process of tradition becomes evident in it. ... whether the truth understood in the new thought form is still identical with the one handed on is a question that can never be proven or indeed ultimately secured. Different thought forms are just not immediately compatible, and a supra-historical vantage point from which human beings could possess the content of the faith without its form of being understood is denied to them. A standpoint from which they could judge, so to speak, in ultimate capacity (*Instanz*), the success of the process of transformation is not available.[447]

By appropriating the categories of freedom, transcendental thinking and history as thought forms typical of modernity, Schleiermacher accepted this risk and succeeded in opening up a new era of theological reflection, responsible to and shaping the modern age.

8.2 Problems with specific argumentations and solutions

While the starting point is taken in the perspective of the human subject, in keeping with the anthropological turn, problems arise in the more specific determinations of the underlying concepts of the self (8.2.1), of the Redeemer (8.2.2), and of God (8.2.3). Some of these can be related to his concern not to contradict a further feature of modernity, the methods and empirical enquiries of the emerging natural sciences (8.2.4).

8.2.1 Overdrawing the result of the analysis of self-consciousness

The decisive achievement of the argumentation of the second edition was to demonstrate that the feeling of absolute dependence is the hermeneutical basis also for the philosophical concept of God. Conducting this enquiry was necessary in the interest of showing that the new opening given to the Introduction, relating dogmatics to the concept of church, could claim a more than empirical status for religious traditions. They are not just social facts. The existence of "pious communities" is shown to be not an "aberration" (cf. BO ²§ 22. 12) but a

---

[447] Thomas Pröpper and Georg Essen, "Aneignungsprobleme der christologischen Überlieferung. Hermeneutische Vorüberlegungen", in Rudolf Laufen (ed.), *Gottes ewiger Sohn. Die Präexistenz Christi* (Paderborn: Schöningh, 1997), 163–178, 176–177. They conclude that in view of this necessary but risky task, trust in the support of the Spirit is needed.

justified feature of communal human life. They arise as formations in consequence of the relationship to God which is presented as a necessary human disposition. The basis for this demonstration is a philosophical analysis of human freedom. The problem noted with the concept of self, which is shown to be a "God-consciousness", is the restriction to the level of existing, concrete freedom, leaving out the formal, unconditioned level.[448] If a more radical understanding of freedom in its unconditionality had been taken as the starting point, it would also have allowed a different perspective on evil as a freely determined deed. This is a lacuna noted by theologians critical of his concept of sin such as Walter Wyman: "Finally, the absence of an exploration of the relationship of sin to moral evil (*das Böse*) is noteworthy and problematic."[449]

8.2.2 Underdetermining the content of Christology

Overdetermining the result of the analysis of self-consciousness is the root problem of Schleiermacher's Christology which can then only serve to confirm an already actualised human consciousness of a reliable, benevolent God. It remains true that F. C. Baur's reading ignores and misrepresents the structure of the first edition's argument, judging it by the requirements of his then supernaturalist position with the expectation that biblical proofs would be harnessed for Christ's divinity; he is correct, however, in his content diagnosis. There is no positive, new, distinctive content in what Christ mediates but only the fullness of the

---

[448] In her comprehensive and insightful study of Schleiermacher's concept of freedom throughout his work, Katharina Gutekunst objects to critiques of his anthropology that are based on this distinction within the concept of freedom. For her analytic philosophical approach, the matter explored is concrete human freedom. She mistakes the distinction as proposing that freedom is unconditioned in both respects, which would imply that humans create their own existence. The transcendental and the empirical levels are not distinguished sufficiently when she concludes: "If in addition the positions mentioned above think of freedom first of all as unconditionality and independence, it indeed becomes inconceivable" (*Freiheit des Subjekts*, 207). "Unconditionality" does not imply "independence" which is an empirical feature. In contrast, the point of the distinction is to show exactly the consciousness of contingency which arises from being able to take a stance to one's concrete history and conditions. This capability is meant by the "formal" level of freedom. The misunderstanding of "unconditioned" as denying the other level of analysis, that is, the concrete, material, embedded, etc. level of analysing freedom, shows, in my view, that approaches like those of Kant, Schleiermacher and Kierkegaard have to be reconstructed within the context of Continental philosophical reflection and cannot be completely grasped with the tools of analytic philosophy.
[449] Walter Wyman, "Sin and redemption", in Mariña (ed.), *Cambridge Companion to Friedrich Schleiermacher*, 129–149, 138.

God-consciousness, submerged up until then in the dominance of the senses, which is interpreted as "sin".[450] This lack of a genuine content – such as being the revelation of God's love – and the substitutive role of the doctrine of sin to supply the reason for the need for Christ leads Thomas Pröpper to judge the *Glaubenslehre* as offering "the classical example for the role of sin as a dogmatic helper in need (*Nothelferrolle*)".[451] At the same time, the subsequent version of Baur's critique remains unconvincing: that no individual can ever be accredited with God's self-revelation. The possibility of a Christology that seeks to do justice both to the human and to the divine in his person hinges on being able to show that the self-communication of God as love was possible in the life and destiny of the individual person of Jesus. Here a disconnection from unspoken Hegelian premises is overdue.

Schleiermacher's insight that "apart from redemption ... the divine love must always remain a matter of doubt" (^{1}§ 182,1. II, 345 and ^{2}§ 166,1. ET 1928, 728) could have enabled a different portrayal of the person of Jesus: his proclamation and symbolic actions at concrete, contingent occasions gave the clearest possible insight into his "consciousness" or understanding of a God of unconditional love. Yet, as Pannenberg observed, the term "love" is not explicated in terms of immediate personal encounter[452] but in terms of the historical breakthrough of what had primordially been implanted into the human creatures. The reason for this reticence is to be found, as outlined in the previous chapter, in his doctrine of God.

8.2.3 Making the case for a changeless God

The priority of a philosophical-metaphysical concept of perfection, implying changelessness as the benchmark for an adequate doctrine of God, has consequences: with the explication of God's agency in terms of a single pre-temporal decree it is the reason for the inability to spell out the freedom of God, of Jesus Christ and of the human subject as the basis of their unique and non-predetermined agencies. Combined with all-causality as the guiding category for God, derived from the feeling of absolute dependence, the explication of God's activity

---

450 For a critique that encompasses both the reduction of sin to natural factors and the problem it contains for the concept of God as the indirect cause of sin, cf. Hermann Fischer's reminder that this solution for otherwise contradictory elements within his dogmatics proved "unconvincing even to many of his adherents" (F. D. E. *Schleiermacher*, 110).
451 Pröpper, *Theologische Anthropologie*, vol. II, 677.
452 Pannenberg, "Schwierigkeiten", 13.

verges on a monism that the specification of other attributes like omniscience and eternity then needs to counteract: a limitation of God's omnipotence by insisting on its complete expression in the world (^{1}§ 68.a. and ^{2}§ 54). The corresponding identification of God's willing with God's doing does not leave any space for eschatological action, neither in relation to the resurrection of Jesus nor to the possibility of a salvation that would rescue the victims of history from the fate they were made suffer.

There would have been other theological avenues available to follow instead of completely taking on board the Fichtean and the Spinozist critiques of personal categories for God. Causality is the lens through which the living God is accessed from the plethora of effects in the world. By endorsing the *ex nihilo* designation as valid, causality is restrained from becoming a necessity of productivity for God which would cancel the "free decision" to create.[453] Only from Part Two does the "purpose" of creating a world become clear, namely "love". While this motivation protects against the impression of a merely anonymous author bent on producing something other, it also robs the concept of revelation of any defining power.[454] Schaefer resumes:

> Well before any revelation – something that would actually be able to give insight into the essence of God –, it has already been decided in the logic of the *Glaubenslehre* how God is in relation to the world. It was decided through an analysis of the finite self-consciousness in correspondence to which the attributes of the First Part of the main dogmatics were developed. Due to the overall design of the *Glaubenslehre*, the event of revelation (*Offenbarungsgeschehen*) in which God becomes known for the first time as love could no longer be of constitutive significance for the teaching on divine attributes.

She concludes with the question whether the distinguishing feature that is typical for Christian piety, the relation to the event of redemption, contains more than a modification, given that the content of God's specific relationship to the world had been decided much earlier: based on the elementary data of the general realisation of piety which was demonstrated by way of philosophy.[455]

---

[453] Daniel J. Pedersen does not account for these corrective moves when he draws the conclusion from ^{2}§ 54,4 that "again following Spinoza, Schleiermacher holds that God acts by the necessity of the divine nature alone. Since freedom and necessity are one in God". He concludes: "As God acts by the necessity of his nature, the world follows of absolute necessity as determinate effect from determinate cause." *The Eternal Covenant*, 123–124.

[454] The implicitly optimising view of the "absolute infinity" of the "Whence" as benign rather than "either an *empty thought* or a *horrifying something*" (ein *leerer Gedanke* oder ein *schreckliches Etwas*)" was noted by Bretschneider, "Ueber das Princip", KGA I.7.3, 380.

[455] Schaefer, *Gottes Sein zur Welt*, 212–213.

8.2.4 Underrating the critical contribution of theological perspectives to the dialogue of the humanities with the natural sciences

Apart from Schleiermacher's commitment to specific positions in the philosophical debate and in the theological tradition, a further reason for the final shape of the doctrines is his wish to avoid conflicts with science. The judgements of commentators on this concern differ, from an interpretation of the *Glaubenslehre* as a project of subsuming the phenomena of religion to scientific explanation, to the view that the compatibility sought with science came at the expense of theology. On the first side is Andrew Dole who sums up his reading of the dogmatics in the context of the determinist position he sees as being put forward in Schleiermacher's work: "he in fact proposed as an interpretation of Christian doctrine a description of processes operating within the mind that he anticipated the natural sciences might someday be able to observe independently".[456] In the context of the one human nature shared by "Adam" and Christ, Robert Sherman points out the advantage of such a position in avoiding to alienate science: Instead of

> two human natures, the first modeled after Adam and the second "remodeled" by Christ ... there is only one, and it is embodied by Christ ... the underlying integrity of the natural order will be made manifest. And once this becomes clear, then the underlying unity and constancy of the divine causality will likewise become apparent ... The natural order can be understood as constant ... viewed from the outset through a christological lens. This is certainly a plus for theology's relation to modernity, because it echoes the latter's assumption of the constancy of the natural causal nexus.[457]

Precisely on the point of natural laws, their status is clarified by Schaefer as presupposing the activity of theoretical reason and of the faculty of judgement (*Urteilskraft*). For

---

[456] Dole, *Schleiermacher on Religion and the Natural Order*, 166. The method he sees him as endorsing is neither hermeneutical nor transcendental, but an unveiling of the natural causes of religion: "Schleiermacher hoped that his dogmatics would demonstrate ... that viewing religion as the scientific mindset requires – as a phenomenon unfolding within the natural order and hence subject to an increasingly sophisticated causal explanatory accounting with the advance of time – could by nature neither destroy Christian faith nor pronounce the final word concerning its content, even if such a posture would require an unaccustomed degree of doctrinal flexibility and epistemic humility" (175).
[457] Sherman, *The Shift to Modernity*, 217. 220.

Kant, the possibility of secure knowledge (*gesicherter Erkenntnis*) was tied to empirical reality conforming to natural laws that could be established apriori. The factual agreement (*Übereinkunft*) of the empirical with a natural law, however, cannot be sufficiently explained by theoretical reason but only by an assessment as purposive (*zweckmäßig*) for the finite use of reason by the teleological faculty of judgement ... Since reason strives to establish the unity of all knowing by understanding (*Verstandeserkenntnis*), it must assume (*ansetzen*) the principle of purposiveness as a regulative principle.[458]

In other words, the regularity of processes in nature is the expectation that is tested; to assess its own status, the conduct of scientific experiments presupposes a philosophical account of reason (*Vernunft*). Also in concrete investigations, scientific rationality interacts with philosophical reason in designing research projects based on hypotheses.[459] Apart from this reminder from a philosophically informed theory of science, the question is whether any dogmatic content was adjusted to fit what were perceived to be the exigencies of science. Subordinating creation to preservation could be motivated by either: a wish for regularity of natural processes, or a specific concept of God's perfection that rules out completely new beginnings and change.

The conclusion of a lecture given at a North American university in 1968 by Gerhard Ebeling is instructive in the greater ambivalence it manifests than Schleiermacher's era did regarding new powers owed to science. Concerning the "contemporary tasks of dogmatic responsibility", Ebeling offers an updated version of Schleiermacher's concern expressed in the *Sendschreiben:* "Is it not the case that the question is posed to us at times in the following form: Should the knot of history be resolved in this way: Christianity with unbelief, and science (*Wissenschaft*) with barbarism?"[460]

From the perspective of an ethics operating within the sciences and the humanities, there are points that theology has the capacity to make, on the strength of the heuristic or problem-spotting potential of traditions that have reflected on conditions of human flourishing, suffering, failure and rescue. Attributes on which philosophical and theological anthropology and ethics can agree are, as the theological ethicist Dietmar Mieth states, human contingency, finitude

---

[458] Schaefer, *Gottes Sein zur Welt*, 245, and 245, n. 167, with reference to Kant, *Critique of Judgement*, (KU B XXXVIII), and to Magnus Striet's considerations in *Das Ich im Sturz der Realität* (Regensburg: Pustet, 1998), 286–303.
[459] Jürgen Habermas has elucidated this interaction where a philosophical idea sparks and guides research with examples such as Durkheim's idea of the sacred, Freud's psychoanalysis and Kohlberg's theory of moral development, in "Philosophy as stand-in and interpreter", *in Moral Consciousness and Communicative Action* (Cambridge, MA: MIT Press, 1990), 1–20.
[460] Ebeling, "Schleiermachers Lehre von den göttlichen Eigenschaften", 342.

and fallibility.⁴⁶¹ They encourage an attitude of precaution and the need to judge the direction of technological innovations by their human value. A specific contribution from Schleiermacher's work could be his high regard for individuality. The human self is ineffable and cannot be captured in a grid of empirical data. Her freedom within the setting of her time manifests itself, among others, in her capability for "divination" when interpreting the meaning intended by a text or a present person. It is tempting to introduce into the ongoing cultural debate on whether parents should be allowed to enhance their children's genes (which began in the late 1990s before the scientific means had become available) the commandment Schleiermacher rewrote in his "Catechism for Noble Women": "Reverence the individuality and the freedom of choice (*Eigentümlichkeit und Willkühr*) of thy children, that they may enjoy health and happiness and live robustly (*kräftig*) on earth."⁴⁶²

The respect for individuality predates the Romantic Age. It is an idea arising in the context of the view of each human being as created in the image of God and envisaged to become a partner and friend of God. As a reminder of the resources of Christian thinking, the final section will offer a look back to the inaugurator of an earlier new departure, John Duns Scotus.

8.3 Opening up a new era: Duns Scotus's conception of a God who creates free counterparts and risks an open history

The work of Duns Scotus has been credited with inaugurating a new era, moving decisively beyond the thought forms of Antiquity and the high Middle Ages. Like Schleiermacher's, his approach is supralapsarian, but for other reasons. I will briefly indicate how the new conceptions he introduces for God (8.3.1), for the human self (8.3.2) and for the difference of Jesus Christ (8.3.3) open up the path to modernity in their categories of freedom. His precise analysis of the

---

461 Dietmar Mieth, "Bioethics and biolaw in the European Union: Bridging or fudging different traditions of moral and legal argumentation?", in Cathriona Russell, Linda Hogan and Maureen Junker-Kenny (eds), *Ethics for Graduate Researchers. A Cross-Disciplinary Approach* (Oxford: Elsevier, 2013), 59–72, 62.
462 Schleiermacher, "Outline of a Reasonable Catechism for Noble Women (1798)", trans. Robert F. Streetman, in *New Athenaeum/Neues Athenaeum* 2 (1991) 175–176. Habermas justifies his rejection of intruding into the "deontologically protected core" with a concept developed by Kierkegaard, the "ability to become a self." Cf. Habermas, *The Future of Human Nature* (Cambridge: Polity Press, 2003).

role of contingency makes it possible to conceive of history as the place of encounter between divine and human freedom (8.3.4). Magnus Striet sums up his epoch-changing role: "The Scotist critique of metaphysics founds the primacy of practical reason over theoretical reason, the primacy of the individual (*des Individuellen*) over what is general (*Allgemeinheit*), and the primacy of contingency over necessity. With this, it is at the same time a metaphysics of freedom, both of God and of the human person."[463]

8.3.1 The distinction between *potentia Dei absoluta* and *potentia Dei ordinata*

These breakthroughs are enabled by a new distinction introduced to the doctrine of God, that of *potentia Dei absoluta*, the full extent of God's power, and *potentia Dei ordinata*, its actual use.[464] It safeguards God's freedom by not collapsing, as Schleiermacher does, the difference between 'will' and 'can' in God. Duns Scotus identifies the power to produce (*producere*) as the supreme capability of the divine will from which God's initiative to "create" (*creare*) is a separate decision. The "*ex nihilo*" relates to "*productio*": In "absolute freedom", God "produces" from "absolute nothingness". The only reason that possible elements for creation, "'*creabilia*', become realities is God's free will in God's contingent *creare*".[465]

These distinctions signify that the world's existence is owed to a contingent divine act arising from the self-determination of God's will and not to a divine necessity for self-expression.

The reason for creation, as in the *Glaubenslehre*, is God's love, but it is defined differently: not as the unification with human nature but as the condition for being able to encounter humans in their freedom; they are destined to become possible "fellow lovers" of one another, of the world and, above all, of God. This understanding of God's work corrects the tendency of positions within the medieval debate between the monotheistic traditions to combine Neo-Platonic and Aristotelian ideas towards a pantheist view:

> It is only with Duns Scotus and Ockham – in a conscious countermove to an increasingly evident Aristotelian determinism – that freedom, grasped in its originality (*Ursprünglichkeit*) in a new and genuine way becomes the core of the doctrine of God and of anthropol-

---

463 Magnus Striet, *Offenbares Geheimnis. Zur Kritik der negativen Theologie* (ratio fidei 14) (Regensburg: Pustet, 2003), 131.
464 Schleiermacher rejects this distinction in ¹§ 68.a., 1. I, 205 and ²§ 54,4. ET 2016, 310–315.
465 Striet, *Offenbares Geheimnis*, 144–145.

ogy, thus leaving the enclosure (*Bannkreis*) of antique philosophy behind. ... A decisive counterweight against the temptation, further strengthened by Neoplatonism, to conceive the aim of becoming like God and the connection with God in the manner of a fusion in which the counterpart relationship of God and humans almost disappears and the human person, losing almost all distinction (*gleichsam differenzlos*), sinks into the Absolute.[466]

8.3.2 The addressees of God's love: Human beings in their freedom

Striet spells out how prioritising God's freedom in creation affects the concepts of the world and of the human creature: "Duns Scotus knows precisely that there can only be human freedom and thus an intellectual alternative to Arabic necessitarianism if God was free in God's act of creation ... In a necessary world there can be no freedom." The category of *potentia Dei ordinata* ensures that God's self is bound to be faithful to the promises to humans, and that they can participate in a trustworthy world order. "Conditioned necessity is exactly not an obstacle to freedom but allows humans to act freely in a contingent world ... presupposing reliable structures."[467]

The achievement of turning practical reasoning away from the preset natural finality that only allowed to choose between goods but not set goals oneself, towards the original spontaneity and concrete self-determination by their will that open up the path to modernity is outlined by Ludger Honnefelder. It belongs to the inherent freedom of the will (*libertas innata*) to be able to freely bind itself to what is good in itself. This "*affectio iustitiae*" is distinguished from an "*affectio commodi*" towards which it operates as "*moderatrix*" revealing a "reflexive self-relationship of the will which founds the moral responsibility of the human being."[468] Reading this portrayal from the background of late modern approaches to ethics, the description of the need and the capability for taking a de-

---

466 Pröpper, *Theologische Anthropologie*, vol. I, 206. He points to the patristic efforts to highlight the "significance of human freedom in the relationship to God which is owed to the memory, testified to in the Bible, of the history of God with humans as the foundation of their faith" (206).
467 Striet, *Offenbares Geheimnis*, 131.
468 Honnefelder, *Woher kommen wir*, 194–195. Against readings that ascribe "voluntarism" and "excessive indeterminism" to his theory of freedom, Honnefelder distinguishes the position of Henry of Ghent from that of Duns Scotus and shows the self-binding of the will as the key capacity discovered. In contrast to the "extreme voluntarism" attributed to Duns Scotus, he identifies "the highest form of freedom in the form of self-determination as consisting in not allowing oneself to be determined by anything but the good as such" (193–194).

ontological stance (*affectio iustitiae*) towards the striving for a flourishing life (*affectio commodi*) is not unlike the function Paul Ricoeur names the "sieve of the norm" in his three-part ethics.[469] The framework of the reconstructions both by Duns Scotus and Ricoeur is one that resists a decisionist or legal positivist approach in which "contingent moral norms are only valid because the normgiver willed them to be".[470]

Pröpper summarises the contrast to antique ethics: "Scotus discovered the unconditionality of freedom and therefore takes the conceptions of rationality (*Verstand*) merely as contingent causes (*Gelegenheitsursachen*) for the decision of the will which is solely moved by itself and avails of original self-determination also in relation to the choice of aims ... Self-originating freedom as irreducible self-determination" opens up an understanding of personhood as being "a counterpart (*Gegenüberstand*) and as realising itself *ab ovo* in relation to other freedom".[471] This understanding of the originating power of the will prefigures Kant's definition of the capability for morality as the ground of human dignity, honouring the pricelessness of every human being.

Dating from the years around 1300, it is a theological conception which prizes the free response of the beloved creature that depends on the self-determination of the human addressee and cannot be necessitated by God. There is no prior coordination of self-active units and no impossibility not to relate to the "Whence"; it can only be a matter of God's hopeful expectation whether the individual will accept the invitation. The risk of a one-sided initiative is not downplayed; the unwavering conviction expressed by Schleiermacher that ultimately, all of humanity will have become Christian[472] is missing, for the good reason of not being able to predict how humans will use their freedom in their ongoing history with God.

8.3.3 The *haecceitas* of Jesus

Finally, a resolution even of the problems with the terminology of the Christological councils comes into sight with the turn Duns Scotus gives to the "hypostatic union" of humanity and divinity in Jesus Christ. It matches the emphasis of his

---

[469] Paul Ricoeur, *Oneself as Another*, trans. Kathleen Blamey (Chicago: University of Chicago Press, 1992), 170.
[470] Honnefelder, *Woher kommen wir?*, 193.
[471] Pröpper, *Theologische Anthropologie*, vol. I, 409.
[472] In ²§ 120,4. ET 1928, 558, Schleiermacher states: "each is fashioned in readiness to become a member of the Christian fellowship, because he is foreseen as a believer."

whole approach on the significance of the factual and the individual over against the general that he applies this thought also to the person of Jesus. He specifies the "humanity" in the formula of Chalcedon not as denoting human nature as such, but the individualised human nature of Jesus. What is assumed in the hypostatic union is Jesus' specificity, his *haecceitas*, that is, his human loving response to God and decision to set his life on God's love.[473]

The Christian ethicist Christoph Hübenthal has interpreted this conception as the theological foundation of a secular world in its own right.[474] It is the result of recognising, in keeping with Chalcedon, Jesus' humanity in his free response to God. For theological ethics it is seen as a liberation from the substantial-ontological terms of an Aristotelian natural order.[475] The relationship between nature and grace can be re-envisaged in terms of freedom, once the pre-modern framework marked by a teleology of striving has been "dispatched for good".[476]

The Scotist conception of the history of salvation is supralapsarian not due to a need to keep God free from change and achieving this by proposing the one decree of creation and redemption; it is so because of God's wish for *alios con-*

---

[473] For a fuller presentation of the "order of love", in which God's love first relates to the Son as the second person of the Trinity, see Dirk Ansorge, *Gerechtigkeit und Barmherzigkeit Gottes. Die Dramatik von Vergebung und Versöhnung in bibeltheologischer, theologiegeschichtlicher und philosophiegeschichtlicher Perspektive* (Freiburg: Herder, 2009), 353–377. Ansorge also points out why Duns Scotus is the dreaded antipode for the Radical Orthodoxy movement in Anglophone theology. In *Kleine Geschichte der christlichen Theologie. Epochen, Denker, Weichenstellungen* (Regensburg: Pustet, 2017), 391, he identifies the independence of philosophy from theology as a key reason for this critique from a school that opposes a positive view of modernity and of human freedom also towards God. He sums up that the Late Middle Ages are made responsible for the "drifting apart of reason and faith, theology and philosophy in modernity. By emphasising the absolute freedom of the divine will, Duns Scotus is said to have facilitated a theology which grasps God as unpredictable and as acting wilfully. At the same time Duns Scotus is seen as overestimating human freedom. Thus, the unity of truth and divine freedom as it was still given in Augustine and Thomas Aquinas was broken up. Immanuel Kant finally justified philosophically through his critique of the scope (*Reichweite*) of human reason the separation of physics from metaphysics that was begun by Duns Scotus; this separation is seen as having become effective in the secularism of modernity."
[474] Christoph Hübenthal, "Ethische Begründung aus dem theologischen Grund des Säkularen. Eine katholische Sicht", in *Ökumenische Ethik*, ed. Thomas Weißer (Fribourg/Würzburg: Academic Press Fribourg/Echter, 2018), 45–63, especially 55–56.
[475] In *Approaches to Theological Ethics. Sources, Traditions, Visions* (London/New York: T & T Clark, 2019), I have compared the philosophical background traditions of five current English- and German-speaking approaches and discussed the frameworks they offer for theological reflection on action in the spirit of Jesus.
[476] Hübenthal, *Grundlegung der christlichen Sozialethik. Versuch eines freiheitsanalytisch-handlungsreflexiven Ansatzes* (Münster: Aschendorff, 2006), 369.

diligentes, genuine others who can freely decide to be fellow lovers. This is the reason for creation and incarnation, and it does not presuppose sin as the determining motive. Sin would not be a worthy enough cause because divine agency "also in its relation to what is outside of God can have no other measure than God's self".[477] Correspondingly, for Duns Scotus, Christ is not "primarily the Redeemer. Rather, he is the personified shape (*Gestalt*), revealed to humans, of the love that God is in God's self", wishing for the response of humans, but "knowing that with the creation of a free being who is able to respond to God's love it is also possible that this free being will close itself off from God." Jesus' death on the cross is taken as his fidelity to his mission. For Schleiermacher, too, it is not his suffering as such that is redemptive but his "loving obedience ... under the conditions of the domination of sin".[478] Duns Scotus redirects the notion of beatitude from the contemplative *visio* which it was for Thomas Aquinas to a "*visio*" and "*scientia practica*". Human beings "know that they are able to respond to the divine love ... due to an enabling and preserving act" of God, and this encounter deserves the name *amicitia*, friendship.[479]

It is a different model of "theocentrism"[480] to that of Schleiermacher's dogmatics.[481] It gives due recognition to the role of human freedom in the interaction with God, called to respond in a contingent world shaped by their actions. The final point of comparison are their views of salvation history.

8.3.4 The outcome of history as an open theological question

A key difference, alluded to before, is the vision of how the mission of Christianity is to proceed and which type of confidence can inspire it. Roger Haight judges Schleiermacher's outlook as basically acceptable, with newly developed insights to be added:

---

477 Ansorge, *Gerechtigkeit und Barmherzigkeit Gottes*, 365.
478 Ansorge, *Gerechtigkeit und Barmherzigkeit Gottes*, 366–367. 370.
479 Ansorge, *Gerechtigkeit und Barmherzigkeit Gottes*, 372–374.
480 Pröpper, *Theologische Anthropologie*, vol. II, 1281.
481 Gockel, *Election*, 103, concludes: "Christ is the universal redeemer and mediator of salvation but his appearance does not contribute specifically to the determination of the divine will and decree. Despite the christologically motivated affirmation of general redemption and rejection of eternal damnation, the overall reconstruction remains theocentric; it is grounded in the belief in God the almighty creator, even though ecclesiology is its context and christology its background."

Schleiermacher's ecclesiology includes an intrinsic orientation outward in mission to the world. This feature, too, flows logically from his Christology and soteriology. A number of adjustments in the theology of religions and mission theology are required in our postcolonial situation, but Schleiermacher's stress on a fundamental facing outward into the world and history remains a Christian exigency.[482]

With his turn towards subjectivity, Schleiermacher laid the foundations for an understanding of God's history with humans in terms of freedom, moving from the objectifying proofs of God from reason to the truth of the person in her complex constitution. To be able to support the Christian practice outlined by Haight, however, a different understanding of God's omnipotence would be needed, as Pröpper specifies:

> In order to conceive of the history between both (God and humans) seriously as open, God must be envisaged as creating, and allowing to be, free beings who take a stance to God ... in every moment of God's *potentia ordinata* the capability must be presupposed of responding to the actions of free humans ... and remaining identical with God's self in the contingent divine decisions. God is the primary subject of an open history which nevertheless does not escape God, which does not decline and split up but that retains its future full of promise, due to God's original power to innovate, with possibilities which are never exhausted.[483]

The philosopher Michael Theunissen concludes an article on monistic philosophies and Christian theology with a similar analysis of the attitude provided by a faith perspective:

> for the philosopher ... only the question remains: Does the self-delivery of God to history not also imply that the outcome of the adventure which God let God's self into is open? Trust in God's goodness includes the certainty: God will do everything to grant it to us (*sie uns angedeihen zu lassen*). But what is uncertain is whether God's power in history will eventually become omnipotence after all, that is, whether the principalities and powers that Paul speaks of will ultimately be subjected (*untertan*) to God at the end. This uncertainty constitutes the basis above which the paradoxical certainty of faith rises. (*Diese Ungewissheit bildet die Basis, über der die paradoxe Gewissheit des Glaubens sich erhebt*).[484]

---

[482] Haight, "Take and Read: The Christian Faith", in *National Catholic Reporter* May 23, 2016, accessed March 1, 2020. https://www.ncronline.org/blogs/ncr-today/take-and-read-christian-faith.
[483] Pröpper, *Theologische Anthropologie*, vol. I, 608, formulating one of the "essentials" that a doctrine of God must encompass.
[484] Michael Theunissen, "Philosophischer Monismus und christliche Theologie", in *Zeitschrift für Theologie und Kirche* 102 (2005) 397–408, 408.

A "paradoxical certainty" of God's greater possibilities beyond the efforts available to the human "fellow lovers" – who are the reason for creation for Duns Scotus – differs significantly from Schleiermacher's equally supralapsarian conception. Francis Fiorenza summarises the confident outlook on how the perfection of creation will be achieved in history: "The Holy Spirit as the common spirit of the Christian community is the present reality of the love of God in Christ and as such the organ or instrument of God's wisdom that gradually brings God's love into history. As an instrument of activity this love works its way out into the future of the world".[485]

How God's omnipotence relates to human freedom belongs to the fundamental issues which to examine in their alternative directions has been the third aim of this study. The idea of a "self-limitation" of God in favour of giving scope to free human agency was incompatible with Schleiermacher's idea of divine perfection. God's design for the world in its sequence of First and Second Adam and the Common Spirit deriving from Christ was irresistible. To open up this circle restores agency and risk in an unpredictable history and the strength of mere hope.[486]

---

485 Francis Fiorenza, "Schleiermacher's understanding of God as triune", in *Cambridge Companion to Friedrich Schleiermacher*, ed. Mariña, 171–188, 182.
486 Cf. also Wendel, "Die Renaissance des Religiösen und der Glaube an Gott", 218–219 and Schaefer, *Gottes Sein zur Welt*, 261.

Bibliography

1 Sources

Schleiermacher, Friedrich. Kritische Gesamtausgabe (= KGA). Berlin/New York: Walter de Gruyter, 1980–2011; Berlin/Boston: Walter de Gruyter, since 2011.
Schleiermacher, Friedrich. Akademievorträge, edited by Martin Rössler, with Lars Emersleben. KGA I/11. Berlin/New York: Walter de Gruyter, 2002.
Schleiermacher, Friedrich. Brief Outline of Theology as a Field of Study [1811 and 1830], trans. and intro. Terrence N. Tice. Lewiston, N.Y.: The Edwin Mellen Press, 1988.
Schleiermacher, Friedrich. Christian Faith. A New Translation and Critical Edition, 2 vols., trans. Terrence N. Tice, Catherine L. Kelsey and Edwina Lawler; edited by Catherine L. Kelsey and Terrence N. Tice. Louisville, KY: Westminster John Knox Press, 2016.
Schleiermacher, Friedrich. Der christliche Glaube 1821/22, 2 vols., Studienausgabe, edited by Hermann Peiter. KGA I/7.1 and 2. Berlin/New York: Walter de Gruyter, 1984.
Schleiermacher, Friedrich. Der christliche Glaube, 1. Auflage 1821/22, Marginalien und Anhang, edited by Ulrich Barth using preparatory works of Hayo Gerdes and Hermann Peiter. KGA I/7.3. Berlin/New York: Walter de Gruyter, 1984.
Schleiermacher, Friedrich. Der christliche Glaube, 2. Auflage 1830/31, edited by Rolf Schäfer. KGA I/13.1 and 2. Berlin/New York: Walter de Gruyter, 2003.
Schleiermacher, Friedrich. Der christliche Glaube, 2. Auflage 1830/31, Studienausgabe, edited by Rolf Schäfer. Berlin/New York: Walter de Gruyter, 2008.
Schleiermacher, Friedrich. Der christliche Glaube, 2. Auflage 1830/31, 2 vols., edited by Martin Redeker. Berlin: Walter de Gruyter, 1960.
Schleiermacher, Friedrich. Dialektik 1811, edited by Andreas Arndt. Hamburg: Meiner, 1986.
Schleiermacher, Friedrich. Dialektik, edited by Rudolf Odebrecht. Leipzig: J.C. Hinrichs, 1942; reprint Darmstadt: Wissenschaftliche Buchgesellschaft, 1976.
Schleiermacher, Friedrich. "Einleitung zur Vorlesung über Dogmatische Theologie (Sommersemester 1811). Nachschrift August Detlev Christian Twesten", edited by Matthias Wolfes. Zeitschrift für Kirchengeschichte 109 (1998): 80–99.
Schleiermacher, Friedrich. Hermeneutics and Criticism and Other Writings, edited by Andrew Bowie. Cambridge: Cambridge University Press, 1998.
Schleiermacher, Friedrich. Hermeneutik und Kritik, mit einem Anhang sprachphilosophischer Texte Schleiermachers, edited by and intro. Manfred Frank. Frankfurt: Suhrkamp, 61995.
Schleiermacher, Friedrich. Kurze Darstellung des theologischen Studiums zum behuf einleitender Vorlesungen. Kritische Ausgabe, edited by Heinrich Scholz. Leipzig: Deichert'sche Verlagsbuchhandlung Nachf., 31910; reprint Darmstadt: Wissenschaftliche Buchgesellschaft, 1993.
Schleiermacher, Friedrich. On Religion. Speeches to its Cultured Despisers, trans. R. Crouter. Cambridge: Cambridge University Press, 1996.
Schleiermacher, Friedrich. On the Glaubenslehre. Two Letters to Dr. Lücke, trans. James O. Duke and Francis Fiorenza. Atlanta: Scholars Press, 1981.
Schleiermacher, Friedrich. "Outline of a Reasonable Catechism for Noble Women (1798)", trans. R. F. Streetman. New Athenaeum/Neues Athenaeum 2 (1991): 175–176.
Schleiermacher, Friedrich. The Christian Faith (1830/31), edited by H.R. Mackintosh and J.S. Stewart, trans. D. M. Baillie et al. Edinburgh: T. & T. Clark, 1928; 1986.

Schleiermacher, Friedrich. *The Life of Jesus*, trans. S. Maclean Gilmour, edited by Jack C. Verheyden. Lives of Jesus Series. Philadelphia: Fortress Press, 1975; reprint Mifflintown: Sigler, 1997.

Schleiermacher, Friedrich. *Theologische Enzyklopädie (1831/32)*, Nachschrift D. F. Strauß, edited by Walter Sachs. Schleiermacher-Archiv 4. Berlin/New York: Walter de Gruyter, 1987.

Schleiermacher, Friedrich. *Theologisch-dogmatische Abhandlungen und Gelegenheitsschriften*, edited by Hans-Friedrich Traulsen, with Martin Ohst. KGA I/10. Berlin/New York: Walter de Gruyter, 1990.

Schleiermacher, Friedrich. "Ueber die Lehre von der Erwählung; besonders in Beziehung auf Herrn Dr. Bretschneiders Aphorismen", edited by Hans-Friedrich Traulsen, with Martin Ohst. KGA I/10, 145–222. Berlin/New York: Walter de Gruyter, 1990.

Schleiermacher, Friedrich. *Über die Religion. Reden an die Gebildeten unter ihren Verächtern* (1799), edited by Günter Meckenstock. KGA I/2, 185–326. Berlin/New York: Walter de Gruyter, 1984.

Über die Religion. Reden an die Gebildeten unter ihren Verächtern, 2nd – 4th editions, edited by Günter Meckenstock. KGA I/12, 1–321. Berlin/New York: Walter de Gruyter, 1995.

Schleiermacher, Friedrich. *Universitätsschriften. Herakleitos. Kurze Darstellung des theologischen Studiums*, edited by Dirk Schmid. KGA I/6. Berlin/New York: Walter de Gruyter, 1998.

Schleiermacher, Friedrich. *Vorlesungen zur Hermeneutik und Kritik*, edited by Wolfgang Virmond, with Hermann Patsch. KGA II/4. Berlin/New York: Walter de Gruyter, 2012.

2 Secondary literature

Albrecht, Christian. *Schleiermachers Theorie der Frömmigkeit. Ihr wissenschaftlicher Ort und ihr systematischer Gehalt in den Reden, in der Glaubenslehre und in der Dialektik.* Schleiermacher-Archiv 15. Berlin/New York: Walter de Gruyter, 1994, reprint 2011.

Ameriks, Karl, ed. *The Cambridge Companion to German Idealism.* Cambridge: Cambridge University Press, 2000.

Ansorge, Dirk. *Gerechtigkeit und Barmherzigkeit Gottes. Die Dramatik von Vergebung und Versöhnung in bibeltheologischer, theologiegeschichtlicher und philosophiegeschichtlicher Perspektive.* Freiburg: Herder, 2009.

Ansorge, Dirk. *Kleine Geschichte der christlichen Theologie. Epochen, Denker, Weichenstellungen.* Regensburg: Pustet, 2017.

Arndt, Andreas, ed. *Schleiermacher in Halle 1804–1807.* Berlin/Boston: Walter de Gruyter, 2013.

Arndt, Andreas. *Die Reformation der Revolution. Friedrich Schleiermacher in seiner Zeit.* Berlin: Matthes & Seitz, 2019.

Arndt, Andreas, Ulrich Barth and Wilhelm Gräb, eds. *Christentum – Staat – Kultur. Akten des Kongresses der Internationalen Schleiermacher-Gesellschaft Berlin März 2006.* Schleiermacher-Archiv 22. Berlin/Boston: Walter de Gruyter, 2008.

Barth, Karl. *The Theology of Schleiermacher: Lectures at Göttingen, Winter Semester of 1923/ 24*, edited by Dietrich Ritschl, trans. Geoffrey W. Bromiley. Grand Rapids: Eerdmans, 1982.
Barth, Karl. *Die kirchliche Dogmatik*, vol. II.1. Zürich: Evangelischer Verlag, ⁴1958.
Barth, Karl."Nachwort." In *Schleiermacher Auswahl*, edited by Heinz Bolli, 290–312. Gütersloh: Gütersloher Verlagshaus, 1968.
Barth, Roderich, and Christopher Zarnow, eds. *Theologie der Gefühle*. Berlin/Boston: Walter de Gruyter, 2014.
Barth, Ulrich. "Schleiermacher-Literatur im letzten Drittel des 20. Jahrhunderts." *Theologische Rundschau* 66 (2001): 408–461.
Barth, Ulrich. "Die subjektivitätstheoretischen Prämissen der 'Glaubenslehre'. Eine Replik auf Konrad Cramers Schleiermacher-Studie." In Ulrich Barth, *Aufgeklärter Protestantismus*, 329–351. Tübingen: Mohr Siebeck, 2004.
Barth, Ulrich, and Claus-Dieter Osthövener, eds. *200 Jahre "Reden über die Religion. Akten des 1. Internationalen Kongresses der Schleiermacher-Gesellschaft Halle, 14.–17. März 1999*. Schleiermacher-Archiv 19. Berlin/New York: De Gruyter, 2000, reprint 2011.
Baur, Ferdinand Christian. *Primae Rationalismi et Supranaturalismi historia capita potiora, Pars II: Comparatur Gnosticismus cum Schleiermacherianae theologiae indole. (Tübinger Osterprogramm)*. Tübingen: Hopferi de l'Orme, 1827); partly reprinted in KGA I/7.3, 243–256.
Baur, Ferdinand Christian. "Anzeige der beiden academischen Schriften." *Tübinger Zeitschrift für Theologie* 1 (1828): 220–264; partly reprinted in KGA I/7.3, 256–277.
Baur, Ferdinand Christian. *Die christliche Gnosis oder die christliche Religions-Philosophie in ihrer geschichtlichen Entwicklung*. Tübingen: Osiander, 1835.
Baur, Ferdinand Christian. *Die christliche Lehre von der Versöhnung in ihrer geschichtlichen Entwicklung von der ältesten Zeit bis auf die neueste*. Tübingen: Osiander, 1838.
Baur, Ferdinand Christian. *Die christliche Lehre von der Dreieinigkeit und Menschwerdung Gottes in ihrer geschichtlichen Entwicklung*, vol. III. Tübingen: Osiander, 1843.
Baur, Ferdinand Christian. *Lehrbuch der christlichen Dogmengeschichte*. Tübingen: Fues, 1847, Leipzig ³1867, reprint Darmstadt: Wissenschaftliche Buchgesellschaft, 1979.
Baur, Ferdinand Christian. *Kirchengeschichte des 19. Jahrhunderts. (Geschichte der christlichen Kirche V)*, ed. by E. Zeller. Tübingen: Fues, 1862.
Beinert, Wolfgang, and Francis Schüssler Fiorenza, eds. *Handbook of Catholic Theology*. New York: Crossroad, 1992.
Beckmann, Klaus-Martin. *Der Begriff der Häresie bei Schleiermacher*. Munich: Chr. Kaiser, 1959.
Berner, Christian. "Religion et rationalité chez Schleiermacher."*Revue de Théologie et de Philosophie* 149 (2017): 153–168.
Birkner, Hans-Joachim. "Beobachtungen zu Schleiermachers Programm der Dogmatik." *Neue Zeitschrift für Systematische Theologie und Religionsphilosophie* 5 (1963): 119–131.
Birkner, Hans-Joachim. Schleiermacher-Studien im Kontext, edited by Hermann Fischer. Schleiermacher-Archiv 16. Berlin/New York: Walter de Gruyter, 2011.
Bongardt, Michael. "Einheit ja – aber welche?" In *Dogma und Denkform. Strittiges in der Grundlegung von Offenbarungsbegriff und Gottesgedanke*, edited by Klaus Müller and Magnus Striet, 85–100. Regensburg: Pustet, 2005.

Bretschneider, Karl G. "Ueber das Princip der christlichen Glaubenslehre des Herrn Prof. Dr. Schleiermacher." *Journal für Prediger* 66 (1825): 1–28; reprinted in KGA 1/7.3, 369–383. Berlin/New York 1984.

Bretschneider, Karl G. "Ueber den Begriff der Erlösung, und die damit zusammenhängenden Vorstellungen von Sünde und Erbsünde in der christlichen Glaubenslehre des Herrn Prof. Dr. Schleiermacher." *Journal für Prediger* 67 (1825): 1–33.

Cappeløm, Niels Jørgen, Richard Crouter, Theodor Jørgensen, and Claus-Dieter Osthövener, eds. *Schleiermacher und Kierkegaard. Subjektivität und Wahrheit/Subjectivity and Truth*. Schleiermacher-Archiv 21. Berlin/New York: Walter de Gruyter, 2006.

Clements, Keith W. *Friedrich Schleiermacher Pioneer of Modern Theology*. London: Collins Liturgical Press, 1987.

Cramer, Konrad. "Die subjektivitätstheoretischen Prämissen von Schleiermachers Bestimmung des religiösen Bewußtseins." In *Friedrich Schleiermacher 1768–1834. Theologe – Philosoph – Pädagoge*, edited by Dietz Lange, 129–162. Göttingen: Vandenhoeck & Ruprecht, 1985.

Danz, Christian. "Der Atheismusstreit um Fichte." In *Philosophisch-theologische Streitsachen. Pantheismusstreit, Atheismusstreit, Theismusstreit*, edited by Christian Danz and Georg Essen, 135–213. Darmstadt: Wissenschaftliche Buchgesellschaft, 2012.

Dahlke, Benjamin. "Die Christologie in Schleiermachers Glaubenslehre." *Catholica* 70 (2016): 278–299.

Deane-Drummond, Celia, and Peter M. Scott, eds. *Future Perfect? God, Medicine and Human Identity*. London: T. & T. Clark, 2006.

Dierken, Jörg. "Individualität und Identität. Schleiermacher über metaphysische, religiöse und sozialtheoretische Dimensionen eines Schlüsselthemas der Moderne." *Zeitschrift für Neuere Theologiegeschichte/Journal for the History of Modern Theology* 15 (2008): 183–207.

Dierken, Jörg, Arnulf von Scheliha and Sarah Schmidt, eds. *Reformation und Moderne. Pluralität – Subjektivität – Kritik. Akten des Internationalen Schleiermacher-Kongresses der Schleiermacher-Gesellschaft in Halle (Saale) März 2017*. Schleiermacher-Archiv 27. Berlin: Walter de Gruyter, 2018.

Dierksmeier, Claus. "Zum Begriff des religiösen Gefühls im Anschluss an Kant." *Zeitschrift für Neuere Theologiegeschichte/Journal for the History of Modern Theology* 8 (2001): 201–217.

Dilthey, Wilhelm. *Leben Schleiermachers*, vol. II, edited by Martin Redeker. Göttingen: Vandenhoeck & Ruprecht, 1966.

Dole, Andrew. *Schleiermacher on Religion and the Natural Order*. Oxford: Oxford University Press, 2010.

Dole, Andrew. "Schleiermacher's theological anti-realism." In *Analytic Theology. New Essays in the Philosophy of Theology*, edited by Oliver D. Crisp and Michael Rea, 136–154. Oxford: Oxford University Press, 2009.

Dorner, Isaak August. *Entwicklungsgeschichte der Lehre von der Person Christi*. Stuttgart: S. G. Liesching, 1839.

Duke, James O. and Francis Fiorenza. "Translators' Introduction" and "Notes" to Schleiermacher, *On the Glaubenslehre. Two Letters to Dr. Lücke*, trans. by Duke and Fiorenza, 1–32. 95–130. Atlanta: Scholars Press, 1981.

Duke, James O., and Robert F. Streetman, eds. *Barth and Schleiermacher: Beyond the Impasse?* Philadelphia: Fortress Press, 1982.

Dupré, Louis. *Religion and the Rise of Modern Culture*. Notre Dame, IN: University of Notre Dame Press, 2008.
Ebeling, Gerhard. "Schleiermachers Lehre von den göttlichen Eigenschaften." In *Wort und Glaube*, vol. II, 305–342. Tübingen: Mohr Siebeck, 1969.
Ebeling, Gerhard. "Schlechthinniges Abhängigkeitsgefühl als Gottesbewußtsein." In *Wort und Glaube*, vol. III, 116–136. Tübingen: Mohr Siebeck, 1975.
Ebeling, Gerhard. "Interpretatorische Bemerkungen zu Schleiermachers Christologie." In *Schleiermacher und die wissenschaftliche Kultur des Christentums*. Edited by Günter Meckenstock, with Joachim Ringleben, 125–146. Theologische Bibliothek Töpelmann 51. Berlin/New York: Walter de Gruyter, 1991.
Essen, Georg. *Die Freiheit Jesu. Der neuchalkedonische Enhypostasiebegriff in neuzeitlicher Subjekt- und Personphilosophie*. ratio fidei 5. Regensburg: Pustet, 2001.
Essen, Georg. "Das Geschichtsdenken der Moderne als Krise und Herausforderung der Christologie. Historische Vergewisserung in systematischer Absicht." In *Der Problemhorizont der Christologie in der Moderne*, edited by Christian Danz and Michael Murrmann-Kahl, 141–155. Tübingen: Mohr Siebeck, 2009.
Essen, Georg. "Die Autorität der Freiheit. Katholische Ortsbestimmungen im Verhältnis von christlichem und neuzeitlichem Freiheitsverständnis." *Ökumenische Rundschau* 62 (2013): 5–23.
Essen, Georg. "Geschichte – Metaphysik – Anthropologie: Diskurskonstellationen der Christologie der Moderne. Eine katholisch-theologische Vergewisserung." In *Dogmatische Christologie in der Moderne. Problemkonstellationen gegenwärtiger Forschung*, edited by Christian Danz and Georg Essen, 9–18. Regensburg: Pustet, 2019.
Essen, Georg, and Thomas Pröpper. "Aneignungsprobleme der christologischen Überlieferung. Hermeneutische Vorüberlegungen." In *Gottes ewiger Sohn. Die Präexistenz Christi*, edited by Rudolf Laufen, 163–178. Paderborn: Schöningh, 1997.
Essen, Georg, and Danz, Christian, eds. *Dogmatische Christologie in der Moderne. Problemkonstellationen gegenwärtiger Forschung*. Regensburg: Pustet, 2019.
Fiorenza, Francis Schüssler. "Schleiermacher's understanding of God as triune." In *The Cambridge Companion to Friedrich Schleiermacher*, edited by Jacqueline Mariña, 171–188. Cambridge: Cambridge University Press, 2005.
Fischer, Hermann. *Subjektivität und Sünde. Kierkegaards Begriff der Sünde mit ständiger Rücksicht auf Schleiermachers Lehre von der Sünde*. Itzehoe: Verlag "Die Spur", 1963.
Fischer, Hermann, *Friedrich Daniel Ernst Schleiermacher*. Munich: Beck, 2001.
Fischer, Hermann. "Rezeption und Kritik 1918–1960" and "Rezeption und Kritik 1960ff." In *Schleiermacher-Handbuch*, edited by M. Ohst, 465–476 und 476–487. Tübingen: Mohr Siebeck, 2017.
Flöel, Ernst. *Der Entwicklungsgedanke in Schleiermachers Lehre von der Sünde*. Darmstadt: C. F. Winter, 1913.
Freyne, Seán. "The Galilean Jesus and a Contemporary Christology." *Theological Studies* 70 (2009): 281–297.
Freyne, Seán. *The Jesus Movement and Its Expansion – Meaning and Mission*. Grand Rapids: Eerdmans, 2014.
Gerdes, Hayo. *Das Christusbild Sören Kierkegaards, verglichen mit der Christologie Hegels und Schleiermachers*. Düsseldorf: Diederichs, ²1974.

Gerdes, Hayo. "Anmerkungen zur Christologie der Glaubenslehre Schleiermachers." *Neue Zeitschrift für Systematische Theologie und Religionsphilosophie* 25 (1983): 112–125.

Gerhardt, Volker. "Individualität bei Leibniz." In *Leibniz heute lesen. Wissenschaft, Geschichte, Religion*, edited by Herta Nagl-Docekal, 89–101. Berlin/Boston: Walter de Gruyter, 2018.

Gerrish, Brian A. "Continuity and Change: Friedrich Schleiermacher on the Task of Theology." In *Tradition and the Modern World. Reformed Theology in the Nineteenth Century*, 1–48. Chicago: University of Chicago Press, 1978.

Gockel, Matthias. *Barth and Schleiermacher on the Doctrine of Election. A Systematic-Theological Comparison*. Oxford: Oxford University Press, 2006.

Gräb, Wilhelm. *Humanität und Christentumsgeschichte. Eine Untersuchung zum Geschichtsbegriff im Spätwerk Schleiermachers*. Göttingen: Vandenhoeck & Ruprecht, 1980.

Grove, Peter. *Deutungen des Subjekts. Schleiermachers Philosophie der Religion*. Theologische Bibliothek Töpelmann 129. Berlin/New York: De Gruyter, 2004, reprint 2013.

Grosshans, Hans-Peter. "Alles (nur) Gefühl? Zur Religionstheorie Friedrich Schleiermachers." In *Christentum – Staat – Kultur*, edited by Andreas Arndt, Ulrich Barth and Wilhelm Gräb, 547–565. Schleiermacher-Archiv 22. Berlin/Boston: Walter de Gruyter, 2008.

Günther, Ernst. *Die Entwicklung der Lehre von der Person Christi im 19. Jahrhundert*. Tübingen: J.C.B. Mohr, 1911.

Gutekunst, Katharina. *Die Freiheit des Subjekts bei Schleiermacher. Eine Analyse im Horizont der Debatte um die Willensfreiheit in der analytischen Philosophie*. Theologische Bibliothek Töpelmann 185. Berlin/Boston: Walter de Gruyter, 2018.

Habermas, Jürgen. "Philosophy as stand-in and interpreter." In *Moral Consciousness and Communicative Action*, trans. Christian Lenhardt and Shierry Weber Nicholson, 1–20. Cambridge, MA: MIT Press, 1990.

Habermas, Jürgen. *The Future of Human Nature*. Cambridge: Polity Press, 2003.

Habermas, Jürgen. "The boundary between faith and knowledge: On the reception and contemporary importance of Kant's philosophy of religion." In *Between Naturalism and Religion*, trans. C. Cronin, 209–247. Cambridge: Polity Press, 2008.

Habermas, Jürgen et al., eds. *An Awareness of What is Missing. Faith and Reason in a Postsecular Age*, trans. C. Cronin. Cambridge: Polity Press, 2010.

Hagan, Anette. "Review of Friedrich Schleiermacher: *Christian Faith. A New Translation and Critical Edition*, 2 vols., trans. Terrence N. Tice, Catherine L Kelsey and Edwina Lawler; ed. Catherine L Kelsey and Terrence N. Tice. Louisville, Kentucky: Westminster John Knox Press, 2016." *International Journal of Systematic Theology* 19 (2017) 377–379.

Haight, Roger, "Take and Read: The Christian Faith", in *National Catholic Reporter*, May 23, 2016, accessed March 1, 2020. https://www.ncronline.org/blogs/ncr-today/take-and-read-christian-faith.

Harvey, Van A. "A Word in Defense of Schleiermacher's Theological Method." *Journal of Religion* XLII (1962): 151–170.

Hastings, Adrian. "F. D. E. Schleiermacher." In The Oxford Companion to Christian Thought, edited by Adrian Hastings, Alistair Mason, and Hugh Pyper, 644–645. Oxford: Oxford University Press, 2000.

Hell, Leonhard. "Dogmatische Theologie als Wissenschaft. Johann Sebastian Drey im Gespräch mit Friedrich Schleiermacher." *Trierer Theologische Zeitschrift* 126 (2017): 136–149.
Helmer, Christine. "Schleiermacher's exegetical theology and the New Testament." In *The Cambridge Companion to Friedrich Schleiermacher*, edited by Jacqueline Mariña, 229–247. Cambridge: Cambridge University Press, 2005.
Henrich, Dieter. "Das Selbstbewusstsein und seine Selbstdeutungen." In *Fluchtlinien. Philosophische Essays*, 99–124. Frankfurt: Suhrkamp, 1982.
Henrich, Dieter. "What is metaphysics – what modernity?" In *Habermas: A Critical Reader*, edited by Peter Dews, 291–319. Oxford: Blackwell, 1999.
Herms, Eilert. "Schleiermachers Eschatologie nach der zweiten Auflage der 'Glaubenslehre'." *Zeitschrift für Theologie und Kirche* 46 (1990): 97–123.
Herms, Eilert. *Menschsein im Werden. Studien zu Schleiermacher*. Tübingen: Mohr Siebeck, 2003.
Herms, Eilert. "Schleiermacher's Encyclopedia, Philosophical Ethics, Anthropology, and Dogmatics in German Protestant Theology." In *Schleiermacher, the Study of Religion, and the Future of Theology. A Transatlantic Dialogue*, edited by Brent W. Sockness and Wilhelm Gräb, 361–374. Theologische Bibliothek Töpelmann 148. Berlin/New York: Walter de Gruyter, 2010.
Hodgson, Peter C., ed. and trans. *Ferdinand Christian Baur on the Writing of Church History*. Oxford: Oxford University Press, 1968.
Hodgson, Peter. "Review of *Christian Faith: A New Translation and Critical Edition*, 2 vols, by Schleiermacher, Friedrich, trans. by Terrence N. Tice, Catherine L. Kelsey, and Edwina Lawler; edited by Catherine L. Kelsey and Terrence N. Tice. Louisville, KY: Westminster John Knox Press, 2016." *Modern Theology* 33 (2017): 692–697.
Honnefelder, Ludger. *Woher kommen wir? Ursprünge der Moderne im Denken des Mittelalters*. Darmstadt: Wissenschaftliche Buchgesellschaft, 2008.
Horst, Thomas. "Konfigurationen des unglücklichen Bewusstseins. Zur Theorie der Subjektivität bei Jacobi und Schleiermacher." In *Poetische Autonomie? Zur Wechselwirkung von Dichtung und Philosophie in der Epoche Goethes und Hölderlins*, edited by Helmut Bachmair and Thomas Rentsch, 185–206. Stuttgart: Klett-Cotta, 1987.
Huber, Eugen. *Die Entwicklung des Religionsbegriffs bei Schleiermacher*. Leipzig: T. Weicher, 1901, reprint Aalen 1972.
Hübenthal, Christoph. *Grundlegung der christlichen Sozialethik. Versuch eines freiheitsanalytisch-handlungsreflexiven Ansatzes*. Münster: Aschendorff, 2006.
Hübenthal, Christoph. "Ethische Begründung aus dem theologischen Grund des Säkularen. Eine katholische Sicht." In *Ökumenische Ethik*, edited by Thomas Weißer, 45–63. Fribourg/Würzburg: Academic Press Fribourg/Echter, 2018.
Jacob, Friedrich. *Geschichte und Welt in Schleiermachers Theologie*. Berlin: Evangelische Verlagsanstalt, 1967.
Jaspers, Karl. *The Origin and Goal of History*. London: Routledge, 1953.
Jørgensen, Theodor H. *Das religionsphilosophische Offenbarungsverständnis des späteren Schleiermacher*. Tübingen: Mohr Siebeck, 1977.
Jørgensen, Theodor. "Selbstbewusstsein und Gesamtbewusstsein im Reich der Sünde und der Erlösung bei Schleiermacher." In *Schleiermacher und Kierkegaard. Subjektivität und*

Wahrheit/Subjectivity and Truth, edited by Niels Jørgen Cappeløm et al., 519–535. Schleiermacher-Archiv 21. Berlin: Walter de Gruyter, 2006.
Junker, Maureen. *Das Urbild des Gottesbewußtseins. Zur Entwicklung der Religionstheorie und Christologie Schleiermachers von der ersten zur zweiten Auflage der Glaubenslehre.* Schleiermacher-Archiv 8. Berlin/New York: Walter de Gruyter, 1990.
Junker-Kenny, Maureen. "The Transcendental Turn. Shifts in Argumentation between the First and the Second Editions of the *Glaubenslehre*." *New Athenaeum/Neues Athenaeum* 3 (1992): 21–41.
Junker-Kenny, Maureen. "Die 'Anschauung des Universums … zur Vollkommenheit ausgebildet'. Zur Christologie der 'Reden'." In *200 Jahre 'Reden über die Religion. Akten des 1. Internationalen Kongresses der Schleiermacher-Gesellschaft Halle 1999*, edited by Ulrich Barth and Claus-Dieter Osthövener, 714–727. Schleiermacher-Archiv 19. Berlin/New York: Walter de Gruyter, 2000.
Junker-Kenny, Maureen. "Genetic Perfection, or Fulfillment of Creation in Christ?" In *Future Perfect? God, Medicine and Human Identity*, edited by Celia Deane-Drummond and Peter M. Scott, 155–167. London: T. & T. Clark, 2006.
Junker-Kenny, Maureen. "Drei Modelle von Religion: Glaubensgewissheit (Habermas), unmittelbares Selbstbewusstsein (Schleiermacher) und praktische Hoffnung (Kant und Ricœur)." In *Religiösen Zweifel denken?*, edited by Veronika Hoffmann, 67–86. Ostfildern: Grünewald, 2017.
Junker-Kenny, Maureen. "Transformations of doctrine as cases of mutual learning between religions and cultures: Schleiermacher's proposal for translating Christology in Modernity." In *Learning to be Human in Global Times*, edited by Brigitte Buchhammer, 25–37. Washington, D.C.: The Council for Research in Values and Philosophy, 2019.
Junker-Kenny, Maureen. "Schleiermacher und Kierkegaard in der Sicht 'nachmetaphysischen' Denkens'." In *Habermas und die Religion*, edited by Klaus Viertbauer and Franz Gruber, 59–77. Darmstadt: Wissenschaftliche Buchgesellschaft, ^{2}2019.
Junker-Kenny, Maureen. "Nicht magisch, sondern kommunikativ durch Ansprechen anderer Freiheit: Erlösung in der 2. Auflage von Schleiermachers Glaubenslehre." In *Dogmatische Christologie in der Moderne. Problemkonstellationen gegenwärtiger Forschung*, edited by Christian Danz and Georg Essen, 69–88. Regensburg: Pustet, 2019.
Junker-Kenny, Maureen. "What scope for ethics in the public sphere? Principled autonomy and the antinomy of practical reason." *Studies in Christian Ethics* 32 (2019): 485–498.
Junker-Kenny, Maureen. *Approaches to Theological Ethics. Sources, Traditions, Visions.* London/New York: T. & T. Clark, 2019.
Junker-Kenny, Maureen. "Person and Work of Christ." In *Oxford Handbook of Friedrich Schleiermacher*, edited by Andrew Dole, Shelli Poe and Kevin Vander Schel. Oxford: Oxford University Press, forthcoming.
Käfer, Anne, *Inkarnation und Schöpfung. Schöpfungstheologische Voraussetzungen und Implikationen der Christologie bei Luther, Schleiermacher und Karl Barth*. Theologische Bibliothek Töpelmann 151. Berlin/Boston: Walter de Gruyter, 2010.
Käfer, Anne. "Review of Pedersen, Daniel J., *The Eternal Covenant. Schleiermacher on God and Natural Science*. Theologische Bibliothek Töpelmann 181. Berlin/Boston: de Gruyter, 2017." *Theologische Revue* 144 (2019): 491–492.
Kant, Immanuel. *Critique of Pure Reason*, trans. Norman Kemp Smith. New York: St. Martin's Press/Toronto: MacMillan, 1965.

Kant, Immanuel. *Religion within the Boundaries of Mere Reason, and Other* Writings, edited by Allen Wood and George di Giovanni, intro. Robert M. Adams. Cambridge: Cambridge University Press, 2010.
Kantzenbach, Friedrich Wilhelm. *Programme der Theologie, Denker, Schulen, Wirkungen. Von Schleiermacher bis Moltmann*. München: Claudius, 1978.
Keller, Pierre. "Two conceptions of compatibilism in the Critical Elucidation." In *Kant's Critique of Practical Reason. A Critical Guide*, edited by Andrew Reath and Jens Timmermann, 119–144. Cambridge: Cambridge University Press, 2010.
Kelsey, Catherine L. *Thinking about Christ with Schleiermacher*. Louisville/London: Westminster John Knox Press, 2003.
Kierkegaard, Søren. *The Sickness unto Death*, trans. with an introduction and notes by Alistair Hannay. London: Penguin, 1989.
Kobusch, Theo, *Christliche Philosophie. Die Entdeckung der Subjektivität*. Darmstadt: Wissenschaftliche Buchgesellschaft, 2006.
Küng, Hans. "Friedrich Schleiermacher: Theology at the Dawn of Modernity." In *Great Christian Thinkers*, 155–184. New York: Continuum, 1994.
Lange, Dietz. *Historischer Jesus oder mythischer Christus. Untersuchungen zu dem Gegensatz zwischen F. Schleiermacher und D. F. Strauss*. Gütersloh: Gütersloher Verlagshaus, 1975.
Lange, Dietz. "Die Kontroverse Hegels und Schleiermachers um das Verständnis der Religion." *Hegel-Studien* 18 (1983): 201–224.
Lange, Dietz, ed. *Friedrich Schleiermacher 1768–1834. Theologe – Philosoph – Pädagoge*. Göttingen: Vandenhoeck & Ruprecht, 1985.
Lange, Dietz. "Das fromme Selbstbewusstsein als Subjekt teleologischer Religion bei Schleiermacher." In *Schleiermacher und die wissenschaftliche Kultur des Christentums*, edited by Günter Meckenstock, with Joachim Ringleben, 187–205. Theologische Bibliothek Töpelmann 51. Berlin/New York: Walter de Gruyter, 1991, reprint 2019.
Lerch, Magnus. *All-Einheit und Freiheit. Subjektphilosophische Klärungsversuche in der Monismus-Debatte zwischen Klaus Müller und Magnus Striet*. Würzburg: Echter, 2009.
Lerch, Magnus. *Selbstmitteilung Gottes. Herausforderungen einer freiheitstheoretischen Offenbarungstheologie*. ratio fidei 56. Regensburg: Pustet, 2015.
Lerch, Magnus. "Hypostatische Union als Freiheitsgeschehen. Zur gegenwärtigen Diskussion um eine transzendentalphilosophische Reformulierung der Christologie." In *Dogmatische Christologie in der Moderne. Problemkonstellationen gegenwärtiger Forschung*, edited by Christian Danz and Georg Essen, 239–261. Regensburg: Pustet, 2019.
Liebing, Heinz. "Ferdinand Christian Baurs Kritik an Schleiermachers Glaubenslehre." *Zeitschrift für Theologie und Kirche* 54 (1957): 225–243.
Livingston, James C. *Modern Christian Thought. The Enlightenment and the Nineteenth Century*. Minneapolis: Fortress Press, ²2006.
Mariña, Jacqueline, ed. *The Cambridge Companion to Friedrich Schleiermacher*. Cambridge: Cambridge University Press, 2005.
Mariña, Jacqueline. "Christology and Anthropology in Friedrich Schleiermacher." In *The Cambridge Companion to Friedrich Schleiermacher*, edited by J. Mariña, 151–170. Cambridge: Cambridge University Press, 2005.
McGrath, Alister. *The Making of Modern German Christology. From the Enlightenment to Pannenberg*. Oxford: Oxford University Press, 1986.
McGrath, Alister. *Christian Theology. An Introduction*. Oxford: Blackwell, 1994.

McGrath, Alister, ed. *The Christian Theology Reader*. Oxford: Blackwell, ³2007.
Meckenstock, Günter, with Joachim Ringleben, eds. *Schleiermacher und die wissenschaftliche Kultur des Christentums*. Theologische Bibliothek Töpelmann 51. Berlin/New York: Walter de Gruyter, 1991, reprint 2019.
Menke, Karl-Heinz. *Jesus ist Gott der Sohn. Denkformen und Brennpunkte der Christologie*. Regensburg: Pustet, 2008.
Mieth, Dietmar. "Bioethics and biolaw in the European Union: Bridging or fudging different traditions of moral and legal argumentation?" In *Ethics for Graduate Researchers. A Cross-Disciplinary Approach*, edited by Cathriona Russell, Linda Hogan and Maureen Junker-Kenny, 59–72. Oxford: Elsevier, 2013.
Mittelstrass, Jürgen. "Leibniz über Forschung zwischen Theorie und Praxis." In *Leibniz heute lesen. Wissenschaft, Geschichte, Religion*, edited by Herta Nagl-Docekal, 55–68. Berlin/Boston: Walter de Gruyter, 2018.
Moxter, Michael. *Güterbegriff und Handlungstheorie. Eine Studie zur Ethik Friedrich Schleiermachers*. Kampen: Kok Pharos, 1992.
Moxter, Michael. "Neuzeitliche Umformungen der Theologie. Philosophische Aspekte in der neueren Schleiermacherliteratur." *Philosophische Rundschau* 41 (1994): 133–158.
Moxter, Michael. "Gefühl und Ausdruck. Nicht nur ein Problem der Schleiermacherinterpretation." In *Theologie der Gefühle.*, edited by Roderich Barth and Christopher Zarnow, 111–126. Berlin/Boston: Walter de Gruyter, 2014.
Müller, Klaus and Magnus Striet, eds. *Dogma und Denkform. Strittiges in der Grundlegung von Offenbarungsbegriff und Gottesgedanke*. Regensburg: Pustet, 2005.
Nagl-Docekal, Herta. *Innere Freiheit. Grenzen der nachmetaphysischen Moralkonzeptionen*. Deutsche Zeitschrift für Philosophie Sonderband 36. Berlin/Boston: Walter de Gruyter, 2014.
Nagl-Docekal, Herta, ed. *Leibniz heute lesen. Wissenschaft, Geschichte, Religion*. Berlin/Boston: Walter de Gruyter, 2018.
Nagl-Docekal, Herta. "Leibniz heute lesen. Eine Einführung." In *Leibniz heute lesen. Wissenschaft, Geschichte, Religion*, edited by H. Nagl-Docekal, 1–21. Berlin/Boston: Walter de Gruyter, 2018.
Niebuhr, Richard R. *Schleiermacher on Christ and Religion*. New York: Ch. Scribner's Sons, 1964.
Niebuhr, Richard R. "Christ, nature and consciousness: reflections on Schleiermacher in the light of Barth's early criticisms." In *Barth and Schleiermacher: Beyond the Impasse?*. edited by James O. Duke and Robert F. Streetman, 23–42. Minneapolis: Fortress, 1988.
Offermann, Doris. *Schleiermachers Einleitung in die Glaubenslehre. Eine Untersuchung der 'Lehnsätze'*. Berlin: Walter de Gruyter, 1969.
Ohst, Martin. "Review of Dole, Andrew, *Schleiermacher on Religion and the Natural Order*. Oxford: Oxford University Press, 2010." *Church History and Religious Culture* 92 (2012): 456–459.
Ohst, Martin, ed. *Schleiermacher-Handbuch*. Tübingen: Mohr Siebeck, 2017.
Martin Ohst. "Rezeption und Kritik. Bei Lebzeiten." In *Schleiermacher-Handbuch*, edited by M. Ohst, 428–442. Tübingen: Mohr Siebeck, 2017.
Osthövener, Claus-Dieter. *Erlösung. Transformationen einer Idee im 19. Jahrhundert*. Tübingen: Mohr Siebeck, 2004.

Osthövener, Claus-Dieter. "Der christliche Glaube – Dogmatik I: Einleitung in die 'Glaubenslehre'" and "Dogmatik II: Materiale Entfaltung der 'Glaubenslehre'." In *Schleiermacher Handbuch*, edited by Martin Ohst, 349–361 and 362–383. Tübingen: Mohr Siebeck, 2017.
Pannenberg, Wolfhart. "The appropriation of the philosophical concept of God as a dogmatic problem of early Christian theology." In *Basic Questions in Theology*, vol. II, 119–184. London: SCM Press, 1971.
Pannenberg, Wolfhart. *Anthropology in Theological Perspective*, trans. M. J. O'Connell. Philadelphia: Westminster, 1985.
Pannenberg, Wolfhart. "Schleiermachers Schwierigkeiten mit dem Schöpfungsgedanken." München: Verlag der Bayerischen Akademie der Wissenschaften, Sitzungsberichte 1996, Heft 3.
Pedersen, Daniel J. *The Eternal Covenant. Schleiermacher on God and Natural Science*. Theologische Bibliothek Töpelmann 181. Berlin/Boston: de Gruyter, 2017.
Pröpper, Thomas. *Der Jesus der Philosophen und der Jesus des Glaubens. Ein theologisches Gespräch mit Jaspers – Bloch – Kolakowski – Gardavsky – Machovec – Fromm – Ben-Chorin*. Mainz: Grünewald, 1976.
Pröpper, Thomas. "Schleiermachers Bestimmung des Christentums und der Erlösung. Zur Problematik der transzendental-anthropologischen Hermeneutik des Glaubens." *Theologische Quartalschrift* 168 (1988): 193–214. Reprint in *Evangelium und freie Vernunft*, 129–152. Freiburg: Herder, 2001.
Pröpper, Thomas. *Erlösungsglaube und Freiheitsgeschichte. Eine Skizze zur Soteriologie*. Munich: Kösel, ³1991.
Pröpper, Thomas. "Art. Allmacht. In *Evangelium und freie Vernunft*, 288–293. Freiburg: Herder, 2001.
Pröpper, Thomas. "Fragende und Gefragte zugleich. Notizen zur Theodizee." In *Evangelium und freie Vernunft*, 266–275. Freiburg: Herder, 2001.
Pröpper, Thomas. *Theologische Anthropologie*, 2 vols. Freiburg: Herder, 2011.
Pröpper, Thomas, and Georg Essen. "Aneignungsprobleme der christologischen Überlieferung. Hermeneutische Vorüberlegungen." In *Gottes ewiger Sohn. Die Präexistenz Christi*, edited by Rudolf Laufen, 163–178. Paderborn: Schöningh, 1997.
Rawls, John. *Lectures on the History of Moral Philosophy*, edited by Barbara Herman. Cambridge, MA: Harvard University Press, 2000.
Reath, Andrew and Jens Timmermann, eds. *Kant's Critique of Practical Reason. A Critical Guide*. Cambridge: Cambridge University Press, 2010.
Richter, Cornelia. "Feeling and sense, ethics and culture." In *Schleiermacher und Kierkegaard. Subjektivität und Wahrheit/Subjectivity and Truth*, edited by Niels Jørgen Cappeløm et al., 159–177. Berlin/New York: Walter de Gruyter, 2006.
Ricken, Friedo, SJ. "Postmetaphysical Reason and Religion." In *An Awareness of What is Missing. Faith and Reason in a Postsecular Age*, trans. C. Cronin, edited by Jürgen Habermas et al., 51–58. Cambridge: Polity Press, 2010.
Ricoeur, Paul. *The Symbolism of Evil*, trans. Emerson Buchanan. Boston: Beacon Press, 1967.
Ricoeur, Paul. *Oneself as Another*, trans. Kathleen Blamey. Chicago: University of Chicago Press, 1992.
Ricoeur, Paul. *Reflections on the Just*, trans. David Pellauer. Chicago: University of Chicago Press, 2007.

Riemer, Matthias. *Bildung und Christentum. Der Bildungsgedanke Schleiermachers.* Göttingen: Vandenhoeck & Ruprecht, 1989.
Röhr, Johann Friedrich. "Rezension." *Kritische Prediger-Bibliothek* 4 (1823): 371–394. 555–579, and in KGA 1/7.3, 505–533. Berlin/New York: Walter de Gruyter, 1984.
Rössler, Martin. *Schleiermachers Programm der Philosophischen Theologie.* Schleiermacher-Archiv 14. Berlin/New York: Walter de Gruyter, 1994, reprint 2012.
Schaefer, Susanne. *Gottes Sein zur Welt. Schleiermachers Subjektanalyse in ihrer Prinzipienfunktion für Glaubenslehre und Dialektik.* ratio fidei 12. Regensburg: Pustet, 2002.
Scheel, Hans. *Die Theorie von Christus als dem zweiten Adam bei Schleiermacher.* Naumburg: G. Pätz'sche Buchdruckerei Lippert, 1913.
Scheliha, Arnulf von, and Jörg Dierken, eds. *Der Mensch und seine Seele. Bildung – Frömmigkeit – Ästhetik. Akten des Internationalen Kongresses der Schleiermacher-Gesellschaft in Münster, September 2015.* Schleiermacher-Archiv 26. Berlin/Boston: Walter de Gruyter, 2017.
Schmidt, Sarah. "Analogie versus Wechselwirkung – Zur 'Symphilosophie' zwischen Schleiermacher und Steffens." In *Schleiermacher in Halle 1804–1807*, edited by Andreas Arndt, 91–114. Berlin/Boston: Walter de Gruyter, 2013.
Sabine Schmidtke. "'Lebendige Empfänglichkeit' als anthropologische Grundbedingung der Frömmigkeit." In *Reformation und Moderne. Pluralität – Subjektivität – Kritik. Akten des Internationalen Kongresses der Schleiermacher-Gesellschaft in Halle (Saale), März 2017*, edited by Jörg Dierken, Arnulf von Scheliha and Sarah Schmidt, 343–360. Schleiermacher-Archiv 27. Berlin/ Boston: Walter de Gruyter, 2018.
Schreiter, Robert. *Constructing Local Theologies.* Maryknoll: Orbis, 1985.
Schröder, Markus. *Die kritische Identität des neuzeitlichen Christentums. Schleiermachers Wesensbestimmung der christlichen Religion.* Tübingen: Mohr Siebeck, 1996.
Schröder, Markus. "Wiedergewonnene Naivität. Protestantismus und Bildung nach Adolf von Harnack. " In *Das protestantische Prinzip. Historische und systematische Studien zum Protestantismusbegriff*, edited by Arnulf von Scheliha and Markus Schröder, 119–135. Stuttgart: Kohlhammer, 1998.
Schrofner, Erich. *Theologie als positive Wissenschaft. Prinzipien und Methoden der Dogmatik bei Schleiermacher.* Frankfurt: P. Lang, 1980.
Schütte, Hans-Walter. "Die Ausscheidung der Lehre vom Zorn Gottes in der Theologie Schleiermachers und Ritschls." *Neue Zeitschrift für Systematische Theologie und Religionsphilosophie* 10 (1968): 387–397.
Schulz, Walter. *Der Gott der neuzeitlichen Metaphysik.* Pfullingen: Neske, ^{6}1978.
Schulze, Martin. *Das Wesen und die Bedeutung der besonderen Offenbarung in Schleiermachers Glaubenslehre.* Niesky: P. Jenke, 1893.
Sherman, Robert J. *The Shift to Modernity. Christ and the Doctrine of Creation in the Theologies of Schleiermacher and Barth.* New York/London: T & T Clark, 2005.
Sierscyn, Armin. *Das Sünde- und Schuldproblem im dogmatischen Denken Schleiermachers.* Diss. theol. Erlangen-Nürnberg 1973.
Slenczka, Reinhard. *Geschichtlichkeit und Personsein Jesu Christi. Studien zur christologischen Problematik der historischen Jesusfrage.* Göttingen: Vandenhoeck & Ruprecht, 1967.

Sockness, Brent W. and Wilhelm Gräb, eds. *Schleiermacher, the Study of Religion, and the Future of Theology. A Transatlantic Dialogue.* Theologische Bibliothek Töpelmann 148. Berlin/New York: Walter de Gruyter, 2010.
Sorrentino, Sergio, "History and temporality in the debate between F. Ch. Baur and Schleiermacher." In *Schleiermacher's Philosophy and the Philosophical Tradition*, edited by S. Sorrentino, 111–132. Schleiermacher: Studies and Translations Vol. 11. Lewiston, N.Y.: Edwin Mellen Press, 1992.
Sorrentino, Sergio. "Feeling as a Key Notion in a Transcendental Conception of Religion." In *Schleiermacher, the Study of Religion, and the Future of Theology. A Transatlantic Dialogue*, edited by Brent W. Sockness and Wilhelm Gräb, 97–108. Theologische Bibliothek Töpelmann 148. Berlin/New York: Walter de Gruyter, 2010.
Stekeler-Weithofer, Pirmin. "Das monadologische Strukturmodell der Welt. Leibniz zwischen Descartes und Kant." In *Leibniz heute lesen. Wissenschaft, Geschichte, Religion*, edited by Herta Nagl-Docekal, 25–54. Berlin/Boston: Walter de Gruyter, 2018.
Stephan, Horst. *Die Lehre Schleiermachers von der Erlösung.* Tübingen: J.C.B. Mohr, 1901.
Steudel, Johann Christian Friedrich. "Die Frage über die Ausführbarkeit einer Annäherung zwischen der rationalistischen und supranaturalistischen Ansicht, mit besonderer Rücksicht auf den Standpunkt der Schleiermacher'schen Glaubenslehre." *Tübinger Zeitschrift für Theologie* 1 (1828), I. Stück, 74–199; 1 (1828), II. Stück, 74–120.
Strickland, Lloyd. *Leibniz's Monadology. A New Translation and Guide.* Edinburgh: Edinburgh University Press, 2014.
Striet, Magnus. *Das Ich im Sturz der Realität. Philosophisch-theologische Studien zu einer Theorie des Subjekts in Auseinandersetzung mit der Spätphilosophie Nietzsches.* ratio fidei 1. Regensburg: Pustet, 1998.
Striet, Magnus. *Offenbares Geheimnis. Zur Kritik der negativen Theologie.* ratio fidei 14. Regensburg: Pustet, 2003.
Sykes, Stephen. *Friedrich Schleiermacher.* London: Lutterworth Press, 1971.
Sykes, Stephen. "Schleiermacher and Barth on the essence of Christianity – an instructive disagreement." In *Barth and Schleiermacher: Beyond the Impasse?*, edited by James O. Duke and Robert F. Streetman, 88–107. Philadelphia: Fortress Press, 1982.
Sykes, Stephen. *The Identity of Christianity. Theologians and the Essence of Christianity from Schleiermacher to Barth.* Philadelphia: Fortress, 1984.
Theunissen, Michael. "Philosophischer Monismus und christliche Theologie." *Zeitschrift für Theologie und Kirche* 102 (2005): 397–408.
Thiel, John. *Imagination and Authority: Theological Authorship in the Modern Tradition.* Minneapolis: Fortress Press, 1991.
Thiel, John. *God and World in Schleiermacher's 'Dialektik' and 'Glaubenslehre'.* Frankfurt/Bern: Peter Lang, 1981.
Thiel, John. "Barth's early interpretation of Schleiermacher." In *Barth and Schleiermacher: Beyond the Impasse?*, edited by James O. Duke and Robert F. Streetman, 11–22. Philadelphia: Fortress, 1982.
Thiemann, Ronald F. *Revelation and Theology. The Gospel as Narrative Promise.* Notre Dame, IN: University of Notre Dame Press, 1985.
Thiemann, Ronald F. "On speaking of God – the divisive issue for Schleiermacher and Barth: A Response to Frei and Sykes." In *Barth and Schleiermacher: Beyond the*

Impasse?, edited by James O. Duke and Robert F. Streetman, 108–113. Philadelphia: Fortress Press, 1982.

Tice, Terrence N. "Schleiermacher's Conception of Religion: 1799 to 1831." *Archivio di Filosofia* 52 (1984): 333–356.

Trillhaas, Wolfgang. "Der Mittelpunkt der Glaubenslehre Schleiermachers." *Neue Zeitschrift für Systematische Theologie und Religionsphilosophie* 10 (1968): 289–309.

Vance, Robert Lee. *Sin and Self-Consciousness in the Thought of Friedrich Schleiermacher.* Lewiston, N.Y.: Edwin Mellen Press, 1994.

Vander Schel, Kevin. *Embedded Grace. Christ, History, and the Reign of God in Schleiermacher's Dogmatics.* Minneapolis: Fortress, 2013.

Van Driel, Edward. *Incarnation Anyway: Arguments for Supralapsarian Christology.* Oxford: Oxford University Press, 2008.

Vial, Theodore. *Schleiermacher. A Guide for the Perplexed.* London/New York: Bloomsbury T. & T. Clark, 2013.

Viertbauer, Klaus. *Gott am Grund des Bewusstseins? Skizzen zu einer präreflexiven Interpretation von Kierkegaards Selbst.* ratio fidei 61. Regensburg: Pustet, 2017.

Voigt, Friedemann. "Die Schleiermacher-Rezeption 1834–1889" and "Die Schleiermacher-Rezeption 1890–1923." In *Schleiermacher-Handbuch*, edited by Martin Ohst, 442–455 and 455–465. Tübingen: Mohr Siebeck, 2017.

Weeber, Martin. "Schleiermachers doppelte Eschatologie." In *Schleiermacher und Kierkegaard. Subjektivität und Wahrheit,* edited by Niels Jørgen Cappelørn et al., 577–598. Berlin/New York: Walter de Gruyter, 2006.

Wehrung, Georg. *Die Dialektik Schleiermachers.* Tübingen: J.C.B. Mohr, 1920.

Wehrung, Georg. *Die philosophisch-theologische Methode Schleiermachers. Eine Einführung in die Kurze Darstellung und in die Glaubenslehre.* Göttingen: Vandenhoeck & Ruprecht, 1911.

Weissenborn, Georg. *Darstellung und Kritik der Schleiermacherschen Dogmatik.* Leipzig: T. O. Weigel, 1849.

Wendel, Saskia. *Affektiv und inkarniert. Ansätze Deutscher Mystik als subjekttheoretische Herausforderung.* ratio fidei 15. Regensburg: Pustet, 2002.

Wendel, Saskia. "Nicht naturalisierbar: Kants Freiheitsbegriff." In *Kant und die Theologie*, edited by G. Essen and M. Striet, 13–45. Darmstadt: Wissenschaftliche Buchgesellschaft, 2005.

Wendel, Saskia. "Die Wurzel der Religionen."*Freiburger Zeitschrift für Philosophie und Theologie* 53 (2006): 21–38.

Wendel, Saskia. "Die Renaissance des Religiösen und der Glaube an Gott." In *Gott im Kommen. Salzburger Hochschulwochen 2006*, edited by Gregor Maria Hoff , 201–238. Graz: Tyrolia, 2006.

Wendel, Saskia. "Die religiöse Selbst- und Weltdeutung des bewussten Daseins und ihre Bedeutung für eine 'moderne Religion'. Was der 'Postmetaphysiker' Habermas über Religion nicht zu denken wagt." In *Moderne Religion?Theologische und religionsphilosophische Reaktionen auf Jürgen Habermas*, edited by Thomas Schmidt and Knut Wenzel, 225–265. Freiburg: Herder, 2009.

Wenz, Gunther. *Geschichte der Versöhnungslehre in der evangelischen Theologie der Neuzeit.* Munich: Kaiser, 1984.

Wenz, Gunther. "Kirchenvater des 21. Jahrhunderts? Schleiermacherliteratur seit 2010." *Theologische Revue* 111 (2015): 351–364.

Wenz, Gunther. "Sünde und Schuldbewusstsein. Zur Hamartiologie in Schleiermachers Glaubenslehre." *Kerygma und Dogma* 63 (2017): 309–337.

Williams, Robert. *Schleiermacher the Theologian. The Construction of the Doctrine of God.* Philadelphia: Fortress, 1978.

Wolfes, Matthias."'Ein Gegensatz zwischen Vernunft und Offenbarung findet nicht statt'. Friedrich Schleiermachers Vorlesung über Dogmatische Theologie aus dem Sommersemester 1811." In *200 Jahre "Reden über die Religion"*, edited by Ulrich Barth and Claus-Dieter Osthövener, 629–667. Berlin? Walter de Gruyter, 2000.

Wolfes, Matthias. "F. Schleiermacher: Einleitung zur Vorlesung über Dogmatische Theologie (Sommersemester 1811). Nachschrift August Detlev Christian Twesten." *Zeitschrift für Kirchengeschichte* 109 (1998): 80–99.

Wyman, Walter E. "Sin and redemption." In *The Cambridge Companion to Friedrich Schleiermacher*, edited by Jacqueline Mariña, 129–149. Cambridge: Cambridge University Press, 2005.

Wyman, Walter E. "The cognitive status of religious consciousness. The nature and status of dogmatic propositions in Schleiermacher's *Glaubenslehre*." In *Schleiermacher, the Study of Religion, and the Future of Theology. A Transatlantic Dialogue*, edited by Brent W. Sockness and Wilhelm Gräb, 189–202. Berlin/New York: Walter de Gruyter, 2010.

Wyman, Walter E. "How critical is Schleiermacher's revisionist dogmatics? Eschatology as a test case." In *Reformation und Moderne. Pluralität – Subjektivität – Kritik*, edited by Jörg Dierken, Arnulf von Scheliha and Sarah Schmidt, 627–644. Berlin: Walter de Gruyter, 2018.

Person Index

Adams, Robert M. 179
Albrecht, Christian XV, 12
Anselm of Canterbury 105
Ansorge, Dirk 251, 252
Aquinas, Thomas 251, 252
Aristotle (*also* Aristotelian) 224, 248, 251
Arndt, Andreas 38
Augustine of Hippo 105, 251

Bachmair, Helmut 56
Balthasar, Hans Urs von 27
Barth, Karl 12, 22, 51, 76, 77, 98, 99, 110, 123, 125, 134, 135, 185, 196, 206, 212, 214, 238, 239
Barth, Roderich 82
Barth, Ulrich XVII, 1, 15, 58, 59
Baur, Ferdinand Christian 69, 93, 98, 99, 102, 107, 109–126, 128–130, 132, 135, 136, 138, 169, 171, 172, 178, 180–182, 185, 194, 212, 242, 243
Beckmann, Klaus-Martin 88
Ben-Chorin, Schalom 125
Berner, Christian 34, 35
Birkner, Hans-Joachim 12
Bongardt, Michael 61, 62
Bretschneider, Karl Gottlieb 21, 69, 105, 106, 154, 155, 165, 201, 232, 244
Bromiley, Geoffrey W. 99
Brunner, Emil 185
Buchanan, Emerson 234
Bultmann, Rudolf K. (Bultmann School) 182

Calvin, Johannes 196, 206
Cappeløm, Niels Jørgen 197
Clement of Alexandria (Titus Flavius Clemens) 105
Cramer, Konrad 36, 37, 41, 48, 49, 56–59, 66
Cronin, Ciaran 234, 235

Dahlke, Benjamin 174, 198
Danz, Christian 149, 176

Deane-Drummond, Celia 184
Descartes, René 149, 210, 226
Dews, Peter 62
Dierken, Jörg 60
Dierksmeier, Claus 65, 66, 127
di Giovanni, George 179
Dilthey, Wilhelm 54, 55, 61, 123, 184
Dole, Andrew 145, 208, 229, 240, 245
Dorner, Isaak August 201, 202, 212
Duke, James O. XVII, 7, 37, 48, 49, 51, 56, 76, 102
Duns Scotus, John 142, 237, 247–252, 254
Durkheim, Émile 246

Ebeling, Gerhard 27, 42, 51, 52, 246
Essen, Georg 61, 64, 65, 125, 149, 176, 240, 241

Feuerbach, Ludwig 1, 50, 56, 125–128, 131, 182, 184, 238
Fichte, Johann Gottlieb (*also* Fichtean) 40, 41, 61, 63, 64, 145, 149, 177, 209, 217, 227, 244
Fiorenza, Francis Schüssler XVII, 7, 37, 48, 49, 56, 102, 254
Fischer, Hermann 7, 11, 12, 102, 146, 163–165, 172, 243
Flöel, Ernst 195
Flückiger, Felix 12
Frank, Manfred 63
Freud, Sigmund 246
Freyne, Seán 75, 182

Gerdes, Hayo XVII, 1, 105
Ghent, Henry of 249
Gockel, Matthias 22, 146, 147, 217, 219, 235, 252
Goethe, Johann Wolfgang von 56
Gräb, Wilhelm XV, 13, 103, 197, 198
Grove, Peter 39, 42, 57, 59
Günther, Ernst 169
Gutekunst, Katharina 41, 42, 57–59, 145, 242

Habermas, Jürgen   62, 234, 235, 246, 247
Haight, Roger   1, 3, 239, 240, 252, 253
Hannay, Alistair   165
Harvey, Van A.   56
Heegewaldt, Johann David   136
Hegel, Georg Wilhelm Friedrich (*also* Hegelian)   18, 102, 105, 110, 112, 117–119, 121, 123–126, 177, 195, 206, 217, 243
Helmer, Christine   73–75, 129
Henrich, Dieter   38, 61–63
Herms, Eilert   13, 14, 145, 204
Hodgson, Peter C.   25, 27, 44, 117
Hoff, Gregor Maria   68
Hogan, Linda   247
Hölderlin, Friedrich   56, 63
Honnefelder, Ludger   237, 249, 250
Horst, Thomas   55–57
Hübenthal, Christoph   251
Huber, Eugen   66

Jacob, Friedrich   189, 196
Jacobi, Friedrich H.   56
Jaspers, Karl   76, 125
Jørgensen, Theodor H.   100, 202, 205
Jüngel, Eberhard   27
Junker-Kenny, Maureen   247
Junker, Maureen   2
Justin Martyr   224

Käfer, Anne   147
Kant, Immanuel (*also* Kantian)   1, 2, 34, 52, 54, 55, 59, 63, 66, 68, 103, 119, 126, 127, 145, 147, 148, 151, 155, 156, 164, 177, 179, 214, 222, 226, 227, 234, 235, 237, 242, 246, 250, 251
Kantzenbach, Friedrich Wilhelm   91, 104, 105, 155, 171
Kasper, Walter   27, 176
Kelsey, Catherine L.   XVII, 1, 25–27, 60
Kierkegaard, Søren A.   12, 63, 105, 163, 165, 197, 242, 247
Kobusch, Theo   76
Kohlberg, Lawrence   246
Krings, Hermann   61

Lange, Dietz   36, 112, 113, 115, 163, 164, 184, 200, 201, 206

Laufen, Rudolf   241
Lawler, Edwina   XVII, 1
Leibniz, Gottfried Wilhelm   145, 147–153, 209–211, 225–228, 234
Lerch, Magnus   61, 63, 64, 75, 125, 138, 176, 196, 197
Lessing, Gotthold Ephraim   105, 111, 177
Liebing, Heinz   111–116
Lücke, Friedrich   XVII, 7, 25
Luther, Martin (*also* Lutheran)   105, 154

Mackintosh, H. R.   XVII, 1
Mariña, Jacqueline   74, 88, 130, 145, 174, 176, 185, 208, 242, 254
McGrath, Alister   1, 2, 110, 125, 126, 128–130, 238
Menke, Karl-Heinz   119, 174–177
Michel, Marc   196
Mieth, Dietmar   246, 247
Moltmann, Jürgen   91
Moxter, Michael   54, 82, 145
Müller, Klaus   61

Nagl-Docekal, Herta   149, 151, 152, 155, 226
Niebuhr, Richard R.   26, 27, 40, 42, 43, 162, 163, 177, 196, 206
Nitsche, Bernhard   64
Novalis (G. P. F. von Hardenberg)   63

Ockham, William of   237, 248
Odebrecht, Rudolf   221, 226
Offermann, Doris   94
Ohst, Martin   12, 102, 208
Osthövener, Claus-Dieter   12, 15, 75, 77
Otto, Rudolf   66

Pannenberg, Wolfhart   2, 67, 176, 190, 213, 215–217, 219, 221–224, 226–228, 243
Pedersen, Daniel J.   147, 208, 244
Peiter, Horst   XVII, 1
Pellauer, David   206
Plato (*also* Platonic)   177, 224, 248, 249
Pröpper, Thomas   27, 28, 37, 46, 48, 49, 51–53, 61, 63–65, 67–69, 72, 118, 123, 125, 130, 131, 165, 176, 182, 184, 199, 203, 208, 210, 215, 217, 228, 233, 236, 240, 241, 243, 249, 250, 252, 253

272 — Person Index

Rahner, Karl 27, 176
Rawls, John 73
Redeker, Martin 38, 54, 210
Reinhard, Franz V. 175
Rémond, Nicolas 151
Rentsch, Thomas 56
Richter, Cornelia 197
Ricken, Friedo S.J. 234
Ricoeur, Paul 206, 234, 250
Riemer, Matthias 82
Ritschl, Albrecht 205
Ritschl, Dietrich 99
Röhr, Johann Friedrich 30, 104–107, 222
Rössler, Martin 14, 84, 93, 94, 218
Russell, Cathriona 247

Sachs, Walter 71
Sartre, Jean-Paul 63, 67
Schaefer, Susanne 58, 130, 131, 141, 145, 150, 153, 176, 208, 211, 213, 214, 219–223, 225, 227, 228, 230, 231, 233, 235, 236, 239, 244–246, 254
Schäfer, Rolf XVII, 1, 44, 64
Scheel, Hans 186, 188
Scheliha, Arnulf von 60
Schelling, Friedrich Wilhelm Joseph 117, 145, 217
Schmidtke, Sabine 60
Schmidt, Sarah 38, 60
Schreiter, Robert 28
Schröder, Markus 73, 75, 99
Schrofner, Erich 162
Schulze, Martin 194, 195
Schütte, Hans-Walter 205
Scott, Peter M. 184
Sherman, Robert J. 212, 214–216, 218, 219, 224, 225, 230, 233–235, 245
Sierscyn, Armin 170, 171
Slenczka, Reinhard 199, 200
Smith, Norman Kemp 214
Sockness, Brent W. 13, 103
Sorrentino, Sergio 103, 111, 114, 126
Spiegel, Yorick 123
Spinoza, Baruch de (also Spinozist/Spinozism) 147, 149, 210, 216, 217, 225, 226, 228, 230, 231, 244
Steffens, Henrich 38

Stekeler-Weithofer, Pirmin 226
Stephan, Horst 54, 184, 189, 190, 195, 200, 201
Steudel, Johann Christian Friedrich 30, 69, 107–109
Stewart, J. S. XVII, 1
Strauß, David Friedrich 71, 110, 112, 123, 126, 129, 178, 182, 184
Streetman, Robert F. 51, 76, 247
Strickland, Lloyd 150, 152
Striet, Magnus 61, 63, 64, 237, 246, 248, 249
Suárez, Francisco 237
Sykes, Stephen 51, 76, 77, 93

Tatian 224
Theophilus of Antioch 224
Theunissen, Michael 253
Thiel, John 12, 13, 56, 146, 147
Thiemann, Ronald F. 51
Tice, Terrence N. XVII, 1, 9, 11, 25–27, 43, 94, 95
Traulsen, Hans-Friedrich 102, 109
Trillhaas, Wolfgang 118, 123
Troeltsch, Ernst 130
Twesten, August Detlev Christian 15, 17, 18, 78

Vander Schel, Kevin 35, 36, 203
Van Driel, Edward 212
Vial, Theodore 22, 178
Viertbauer, Klaus 63
Voigt, Friedemann 102

Weeber, Martin 12
Wehrung, Georg 22, 31, 40, 50
Weissenborn, Georg 135, 136
Weißer, Thomas 251
Wendel, Saskia 61, 63, 64, 68, 127, 254
Wenz, Gunther 166, 200, 216
Wolfes, Matthias 15, 17–19, 23, 24, 34, 78–81
Wolff, Christian (Wolffian) 104, 145, 237
Wood, Allen 179
Wyman, Walter E. 242

Zarnow, Christopher 82
Zeller, E. 118

Subject Index

abstraction   90, 146
aesthetic   78, 82, 83
agency   7, 23, 30, 34, 44, 61, 68, 76, 105, 108, 124, 127, 145–147, 149, 155–157, 162, 164, 166, 174, 182, 205, 207, 209, 211, 221, 227, 233, 234, 239, 243, 252, 254
analysis of self-consciousness   2, 29, 34, 41, 203, 241, 242
anthropological turn   1, 5, 29, 102, 110, 112, 125, 131, 156, 192, 204, 205, 208, 231, 237, 241
anthropology
– theological ~   3, 9, 28, 67, 134–136, 141, 143, 144, 146, 152, 170, 172, 246
anthropomorphism   146, 202, 227
antinomy of practical reason   31, 147, 155
apokatastasis panton   206, 231, 235
apriori   79, 93, 96–99, 109, 115, 116, 119, 133, 163, 166, 203, 238, 246
– ~ demonstration   109, 133
archetype (*also* archetypal)   104, 112–130, 169, 170, 173, 177–184, 193, 200
– ideal vs. historical   76, 93, 98, 102, 110–120, 179, 180, 183
atheism   65, 69, 149
atonement   105, 198, 199
authority   7, 12, 13, 18, 26, 73, 79, 105, 107, 108, 116, 177, 199
– ~ of Scripture (*see also* revelation)   7, 13, 18, 116
authorship   12, 13, 160
autonomy   63, 155

Bible   7, 26, 71, 73–75, 80, 116, 138, 182, 249
biblical monotheism   62, 76, 223
body/embodiment   32, 92, 103, 133, 157, 159, 164, 202
Brief Outline   XVII, 9–15, 17, 46, 78, 80, 94, 129, 240

causality   77, 101, 124, 134, 136, 144–146, 151, 153, 156, 160, 163, 170, 182, 199, 205–207, 209–212, 218, 220, 222, 224, 225, 228, 230, 231, 243–245
cause   16, 33, 43, 49, 60, 74, 76, 83, 101, 105, 109, 118, 119, 121, 129, 145, 146, 160, 168, 173, 175, 178, 199, 221, 236, 239, 243, 244, 252
Christ, Jesus   XV, XVII, 1–5, 7–24, 26–30, 34, 35, 40, 43, 46, 49, 55, 57, 60, 69–107, 109–139, 141, 143–146, 150, 152–158, 162–208, 212–225, 229, 232, 234, 237–247, 250–254
Christology
– completion of creation (*see also* Second Adam)   169, 170, 180–184, 187, 188, 197
– ideal Christ/idea of redemption   80, 102, 110, 112, 114, 117, 132, 172
– method of inference (*Rückschluss*)   112, 118, 122, 125, 128, 173, 178
– strength of God-consciousness (*Kräftigkeit*)   86, 122, 123, 131, 137, 161, 167, 177, 183, 187, 193–195, 198–202, 239
– two-natures doctrine   173, 175, 176, 237, 238
church (*see also* ecclesiology)   10–13, 19, 22–23, 26, 28, 38, 75, 77, 80, 84, 85, 95, 115, 117, 132, 154, 171, 178, 181, 189, 193, 204, 205, 208, 218, 240, 241
community   11, 19, 20, 22, 24, 28, 30, 38, 39, 52, 62, 72, 73, 75, 84, 90, 94, 112, 115, 117, 118, 121, 129, 130, 132, 172, 180, 181, 191, 205, 240, 254
conscience   34, 162
constructed vs. historically given   11, 17, 73, 75, 80, 85, 88–89, 83, 93–99, 112, 115, 121, 133, 151, 204, 238
contingency (*see also* facticity)   2, 35, 36, 47, 50, 56–58, 64, 66, 67, 69, 119, 124, 127, 165, 193, 201, 202, 210, 213, 220, 221, 227, 242, 246, 248

https://doi.org/10.1515/9783110715989-017

Creator   2, 28, 49, 50, 64, 69, 132, 152, 156, 197, 209, 213, 215, 219, 222, 227, 252
culture   2, 10, 28, 29, 74, 77, 127, 146, 193, 196, 197, 208, 234, 235

decree, divine   4, 101, 117, 124, 125, 130, 134, 145, 164, 168, 169, 172, 185, 188, 202, 205, 209, 212, 216, 217, 224, 234, 239, 243, 252
deontology   156, 247, 250
dependence
– absolute ~   29, 32–37, 44–59, 65–69, 82, 96, 106–109, 113–117, 124, 127, 132, 135, 136, 144, 145, 163, 186, 187, 196, 207–215, 218–223, 226–233, 238, 241–243
– partial ~   29, 33–36, 44, 55, 56, 65, 229, 232
Dialectic   37, 54, 127, 145, 217, 220, 221, 224, 226
dialectical   2, 21, 22, 143, 150
disciplines   10, 11, 14, 15, 19, 23, 46, 78, 93, 94, 132, 133, 218, 240
– comparative   10, 11, 14, 46, 84, 97, 1, 186, 218
– critical   11, 14, 18, 23, 25, 80, 94, 240, 242
dogmatics
– material ~   3, 9, 19, 21, 46, 61, 67, 69, 73, 79, 95, 111, 116, 126, 128, 131–133, 139, 141, 143, 146, 154, 164, 172, 192, 206–208, 212, 218, 238
– sequence of parts   10, 15, 26–28, 72, 212
– duty   77, 183, 240

ecclesiology   193, 203, 204, 218, 240, 252, 253
editions of *Glaubenslehre*
– first   2, 3, 8, 9, 13–17, 20–24, 29, 33, 36–39, 47–55, 78–81, 84–86, 89–92, 95–104, 114, 130, 133–135, 147–149, 157–160, 164–166, 169–170, 174, 178–179, 186, 190–193, 199, 207–212, 217–218, 232, 242

– second   2, 3, 8–13, 18–25, 29, 33–37, 40–42, 49–52, 59, 60, 84–86, 91–100, 108, 116, 124–128, 145, 148, 156–158, 168–171, 174–176, 182–188, 191–193, 204, 205, 210, 211, 217, 218, 222, 229, 232, 237, 238, 241
election   21, 22, 105, 146, 147, 154, 155, 170, 194, 206, 217, 219, 235, 252
empirical method   50, 81, 94, 95,123, 241
Enlightenment   2, 7, 80, 90, 103, 104
epistemology   1, 3, 27, 50, 66, 68, 145–147, 156, 164, 221
eschatology   12, 204, 228, 235, 244
essence
– ~ of Christianity   11, 13, 16, 21, 23, 24, 26, 71–73, 76, 78, 80, 81, 83–85, 97, 114, 125, 133–135, 144, 154, 172, 221, 238
– ~ of piety/religion   7, 13, 24, 29, 31, 36, 39, 72, 95, 106, 208, 220, 238, 240
eternal   55, 74, 89, 91, 101, 124, 134, 147, 152, 164, 171, 174, 185, 194, 202, 205, 206, 209, 212, 216, 230, 233, 235, 239, 244, 252
– pre-temporal   101, 117, 125, 145, 205, 243
ethics   10, 11, 13, 20–22, 38, 46, 93, 94, 133, 145, 146, 155, 156, 165, 197, 246, 247, 249–251
evil   28, 89, 95, 156, 158, 162, 169, 231, 234, 242
evolution   80, 114, 163
exegesis   9, 10, 75
exemplar   138, 181
extrinsicism   3, 78, 131, 138, 141, 235, 238

facticity   36, 45, 47, 57, 58, 60, 65–67, 69, 124, 127, 155, 203, 233
fallibility   247
feeling of absolute dependence   29, 32, 33, 35–37, 46–49, 51, 53, 55–57, 59, 68, 69, 106, 108, 109, 113, 115, 117, 124, 132, 135, 136, 144, 145, 163, 186, 187, 196, 207–210, 212, 215, 218, 219, 221, 223, 226, 229–231, 233, 238, 241, 243
finitude   35, 36, 59, 117, 119, 162, 175, 209, 212, 230, 246, 247
forgiveness   188, 201, 236, 239

Subject Index — 275

freedom, divine   4, 32, 224, 227, 228, 230, 243, 248, 249, 251
freedom, human   2, 4, 28, 33–37, 45, 46, 52, 53, 65, 108, 132, 153, 156–162, 180, 184, 192, 215–218, 231–238, 242, 248–254
– concrete, finite, historical   42, 45, 62, 109, 130, 132, 133, 156, 165, 171, 180, 186, 192, 210, 215, 227, 230–234, 242
– formal, transcendental   45, 47, 52, 53, 55, 58, 59, 66, 132, 133, 162, 233, 234, 237, 238, 241, 242
– spontaneity   34, 35, 41, 42, 57, 63, 180, 249
friendship   252

Genesis   61, 146, 234
German Idealism   61
God
– action, agency   7, 22, 23, 30, 31, 34, 35, 41, 44, 45, 48, 59–62, 68, 76, 90–93, 101, 105, 108, 119, 124–129, 145–150, 153–166, 172–175, 182–185, 191, 194, 198–200, 203–215, 221, 222, 227, 228, 232–235, 238–240, 243–246, 251–254
– attributes   16, 54, 111, 124, 133, 143, 144, 151, 153, 198, 207, 213, 215, 216, 219, 222–225, 227, 230, 244
– causality   77, 101, 124, 134, 136, 144–146, 151, 153, 156, 160, 163, 170, 182, 199, 205–207, 209–212, 218, 220, 222, 224, 225, 228, 230, 231, 243–245
– decree   4, 101, 117, 124, 125, 130, 134, 145, 164, 168, 169, 172, 185, 188, 194, 202, 205, 209, 212, 216, 217, 224, 234, 239, 243, 251, 252
– doctrine of ~   3, 9, 16, 28, 104, 124, 131, 138, 141, 143, 144, 155, 163, 170, 172, 173, 196, 197, 200, 202, 205–209, 213, 214, 217, 218, 222, 225, 229, 230, 243, 248, 253
– freedom of ~   4, 32, 58, 224, 227, 228, 230, 243, 248, 249, 251
– love   92, 106, 124, 153, 171, 182, 198–200, 202, 207, 212, 216, 222, 224, 225, 237, 243, 244, 248–252, 254
– will of ~   176, 225, 227, 235, 248, 251, 252
God-consciousness
– actualised   132, 133, 137, 172, 194, 203, 211, 242
– constant potency   177
grace   3, 16, 17, 19, 24, 26, 28, 35, 36, 72, 79, 113, 115, 141, 145, 146, 156, 164, 171, 172, 198, 203, 205, 207, 216, 219, 251
guilt   162

haecceitas   250, 251
hamartiology   216
happiness   247
Hegelianism   110, 112, 117–126, 177, 243
heresy   11, 26, 73, 77, 87–89, 135, 154, 156
– natural ~   26, 77, 88, 154
hermeneutical circle   85, 95
hermeneutics   10, 62, 203, 230, 240
heteronomy   64
history of effects   74, 75, 102, 119, 210
hope   68, 124, 127, 155, 235, 236, 254
human dignity   113, 173, 235, 236, 250
humanity, human species   3, 26, 28, 53, 86, 87, 89–91, 101, 105, 118, 123, 124, 127, 134, 137, 138, 145, 156, 161, 162, 171, 184, 188–190, 196, 197, 201, 205, 208, 212, 214, 238, 239, 250, 251

identity   3, 41, 42, 57, 74, 81, 88, 89, 100, 129, 144, 168, 184, 194, 222, 223, 228
imagination   12, 13, 119
imago Dei (image of God)   146, 150–152, 153, 247
immediate self-consciousness   3, 30, 31, 35, 38–40, 42, 44, 46, 48–53, 57, 60–63, 65, 67, 68, 82, 83, 93, 111, 115, 116, 127, 135, 136, 161, 169, 195
individuality   2, 62, 79, 83, 95, 113, 145, 147, 148, 150, 153, 217, 225, 226, 228, 230, 247
infinity   33, 49, 106, 127, 183, 214, 222, 238, 244
intentionality   48, 66
intersubjectivity   62, 147, 152

Subject Index

Introduction
- sequence of the ~   19–28, 72, 103, 111, 132
- tasks of the ~   3, 7, 9–28, 240

intuition   17, 18, 21, 23, 51, 64, 81, 126

Jesus
- cross   198, 199, 201, 252
- Life of ~   75, 77, 107, 112, 116, 118, 129, 168, 177, 180, 181, 192, 198–202, 239, 251
- self-proclamation   22, 75, 79, 132, 199, 205
- total impression (*Totaleindruk*)   3, 74, 75, 199, 212, 238

justice   49, 55, 80, 95, 99, 134, 149, 166, 182, 190, 212, 213, 223, 230, 236, 239, 243

justification   13, 20, 26, 60, 62, 91, 93, 97, 105, 110, 118, 120, 126, 130, 141, 171, 173, 181, 184, 196, 232

kingdom of God (*see also* reign of God)   83, 204, 205, 218

language   21, 22, 59, 62, 74, 174, 183, 217
love   92, 106, 124, 153, 171, 182, 198–200, 202, 207, 212, 216, 222, 224, 225, 237, 243, 244, 248–252, 254

meaning, question of   31, 54, 58, 127, 155, 214
mediation of redemption   169, 180, 190
metaphysics   39, 53, 62, 225, 237, 248, 251
miracle   108
modernity   XV, 62, 142, 212, 215, 216, 219, 224, 225, 230, 231, 233–235, 240, 241, 245, 247, 249, 251
monads   148–150, 153, 227
monism   61, 149, 163, 217, 222, 225, 244, 253
- monist vs. egological   29, 53, 60, 61
monotheism   62, 76, 82, 83, 86, 221, 223
morality   32, 39, 53, 154, 155, 250

naturalism   14, 78, 102, 108, 110, 121, 162, 163, 235

necessity   34, 38, 39, 108, 120, 129, 132, 133, 137, 147, 152, 168, 170, 180, 184, 210, 213, 220, 228–230, 240, 244, 248, 249
New Testament   73–76, 108, 110, 114, 115, 119, 120, 123, 128, 129, 155, 171, 174, 178, 181, 182, 201, 204
nexus of nature, natural connectedness (*Naturzusammenhang*)   4, 104, 145, 146, 148, 150, 154, 156, 208–211, 215, 227, 230

objectivity   43, 44, 69, 74, 117, 186, 189, 205
obligation   62
omnipotence   209–211, 216, 227, 230, 233, 244, 253, 254
omniscience   210, 215, 216, 228, 230, 244

pantheism   124, 149, 209, 222, 226–228
particularity   72, 79, 83, 84, 90, 104, 119, 193, 205, 207
perfection   16, 28, 32, 83, 113, 117, 118, 120, 122, 127, 141, 143–147, 149–159, 167, 168, 170–172, 181–184, 189–192, 194, 197, 209, 211, 212, 220, 225, 234, 238, 243, 246, 254
philosophy
- ~ of religion   10, 11, 15, 18, 20, 21, 46, 68, 86, 93, 94, 97, 98, 103, 105, 126, 133, 202, 222
piety   7, 16, 20, 22, 24, 29–33, 36, 38, 39, 45, 46, 48, 50, 53, 55, 65, 66, 71–73, 75, 81–83, 85, 86, 89, 90, 95, 97, 106, 108, 109, 114, 116, 127, 133, 135, 137, 146, 153, 156, 163, 164, 195, 203, 208, 214, 218–221, 228, 229, 231, 232, 244
pluralism   240
pneumatology (Holy Spirit)   77, 254
polytheism   82
positive science   9, 10, 162, 220
positivism   250
postulate of God   54, 63, 103, 155, 158, 169, 196, 229
practical reason   31, 32, 54, 67, 68, 155, 158, 179, 248, 249
predestination   235

Subject Index

pre-established harmony 150, 153, 227
preservation 16, 19, 77, 170, 185, 190, 209, 212–214, 218, 221, 226, 227, 246
principle
– general v. individualising 72, 81, 90
– *principium cognoscendi* 114, 143, 163, 173
progress 36, 51, 53, 80, 83, 89, 91, 105, 128, 155, 159, 168, 181, 182, 184, 196, 235, 236
projection 1, 50, 98, 103, 119, 125–128, 130–132, 179, 194, 238
Protestantism 13, 16, 59, 71, 73, 105, 154, 155
psychological 50, 60, 105, 107, 125, 126, 239
public 129, 155, 234

Rationalism 14, 78, 102–105, 108–111, 121, 128
receptivity 32, 34, 35, 37, 39, 41, 42, 45, 55, 57, 88, 92, 134, 136, 143, 156, 168, 171, 185–187, 191, 215, 233
reciprocity 33, 108, 215
– relationship of ~ 33, 108, 215
Redeemer 16, 70, 74–77, 81, 86, 87, 89, 91, 93, 96, 99–101, 108, 110–115, 117, 119, 120, 124, 130, 132–134, 136, 137, 146, 158, 167, 168, 172–174, 176–181, 184, 186, 189, 191–195, 198, 203, 204, 208, 209, 211, 212, 218, 238, 241, 252
Reformation 60
regeneration 158
reign of God 35, 89, 203
religion
– positive ~ 18, 46, 79, 83, 90, 94, 113, 114
resurrection 12, 77, 198, 200, 244
revelation 14, 18, 46, 50–52, 73, 78–80, 87–92, 97–117, 122, 124, 127, 131, 133, 137, 138, 163, 176, 186, 187, 192–194, 197–202, 207, 219, 220, 224, 235, 238, 243, 244
Romanticism 80, 149

salvation 1, 2, 28, 101, 134, 137, 144, 170, 189, 193, 196, 199, 205, 206, 212, 239, 244, 251, 252

sanctification 228
sciences 1, 10, 19, 21, 23, 80, 94, 102, 129, 138, 208, 220, 241, 245, 246
Scriptures 163
Second Adam 163, 166, 169, 172, 185, 188, 197, 254
self-activity 43, 45, 55–57, 109, 124, 147, 168, 211, 216, 233
self-consciousness
– higher ~ 82, 86, 87, 93, 96, 97, 137, 156, 158, 159, 161
– immediate ~ 3, 30, 31, 35, 38, 40, 42, 44, 46, 48–53, 57, 60–63, 65, 67, 68, 82, 83, 93, 111, 115, 116, 127, 135, 161, 169, 195
– lower ~ 89, 156, 158, 161
– sensible ~ 81, 82, 86, 96, 97, 158, 179, 187
selfhood 126
self-legislation 167
self-reflection 2, 35, 43, 46, 49, 51, 61–64, 69, 76, 95, 121, 126, 132, 197, 204, 234
self-revelation, divine 176, 192, 198, 199, 243
self-understanding 2, 7, 13, 52, 65, 67, 72, 75, 76, 80, 85, 176, 177, 179, 188, 192, 204
Sendschreiben, Letters 7, 21, 25–27, 36, 37, 48, 49, 56, 63, 76, 80, 102, 104, 109, 110, 116, 209, 215, 239, 240, 246
sin 3, 16–19, 24–28, 72, 77, 96, 97, 105, 106, 113–117, 126, 137, 141–146, 154–173, 179, 188, 189, 193–198, 201, 206, 207, 214, 219, 233, 234, 239, 242, 243, 252
– doctrine of ~ (*see also* hamartiology) 3, 17, 24, 26, 28, 105, 141, 144, 154–157, 161–166, 172, 207, 243
singularity 119, 138, 201
society 152, 183
soteriology 105, 141, 143, 198, 199, 204, 239, 253
speculation 32, 55, 80, 183, 184, 202, 240
Speeches 15, 18, 29, 32, 54, 55, 78, 79, 103, 126, 149, 208, 217

Spirit   XV, 30, 32, 39, 51, 71, 77, 80, 99, 100, 105, 116, 134, 155, 157–159, 161, 162, 165, 166, 175, 195, 210, 217, 218, 239, 241, 251, 254
state   15, 16, 24, 35, 41, 43, 50, 61, 72, 90, 93, 95, 98, 106, 115, 137, 150, 152–154, 156, 157, 159, 162, 164, 167, 180, 185, 188, 190, 197, 201
subjectivity   2, 9–11, 29, 37, 38, 42, 53, 54, 59, 62–65, 68, 95, 103, 117, 126, 133, 143, 156, 177, 197, 203, 205, 213, 217, 218, 220, 227, 229, 238, 253
– theory of ~   9, 29, 37, 38, 42, 59, 63–65, 103, 133, 143, 156
supernaturalism   14, 78, 102, 108, 110, 121
supralapsarianism   205, 212, 239, 247, 251, 254
symbolic   80, 234, 243

teleological   31, 72, 78, 82–86, 95, 99, 204, 208, 246
theocentrism   252
theology
– historical ~   9–14, 17, 20, 73–75, 80, 81, 110, 128, 129
– modern ~   XV, 1, 2, 12, 27, 44, 62, 66, 125, 126, 131, 176, 198, 212, 219, 235, 240, 241, 251
– philosophical ~   2, 9–11, 13–15, 17, 28, 46, 52, 57, 62, 94, 104, 105, 151, 203, 218–220, 223, 238, 241, 246
– practical ~   10, 12, 54, 67, 68, 158
– systematic ~   1, 11–14, 19, 22, 64, 80, 125, 176, 204
tradition   7, 12–14, 20, 28, 59, 73, 75, 77, 80, 84, 95, 111, 138, 196, 199, 213, 223, 224, 240, 241, 245

transcendence   55, 56, 134, 211
transcendental method   29, 36, 41, 52–58, 132, 220, 238
transformation   74, 77, 81, 105, 172, 241
translation   XVII, 1–3, 25–27, 39, 40, 42–44, 50, 78, 111, 146, 150, 177, 191, 192, 225
Trinity, doctrine of   175
truth   2, 3, 14, 20, 26, 32, 52, 74, 94, 102, 107, 111, 126, 131, 138, 167, 177, 185, 187, 193, 197, 198, 206, 211, 214, 223, 237, 240, 241, 251, 253

unconditionality   39, 45, 46, 59, 66, 165, 177, 198, 232–234, 242, 243, 250
universality, universalism   156, 227
universe   151, 152, 227, 229
unsurpassibility   85, 172, 188, 193

validity   39, 53, 61, 87, 93, 94, 109, 113, 121, 132, 135, 137, 144, 157, 177, 194
virtue   95, 103, 168, 198

Whence of existence   37, 56, 232
will   65, 67, 109, 153, 155, 159, 160, 161, 176, 179, 191, 192, 202, 211, 225–228, 235, 248–251, 253
– divine ~   176, 225, 227, 235, 248, 251, 252
– human ~   4, 33, 35–37, 45, 46, 52, 53, 65, 67, 109, 136, 155, 160–162, 171, 175, 176, 179, 191, 192, 225, 248–250
wisdom   22, 28, 75, 166, 210, 216, 254
Word of God   125
worldviews   105, 150, 232

www.ingramcontent.com/pod-product-compliance
Lightning Source LLC
Chambersburg PA
CBHW031423150426
43191CB00006B/370